Toxic Mold Litigation

Second Edition

AF886599

Edited by

Joel L. Herz, Esq.
Ernest Greer, Esq.
Richard Valladares, Esq.
Ryan Grelecki, Esq.

Contributors

Sean P. Abbott, Ph.D.
Julie Beddingfield, Esq.
Barry L. Bellovin, Esq.
Marianne E. Brown, Esq.
Mark P. Buttner
Kristy Byrd, Esq.
Abigail A. Clapp, Esq.
Edward Eshoo, Jr., Esq.
Eric S. Fisher, Esq.
Eric G. Fosmire, Esq.
David M. Governo, Esq.
Ander Krupa, Esq.
Ryan C. Kuhn, Ph.D.
Matthew J. Levinstein
Kimberly A. Mello, Esq.
Stephanie L. Oginsky, Esq.
Sarah E. O'Leary, Esq.
Stephen Pate, Esq.
Patrick J. Perrone, Esq.
Douglas F. Schleicher, Esq.
Rhonda M. Sigman, Esq.
Linda D. Stetzenbach
Ashley Turner
Kelly Vance, Esq.
David B. Weinstein, Esq.
Dennis I. Wilenchik, Esq.

Lawyers & Judges Publishing Company, Inc.

Tucson, Arizona

Lawyers & Judges Publishing Company, Inc.

P.O. Box 30040 • Tucson, AZ 85751-0040
(800) 209-7109 • FAX (800) 330-8795
e-mail: sales@lawyersandjudges.com
www.lawyersandjudges.com

Library of Congress Cataloging-in-Publication Data

Toxic mold litigation / Joel Herz ... [et al.] ; contributors Sean P. Abbott ...[et al.]. -- 2nd ed.

p. cm.
Includes index.
ISBN-13: 978-1-933264-37-0 (softcover : alk. paper)
ISBN-10: 1-933264-37-3 (softcover : alk. paper)
1. Personal injuries--United States. 2. Molds (Fungi)--Law and legislation--United States. 3. Actions and defenses--United States. 4. Insurance claims--United States. I. Herz, Joel. II. Abbott, Sean P.
KF3827.R4H47 2009
346.7303'23--dc22

2009030899

Printed in the United States of America
10 9 8 7 6 5 4 3 2 1

Contents

Part II

Acknowledgments

The authors wish to express their appreciation to everyone who played a role in the publication of this book. In particular, we give thanks to the contributors to this publication who withstood our tireless prodding and to the staff at Lawyers & Judges Publishing for their editorial insights. We also must highlight the substantial contribution of Steven Weintraub and Eric Salo, whose patience, attention to detail, and management skills have made this book a reality. Additional thanks must go to our families, friends, and colleagues for providing support and inspiration.

Joel L. Herz in particular, wishes to thank his wife Jane, and his children, Jordan and Abigail, for their unending patience, love and support. Also, special thanks goes to his parents, Myra and Stuart, for their guidance and wisdom. Finally, Joel wishes to thank his paralegals, Leslie Grant and Monique Moran, for their incredible attention and detail in proofreading, and coordinating with all of the contributing authors.

Ernest Greer thanks his wife Patrice for twenty years of standing by his side with love and support, and for still believing he can do anything. He also thanks his daughters Kendall and Lauryn for their love and believing that he is the coolest Dad ever. Finally, special thanks goes to the law firm of Greenberg Traurig, LLP, particularly the Commercial Litigation and the Products Liability Departments for their support of this project.

Richard Valladares wishes to thank his wife Melissa for fourteen years of love and friendship. It is because of her work and sacrifice that endeavors such as this book are ever achieved. He also wishes to thank his sons Jack, Andrew and Matthew for their unconditional love, they are his source of inspiration. Special thanks goes to his father Guillermo and his mother Elizabeth for their constant love, guidance and encouragement. Finally, he thanks Manlio and Loly Leyva for their years of love and support.

Ryan Grelecki wishes to thank his wife, Crysie, for her unconditional love and support. Her hard work and dedication makes his work meaningful. He also wishes to thank his son, Parker, whose endurance and strength is a constant encouragement and continual reminder of what is truly important.

Introduction

Since the first edition of *Toxic Mold Litigation* was published in 2005, mold litigation in many respects has matured and become more predictable. Nevertheless, mold litigation remains extremely complicated. The second edition of *Toxic Mold Litigation* is intended to act as a more comprehensive guide and a resource manual for those facing mold litigation issues. The complexity of addressing mold litigation stems, in part, from the large number of professional disciplines involved, as well as the lack of detailed information readily available about newly emerging state laws. Therefore, this book was developed to provide both information and strategic advice to assist parties in mold litigation.

As with the first edition of *Toxic Mold Litigation*, this book is divided into three parts.

Part I explains critical background information to put the "mold issue" in context. Part II offers a detailed look at the most important elements of mold litigation in critical states where mold litigation has been prevalent.

Part I is designed to be read "cover-to-cover" and will provide the reader with not only essential information important to understanding the issues, but also with strategic advice toward addressing the problems posed by mold. The authors did not intend for the reader to read Part II "cover-to-cover." Rather, this section of the book should serve as critical reference material and offers tremendous insight into any particular state of interest to the reader. Additionally, Part II of the book may be used to compare one state's laws with another state's.

This book is intended to function as a practical reference for persons interested in participating in mold litigation. The authors further intend to update and supplement the book periodically, to keep readers abreast of the latest developments, new laws, and strategies for practically addressing mold issues. ***As this area of law continues to develop at a rapid pace, the reader should carefully check the status of any particular law, or regulation described in the book before relying on the accuracy of any particular reference.***

Part I

Chapter 1

Mold

Barry L. Bellovin, Esq.

Synopsis

It is now eight years since the June 2001 Ballard verdict—a $32-million mold verdict in Texas—started an influx of mold litigation. The Ballard case was an insurance dispute involving claims of bad faith denial of coverage relating to mold in a 7,400-square-foot house. The $32-million verdict was later reduced to $4 million. The verdict set off a frenzy of press and attention on mold litigation.

Prior to Ballard, there were relatively few mold claims filed. Claims could be, and were, routinely settled for relatively nominal amounts. After Ballard, mold claims routinely exceeded $100,000, and mold claims in the commercial setting often exceeded $1 million. In its wake, insurance carriers have almost uniformly inserted various mold exclusions or limitations into insurance policies.

Anecdotally, it appears that the post-Ballard pendulum is beginning to swing back in a different direction. Post-Ballard, it is becoming increasingly clear that mold claims are often expensive to litigate and difficult to win. Mold has not turned into the next wave of asbestos litigation. The likely reasons include:

- The high costs of mold inspections and documenting the existence and cause of the alleged mold.
- The large number of claimants (e.g. in cases involving schools or office buildings) and defendants who must be deposed.
- The fact that claimants are subjected to one or more physical examinations.

- The complex subject matter requiring numerous expert witnesses (e.g. industrial hygienists, architects, engineers, allergists, neurologists, toxicologists, epidemiologists, contractors) to address who caused the mold and whether the mold caused physical injuries.

Regardless, mold claims and litigation are not likely to disappear in the near future. That is because mold is found virtually everywhere in our environment—both indoors and outdoors and in both new and old structures. Molds are naturally occurring microscopic organisms, which reproduce by spores and have existed practically from the beginning of time. Any doubt as to the long-standing nature of mold problems can be resolved by reference to the Old Testament, Leviticus Chapter 14, verses 39–47:

> On the seventh day the priest shall return to inspect the house. If the mildew has spread on the walls, he is to order that the contaminated stones be torn out and thrown into an unclean place outside the town. He must have all the inside walls of the house scraped and the material that is scraped off dumped into an unclean place outside the town. Then they are to take other stones to replace these and take new clay and plaster the house. If the mildew reappears in the house after the stones have been torn out and the house scraped and plastered, the priest is to go and examine it and, if the mildew has spread in the house, it is a destructive mildew; the house is unclean. It must be torn down and taken out of the town to an unclean place. Anyone who goes into the house while it is closed up will be unclean until evening. Anyone who sleeps or eats in the house must wash his clothes.

The molds *Stachybotrys chartarum* and *aspergilis* have been implicated in some of the most severe injury and property mold claims. Confounding mold litigation is that the effect of mold exposure varies dramatically between individuals. For example, children generally tend to be more susceptible to mold than adults. Those with pre-existing asthma and allergies tend to react more severely than others with no pre-existing condition, all other variables being equal. Confounding the situation further, is that mold exposure can come in combination with exposure to multiple molds and other substances at the same time. In addition, mold exposure varies significantly in terms of the intensity and length in time of exposure. Generally speaking, the lower the duration of exposure and the lower the spore count the greater chance there is for full recovery of person and property upon removal of the offending mold. Obviously, the reverse tends to be generally true. That is, the longer the exposure and the greater the spore count, the higher chance of illness and damage, assuming we are talking about a destructive species of mold.

1.1 Legal Aspects of Mold Litigation

Whether we are considering an injury or property damage mold claim or a combination thereof, a key consideration is the existence and handling of the evidence. Evidence of mold species and spore count can make or break either a plaintiff's or defendant's case. The best evidence is the mold itself, assuming the structure has not been remediated or repaired. The question of how to preserve this evidence should be considered carefully. Chain of custody issues must be considered. Lack of a tightly documented chain of custody places any scientific testing results in doubt and subject to cross-examination, challenges to legal foundation, and potentially exclusion from evidence. There are different types of industries that have sprung up around the mold issues. The first type is a mold testing company, which can consist of an industrial hygienist. These types of companies who are meritorious, carefully gather evidence, document, and use reputable labs to establish the existence of mold, its variety, spore count, etc. There is another type of company known as a remediation company that resembles a specialized contractor who removes the mold and rebuilds. Mold can be removed in a variety of ways. The classic attack on mold is to stop its source of moisture, remove damaged materials, and dry out the affected environment. There are contractors who can literally seal up a property and then, using a suctioning device, extract the moisture. Remedies dealing effectively with mold continue to be developed.

In the case of a product liability defect in an automobile case, the key is to secure the automobile. The result of not securing the automobile in a product liability case often leads to there being no case at all. It is the same with mold litigation for the same reasons, as mold litigation has a great deal of similarity to product liability. Simply put: no product, no case. The exceptions are few. This is a reality for both plaintiff and defendant. If the plaintiff has evidence of the presence of a harmful species of mold, high spore count, significant exposure time and prompt medical reporting to a qualified physician who can establish causation, the plaintiff may have a viable case. However, if any of these elements are lacking, the defendant has strong avenues of defense.

A plaintiff who may have suffered mold injury should report their symptoms to their primary care physicians. The plaintiff should also consult the various professionals who are experts in evaluation, diagnosis, and treatment of mold exposure and who are willing to provide testimonial support. The health professionals involved in these types of cases often bear the titles of toxicologist, occupational medicine physicians, and/or pulmonologist. These physicians should provide the necessary diagnostic testing to determine causation. The earlier that mold is detected and removed the better the prognosis for both property and patient. Testing can also rule out the presence of a mold-related injury. The types of injuries often claimed to be associated with mold exposure include pulmonary dysfunction, asthma, allergies, chemical pneumonitis, phenomena, headache, rash, mental disorientation and memory loss, and multiple chemical sensitivity. The relationship of these symptoms to mold exposure remains controversial. Experts in the medical field differ strongly on whether mold is the culprit for this constellation of symptoms. This leaves ample room for argument by experts on all sides of the table. On the liability side, experts such as contractors, plumbers, landlords and property managers can be necessary experts to establish the standards for maintenance and the breaches thereof. In a defect case, an architect is also an appropriate expert.

In today's legal climate, experts must be selected with great care. The penalty of disqualification can leave a lawyer with no expert or expert testimony. Ideally, an expert toxicologist, industrial hygienist, or other professional expert will have been previously qualified in a court of law to testify and will have been published in several peer-reviewed books, articles or publications. Any expert selected must not only be able to support their opinions, but also the underlying scientific methodology for the assumptions that form the foundations for their opinions. This is a challenge in the mold litigation arena because the science of diagnosis and remediation is still developing. The witness should be able to scientifically support the scientific validity of the underlying sampling, data collection, and the efficacy of the equipment used to test and analyze data.

1.2 Legal Theories

Mold cases are different from other types of accidental injury cases in major respects. Mold cases develop slowly, and often silently. To prevent mold it often takes due diligence by the property owner. When this due diligence is absent, legal liability for harm caused can attach. Mold results from chronic moisture conditions or from the remnants of a flood where the moisture was allowed to remain. It does not take a great deal of moisture to create mold. A small roof leak, leaky plumbing pipe, or cracks or openings around window and door frames are typical sources of water intrusion on a chronic basis leading to mold development. This situation can be compounded by the leaks remaining within walls of the structure, and developing unseen. The need for due diligence stems from ongoing maintenance obligations. There can also be a defect in construction or repair that creates the same obligations and liabilities as lack of maintenance. For example, a defective roof might have a gap in drainage that allows water to escape into the walls. Such a defect can be caused by design error, roofer error, or both. A maintenance or design defect can easily develop serious consequences by the presence of other hazards. For example, a carpet floor in a bathroom can become dangerously contaminated by a plumbing leak due to the bacterial environment of the bathroom. In addition, a heating and cooling system in a home or office can easily spread contamination throughout the structures and to a larger group of people. The threat of mold can be underestimated in a dry climate. However, dry climates can have significant mold issues due to plumbing leaks which are not climate sensitive, and cracking can occur due to temperature extremes allowing for water intrusion.

There are various legal theories which can be applied through tort and contract law. With regard to tort theories, negligence is the most prevalent. The negligence typically is based upon lack of due diligence due or lack of maintenance. When this lack of maintenance leads to chronic water intrusion and high moisture conditions which leads to causative injury to person or property, a negligence claim is appropriate. If there are any statutes that are violated, negligence per se can be pleaded. Strict liability can also be plead in certain circumstances. Under certain conditions, a nuisance claim may be similarly plead. A nuisance is an interference with the use and enjoyment of property.

Breach of contract and breach of warranty also can and should be plead in a mold claim where appropriate. If the home had mold that the seller knew about and did not disclose prior to purchase, the buyer has a potential misrepresentation claim. The essence of these claims is that the purchaser did not receive the wind- and water-tight home and healthful environment that they expected they purchased. General contractors and other building professionals are similarly exposed for defective construction that promotes mold growth. Similar to a termite infestation that is cured, there is an issue of whether an owner must disclose on sale even a remediated mold infestation. Tenants who are subjected to mold may have claims for negligence and breach of contract under their leases. Tenants may also be able to assert a claim for any personal property damaged by mold. Various landlord tenant acts may apply in your jurisdiction. Workers' compensation claims, sometimes with third-party liability, can often arise in an office setting where there is the presence of mold.

1.3 Insurance Issues

The applicability of insurance coverage, or lack thereof, is often actual with regard to mold claims and litigation.

In third-party claims the insurance industry in commercial general liability policies has relied on an absolute pollution exclusion. These clauses generally state that the insurance policy does not cover "bodily injury or property damage arising out of the actual, alleged, or threatened discharge, disbursal, or escape of pollutants at or from premises you own, rent, or occupy." These clauses broadly define pollutants. In third-party claims the application of this absolute pollution exclusion has met with inconsistent results and the validity of the exclusion has often depended upon the exact wording contained in the exclusion, the specific policy, and the exact facts of the underlying claim.

With regard to first-party claims under the homeowners policy for property damage caused by mold contamination there is typically a finding of coverage despite exclusion language in the policy. This is especially the case if the mold was the result of a covered loss caused by broken plumbing pipes, or rain damage associated with roof and window leaks.

As is often the case with the rise in number and magnitude of a class of cases, insurers often race to send their policyholders notices of exclusion for coverage. Mold is no exception. Insurers, in an effort to limit their liability, have been especially aggressive in excluding claims for mold from coverage. This presents many challenges for the legal practitioner. The policy language must be researched thoroughly. In addition, one should look to other policies including umbrella coverage that do not contain such exclusions. Another source of mold litigation is insurance carriers' wrongful refusal to pay claims or their failure to pay the claims fully. The insurers can also be held liable for a failure to completely and adequately remediate. Contractors who do not properly repair and remediate can also have independent liability.

1.4 Statute of Limitations

The statute of limitations varies from jurisdiction to jurisdiction. However, one interesting aspect of mold claims is that it can be argued that the statute does not begin to run until discovery of the damage or illness.

What follows in this book is an in-depth discussion of mold law in various states. The current legal cases and trends are cited and analyzed. The requirements for the admission of expert testimony under current law is also discussed.

Chapter 2

Evidentiary Standards in Toxic Mold Litigation

Dennis I. Wilenchik, Esq.

Synopsis

2.1 Introduction

Approximately ten years ago, the nation was gripped by near panic talk about toxic mold, including a particular species called *Stachybotrys chartarum*. The media featured stories on homes filled with this dangerous black mold, and large jury verdicts fueled the fear of mold. Even today, home buyers inspect for mold and home sellers are usually required to disclose the existence of mold. However, the truth is that mold exists all around us, both in nature and in our homes. More than 1,000 different species of mold are found indoors, most of which are not harmful. Like many other molds, *Stachybotrys chartarum* is typically found in water-damaged structures and typically grows in moist, dark places. While it is generally thought that mold should be remediated from residences, schools, office buildings, and other structures, most scientific reports have found no conclusive link between *Stachybotrys chartarum* and injury or disease. These scientific studies have greatly affected strategy among parties litigating mold cases because they dictate what kind of information the jury hears. This chapter will focus on the evidentiary standards applicable in mold litigation.

2.2 Expert Witness Evidentiary Standards

In a mold case, an expert witness is the most important witness to take the stand. Both Plaintiffs and Defendants will undoubtedly fight to have their expert witnesses testify in front of the jury. At the same time, both parties will attempt to exclude the other side's expert witnesses for obvious reasons. An expert witness will be able to prove or disprove a causal link between the presence of mold and injury or illness or testify to an applicable standard of care or damages. More importantly, a good expert will be able to explain the complexities and subtleties of mold in plain English to the jury. If the trial court excludes such an expert, there may be a large hole in counsel's case. Before an expert can take the stand, however, the trial court judge must act as a "gatekeeper" and determine if the witness can be allowed to testify. Trial court judges typically have the power to exclude experts under theories which come from two cases: *Frye* and *Daubert*. Most states follow either *Frye* or *Daubert*, but some states follow their own line of cases or statutes.

A. The Frye "General Acceptance" Test

Frye v. United States[1] was the first major case to establish a standard for the admissibility of new or novel scientific evidence. In fact, *Frye* came years before the enactment of Rule 702 of the Federal Rules of Evidence in 1975. The sole issue on appeal in *Frye* was whether the defense in a murder case could offer an expert witness to testify regarding the systolic blood pressure deception test.[2] The defense proposed to have the expert witness conduct this test and perform it in the presence of the jury, but the Court held that the systolic blood pressure deception test had not gained "general acceptance" in the scientific community to justify admission of expert witness testimony.[3] In other words, the Court did not know whether the test was accurate; and, therefore, if evidence from it was presented to the jury, it could be reversible error. As part of the holding in *Frye*, the Court created the "general acceptance test" and stated that:

> Just when a scientific principle or discovery crosses the line between the experimental and demonstrable stages is difficult to define. Somewhere in this twilight zone the evidential force of the principle must be recognized, and while courts will go a long way in admitting expert testimony deduced from a well-recognized scientific principle of discovery, the thing from which the deduction is made must be sufficiently established to have gained general acceptance in the particular field in which it belongs.[4]

The *Frye* general acceptance standard was prevalent for many years in both state and federal courts up until Federal Rules of Evidence Rule 702 was enacted. Following the enactment of Rule 702 of the Federal Rules of Evidence, some federal district and appellate courts rejected the *Frye* test. The Supreme Court resolved the conflict among these courts in *Daubert v. Merrell Dow Pharmaceuticals, Inc*,[5] discussed *infra.*

Although a slight majority of states follow the *Daubert* ruling, the 1923 *Frye* decision still remains the law in many state courts. The states that still use *Frye's* "general acceptance" test include Arizona, California, the District of Columbia, Florida, Illinois, Kansas, Maryland, Michigan, Minnesota, Mississippi, Missouri, New York, North Dakota, Pennsylvania, and Washington.[6]

1. The *Frye* procedure

The procedure courts utilize in deciding whether to allow an expert to testify is rather straightforward. Courts will hold a *Frye* hearing before or during a trial in order to determine whether an expert should testify. The purpose of a *Frye* hearing is to resolve the issue of "general acceptance" of the theories relied upon before trial. The advantage of conducting a *Frye* hearing before trial is that the results of the hearing may lead to further settlement negotiations, and the hearing itself takes place out of the presence of the jury. Parties preparing for a *Frye* hearing should ideally prepare notebooks with various scientific reports and case law rulings on similar evidentiary matters.

2. The trial court's discretion under *Frye*

In general, the trial court is afforded great discretion in evidentiary matters and in its assessment of the credibility and weight of the expert testimony. An appellate court will review *de novo* a lower court's determination that a scientific principle meets the *Frye* requirement of general acceptance.[7] If the trial court allows an expert to testify at trial, the jury will still be able to decide the appropriate weight to be given to the expert's testimony.

B. The *Daubert* Test

In *Daubert v. Merrell Dow Pharmaceuticals, Inc.*, the United States Supreme Court defined a new standard for the admissibility of novel scientific evidence. In this action, the parents of two boys alleged that the prescription and ingestion of anti-nausea drug Bendectin during the mother's pregnancy caused birth defects.[8] The evidentiary issue decided by the Court involved whether expert evidence relying on a particular type of blood test was admissible.[9]

At the trial court level, the defendant's expert witness executed an affidavit in which he stated that, based upon his review of the published literature, Bendectin did not pose a risk of birth defects.[10] Plaintiffs sought to refute defendant's expert witness' affidavit by introducing the testimony of eight experts who had come to the opposite conclusion.[11] In ruling plaintiffs' expert testimony inadmissible, the trial judge determined that plaintiffs' experts' methodologies did not meet the *Frye* general acceptance test.[12] The trial judge granted defendant's motion for summary judgment and the D.C. Circuit Court of Appeals affirmed.[13]

The United States Supreme Court reversed, holding that Rule 702 of the Federal Rules of Evidence superseded *Frye*, and that the general acceptance test set forth by *Frye* was no longer a precondition to the admissibility of scientific evidence.[14] The Supreme Court set forth four criteria for the evaluation of experts: (1) whether the theory or technique has been or can be tested; (2) whether it has been subjected to peer review and publication; (3) the known or potential rate of error; and (4) whether the theory or technique has been generally accepted by the scientific community.[15] These four factors are non-exhaustive but reflect the goal of the Supreme Court to only allow expert witnesses to testify if they are qualified and have a reasonable foundation for their testimony.[16]

The Supreme Court in *Daubert* also created a two-prong test relying upon Rule 104(a) of the Federal Rules of Evidence. Trial courts applying *Daubert* must (1) make a preliminary assessment of whether the reasoning or methodology underlying the expert's testimony is scientifically valid and applicable to the facts of the case; and (2) decide whether the expert's testimony would be helpful to the jury.[17]

The introduction of *Daubert's* four criteria has prompted a looser standard in admitting scientific evidence, and some critics fear that "junk science" is being admitted into the courtroom. The Supreme Court tried to address these fears by stating its belief that cross-examination, care in instruction on the burden of proof, and presentation of contrary evidence will act as balancing tools against the evidence.[18]

The states that have adopted *Daubert* include Alaska, Arkansas, Colorado, Connecticut, Delaware, Idaho, Indiana, Iowa, Kentucky, Louisiana, Maine, Montana, Nebraska, New Mexico, North Carolina, Ohio, Oklahoma, Oregon, Rhode Island, South Carolina, South Dakota, Tennessee, Texas, Vermont, West Virginia, and Wyoming.[19]

1. Subsequent case law interpreting *Daubert*

The Supreme Court has reaffirmed the *Daubert* decision in subsequent cases. The Court has stated that "abuse of discretion" is the proper standard of review for appeals of *Daubert* rulings,[20] and that experts cannot draw unreasonable conclusions based upon well-accepted and reliable methodology.[21] More recently, the Court decided that the ruling in *Daubert* extended to non-technical experts.[22] In December 2000, an amended version of Rule 702 of the Federal Rules of Evidence went into effect incorporating the *Daubert* decision. Rule 702 of the Federal Rules of Evidence now provides:

> If scientific, technical or other specialized knowledge will assist the trier of fact to understand the evidence or to determine a fact in issue, a witness qualified as an expert by knowledge, skill, experience, training, or education, may testify thereto in the form of an opinion or otherwise, if (1) the testimony is based upon sufficient facts or data, (2) the testimony is the product of reliable principles and methods, and (3) the witness has applied the principles and methods reliably to the facts of the case.[23]

State courts, including *Frye* states, may adopt variations of this rule. While the actual rule may vary from state to state, the general premise remains the same: expert witnesses may testify if their specialized knowledge will be helpful to the trier of fact.

2. The *Daubert* procedure

To challenge the admissibility of scientific evidence in a *Daubert* state, an attorney should draft a concise motion pursuant to Rule 702 of the Federal Rules of Evidence. In order to preserve judicial economy, the motion should also include or incorporate all other bases for challenging the admissibility of the evidence. The purpose of a *Daubert* motion is to establish that the proffered evidence lacks scientific validity and reliability. Such a motion often attacks the means of an expert rather than the opinions or conclusions of the expert.

The accompanying memorandum to the motion should provide the court with the general principles of admissibility of expert testimony and discuss each of the four factors enumerated by *Daubert.* If possible, the expert should submit an affidavit in support of the *Daubert* motion. The affidavit should serve to provide the court with admissible, evidentiary bases for excluding the testimony of the expert. After providing the court with a general road map of the case, the affidavit should demonstrate specifically step by step why or how the proffered expert's testimony lacks the scientific validity and reliability required by *Daubert's* four factors.

The Federal Rules of Evidence provide that full hearings outside the presence of the jury are only mandated "when the interests of justice so require."[24] Thus, a preliminary hearing pursuant to Rules 104(a) and (c) of the Federal Rules of Evidence is the most practical approach. If such a hearing is scheduled before trial begins, the result of the hearing could affect settlement negotiations. Some courts are reluctant to spend time conducting a *Daubert* hearing. In those instances, the *Daubert* motion and accompanying documents carry even more importance.

C. States Applying a Hybrid System or Their Own Evidentiary Standards

As stated above, states generally either follow the *Daubert* or *Frye* line of cases. In total, 26 states follow *Daubert* and 14 states plus the District of Columbia follow *Frye*. This means that 10 states either use a combination of both *Frye* and *Daubert* or have devised their own system for determining the admissibility of novel scientific evidence. The states that fall under this category include Alabama, Georgia, Hawaii, Massachusetts, Nevada, New Hampshire, New Jersey, Utah, Virginia, and Wisconsin.[25]

Often times, a particular state's standard is loosely based on *Frye* or *Daubert* or a combination of both. For example, Alabama has neither abandoned *Frye's* "general acceptance" test, nor has it adopted the *Daubert* standard. Alabama uses *Frye* with respect to expert scientific testimony on subjects other than DNA,[26] but in dealing with DNA evidence, Alabama uses a statute based on *Daubert.*[27] Hawaii determines the admissibility of evidence based on Rules 702 and 703 of its own Rules of Evidence, which seem to give some credence to both *Frye* and *Daubert.*[28] Because each of these states has its own standards, it is important to check with each state's rules of evidence.[29]

D. Rule 703 of the Federal Rules of Evidence

Rule 703 of the Federal Rules of Evidence essentially allows a testifying expert to rely on facts or data not otherwise admissible. Thus, even if the judge does not allow scientific evidence regarding the effects of mold to come in directly, the expert testifying at trial can still base his opinion on such data if the data is reasonably relied upon by similar experts in the field. The current Rule 703 of the Federal Rules of Evidence provides:

> The facts or data in the particular cause upon which an expert bases an opinion or inference may be those perceived by or made known to the expert at or before the hearing. If of a type reasonably relied upon by experts in the particular field in forming opinions or inferences upon the subject, the facts or data need not be admissible in evidence in order for the opinion or inference to be admitted. Facts or data that are otherwise inadmissible shall not be disclosed to the jury by the proponent of the opinion or inference unless the court determines that their probative value in assisting the jury to evaluate the expert's opinion substantially outweighs their prejudicial effect.[30]

Experts are provided wide latitude in offering opinions, and may state opinions not based on first-hand knowledge or observation.[31] Rule 703 may vary among states. Like Federal Rules of Evidence Rule 702, it would be wise to check the local rules of practice. Specifically, some jurisdictions following *Frye* hold that opinion evidence relying upon scientific principles *must* meet the *Frye* standards.[32]

2.3 Evidentiary Standards for Mold-Related Injuries and Diseases

Claims of mold-related injury are based upon a wide range of allegations of injury. With the boom of mold litigation over the past several years, courts have had many opportunities to decide whether to admit or exclude expert testimony on mold issues. In evaluating whether to admit such testimony, courts often turn to the Manual of Scientific Evidence, which provides an outline for dealing with toxicology subjects like mold.

A. Manual of Scientific Evidence

Understanding toxicology, or the science of poisons, is crucial to the science of mold. "There are three central tenets of toxicology. First, 'the dose makes the poison'; this implies that all chemical agents are intrinsically hazardous—whether they cause harm is only a question of dose. Even water, if consumed in large quantities, can be toxic. Second, each chemical agent tends to produce a specific pattern of biological effects that can be used to establish disease causation. Third, the toxic responses in laboratory animals are useful predictors of toxic responses in humans."[33] While some scientists debate the usefulness of testing toxic responses in animals, it is unethical to purposefully expose humans to chemical agents.[34]

In evaluating mold or other poisons, toxicologists consider the hazards presented to the human population and environment and the degree of risk associated with exposure at a specific dose.[35] Furthermore, toxicologists analyze risk, specifically the risk of contracting a disease at a given dose.[36] In the courtroom, toxicologists offer evidence to support or refute a claim that exposure to chemicals caused a plaintiffs' injuries.[37] Courts consider several factors in evaluating the testimony presented by toxicologists.

First, courts consider the species of animal tested along with the biological links to humans.[38] Overall, humans and other mammals share a similar biological bond.[39] Problems arise, however, where humans complain about nonspecific symptoms like nausea and headaches because it is difficult to test laboratory animals for these symptoms.[40] It is also problematic where the laboratory animals differ from humans. For example, rats do not have gall bladders.[41]

Second, courts consider whether the research indicates that a chemical agent affects a specific organ in a laboratory animal, and whether there is a similar link in humans.[42] Toxicologists have found that certain chemical agents only affect a single organ, and some chemical agents affect multiple organs.[43]

Third, courts consider the chemical structure of the compound and its relationship to toxicity.[44] Toxicologists compare the chemical structures of compounds with a known toxicity with chemical structures of compounds with an unknown toxicity, and estimate toxicity based on the molecular similarities between the two compounds.[45]

Fourth, courts consider whether the compound has been subject to in vitro research and whether such findings are relevant.[46] Often times, toxicologists have used in vitro tests to test new products, and in vitro tests often provide early warning detection for toxicity.[47]

Fifth, courts consider whether the association between exposure to a chemical agent and a disease is biologically plausible.[48]

For each mold injury listed below, courts should consider these factors to determine whether an association exists between exposure to mold and risk of inheritance of a disease. These days, any injury claim will be comprised of one or more types of injuries from allergic, infectious, or toxic reactions to mold.

B. Allergic Reactions Resulting From Exposure to Mold

Mold allergies and allergic reactions are common and are well documented. The most common types of allergic responses are immunoglobulin E (IgE) and immunoglobulin G (IgG).[49]

The allergic response IgE, which is the more common of the two types, can lead to allergic asthma or allergic rhinitis.[50] People with this type of mold allergy are generally susceptible to a host of other indoor and outdoor allergens, including animal dander, dust mites, and weed, tree, and grass pollens.[51] Mold is just one environmental agent that is problematic for these people. Approximately 40 percent of the population has the allergic response IgE.[52] In addition, approximately 10 percent of the population has allergic antibodies to common inhalant molds and about 5 percent of the population will develop allergic symptoms from molds during their lifetime.[53]

The second allergic response, IgG, can lead to hypersensitivity pneumonitis (HP).[54] "HP results from exaggeration of the normal IgG immune response against inhaled foreign (fungal or other) proteins."[55] Although most cases of IgG derive from exposure to mold at work, some cases have been linked to pet birds, humidifiers, and heating, ventilating, and air conditioning systems.[56]

In sum, allergic reactions to mold, unlike toxic reactions discussed *infra*, are rather common. Courts have often allowed experts to testify regarding allergic reactions.

For example, in *New Haverford Partnership v. Stroot*,[57] the Supreme Court of Delaware affirmed the trial court's decision to allow the admission of the testimony of a physician who opined that the mold found in the apartment of plaintiffs increased the severity of plaintiffs' asthma.[58] In admitting this evidence, the Court followed the standard set forth by *Daubert.*[59]

In *Mondelli v. Kendel Homes Corp.*,[60] the Supreme Court of Nebraska, applying *Frye*, held that the trial court abused its discretion in excluding plaintiffs' proffered expert testimony. Plaintiffs claimed that mold found in their home caused several asthmatic attacks that required hospitalization.[61] The Court found that plaintiffs' experts were qualified to testify and their testimony was relevant and helpful to the jury.[62]

Not all cases, however, allow expert testimony regarding allergies or asthma. In *Roche v. Lincoln Property Co.*,[63] a United States District Court held that a physician's testimony, that mold within a tenants' apartment caused respiratory and other ailments, was inadmissible under *Daubert.*[64] Plaintiffs' expert was a doctor that was board-certified in internal medicine and pulmonary diseases.[65] The court excluded plaintiffs' expert for three reasons. First, he failed to follow the established methodology for differential diagnosis.[66] Second, he failed to explain how published reports showing a link between mold and allergic reactions related to the plaintiffs.[67] Third, he relied solely on the time frame between plaintiffs' exposure to molds and plaintiffs' symptoms, without accounting for flu-like symptoms that happened shortly before plaintiffs moved into the apartment.[68] Plaintiffs' expert failed to "provide any evidence that a particular mold in the [apartment] had a greater possibility than cigarettes, dust mites, fibers [cat dander],...or any number of present environmental allergens, of causing health effects in [plaintiffs]."[69]

C. Infection Resulting From Exposure to Mold

Like allergic reactions to mold, infections related to mold exposure are fairly common. Those with compromised immune systems are more susceptible to infections from exposure to mold than most people. Specifically, people undergoing chemotherapy, people with uncontrolled diabetics, people with advanced AIDS, and people with lymphoproliferative disorders, including acute leukemia, are at risk for fungal infections that invade deep tissue.[70] Only people with severe immune system problems should be concerned about this exposure to mold, and these cases are easy to spot and diagnose.

In addition, certain infections are common to people with more normal immune systems. These infections, albeit less severe than those mentioned in the previous paragraph, are extremely common.[71] Some of these infections include "infection of the feet (*tinea pedis*), nails (*tinea onychomycosis*), groin (*tinea cruris*), dry body skin (*tinea corporis*), and infection of the oral or vaginal mucosa."[72] Often times, the particular fungus involved can be found growing as an indoor mold or on indoor pets like dogs and cats.[73] Like the typical allergic reaction to mold, the infectious reaction is rather mild.

D. Injury and Disease Resulting from Exposure to Toxic Mold

As noted in the introduction, much of the press coverage surrounding mold in recent years has centered on *Stachybotrys chartarum*. Although *Stachybotrys chartarum* has been found in homes, schools, and offices, other indoor molds also produce mycotoxins, which are metabolites that some people believe cause various injuries and diseases.[74] More importantly, recent scientific publications have "concluded that indoor airborne levels of microorganisms are only weakly correlated with human disease or building-related symptoms and that a causal relationship has not been established between these complaints and indoor exposures to [*Stachybotrys*] *chartarum*."[75] Previous studies regarding infant lung hemorrhages noted *infra* arrived at the opposite conclusion.

"If mycotoxins are to have human health effects, there must be an actual presence of mycotoxins, a pathway of exposure from source to susceptible person, and absorption of a toxic dose over a sufficiently short period of time."[76] At the present time, however, scientists have not established standards for what constitutes harmful levels of mold exposure.[77] While studies have been conducted on rats, mice, and guinea pigs, the results of these tests are not particularly helpful for a plaintiff in a mold case.[78]

Hypothetically, even if a plaintiff could establish such standards for mold exposure, they would not necessarily be relevant because mold found indoors is made up of both indoor and outdoor mold.[79] In addition, outdoor molds are more prevalent and significant in airway allergic disease than indoor molds.[80] And, if outdoor molds are shown to be the "cause" of a plaintiff's problems, the plaintiff has no case for negligence, breach of warranty, or the like.

Scientists have also not found a method to determine exposure levels by examining a specific quantity of mold.[81] In examining a mold sample, the amount of mycotoxin produced depends on several variables, including "the species and strain of mold, length of time the mold has been growing, the amount of available food and water, temperature, and the amount (and even wavelength) of available light."[82] In addition, different varieties of mold move differently.[83] *Stachybotrys chartarum* is a rather idle form of mold that requires some mechanical disturbance in order for it to become airborne.[84] Some laboratories have recently developed procedures to measure the level of mycotoxins in the air, but the level of success of these laboratories is currently unknown.[85]

Finally, no biomarker exists to determine if a person has been exposed to mold.[86] Although some plaintiffs may claim that a high level of a specific antibody exists in their blood work, a small percentage of people "have levels above the reference value for any one tested material. Consequently, a panel of tests has a high probability of producing a false-positive result."[87] In sum, our knowledge regarding toxic mold, including *Stachybotrys chartarum*, is incomplete. Despite the lack of knowledge regarding *Stachybotrys chartarum*, some scientists have developed a protocol in evaluating patients who have possibly been exposed to this toxic mold.[88]

As the following summary indicates, plaintiffs have alleged a large number of injuries and diseases resulting from exposure to mold. Accompanying each description is a summary of the state of the science regarding the disease or injury, as well as the likelihood of admission of such evidence in court under *Daubert* and *Frye*.

1. Infant lung hemorrhage

In 1994, a pediatric pulmonologist alerted the Centers for Disease Control and Prevention (CDC) to eight babies in Cleveland, Ohio, who all had developed a rare disorder: all eight of these babies had bleeding lungs. In investigating these cases, the CDC noted that the babies all lived in homes with water damage. Thereafter, the investigation centered on mold, particularly *Stachybotrys chartarum.*

In its initial report, the CDC concluded that mold *could* be responsible for the lung bleeding.[89] By 1995, the CDC began conducting press conferences discussing the possible link.[90] In 1997, the CDC issued its second report on the Cleveland case study.[91] Although the second report was still cautious and indicated that further studies were necessary, the media ferociously began to warn America of the "dangers" of mold.[92] Television stations including ABC and CNN devoted news segments to the 1997 report published by the CDC.[93] In addition, print media including the Wall Street Journal, the New York Times, and the Chicago Tribune published articles about the possible link between mold and bleeding lungs,[94] and people created mold awareness websites and Internet message boards to discuss emerging mold issues.

The sensationalism and publicity surrounding the possible link helped lead the CDC to form two expert panels to further study the epidemic.[95] The results from these studies forever changed everything we know about the relationship between mold and human illness. A 1999 report rejected the link between mold and infant pulmonary hemorrhage, stating that the illnesses of the eight infants were not compatible with illnesses known to have been caused by *Stachybotrys chartarum.*[96] The 1999 report also questioned how no other family members exhibited any illness or symptoms related to the mold.[97] An additional report published in 2000 by the CDC further disaffirmed any definitive link between *Stachybotrys chartarum* and pulmonary hemorrhage.[98] Further studies, not commissioned by the CDC, doubt any such link because *Stachybotrys chartarum* mold spores are unlikely to become airborne.[99] Furthermore, even if *Stachybotrys chartarum* spores were to become airborne, the spores are too large to reach someone's lower respiratory tract.[100]

Based on current research, the possible link between mold and lung hemorrhage cannot satisfy a *Daubert* analysis.[101] Similarly, under a *Frye* analysis, there has been no general acceptance of a purported link between mold and lung damage.

2. Cancer

Any purported link between mold and cancer is even more unrealistic,[102] and purported claims that exposure to *Stachybotrys chartarum* caused cancer are very rare because of the lack of supporting science. While some studies have found that certain fungi and mycotoxins have caused tumors in monkeys, there are only limited studies regarding the carcenogenicity of inhaled aflaxins such as *Stachybotrys chartarum.*[103] These limited studies involving inhaled aflaxins were all flawed in some aspect or another.[104] As such, courts must exclude expert testimony regarding the purported link between mold and cancer as unreliable under both *Daubert* and *Frye*.[105]

3. Brain damage and other cognitive deficiencies

Some courts have allowed experts to testify regarding Toxic Encephalopathy. Toxic Encephalopathy is an impairment that affects intellect, memory, emotions, and personality.[106] In a case decided by a Delaware superior court, the judge allowed plaintiff's expert to discuss Toxic Encephalopathy, but allowed the defendants to cross-examine plaintiff's expert as to any defects in the diagnostic methods.[107] Other courts, however, have excluded evidence regarding Toxic Encephalopathy. In *Allison v. Fire Insurance Exchange*,[108] the court relied on *Daubert* and its progeny to exclude the testimony of plaintiff's expert witnesses.[109] One of plaintiff's experts could not say whether his techniques were generally accepted in the scientific community.[110] Furthermore, both experts' testimony was based on unreliable foundational data.[111] Other courts previously allowed the admission of expert testimony regarding cognitive deficits based on exposure to atypical molds, but these cases are likely irrelevant because they are outdated.[112]

On the other hand, there is some support for brain damage based on people *eating* moldy foods. Centuries ago, people feared ergotism, an illness caused by eating moldy grain products.[113] Ergot is a fungal disease of rye grass. Ergotism is a form of fungal poisoning caused by ingesting ergot.[114] The symptoms of ergotism include muscle spasms, seizures, and hallucinations.[115] In fact, the drug LSD can be extracted from ergot.[116] In the past, people whose diet depended on grain products including rye were susceptible to ergotism.[117] Some scholars propose that ergotism contributed to the Salem Witch Trials in early America and the Black Death in the late middle ages.[118] As recently as 1975, ergotism was reported in India.[119] Nevertheless, there is no scientific support that links the rare disease of ergotism to the inhalation of airborne mold spores.[120] Therefore, any expert testimony regarding a connection between ergotism and inhalation of airborne toxic mold spores may be excluded under both *Daubert* and *Frye*.

4. Fibromyalgia

Most courts will also likely exclude evidence regarding a link between mold and Fibromyalgia. In brief, Fibromyalgia is a disorder where people develop muscle and soft tissue pain, tenderness, and fatigue.[121] People with Fibromyalgia also report morning stiffness and trouble sleeping.[122] Doctors may have trouble diagnosing Fibromyalgia because its symptoms are indistinguishable from symptoms of other disorders.[123] Like many other illnesses mentioned in this section, scientists have not identified a cause associated with Fibromyalgia.[124] As such, some courts have chosen to exclude evidence regarding Fibromyalgia.[125]

5. Multiple Chemical Sensitivity

Some plaintiffs have hired expert witnesses to testify that they have Multiple Chemical Sensitivity. Multiple Chemical Sensitivity is a condition used to describe a person who has been exposed to a number of chemicals, including mold.[126] Although scientists debate whether Multiple Chemical Sensitivity is a "real disorder," some people have complained of symptoms including headaches, fatigue, nausea, confusion, and dizziness.[127] People who claim they have developed Multiple Chemical Sensitivity do not develop antibodies in response to chemical exposure.[128] Most courts have declined to recognize the diagnosis of Multiple Chemical Sensitivity as a valid condition.[129] At the very least, some courts following *Daubert* have not allowed experts to testify regarding Multiple Chemical Sensitivity.[130]

6. Sick Building Syndrome

Sick Building Syndrome, often related to Multiple Chemical Sensitivity, refers to a set of symptoms that are attributed to occupancy in a building. Like Multiple Chemical Sensitivity, some courts have refused to allow experts to testify regarding Sick Building Syndrome. Plaintiffs often claim that their illness is a result of working in a poorly ventilated building. Typical symptoms of Sick Building Syndrome include itchy eyes, dry throat, headache, and lethargy.[131] Courts not allowing experts to testify regarding Sick Building Syndrome cite the lack of scientific knowledge regarding the alleged syndrome.

> [N]o specific causative agent has been identified for the symptoms occurring in patients with the Sick Building Syndrome....The lack of agreement by workers in this field over the definition of Sick Building Syndrome and inclusion and exclusion criteria for patients suspected of having this syndrome has hampered efforts to design well-controlled studies. Evidence that this syndrome exists as a separate disease entity is weak. Some have claimed that mass hysteria and other psychological factors are responsible for symptoms.[132]

A Delaware court applying *Daubert* placed Sick Building Syndrome in the same boat with Multiple Chemical Sensitivity and refused to allow testimony regarding either because of problems with proof of causation.[133] While some courts have allowed expert testimony in "sick building cases," it should be noted that these cases were published at a time when scientific evidence regarding exposure to mold was less complete.[134]

7. Chronic Fatigue Syndrome

Unlike Sick Building Syndrome and Multiple Chemical Sensitivity, Chronic Fatigue Syndrome is a diagnosable disease. Chronic Fatigue Syndrome symptoms often resemble the symptoms of the flu and include headache, fatigue and muscle weakness, mild fever, and difficulty concentrating.[135] Although doctors can diagnose Chronic Fatigue Syndrome, there is no known cause of the disease.[136] In a mold case, where an expert cannot pinpoint the actual cause of Chronic Fatigue Syndrome, expert testimony suggesting that exposure to mold caused the Chronic Fatigue Syndrome should be excluded under both *Daubert* and *Frye*.[137]

8. Reactive Airway Dysfunction Syndrome

Unlike most mold-related illnesses and diseases, some courts have allowed experts to testify regarding Reactive Airway Dysfunction Syndrome (RADS). RADS is similar to asthma, but is induced by exposure to a high-level irritant, gas, vapor, or fume.[138] Some scientists believe that dusts can cause RADS.[139] In *Minner*,[140] the court allowed expert testimony regarding RADS because plaintiffs made a sufficient showing that the air quality in the building *could* have caused RADS.[141] Although the court in *Minner* allowed expert testimony regarding RADS, some courts have not admitted expert testimony regarding RADS.[142] Whether exposure to mold can cause RADS is certainly debatable at this point.

2.4 Causation

Plaintiffs bringing mold claims must demonstrate that exposure to mold caused illness or injury. This can be a difficult proposition because, after all, mold is literally everywhere. In order to overcome this burden, plaintiffs in mold cases must demonstrate both general and specific causation.[143]

A. General Causation

An expert testifying to general causation must show that a substance like mold is capable of causing a certain physical effect in the general population.[144] "One can prove general causation either through experiments to show that a substance is capable of causing a particular injury or by attempting to show that exposure to a substance increases the risk of a particular injury."[145] As noted earlier, existing scientific studies have not determined a definitive link between exposure to mold and illnesses such as lung hemorrhages, brain damage, and cancer. Therefore, plaintiffs attempting to show general causation with regards to these injuries will be unsuccessful and need not attempt to show specific causation.

In *Allison v. Fire Insurance Exchange*,[146] noted *supra*, two doctors conducted epidemiological studies to examine whether a link existed between exposure to mold and Toxic Encephalopathy.[147] In evaluating whether epidemiological studies have a reliable foundation, the factors courts examine include whether the study was properly designed, biased, capable of repetition with the same results 95 percent of the time, and whether exposure to the substance more than doubles the risk of injury.[148] The court in *Allison* determined that the epidemiological tests used by plaintiffs' experts failed, could not be repeated with the same results 95 percent of the time, and could not show that exposure to the substance more than doubled the risk of injury.[149] The court therefore found that there was no reliable foundation for the general causation evidence and, as a result, did not even address the issue of specific causation.[150]

B. Specific Causation

Specific causation requires that the plaintiff prove that the substance actually caused the plaintiff's alleged injury.[151] One of the biggest hurdles in proving specific causation is to show that a plaintiff was exposed to a sufficient level of mold over a sufficient amount of time to cause the injury claimed.[152] Mold exists in virtually every home or building in some quantity. Although almost any substance can be toxic above a certain level of exposure, certain molds like *Stachybotrys chartarum* do not normally become airborne. Moreover, scientists have not developed standards for harmful mold exposure.

Nevertheless, in order to prove specific causation in a mold case, some commentators suggest that a plaintiff (1) properly identify the mold and mold byproduct allegedly causing a plaintiff's injury; (2) determine plaintiff's proximity to the mold; (3) determine the amount of time a plaintiff was exposed to the mold; (4) determine the alleged exposure pathway; and (5) analyze plaintiff's medical history including the specific details of plaintiff's symptoms and the corresponding timeframes.[153]

1. Case law illustrating causation principles

Most reported cases evaluating causation have determined that causation had not been established. For example, in *Roche v. Lincoln Property Co.*,[154] plaintiffs claimed that mold exposure caused them to develop certain respiratory ailments.[155] Plaintiffs moved into their apartment on April 4, 2001, but one of the plaintiffs had related health problems *prior* to moving into the apartment.[156] In deciding to exclude plaintiffs' expert witnesses, the court noted that one plaintiff had asthma since she was a child, and visited the hospital for flu-like symptoms several times before moving into the apartment.[157] That particular plaintiff even visited the emergency room complaining of bronchitis on March 4, 2001, less than one month before moving into the apartment.[158] In a separate opinion granting defendant's motion for summary judgment, the court in *Roche* further discussed causation as it related to the case.[159] Regarding a different expert, the court identified several more problems evidencing a lack of specific causation. Plaintiffs' expert performed his test one year after a sample was removed from plaintiffs' apartment and the test itself was not performed at the apartment.[160] In addition, plaintiffs' test failed to determine the actual level of mycotoxins in the apartment—it only determined that mycotoxins grew out of one of the samples collected a year before the test.[161]

Similarly, in an unpublished decision from California, an appellate court found that causation did not exist. In that case, plaintiff claimed that a broken sewer pipe outside her town home and mold in her garage caused her bronchitis.[162] Plaintiff saved the contents of her vacuum cleaner bag and a filter from her air purifier, and later tested these samples to show causation.[163] The trial court found that the link between the evidence, tested 18 months after plaintiff collected it, and plaintiff's illness was too tenuous.[164] The California Court of Appeals sided with the lower court but remanded the case to determine if the premises became uninhabitable and to calculate the amount of rent to be abated.[165]

An unpublished Ohio opinion also declined to find causation. There, plaintiff alleged that defendants negligently and recklessly contributed to the damp and moldy conditions in her basement office space, which caused her lung disease.[166] Plaintiff worked for a non-profit organization that rented office space in a basement from defendants at *no charge* as long as the non-profit organization assumed responsibility to care for the space.[167] In her absence, plaintiff claimed that mold growth accumulated in the basement.[168] Plaintiff claimed that the mold in the basement caused her lung disease, but the court found that basements, by nature, are more conducive to mold growth than other areas.[169] The defendants did not act in a willful, wanton, or reckless manner, and the fact that mold grows in a basement does not give rise to a dangerous condition.[170] The trial court granted defendant's motion for summary judgment and the appellate court affirmed.[171]

Some courts have denied motions for summary judgment brought by plaintiffs because a material issue a fact existed as to causation. In *Watters v. Department of Social Services*,[172] the Louisiana Court of Appeals found that a genuine issue of material fact existed as to whether an office-building worker was exposed to mold.[173] Approximately 680 plaintiffs had brought a class action against the Department of Social Services alleging injuries as a result of being exposed to mold and asbestos in an office building.[174] Plaintiff Christine Songy filed a motion for summary judgment and the trial court denied the motion.[175] One of plaintiff's experts indicated that she was exposed to mold, but the expert could not determine if the exposure occurred at the office building in question.[176] Additional experts also testified at depositions that plaintiff was exposed to mold.[177] On review, the Court of Appeals concluded that a genuine issue of material fact existed because there was no definitive finding of mold in any area of the building which plaintiff frequented.[178] Therefore, the trial court properly denied plaintiff's motion for summary judgment on the issue of whether she was exposed to mold at work and whether her exposure to mold was a contributing factor to her injuries.[179]

Not all courts, however, have ruled in favor of defendants on the issue of causation. In *New Haverford Partnership*,[180] the Supreme Court of Delaware held that the expert opinion of a physician certified in environmental medicine, that excessive mold in apartments *proximately caused* tenants' health problems, was admissible.[181] Although the physician neglected to conduct tests to exclude other possible causes of plaintiffs' health problems, the physician followed the scientifically accepted procedure of obtaining medical histories and patient questionnaires.[182] The court also found that the foundation for an expert's causation opinion need not be established with the precision of a laboratory experiment.[183] Plaintiffs' expert did not conduct extensive baseline tests regarding the mold levels inside and outside the apartment building.[184] The court found that plaintiffs' expert's oversight went to the weight and not the admissibility of the opinion.[185]

2.5 Preparing Data for Trial

The New York City Department of Mental Health & Hygiene proposed guidelines for inspecting and sampling mold in 1993.[186] These guidelines were developed in response to mold growth problems in several New York City buildings in the 1990s. The report initially proposed that residents visually inspect and assess any problem areas. In particular, residents are advised to inspect ventilation systems, ceiling tiles, wallboard, cardboard, and other paper surfaces for evidence of mold. The report also suggests that a trained professional obtain bulk or surface samples to identify the particular fungal contaminants. According to the report

> [b]ulk samples are usually collected from visibly moldy surfaces by scraping or cutting materials with a clean tool into a clean plastic bag. Surface samples are usually collected by wiping a measured area with a sterile swab or by stripping the suspect surface with clear tape. Surface sampling is less destructive than bulk sampling. Other sampling methods may also be available. A laboratory specializing in mycology should be consulted for specific sampling and delivery instructions.[187]

With regard to air monitoring samples, the report stated that if a resident chose to monitor air samples inside her home, she should concurrently take an air sample from outside.[188] The report further stated that someone trained in air sampling methods for microbial contaminants should perform the test and that a laboratory specializing in mycology should analyze the air samples.[189] The report, however, did not recommend that everyone conduct air samples of their homes for contamination. Air monitoring is appropriate if the resident has been diagnosed with a disease that may be associated with exposure to mold or fungus, if the resident suspects that the ventilation systems are contaminated, or if the resident suspects mold is present but cannot visually verify the presence of mold.[190]

Once an air sample is collected, the sample should be sent to a laboratory, preferably one accredited by the American Industrial Hygiene Association (AIHA).[191] While laboratories can compare the indoor samples against the outdoor samples, there are no guidelines in the industry. Laboratory test results by themselves are not sufficient to offer any medial diagnoses.[192]

As of this publication, and over ten years after these guidelines were proposed, there are still no uniform standards or findings concerning "safe" or "unsafe" levels of mold exposure. Furthermore, the mere presence of mold in a building does not necessarily mean that mycotoxins are present, or that they are present in any harmful quantities.[193] Indeed, the American College of Occupational and Environmental Medicine concluded that inhalation of a toxic dose of mycotoxins is "highly unlikely at best, even for the hypothetically most vulnerable subpopulations."[194]

2.6 Conclusion

The state of the science regarding toxic mold is, at best, inconclusive. While several years ago scientists claimed a link between *Stachybotrys chartarum* and disease or injury, scientists have since backed away from that conclusion. At the moment, scientists continue to research the potential harms related to toxic mold, but have not published any definitive findings. In order to avoid admitting "junk science" into evidence, courtrooms have to be cautious by not allowing evidence regarding toxic mold to be presented to the jury. Whether a court follows the *Daubert* or *Frye* methodology, or its own hybrid standard, courts must act as gatekeepers and deny the admission of such evidence, even with their broad discretion.

Regardless of the difficult evidentiary hurdles plaguing plaintiffs, the threat of mold exposure should be taken seriously. People discovering mold in homes, schools, offices, or other buildings should take careful steps to remediate the problem. In addition, professionals with the proper equipment should perform remediation procedures. As long as scientists debate the threat of mold exposure, people should take steps to protect themselves and their families.

Endnotes

1. *Frye v. United States*, 293 F. 1013 (D.C. Cir. 1923).

2. *Id.*

3. *Id.* at 1014.

4. *Id.*

5. *Daubert v. Merrell Dow Pharmaceuticals, Inc.*, 509 U.S. 579 (1993).

6. Alice B. Lustre, Annotation, *Post-Daubert Standards for Admissibility of Scientific and Other Expert Evidence in State Courts*, 90 A.L.R.5th 453 (2001).

7. *See e.g.*, *State v. Marshall*, 193 Ariz. 547, 549, 975 P.2d 137, 139 (App. 1998).

8. *Daubert*, 509 U.S. at 579.

9. *Id.* at 582.

10. *Id.*

11. *Id.* at 583.

12. *Id.*

13. *Id.* at 583-84.

14. *Id.* at 579.

15. *Id.* at 593-94.

16. *Id.* at 594.

17. *Id.* at 592-93.

18. *Id.* at 596.

19. Lustre, *supra* Note 6.

20. *General Electric Co. v. Joiner*, 522 U.S. 136, 143 (1997).

21. *Id.* at 146.

22. *Kumho Tire Co. v. Carmichael*, 526 U.S. 137, 147-149 (1999).

23. FED. R. EVID. 702.

24. FED. R. EVID. 104(c).

25. Lustre, *supra* Note 6.

26. *Parker v. State*, 777 So. 2d 937 (Ala.Crim.App. 2000); *Hoosier v. State*, 612 So.2d 1352 (Ala.Crim.App. 1992).

27. *See*, ALA. CODE § 36-18-30.

28. *State v. Ito*, 90 Hawaii 225, 978 P.2d 191 (App. 1999) (the following factors should be considered in determining the admissibility of scientific evidence at trial: (1) the evidence will assist the trier of fact to understand the evidence or to determine a fact in issue; (2) the evidence will add to the understanding of the jury; (3) the underlying theory is generally accepted as valid; (4) the procedures used are generally accepted as reliable if properly performed; (5) the procedures were applied and conducted properly in the present instance; and (6) whether admitting such evidence will be more probative than prejudicial).

29. *See*, Lustre, *supra* Note 6.

30. FED. R. EVID. 703.

31. *Daubert v. Merrell Dow Pharmaceuticals, Inc.*, 509 U.S. 579, 591 (1993). *See also, Gussack Realty Co. v. Xerox Corp.*, 224 F.3d 85, 94-95 (2d Cir. 2000) (even though experts did not conduct their own tests and relied primarily on data provided by others, testimony of expert admissible under *Daubert* standard).

32. *See*, *State v. Boles*, 183 Ariz. 563, 905 P.2d 572 (App. 1995) (where *Frye* test is applicable, opinion testimony not based on generally accepted principles is inadmissible regardless of the fact that the expert rendering opinion is subject to cross-examination).

33. BERNARD D. GOLDSTEIN AND MARY SUE HENIFIN, *Reference Guide on Toxicology*, REFERENCE MANUAL ON SCIENTIFIC EVIDENCE 401, 403 (2d ed. 2000) available at http://air.fjc.gov/public/fjcweb.nsf/pages/16.

34. *Id.* at 405.

35. *Id.* at 403.

36. *Id.*

37. *Id.* at 404.

38. *Id.* at 419.

39. *Id.* at 420.

40. *Id.*

41. *Id.*

42. *Id.*

43. *Id.*

44. *Id.* at 421.

45. *Id.*

46. *Id.* at 422.

47. *Id.*

48. *Id.*

49. American College of Occupational and Environmental Medicine, *Adverse Human Health Effects Associated with Molds in the Indoor Environment* (2002) available at http://www.acoem.org/position/statements.asp?CATA_ID=52.

50. American College of Occupational and Environmental Medicine, *supra* note 49. Allergic rhinitis includes nasal discharge, sneezing, and conjunctivitis. O. Edwin McClusky, *Black Mold and Human Illness*, Report of Council on Scientific Affairs. Asthma includes bronchospasm, wheezing, mucous secretion, and plugging. *Id.*

51. American College of Occupational and Environmental Medicine, *supra* note 49.

52. *Id.*

53. *Id.*

54. *Id.* Hypersensitivity pneumonitis includes farmer's lung (a lung tissue inflammation occurring from exposure of an inhaled antigen) and allergic aspergillosis (a rare lung tissue inflammation involving both airways and tissues in the lungs). O. Edwin McClusky, *supra* note 50.

55. American College of Occupational and Environmental Medicine, *supra* note 49 citing Fink J, Zacharisen MC. Hypersensitivity Pneumonitis. In: Middleton E, Jr. et al., eds *Allergy: Principles and Practice*. St. Louis: Mosby Co.; 1998-994-1004.

56. American College of Occupational and Environmental Medicine, *supra* note 49.

57. *New Haverford Partnership v. Stroot*, 772 A.2d 792 (Del. 2001).

58. *Id.* at 796, 799.

59. *Id.* at 799.

60. *Mondelli v. Kendel Homes Corp.*, 262 Neb. 263, 631 N.W.2d 846 (2001).

61. *Mondelli*, 262 Neb. at 266, 631 N.W.2d at 852.

62. *Mondelli*, 262 Neb. at 270-276, 631 N.W.2d at 854-859.

63. *Roche v. Lincoln Property Co.*, 278 F.Supp.2d 744 (D.Va. 2003).

64. *Id.* at 750-52.

65. *Id.* at 749.

66. *Id.* at 746.

67. *Id.*

68. *Id.*

69. *Id.* at 765 citing *Flores v. Allstate Texas Lloyd's Co.*, 229 F.Supp.2d 697, 702 (S.D. Tex. 2002).

70. American College of Occupational and Environmental Medicine, *supra* note 49.

71. *Id.*

72. *Id.*

73. *Id.*

74. *Id.*

75. *Id.* citing Tobin RS, et al. Significance of fungi in indoor air: report of a working group. *Can J Public Health.* 1987; 78: S1-S32; Menzies D, Bourbeau J. Building-related illnesses. *N Engl J Med.* 1997; 337: 1524-31.; Fung F, Clark R, Williams S. *Stachybotrys*, a mycotoxin-producing fungus of increasing toxicologic importance. *J Toxicol Clin Toxicol.* 1998; 36: 79-86; Robbins CA, et al. Health effects of mycotoxins in indoor air: a critical review. *Appl Occup Environ Hyg.* 2000; 15: 773-84; Sudakin DL. *Stachybotrys chartarum*: current knowledge of its role in disease. *MedGenMed.* 2000; E11; Page EH, Trout DB. The role of *Stachybotrys* mycotoxins in buildings related illness. *Am Ind Hyg Assoc J.* 2001; 62: 644-8; Terr Al. *Stachybotrys*: relevance to human disease. *Ann Allergy Asthma Immunol.* 2001; 87: 57-63; Burge HA. Fungi: toxic killers or unavoidable nuisances? *Ann Allergy Asthma Immunol.* 2001; 87: 52-56.

76. American College of Occupational and Environmental Medicine, *supra* note 49.

77. Cliff Hutchinson and Robert Powell, *A New Plague—Mold Litigation: How Junk Science and Hysteria Built an Industry*, commissioned by the U.S. Chamber Institute for Legal Reform and the Center for Legal Policy at the Manhattan Institute, 27 (2003).

78. American College of Occupational and Environmental Medicine, *supra* note 49.

79. Cliff Hutchinson and Robert Powell, *supra* note 77, at 27.

80. American College of Occupational and Environmental Medicine, *supra* note 49.

81. Cliff Hutchinson and Robert Powell, *supra* note 77, at 27.

82. *Id.* citing Jonathan S. Rutchick, *Evaluating Mold Exposure and Neurologic Complaints: No Easy Answers*, CLAIMS MAGAZINE 53 (March 2003).

83. Cliff Hutchinson and Robert Powell, *supra* note 77, at 27 citing Harriet A. Burge, *Fungi: Toxic Killers or Unavoidable Nuisances?*, 87 ANNALS OF ALLERGY, ASTHMA & IMMUNOLOGY 33, 36 (Dec. 2001).

84. *Id.*

85. For example, http://www.aerotechlabs.com offers a service to measure the amount of *Stachybotrys chartarum.*

86. Cliff Hutchinson and Robert Powell, *supra* note 77, at 28.

87. American College of Occupational and Environmental Medicine, *supra* note 49.

88. The protocol includes the following steps:

1. A thorough history, including the duration and nature of symptoms, home environmental and workplace history, past medical history, and family history.
2. A physical exam.
3. Exclusion of more common infectious causes.
4. Phenotyping the patient as atopic versus non-atopic, which includes skin testing.
5. Perform a chest x-ray or high-resolution CT of chest.
6. Supportive testing including serologic testing for specific IgG, IgE, or IgA to mold, hypersensitivity pneumonitis screen, and consideration of humoral and cell-mediated immune system evaluation.
7. Environmental assessment including walkthrough, air sampling, and measurement of known perennial allergens, irritants, dew point, and mycotoxins.
8. Measurement of total symptom scores in and out of the environment.
9. Measurement of peak expiratory flow rates in and out of the environment event every 2 to 3 hours while awake, and correlation with environmental exposure measurements.
10. Consideration of specific provocation test.

O. Edwin McClusky, *supra* note 50 citing J.A. Bernstein, *The Role of the Allergist in Building Related Illness* in American Academy of Allergy, Asthma, and Immunology 58th Annual Meeting handout materials (2002).

89. Cliff Hutchinson and Robert Powell, *supra* note 77, at 12.

90. Cliff Hutchinson and Robert Powell, *supra* note 77, at 12 citing *Science Update*, DALLAS MORNING NEWS at 8D (April 3, 1995); *see also*, Cleveland Plain Dealer at 12B (Sept. 14, 1995) (researchers "99.999 percent certain they've pinpointed" fungus as cause).

91. *See*, Update: Pulmonary Hemorrhage/Hemosiderosis Among Infants—Cleveland, Ohio 1993-1996 46(2) MORBIDITY & MORTALITY WEEKLY REPORT 33 (Jan. 17, 1997).

92. Cliff Hutchinson and Robert Powell, *supra* note 77, at 12.

93. *Id.*

94. *Id.*

95. *Id.*

96. *Id.* at 14 citing *Report of the CDC Working Group on Pulmonary Hemorrhage/Hemosiderosis* (June 17, 1999).

97. Cliff Hutchinson and Robert Powell, *supra* note 77, at 14.

98. *Id.* citing *Update: Pulmonary Hemorrhage/Hemosiderosis Among Infants—Cleveland, Ohio*, 1993-1996, 49(09) MORBIDITY & MORTALITY WEEKLY REPORT 180 (Mar. 10 2000).

99. *See e.g., Clearing the Air: Asthma and Indoor Air Exposures* at 163, NATIONAL ACADEMY OF SCIENCES, INSTITUTE OF MEDICINE (2000).

100. Cliff Hutchinson and Robert Powell, *supra* note 77, at 30 citing D.M. Kuhn and M. A Ghannoum, *Indoor Mold, Toxigenic Fungi, and Stachybotrys chartarum: Infectious Disease Perspective*, 16(1) CLINICAL MICROBIOLOGY REVIEWS 144, 159 (2003)

101. Cliff Hutchinson and Robert Powell, *supra* note 77, at 30.

102. *Id.*

103. *Id.* citing D.M. Kuhn and M. A Ghannoum, *Indoor Mold, Toxigenic Fungi, and Stachybotrys chartarum: Infectious Disease Perspective*, 16(1) CLINICAL MICROBIOLOGY REVIEWS 144, 159-162 (2003)

104. Cliff Hutchinson and Robert Powell, *supra* note 77, at 30.

105. *Id.*

106. *Minner v. American Mortgage & Guaranty Co.*, 791 A.2d 826, 857 (Del. Super. 2000) citing WHO & Nordic Council of Ministers, *Chronic Effects of Organic Solvents on the Central Nervous System and Diagnostic Criteria*, 8 (1985).

107. *Id.*

108. *Allison v. Fire Insurance Exchange* 98 S.W.3d 227 (Tex. App. 2002).

109. *Id.* at 239-40.

110. *Id.* at 239.

111. *Id.* at 240.

112. *New Haverford Partnership v. Stroot*, 772 A.2d 792 (Del. 2001) (applying *Daubert*, the Supreme Court of Delaware found that evidence opined by experts was accepted in the scientific community).

113. Cliff Hutchinson and Robert Powell, *supra* note 77, at 28.

114. *Poisons of the Past/Ergotism* at http://www.uic.edu/classes/osci/osci590/5_1Poisons%20of%20the%20Past%20Ergotism.htm

115. Cliff Hutchinson and Robert Powell, *supra* note 77, at 28-29 citing D.M. Kuhn and M. A Ghannoum, *supra* note 103 at 159-60.

116. *Poisons of the Past/Ergotism*, *supra* note 114.

117. *Id.*

118. *Id.*

119. Cliff Hutchinson and Robert Powell, *supra* note 77, at 29 citing D.M. Kuhn and M. A Ghannoum, *supra* note 103 at 159.

120. Cliff Hutchinson and Robert Powell, *supra* note 77, at 29.

121. *Fibromyalgia Topic Overview*, available at http://my.webmd.com/content/healthwise/10/2429.htm?lastselectedguid={5FE84E90-BC77-4056-A91C-9531713CA348}.

122. *Id.*

123. *Id.*

124. *Id.*

125. *See e.g., Minner v. American Mortgage & Guaranty Co.*, 791 A.2d 826, 855 (Del. Super. 2000) ("This sort of speculative testimony in stating that the environmental material in the building was a causal factor in the Plaintiffs' development of [Fibromyalgia], without the sufficient exclusion of other causative factors, is precisely the type of testimony that should be kept from the jury under the principles of *Daubert*").

126. *Multiple Chemical Sensitivity* at http://my.webmd.com/content/article/61/67473.htm?lastselectedguid={5FE84E90-BC77-4056-A91C-9531713CA348}.

127. *Id.*

128. *Id.*

129. *See e.g., Minner*, 791 A.2d at 850.

130. *Id.* ("Dr. Ziem's testimony concerning MCS must be excluded from the jury as unreliable on two fronts under the *Daubert* standard. First, the Court is satisfied that MCS is not a scientifically valid diagnosis. Second, the Court opines that Dr. Ziem's testimony that the Discover Card building somehow caused Plaintiffs' MCS seems to be based on nothing other than speculation"). *See also*, *Bradley v. Brown*, 42 F.3d 434 (7th Cir. 1994) (testimony of physician that Multiple Chemical Sensitivity was the result of pesticide exposure properly excluded); *Summers v. Missouri Pac. R.R.*, 132 F.3d 599, 603 (10th Cir. 1997) ("MCS is a controversial diagnosis that has been excluded under *Daubert* as unsupported by sound scientific reasoning or methodology").

131. *Are You a Victim of Sick Building Syndrome?* Available at http://my.webmd.com/content/article/35/1728_97473.htm?lastselectedguid={5FE84E90-BC77-4056-A91C-9531713CA348}

132. *Minner*, 791 A.2d at 852 citing 268 JAMA, Dec. 23/30, Clinical Ecology-Council on Scientific Affairs 3455, 3466 (1992).

133. *Minner*, 791 A.2d at 867-68.

134. *See e.g. Centex-Rooney Const. Co., Inc. v. Martin Country*, 706 So.2d 20 (Fla. App. 1998) (Relying on *Frye*, the Florida Appellate Court affirmed the lower court's decision to admit the expert testimony of two doctors who suggested the existence of health hazards based on toxic mold found in several buildings. The Florida Appellate Court's decision to allow two experts to testify was not based on any blanket rule on the admissibility of "toxic mold" testimony but on the fact that the experts in question provided specific references to published medical support of their claims and methodology at a *Frye* hearing).

135. *Newly Diagnosed: Chronic Fatigue Syndrome (CFS)* available at http://my.webmd.com/content/article/70/81020.htm?lastselectedguid={5FE84E90-BC77-4056-A91C-9531713CA348}

136. *Id.*

137. *See e.g., Minner*, 791 A.2d at 853-54.

138. *Id.* at 856 citing Stuart M. Brooks et al., *The Spectrum of Irritant-Induced Asthma*, 113 Chest/1/Jan.1998, 42 (1998).

139. *Minner*, 791 A.2d at 857.

140. *Minner v. American Mortgage & Guaranty Co.*, 791 A.2d 826, 855 (Del. Super. 2000)

141. *Id.*

142. *See e.g., Schmaltz v. Norfolk & W. Ry.*, 878 F.Supp. 1119 (D.Ill. 1995) (Plaintiff's expert failed to come forward with sufficient empirical support for causation opinion that plaintiff's condition, diagnosed as RADS, was caused by exposure to herbicides).

143. *Merrell Dow Pharms., Inc. v. Havner*, 953 S.W.2d 706, 714 (Tex. 1997).

144. Cliff Hutchinson and Robert Powell, *supra* note 77, at 24 citing *Cavallo v. Star Enterprise*, 892 F.Supp. 756, 771 n. 34 (D.Va. 1995).

145. *Allison v. Fire Insurance Exchange*, 98 S.W.3d 227, 239 (Tex. App. 2002) citing *Havner*, 953 S.W.2d at 714-15.

146. 98 S.W.3d 227 (Tex. App. 2002).

147. *Id.* at 239.

148. *Havner*, 953 S.W.2d at 717-23.

149. *Allison*, 98 S.W.3d at 239-40.

150. *Id.* at 240.

151. *Havner*, 953 S.W.2d at 714.

152. Cliff Hutchinson and Robert Powell, *supra* note 77, at 25.

153. *Id.* at 26.

154. *Roche v. Lincoln Property Co.*, 278 F.Supp.2d 744 (D.Va. 2003).

155. *Id.* at 745-46.

156. *Id.* at 764.

157. *Id.*

158. *Id.*

159. *Roche v. Lincoln Property Co.*, 2003 WL 22002716 (E.D. Va. 2003)

160. *Id.* at 4.

161. *Id.*

162. *Dick v. Pacific Heights Townhouses*, 2002 WL 31117253 (Cal. App. 2002).

163. *Id.* at 2.

164. *Id.* at 3.

165. *Id.* at 9.

166. *Alberty v. J.C. Partners Limited*, 2000 WL 1807273 (Ohio App. 2000).

167. *Id.* at 1.

168. *Id.*

169. *Id.* at 3.

170. *Id.*

171. *Id.* at 4.

172. *Watters v. Department of Social Services,* 849 So.2d 724 (La. App. 2003).

173. *Id.* at 733.

174. *Id.* at 725.

175. *Id.*

176. *Id.* at 732-33.

177. *Id.* at 733.

178. *Id.*

179. *Id.* at 734.

180. *New Haverford Partnership v. Stroot,* 772 A.2d 792 (Del. 2001). (NEW HAVERFORD)

181. *Id.* at 800.

182. *Id.*

183. *Id.*

184. *Id.*

185. *Id.*

186. *See*, http://www.nyc.gov/html/doh/epi/moldrpt1.html.

187. *Id.*

188. *Id.*

189. *Id.*

190. *Id.*

191. *Id.* The American Industrial Hygiene Association has a listing of accredited laboratories available on their website at http://www.aiha.org

192. *See*, Frederick Fung, M.D., M.S., *What is Mold all about?* In Mold and Related Toxin Litigation and Claims Handling, April 2002 at 159.

193. ENVIRONMENTAL PROTECTION AGENCY, MOLD REMEDIATION IN SCHOOLS AND COMMERCIAL BUILDINGS, APPENDIX B, INTRODUCTION TO MOLDS (2001). *See also*, http://www.epa.gov/iaq/molds/appendb3.html.

194. American College of Occupational and Environmental Medicine, *supra* note 49.

Chapter 3

Sampling and Analysis for Mold Contamination in the Indoor Environment*

Linda D. Stetzenbach, Mark P. Buttner, and Sean P. Abbott, Ph.D.

Synopsis

---

*Original chapter written by Linda D. Stetzenbach and Mark P. Buttner. Revised and updated in 2008 by Sean P. Abbott.

3.1 Introduction

Fungi are ubiquitous and contribute to the decomposition of organic material and the natural recycling of nutrients from wood, wood-products, and detritus in the environment. They are microscopic organisms that form visible colonies or other structures when growing on a suitable substrate under favorable environmental conditions. Filamentous fungi, also termed molds, reproduce through the production of microscopic spores, many of which are dispersed by wind, rainfall, insect/arthropod vectors, and physical disturbance. Mold spores are generally present in indoor environments as mixtures of fungal genera with no one organism predominating. However, molds can colonize and grow in indoor environments that have been subjected to water accumulation or water damage, resulting in elevated concentrations or the predominance of some species that may cause in humans adverse health effects. Monitoring in indoor environments is performed to determine if unusual fungal populations or concentrations are present. Monitoring is also performed following remediation of mold-contaminated indoor environments to verify the efficacy of the remediation. This chapter focuses on currently used methods for sampling and analysis of air and surfaces in office, residential, and classroom environments.

3.2 Planning for the Monitoring of an Indoor Environment

Prior to collecting samples in an indoor environment, a plan should be prepared that outlines the reasons for the monitoring and the goals of the investigation. This planning is necessary for the selection of meaningful sampling and analysis methods. Additionally, all sample analysis should aid in proper planning for mold remediation, if necessary, to be performed in accordance with the IICRC S520 Standard and Reference Guide to Professional Mold Remediation (2008, in press). There are three main reasons to conduct an on-site investigation for mold contamination in a building. The first two are focused on the hypothesis that contaminant mold(s) may be present in the indoor environment. The third reason is to verify clean up of a mold-contaminated environment. The first reason for an investigation is concern regarding indoor quality and potential health effects. In some cases, this may be in response to complaints from employees or occupants of a building that indoor air quality is poor or the belief that fungal contaminants are causing adverse indoor environmental quality. In other cases, it may be in response to a physician reporting that a patient's symptoms are consistent with exposure to mold. The second reason, evidence or suspicion of water damage, is the most compelling. A sudden incidence of indoor water damage such as flooding, plumbing overflow or backup, or structural damage during a rainstorm are among the obvious water damage events that prompt indoor surveys for mold, but insidious water damage resulting from hidden plumbing problems, roof leaks, condensation, or construction defects is often not found until the survey has identified the presence of mold contamination. The third reason is to verify that remediation of a mold-contaminated environment has been effective. Regardless of the reason for the investigation, an on-site investigation should be conducted to visually assess the physical parameters of the building and to obtain information from the building occupants. On-site inspections in commercial buildings and schools can also provide a forum for discussions with building operators and maintenance staff. The on-site investigation conducted in post-remediation monitoring is also an opportunity for discussions with the remediation contractor. Once a decision to conduct an investigation has been made, it is important to determine the goals of the monitoring so that the proper types of data can be obtained. The types of data that are usually desired in the investigation of indoor environments are:

1. documentation of the presence of moisture accumulation/water damage conditions that are likely to lead to mold contamination;
2. documentation of visible contamination on surfaces; and
3. quantitative and qualitative measurements of the concentration and composition of airborne and surface-associated fungal populations; and/or the presence of fungal allergens, toxins or other by-products (e.g., ergosterol, ß-1,3 glucan) of fungal metabolism that indicate fungal growth.

The documentation of moisture intrusion or accumulation is provided through visual assessment of water-damaged areas and by using commercially available moisture meters for surrounding areas that do not appear to have overt water accumulation. In addition, the collection of a photographic record of surfaces is useful to document the presence of visible contamination. However, quantitative and qualitative measurements of mold populations require the sampling and analysis of the air and of surfaces. Selection of methods to be used in the monitoring must include considerations of the performance evaluation of the methods, the number of samples to be collected, the locations of sample sites, the cost of monitoring, and the types of data that are needed. The expertise of the sampling team and the analytical laboratory is also an important consideration.

3.3 Methods for Sampling and Analysis

Monitoring of air and surfaces requires consideration of both sampling and analysis techniques, with the selection of a sample collection method dependent on the analytical method(s) to be used. It is important to note that consultation with the environmental laboratory that will be responsible for the analysis is critical before conducting an investigation.

A. Analysis

Samples for airborne and surface-associated fungi have traditionally been analyzed by culture and/or by microscopic examination (ACGIH, 1999; Buttner et al., 2002a). Determination of mycotoxins, fungal allergens, ergosterol and ß-1,3 glucan indoors is not routinely conducted in indoor monitoring, but this may be useful in particular situations or for research applications.

1. Culture analysis

Culturing involves growing the mold on laboratory culture media and counting the resulting colonies. Selection of the media used to grow the colonies is critical when monitoring for culturable mold. Malt extract agar is a broad-spectrum growth medium commonly used for culture of mold in indoor environments (ACGIH, 1999), but a variety of other agar media has also been recommended. It is important to remember that no single growth medium will support the growth of all fungi. A minimal medium with glycerol (e.g., Dichloran Glycerol 18 percent agar) has been suggested to increase the likelihood of culturing xerophilic (dry-tolerant) fungi (Pasanen, 1992; Smid et al., 1989; Verhoeff et al., 1990) and antibiotic-amended media are useful in inhibiting the growth of bacteria that may prevent or obscure the culturing of slower growing fungi. Cellulolytic fungi, including *Stachybotrys chartarum*, may be optimally cultured on an agar medium containing cellulose.

In general, samples for culture analysis are inoculated onto agar and incubated at room temperature (23-25°C) for five to ten days with daily inspection and analysis. Species identification may require additional incubation time or transfer to optimal media. Incubating additional agar plates at elevated temperatures permits the selective isolation of some thermotolerant fungi (e.g., *Aspergillus fumigatus*) that grow optimally at high temperatures. Sampling for potential thermotolerant opportunistic fungal pathogens is prudent in healthcare-related facilities.

Thus, appropriate use of culturable analyses will recover a wide range of possible mold contaminants and identification of fungal species is possible to provide detailed analytical data. This can be used for making informed decisions regarding potential health effects and remediation needs.

Data are reported as the number of colony forming units (CFU) with the assumption that each colony arose from a single fungal spore or fragment of vegetative hyphae. Air samples collected using a volumetric air sampler result in data that are reported as CFU per cubic meter of air (CFU/m^3). Surface sample data may be qualitative or quantitative, and may be reported as the number of CFU/gram of sample collected or as the number of CFU/area (e.g., CFU/cm^2).

2. Microscopic analysis

Microscopic analysis provides information on the total fungal population in a sample, both culturable and non-culturable. Fungal contaminants that may not readily grow in culture (e.g., basidiospores) or those that are difficult to grow can be detected, as this method does not require the formation of colonies on an agar surface. Microscopic analysis is usually performed using standard light microscopy while other microscopic methods, such as interference, phase contrast, and scanning electron microscopy, are mostly limited to research settings.

Air samples for light microscopic analysis are collected by impacting particles directly onto a glass slide coated with an adhesive medium. Surface samples are collected by pressing surfaces with transparent tape. These samples are often referred to as "tape samples." Samples collected for microscopic analysis are generally prepared using a mounting medium with a stain (e.g., lacto cotton blue; Sime et al., 2002) to enhance examination of fungal structures and enumeration of spores. Microscopic preparations must be carefully examined since airborne particles are not necessarily deposited homogenously on the slide and surface—associated fungi collected on tape samples may not be uniformly distributed.

The results of air samples are reported as the total number of spores/m^3 of air, using the volume of air sampled to convert the data, and recognizable spores are identified and enumerated. Surface analyses from tape samples are generally reported as qualitative assessments using a numerical scoring system (e.g., Levels 1-5 corresponding to increasing density or extent of growth). Growth and reproductive structures (e.g., hyphae and conidiophores, respectively) are important to note as these structures demonstrate the growth and colonization of fungi on the sampled surface, and must be differentiated from occasional spores that may be present on surfaces as part of settled dust. Additionally, in both air and surface samples, reporting of insect parts, pollen, skin cells, fiber glass, non-biological particulate, or other fragments assist in evaluation of the condition of the sampled location.

Microscopic analytical methods allow for rapid detection of airborne spores and are not limited by viability of spores, culturability of the various types of fungi, or competition on laboratory media. Additionally, direct microscopy of surface samples (e.g., tape samples) allows for rapid confirmation of fungal growth and determination of actual growth of contaminant fungi on specific substrata within buildings.

3. Additional analytical methods

Analytical chemistry methods (e.g., high performance liquid chromatography [HPLC], gas chromatography with mass spectrophotometry [GC-MS]) can be used to detect ergosterol as indicators of the presence of fungal biomass (Douwes et al., 1999; Pasanen et al., 1999). However, identification of the types of fungi present is not possible and these methods are generally limited to analysis of surface samples. Similarly, detection of (1-3)-ß-D-glucan (a structural component of fungal cell walls) as an indicator of fungal biomass can be performed using an enzyme inhibition method (Douwes et al., 1996; Rylander, 1999). Analytical chemistry methods are also used to detect mycotoxins, toxic chemicals produced by fungi (e.g., Jarvis et al., 1998, Vesper et al., 2001). While the presence of these compounds has been associated with spores and reports of adverse human health in exposed building occupants (Sorenson et al., 1987), routine assay for these compounds in samples from indoor environments has not been widely adopted. More commonly, inference regarding the potential presence of mycotoxins is made based on identification of fungal contaminants by culturable and microscopic analytical methods.

Immunochemical methods such as enzyme-linked immunosorbent assay (ELISA) and multiplex array (Chapman, 2003; Earle et al., 2007) rely on specific antigen-antibody recognition. This type of assay can be used to detect the presence of specific fungal antigens present in a sample, and is a useful tool for monitoring for allergens in indoor environments (Chapman, 2003; Douwes et al., 1999). Allergens are best analyzed from samples of collected dust. Tests for allergens such as *Aspergillus fumigatus* and *Alternaria alternata* in household dust may be correlated with medical data obtained from allergy tests of sensitive occupants. These methods are currently not available for air samples, but inferences regarding exposure to airborne allergens can be made by analysis for a complete screen of biological particles in a spore trap sample and the detection of allergens in settled dust.

4. Molecular biology

The application of polymerase chain reaction (PCR) amplification for the detection and quantitation of contaminant fungi in indoor environments has recently developed. This technology relies on the amplification of a known gene sequence that is unique to a particular mold to detect and enumerate an organism of interest in a sample (e.g., Haugland et al., 1999), and it is not dependent on the viability of the collected material. As such, PCR may be appropriate to determine levels of specific contaminants, but does not look comprehensively for all possible fungal contaminants in a sample, and may underestimate the total levels of fungi or may miss specific significant fungal contaminants altogether. PCR decreases the analysis time and increases specificity and sensitivity, but concerns for inhibition by environmental substances present in samples requires development of additional strategies for sample processing (Cruz et al., 2001a, 2001b). Therefore, PCR is primarily used in research applications (e.g., Haugland et al., 2001; Pietarinen et al., 2008), but some commercial laboratories offer this supplemental analysis for indoor samples. The EPA has developed molecular techniques and a limited profile of fungal species to report a type of mold index, the Environmental Relative Moldiness Index (ERMI)(Vesper et al., 2007, 2008). While still limited by the factors discussed above, molecular analyses may provide additional data to help detect reservoirs of specific contaminant fungi in indoor environments. PCR provides an additional analytical tool, but it is recommended that this be used in combination with culturable and non-culturable methods.

5. Limitations to current analysis methods

There are limitations to all analysis methods. Culture depends on the ability of every spore to germinate and grow into a recognizable colony. Successful culture depends on the viability of the spore, and on the nutritional and environmental requirements imposed by the laboratory conditions. No single culture medium or set of environmental conditions will detect all the viable spores in a sample. In addition, fast-growing species will often dominate cultures of environmental samples, preventing the detection of slower growing organisms. These problems may result in underestimation of the fungal population in the sample as only the culturable spores are detected. Dead mold spores may also represent a health concern since the allergens and mycotoxins contained in the spores are still present. Because not all mold spores have to be living (e.g., *Alternaria alternata, Stachybotrys chartarum*) to cause allergic and toxigenic effects, the detection of total spores using microscopy is useful. However, fungal genera with spores of similar appearance (e.g., *Aspergillus* and *Penicillium*) cannot be distinguished using traditional light microscopy. Therefore, it is recommended that microscopic and cultural methods be used in combination in order to provide a reasonable representation of fungal populations. Methods to detect fungal biomass indicators (i.e., ergosterol, (1-3)-ß-D-glucan) do not provide information on the populations of fungi, and immunoassay methods have relatively poor sensitivity requiring large quantities of antigen to be present before a positive result is obtained. PCR, which has greater sensitivity than other assays and exquisite specificity, currently is hampered by interferences from environmental background, and it only detects the specific organisms for which the assay is designed.

B. Air Sampling

Air sampling is performed to document the concentration and composition of airborne fungi. It is important to remember that molds grow on surfaces and the spores are dispersed from these surfaces as a result of air movement and physical disturbance (e.g., removal of contaminated walls, walking on contaminated flooring). Therefore, negative results obtained from air samples do not ensure that a fungal biocontaminant is not present in the indoor environment. Because there are no recognized instruments for the direct reading of airborne fungal levels in residential or commercial buildings, it is necessary to collect samples in the field for later analysis at the laboratory. A variety of sampling methods have been used in monitoring of indoor environments (Table 3.1).

1. Impactor samplers for culture-based analysis

A variety of air samplers are commercially available (Buttner et al., 2002a; Jensen et al., 1992; Pasanen, 2001), but the most commonly used for routine indoor air quality monitoring of culturable fungi is a single-stage impactor sampler. The Andersen single-stage impactor sampler was developed in the late 1950s (Andersen, 1958), and is still widely used; but since the patent on this device has expired, other similar samplers are now available. The Andersen sampler requires a vacuum pump, an electrical power source, and a pre-filled agar petri plate. Air is drawn through 400 small holes in a sieve plate that accelerates the air stream. Particles are collected when the velocity of the air through the holes propels the particles with sufficient inertia to leave the air stream and impact onto the agar surface. The distance from the sieve plate to the agar surface is critical, and is controlled by the amount of agar in the petri plate (40 ml of agar in a 100 mm petri plate is required for the traditional single-stage sampler). The sampler is usually placed on a tripod at the breathing zone (i.e., 1.5 meters from the floor), although occasionally the sampler may be placed on a tabletop or a sampling cart during monitoring. The lower limit of detection (LLD) for this impactor sampler operating at 28.3 liters/minute for a 2-minute sampling time is 18 CFU/m^3 of air. Increasing the sampling time may increase the sensitivity, but the agar surface may become overloaded with increased levels of fungi and the agar surface may dry out leading to increased sampling stress and particle bounce, resulting in underestimation of airborne concentrations.

Table 3.1 Overview of Monitoring Methods for Mold in Indoor Environments

Method	Principle	Analysis	Advantages	Limitations
Air Sampling				
Impaction	deposition onto agar surface	culture	enumeration of culturable airborne fungal spore concentrations; species identification of colonies	dependent on physiological state of organism, selection of growth media and temperature; takes days to weeks for growth and identification; agar surface may become overcrowded with high airborne concentrations of spores or non-biological debris
	deposition onto adhesive-coated slide surface	microscopy	enumeration of airborne fungal spore concentrations; not dependent on culture	cannot discriminate between some spores at the genus level and cannot identify to the species level; may become overloaded in conditions of high airborne concentrations
Impingement	deposition into liquid	culture, microscopy, analytical chemistry, molecular biology	enumeration of culturable airborne fungal spore concentrations; variety of analytical methods; can dilute sample to avoid overloading during analysis	difficult to manipulate in the field due to glass construction and liquid sample; may induce increased sampling stress
Filtration	deposition onto filter material	culture, microscopy, analytical chemistry, molecular biology	variety of analytical methods; can dilute sample to avoid overloading during analysis	may result in dessication of organisms and culturability losses

Table 3.1 (continued)

Method	Principle	Analysis	Advantages	Limitations
Surface Sampling				
Contact	direct plating from surface onto agar	culture	inexpensive collection	representative of a limited area due to small contact area; dependent on physiological state of organism, selection of growth media and temperature; takes days to weeks for growth and identification; agar surface may become over-crowded with high concentrations
Swab	collection of material from a surface using a sterile swab	culture, microscopy, analytical chemistry, molecular biology	inexpensive collection; can dilute sample to avoid overloading during analysis; variety of analytical methods	representative of a limited area to small sample size; not optimal method for microscopy due to disarticulation of fungal structures during collection
Bulk	collection of building material	culture, microscopy (analytical chemistry, molecular biology of eluted sample)	variety of analytical methods; can dilute sample to avoid overloading during analysis	destructive method requiring removal of building material from structure; representative of a limited area due to small sample size
Dust	collection of settled dust	culture, microscopy, analytical chemistry, molecular biology	variety of analytical methods; can dilute sample to avoid overloading during analysis	representative of a limited area due to small sample size
Tape	collection of material from a surface	microscopy	inexpensive, non-destructive collection, direct examination of surfaces within the building	samples not culturable, cannot identify to species level; representative of a limited area due to small sample size

2. Impactor samplers for microscopic-based analysis

Collection of total airborne fungal spores is generally accomplished using a spore trap sampling device (Buttner et al., 2002a; Grinshpun et al., 2007; Pasanen, 2001). A variety of sampling pumps and collection materials are available. These may function as slit impactors (Grinshpun et al., 2007) or circular impactors (Grinshpun et al., 2005) and these may be portable devices that are re-loadable (e.g., Allergenco, BioSIS, Burkard, Cyclex) or be in the form of disposable cassettes attached to a vacuum pump (e.g., Allergenco-D, Air-o-cell, Cyclex-d, Micro-5, Versa Trap). Particles are collected on an adhesive-coated glass cover slip internal to the cassette. The sampling pump is operated at 5-20 liters/minute, depending on the flow rate designed for various devices, for a predetermined interval, generally 5-10 minutes. These cassettes can be easily shipped to the laboratory for analysis and there is little concern for cross-contamination between samples; but there is no provision for examining the sample in the field to determine if the slit is overloaded with particles, in which case an additional sample with a smaller volume could be collected. Portable, battery-powered or electric samplers collect short-term (1-15 minute) samples through a slit onto an adhesive-coated glass slide and operate at 10-15 liters/minute. This type of sampler is small and lightweight, and the glass slide can be examined to determine the amount of sample collected, thereby avoiding overloading of the viewing area.

3. Filter sampling

Collection of airborne particles using filter cassettes provides a means to sample for extended periods of time without overloading an agar surface or microscopic field of view (Buttner et al., 2002a; Pasanen, 2001), and filter sampling has been used to detect airborne mycotoxin (Pasanen et al., 1993). However, some concern for dessication and subsequent loss of viability is inherent in the method when used with culture-based analysis. For examination of air samples by microscopic analysis, filters used for detection of fungal spores have not proven as useful as that of the adhesive spore trap design. The collected material is returned to the laboratory for processing in a manner similar to that for bulk or dust samples (see below).

4. Gravity / settle plate sampling

Gravity or settle plate sampling is the exposure of agar-filled petri plates or greased slides to the air. There is no volumetric measurement of the air from which spores are deposited. Therefore, this is a non-quantitative sampling method. This type of sampling has been used for assessing airborne fungal presence because it does not require expensive sampling equipment and can be performed by building occupants. However, it relies on the settling of airborne particles and ignores the differential settling of spores due to differences in size and shape. In addition, air current fluctuations over the sampling surface can drastically change collection characteristics. Studies have shown that gravity/settle plate sampling poorly represents the populations of microorganisms in aerosols (Sayer et al., 1969, 1972; Solomon, 1975) and it is not recommended for use to determine fungal populations in indoor environments.

5. Limitations to air sampling

Unfortunately, all currently available methods of air sampling often underestimate the presence of fungal contaminants in indoor environments (ACGIH, 1999) due to issues with biological and physical efficiency of the instruments. Capture of airborne particles by inertial impactors is influenced by the physical size, density and aerodynamic shape of the fungal spores. Biologically, a culture-based collection method may stress the organism(s), resulting in the inability of the colony to grown under the conditions provided. Physically, the sampling method may not efficiently collect the particle size of the contaminate organism or permit discrimination from other organisms or abiotic material. Therefore, investigations of indoor environments should combine the use of a culture-based air sample and a non-culturable, spore trap method, and the investigation should include surface sampling (dust sample, tape sample) for the determination of possible sources of fungal contamination.

C. Source/Surface Sampling

Source/surface sampling can be used to identify the kinds of mold-colonizing surfaces and can provide an indication of the reservoir of fungal material that may be dispersed into the air. A variety of source/surface sampling methods are available to detect mold indoors (Table 3.1).

1. Culture-based surface sampling

One traditional method for evaluating surfaces for microbial contamination is the use of a contact plate in which a convex agar surface is pressed against the surface to be sampled. After incubation, colonies that grow on the agar are counted and identified. Commercially prepared contact plates are available which can contain any one of a variety of culture media, or the laboratory conducting the analysis may prepare the plates for the specific monitoring project. Results are often extrapolated to larger surfaces providing semi-quantitation of contamination. However, this information is only valid if there is uniform distribution of organisms, which rarely occurs for fungal contamination indoors and this practice can over- or underestimate the amount of contamination present. Contact plates are also useful to monitor before and after remedial activity to establish post-remediation verification criteria.

Irregular, uneven, textured, and smooth surfaces are often sampled using commercially available sterile swabs. Swabs may be used directly or pre-moistened in sterile liquid. The swab is wiped across the surface to be sampled and then placed into a sterile transport container and shipped to the laboratory for analysis using culture. Semi-quantitative results can be achieved but, as with contact plates, extrapolation to surfaces beyond those actually sampled is generally not possible due to uneven distribution of fungi on surfaces.

Bulk sampling refers to the collection of sections of building materials and furnishings (e.g., ceiling tile, wallpaper, wallboard, carpet) that are transported in labeled plastic bags to the analytical laboratory where the material can be analyzed by microscopy or by culture. For culture analysis, pieces of the sample are suspended in buffer, and mixed to dislodge fungal material. The buffer can then be used to inoculate a variety of growth media. Microscopic analysis is generally performed using a stereomicroscope to scan the surface of the material followed by the collection of transparent tape samples from selected areas of the bulk sample. Removal of plug segments of insulation materials (Buttner et al., 2002b) or flooring (Buttner et al., 1999) has been used to quantify fungal contamination in air handling duct materials, but bulk sampling is a destructive method necessitating the removal of material from the site where the sample is collected.

A non-destructive method that is useful in identification and quantitation of surface-associated fungi is dust sampling (AIHA, 2001). Dust sampling involves collecting material from porous surfaces (e.g., carpet, contents, air handling duct liner, air filter) and non-porous surfaces (e.g., vinyl flooring, horizontal surfaces of bookcases, cabinets). Samples are collected with a commercial single-use filter cassette using a vacuum device or an adapter to a traditional vacuum cleaner. After collection, the samples are usually prepared to remove debris (e.g., hair, textile fibers) and the fine dust is weighed and suspended in a detergent solution (e.g., sterile water with 0.05 percent tween) with serial dilution and plating to culture media (Macher, 2001). Although the dust is usually analyzed by culture, some laboratories will also examine the sample microscopically. Microscopic analysis is not recommended as a replacement to culturable analyses, but may provide useful supplemental data.

2. Microscopy-based surface sampling

Transparent adhesive tape can be used to sample visible fungal growth on surfaces. The tape is pressed against the visible growth and then mounted on a glass slide for microscopic examination. The method is qualitative providing a means to observe recognizable fungal structures sufficient for identification of many fungal genera without the need for culture. This method has been successfully used for identifying fungal contamination on carpet backing and woven baskets when the fungi were not readily culturable (Kozak et al., 1980).

D. Interpretation of Data

No exposure limits have been established for airborne or surface-associated fungi in commercial or residential indoor environments. Several years ago, some guidelines for interpretation of data were published with the general consensus that indoor fungal levels should be lower than those outdoors and the populations should be similar indoors and outdoors. In a review of published reports, Rao et al. (1996) noted that many investigators agree with Miller et al. (1988) that the presence of some fungi (e.g., pathogens and certain toxigenic fungi) are unacceptable in indoor air. However, the American Conference of Governmental Industrial Hygienists does not support any numerical criteria for interpreting air or surface data, but discusses interpretation of data that are indicative of environmental contamination and exposure of building occupants (Burge et al., 1999). This and other documents also present perspectives on comparisons of data with known databases, comparisons of compliant and non-compliant areas within buildings, and on indoor/outdoor ratios (Codina et al., 2008). The lack of adequate dose/response data contributes to the current disagreement among those attempting to formulate guidelines for acceptable environmental levels of fungi. The goal of sampling and analysis is to detect evidence of indoor proliferation of mold. However, as sampling and analytical protocols are developed to allow estimation of actual exposure and standardized protocols are established, it is likely that reliable assessments of the risk associated with fungal exposure will be obtained.

References

American Conference of Governmental Industrial Hygienists (ACGIH). 1999. "Sample Analysis." In J.M. Macher, ed. *Bioaerosols: Assessment and Control.* Cincinnati, OH, pp. 6-1–6-13.

Ameican Industrial Hygiene Association (AIHA). 2001. Report of microbial growth task force. American Industrial Hygiene Association, pp. 1-64.

Andersen, A.A. 1958. New sampler for the collection, sizing, and enumeration of viable airborne particles. *Journal of Bacteriol*ogy. Vol. 76, pp. 471-84.

ANSI/IICRC. 2008. IICRC S520 *Standard and reference guide for professional mold remediation, 2nd Edition.* Institute of Inspection, Cleaning and Restoration Certification, Vancouver, WA.

Burge, H.A., J.M. Macher, D.K. Milton, and H.A. Ammann. 1999. "Data Evaluation." In J.M. Macher, ed. *Bioaerosols: Assessment and Control.* American Conference of Governmental Industrial Hygienists, Cincinnati, OH, pp. 14-1–14-11.

Buttner M.P., P. Cruz-Perez, P.J. Garrett, and L.D. Stetzenbach. 1999. Dispersal of fungal spores from three types of air handling system duct material. *Aerobiologia*, Vol.15, pp. 1-8.

Buttner M.P., K. Willeke, S.A. Grinshpun. 2002a. "Sampling and Analysis of Airborne Microorganisms." In C.J. Hurst, R.L. Crawford, G.R. Knudsen, M.J. McInerney, and L.D. Stetzenbach, ed. *Manual of Environmental Microbiology, Second Edition.* ASM Press, Washington DC, pp. 814-826.

Buttner M.P., P. Cruz-Perez, L.D. Stetzenbach, P.J. Garrett, and A.E. Luedtke. 2002b. Measurement of airborne fungal spore dispersal from three types of flooring materials. *Aerobiologia*, Vol.18, pp.1-11.

Chapman, M.D. 2003. Indoor Allergens. In Leung, Sampson, Geha and Szefler, ed. *Pediatric Allergy Principles and Practices.* Mosby Publishing. pp. 261–268.

Codina R., R.W. Fox, R.F. Lockey, P. DeMarco, and A. Bagg. 2008. Typical levels of airborne fungal spores in houses without obvious moisture problems during a rainy season in Florida, USA. J Investig Allergol Clin Immunol., Vol. 18, pp. 156-62.

Cruz-Perez P., M.P. Buttner, and L.D. Stetzenbach. 2001a. Specific Detection of *Aspergillus fumigatus* in Pure Culture using Quantitative Polymerase Chain Reaction. *Molecular and Cellular Probes*, Vol. 15, pp. 81-88.

Cruz-Perez P., M.P. Buttner, and L.D. Stetzenbach. 2001b. Specific Detection of *Stachybotrys chartarum* in Pure Culture using Quantitative Polymerase Chain Reaction. *Molecular and Cellular Probes*, Vol. 15, pp. 129-138.

Douwes J., B. van der Sluis, G. Doekes, F. van Leusden, L. Wijnands, R. van Strien, A. Verhoeff, and B. Brunekreed. 1999. Fungal extracellular polysaccharides in house dust as a marker for exposure to fungi: relations with culturable fungi, reported home dampness, and respiratory symptoms. *Journal of Allergy Clinical Immunology*; Vol. 103, pp. 494-500.

Douwes J, G. Doekes, R. Montijn, D. Heederik, and B. Brunekeef. 1996. Measurement of ß(1-3)-glucan in occupational and home environments with an inhibition enzyme immunoassay. *Applied and Environmental Microbiology*, Vol. 62, pp. 3176-3182.

Earle C.D., E.M. King, A. Tsay, K. Pittman, B. Saric, L. Vailes, R. Godbout, K.G. Oliver, and M.D. Chapman. 2007. High-throughput fluorescent multiplex array for indoor allergen exposure assessment. J. Allergy Clin. Immunol., Vol. 119, pp. 428-433.

Grinshpun S.A., G. Mainelis, M. Trunov, R.L. Górny, S.K. Sivasubramani, A. Adhikari, and T. Reponen. 2004. Collection of air samples by circular single-stage impactors with small jet-to-plate distance. Journal of Aerosol Science, Vol. 36, pp. 575-591.

Grinshpun S.A., A. Adhikari, S. Cho, K. Kim, T. Lee and T. Reponen. 2007. A small change in the design of a slit bioaerosol impactor significantly improves its collection characteristics. J. Environ. Monit., Vol. 9, pp. 855–861.

Haugland, R.A, S.J. Vesper, and S.M. Harmon. 2001. Phylogenetic relationships of *Memnoniella* and *Stachybotrys* species and evaluation of morphological features from *Momnoniella* species identification. *Mycologia*, Vol. 93, pp. 54-65.

Haugland, R.A, S.J. Vesper, and L.J. Wymer. 1999. Quantitative measurement of *Stachybotrys chartarum* using real time detection of PCR products with the TaqMan fluorogenic probe system. Molecular and Cellular Probes, Vol. 13, pp. 329-340.

Jansen P.A., W.F. Todd, G.N. Davis, and P.V. Scarpino. 1992. Evaluation of eight bioaerosol samplers challenged with aerosols of free bacteria. Am. Ind. Hyg. Assoc. J., Vol 53, pp. 660-667.

Jarvis B.B., W.G. Sorenson, E. Hintikka, M. Nikulin, Y. Zhou, J. Jiang, S. Wang, S. Hinkley, R.A. Etzel, and D. Dearborn. 1998. Study of toxin production by isolates of *Stachybotrys chartarum* and *Memnoniella echinata* isolated during a study of pulmonary hemosiderosis in infants. Applied and Environmental Microbiology, Vol. 64, pp. 3620-3625.

Kozak P.P, J. Gallup, L.H. Cummins, S.A. Gillman. 1980. Currently available methods for home mold surveys. II. Examples of problem homes surveyed. *Annals of Allergy*, Vol. 45, pp.167-176.

Macher, J.M. 2002. Evaluation of a procedure to isolate culturable microorganisms from carpet dust. *Indoor Air*, Vol. 11, pp. 134-140.

Miller J.D, A.M. Laflamme, Y. Sobol, P. Lafontaine, and R. Greenhalgh. 1988. Fungi and fungal products in some Canadian houses. *Internatnational Biodeterioration*; Vol. 24, pp.103-20.

Pasanen A.L. 2001. A review: fungal exposure assessment in indoor environments. *Indoor Air*, Vol. 11, pp. 87-98.

Pasanen A.L. 1992. Airborne mesophilic fungal spores in various residential environments. *Atmospheric* Environment, Vol. 26, pp.2861-2868.

Pasanen A.L, K. Yli-Pietila, P. Pasanen, P. Kalliokoski, and J. Tarhanen. 1999. Ergosterol content in various fungal species and biocontamianted building materials. *Applied and Environmental Microbiology*, Vol. 65, pp. 138-142.

Pasanen A.L, M. Nikulin, M. Tuomainen, S. Berg, P. Parikka, and E.L. Hintikka. 1993. Laboratory experiments on membrane filter sampling of airborne mycotoxins produced by *Stachybotrys atra* corda. *Atmospheric Environment*, Vol. 27, pp. 9-13.

Pietarinen V., H. Rintala, A. Hyvärinen, U. Lignell, P. Kärkkäinen and A. Nevalainen. 2008. Quantitative PCR analysis of fungi and bacteria in building materials and comparison to culture-based analysis. J. Environ. Monit., Vol. 10, pp. 655–663.

Rylander, R. 1999. Indoor air-related effects and airborne (1-3)-ß-D-glucan. *Environmental Health Perspectives*, Vol. 107, pp. 501-503.

Sime, A.D., L.L. Abbott and S.P. Abbott. 2002. A mounting medium for use in indoor air quality spore-trap analyses. Mycologia, Vol. 94, pp. 1087-1088.

Sorenson WG, D.G. Frazier, B.B. Jarvis, J. Simpson, and V.A.Robinson. 1983. Trichothecene mycotoxins in aerosolized conidia of *Stachybotrys atra. Applied and Environmental Microbiology*, Vol 53, pp.1370-1375.

Stetzenbach LD. 2002. "Introduction to Aerobiology." In C.J. Hurst, R.L. Crawford, G.R. Knudsen, M.J. McInerney, and L.D. Stetzenbach, ed. *Manual of Environmental Microbiology, Second Edition*, ASM Press, Washington DC, pp. 801-813.

Vesper S., M.L. Magnuson, D.G. Dearborn, I. Yike, and R.A. Haugland. 2001. Initial Characterization of the Hemolysin Stachylysin from *Stachybotrys chartarum*. Infection and Immunity, Vol. 69, pp. 912-916.

Vesper S., C. McKinstry, R.A. Haugland, L. Wymer, P. Ashley, D. Cox, 2007. Development of an environmental relative moldiness index for homes in the U.S., J. Occup. Environ. Med., Vol. 49, pp. 987-990.

Vesper S., C. McKinstry, R. Haugland, L. Neas, E. Hudgens, B. Heidenfelder, and J. Gallagher. 2008. Higher environmental relative moldiness index (ERMI) values measured in Detroit homes of severely asthmatic children. Science of the Total Environment, Vol. 394, pp. 192-196.

Chapter 4

The Current Science of Mold

Ryan C. Kuhn, Ph.D.

Synopsis

4.1 Introduction to Mold

Fungi are an integral part of the world's ecology. Without the wide variety of fungi, accumulation of organic materials would overwhelm the planet's surface. Fungi are a distinct group of organisms that rely on adsorption of nutrients from their environment for survival. The kingdom of Fungi can be broken down further into smaller groups (i.e., yeasts, molds, and macrofungi) based on the physical appearance of the organism. Mold is a term used to classify a group of microscopic fungi that grow in the form of multi-cellular filaments called hyphae. Molds can be found in just about every ecological niche on the planet. Currently there have been over 100,000 species of molds already identified with new species continuing to be identified on a constant basis.

While molds are capable of growth in just about any environment, they are limited by one factor: moisture. To obtain food from the surrounding environment, molds must secrete a number of enzymes from their cells to break down the growth substrate. Liquid water is required to allow enzyme transport from the cell and transport of the nutrient to the cell. Therefore, even in the presence of an optimal food source, mold will not develop without adequate liquid water. It is important to stress the word "liquid" when describing the moisture required for mold growth. Moisture in vapor form is not sufficient to allow mold to grow. Vapor must condense or be concentrated on the growth surface to allow for growth.

The lifecycle of a mold begins with a spore. Spores are environmentally resistant structures that allow the mold to exist in unfavorable conditions (e.g., drought) for long periods of time. When a spore finds a favorable condition for growth, the spore will germinate and begin to produce hyphae. As the hyphae begin to grow, they begin to branch out, thereby forming a group of interconnected hyphae called mycelium. The mycelium will continue to grow and spread across the surface of the food source. It is at this point that most molds become visible to the naked eye. This large mass of interconnected hyphae is referred to as a colony. Typically the hyphae have a clear or white cottony appearance. As the colony matures and develops, reproductive structures begin to develop. At this point, large numbers of spores are produced. The spores produced by most molds typically contain some pigment. The combined pigment production from millions and millions of spores will result in the development of color on the colony. The commonly seen black, green, brown, yellow, and red colors associated with mold are primarily due to the spore production. Upon maturation, the spores will then be released into the environment. The method of spore dispersion will vary depending on the type of mold. Molds such as *Aspergillus* and *Penicillium* species disseminate spores via air movement or wind. Other fungi such as *Stachybotrys* rely on water droplets or insect transport for spore dispersion. Spores dispersed into the environment will then sit dormant until optimum conditions are present to allow germination and colonization of a new substrate.

Scientists historically have classified organisms, such as molds, based primarily on similar appearance or traits. Recent developments in DNA technology have changed the classification scheme from shared physical traits to shared DNA markers. As such, the classification of fungi is a continually evolving process. Typically when conducting analysis for an indoor mold assessment, laboratories will focus their classification at three levels: group, genera and species depending on the type of analysis requested. Most commonly used analytical techniques used for mold evaluations include direct microscopic examination and culture. Under direct microscopic examination, the laboratory analyst will identify the molds collected based on the physical characteristics of the spores in the sample. Culture method will allow the analyst to view colony traits in addition to the spore traits for a more defined classification. An example of a group would be when a lab analyst observes a basidiospore under the microscope. Basidiospores are spores produced by fungi such as mushrooms and toadstools. The analyst can determine that the spore is that produced by a mushroom but cannot determine which of the thousands of species of mushrooms produced the spore. Similarly, if the analyst observes a *Stachybotrys* spore under the microscope, the analyst can determine that the spore is from the genera *Stachybotrys*, but she cannot tell which of the estimated 13 species of *Stachybotrys* produced that spore. However, if the analyst cultures a sample and observes a colony, not only can the analyst determine that the colony is from the genera *Aspergillus*, but she can also determine that the colony is that of species flavus. As such, the lab will report the finding as *Aspergillus flavus*. The level of classification is extremely important in terms of litigation and will be discussed later in this chapter.

Experienced investigators will typically look for certain genera or species of mold in indoor environments. Typically there are a small number of mold genera that are isolated from wet building materials. Many people have termed these molds "indicator species" or "water indicator molds." The most frequently isolated genera include: *Penicillium*, *Aspergillus*, *Chaetomium*, *Ulocladium*, *Stachybotrys* and *Cladosporium* (Andersson et al., 1997; Horner et al., 2004; Krause et al., 2006). It should be noted, however, that all of these molds also exist naturally in the outdoor environment and that simply isolating spores of these genera does not provide conclusive evidence of moist conditions in a building. Mold spores from these genera can enter a structure by air currents into the building, on the occupants of the building (humans and animals) and can be incorporated into the building materials at the time of construction.

4.2 Conducting a Mold Investigation

When asked to investigate moisture and mold damage in a building, it is essential that the investigator develop a comprehensive sampling plan prior to starting the investigation. Many times an investigator will inadvertently collect useless data or negatively impact their samples. A non-invasive/non-disruptive visual inspection should be conducted prior to any sampling or disruption of the environment. This inspection should be used by the investigator to determine what type of information needs to be collected (moisture readings, observe carpet tack strips, etc.), to develop a sampling plan and to determine the order in which samples should be collected. Currently, there are no widely accepted standards for site investigation or sampling protocol. ASTM International, one of the largest voluntary standards development organizations in the world, published the "Standard Guide for Readily Observable Mold and Conditions Conducive to Mold in Commercial Buildings: Baseline Survey Process." However, this document is not commonly cited by consultants conducting mold investigations. In contrast, mold investigators commonly cite and rely upon the following documents: "Guidelines on Assessment and Remediation of Fungi in Indoor Environments" by the New York Department of Health and Mental Hygiene; "Mold Remediation in Schools and

Commercial Buildings" by the United States Environmental Protection Agency (EPA); "Bioaerosols Assessment and Control" by the American Conference of Governmental Industrial Hygienists (ACGIH); "Assessment, Remediation, and Post-Remediation Verification of Mold in Buildings" by the American Industrial Hygiene Association (AIHA); and "Field Guide for the Determination of Biological Contaminants in Environmental Samples" also by the AIHA. While both "Bioaerosols Assessment and Control" and "Field Guide for the Determination of Biological Contaminants in Environmental Samples" texts provide detailed information concerning sampling plans and information concerning sample numbers, very few investigators follow these recommendations and collect the appropriate number of samples so as to provide reliable and useful data.

Currently there is some debate on the usefulness of sampling while conducting a mold investigation. Guidelines from both the EPA and the New York Department of Health and Mental Hygiene recommend against sampling as part of an initial investigation. When making a decision whether or not to sample, it is important for an investigator to be aware of the sampling methodologies currently available and to understand the advantages and disadvantages of each method. Common sampling methods can be broken down into two categories: surface samples and air samples. Each of these categories can be further broken down to describe specific methodologies.

4.3 Air Sampling

Air sampling is by far the most common method used by investigators to sample for mold. A number of investigators heavily rely on air sampling to characterize the mold conditions in a building. Before collecting air samples, the investigator should understand the limitations of air sampling. Air sampling alone is insufficient to determine the nature and extent of fungal growth within a structure. It is important to consider three important factors prior to employing the air sampling methods: 1) air sampling is a snapshot in time and will only provide information concerning the conditions at the time of sampling; 2) air samples have a high degree of variation (up to 10-fold) between individual samples collected concurrently (that is, samples collected at the same time in the same space); and 3) a large number of samples are required to estimate inhalation exposures. Currently, there are three different analytical methods used for evaluating airborne mold levels; spore trap (including WallChek™ sampling), culture, and polymerase chain reaction (PCR).

Spore Trap Samples

Spore trap or particulate samples are probably the most commonly used method by investigators today. A spore trap sample is collected using a cassette that contains a microscope slide coated with a greasy or sticky substance. Air is then pulled over the slide, allowing the spores and other particulate materials to come into contact with the coating on the slide, thus trapping the spore on the surface of the slide. The laboratory analyst can then take the slide and conduct a direct microscopic exam and count of the materials collected on the surface of the slide. Commonly used spore trap cassettes include: Air-O-Cell™, Burkard, Cyclex-D, Micro 5, and Buck BioAire to name a few. Spore trap samples have become popular with investigators primarily because they are easy to use; require very little specialized equipment; can be quickly analyzed; can capture spores that may not be readily culturable; and have very little risk of contamination. The major disadvantage of a spore trap sample is the laboratory's inability to classify the collected spores down to a specific species. In a number of cases, the laboratory was unable to even classify the spores to genera. For example, the detection of spores from the genera *Aspergillus*, *Penicillium*, *Trichoderma* and others look identical under the microscope. As such, most laboratories will group the spores and classify them as "*Aspergillus/Penicillium-like*" spores. Other disadvantages include the potential for misclassification of the spores by analysts and high sample variation due to the fact that mold spores are not equally distributed in the air.

Currently there exist no numerical standards against which one may compare spore trap data. Current guidelines recommend that spore types and counts in the indoor air be similar to those of the outdoor air or the non-impacted portion of the building on the day of sampling. In most cases, when interpreting spore trap data, investigators do not take into consideration sample variation and error levels associated with the data. For example, an investigator receives data back from a sampling event. The investigator collected three samples, one outdoor sample and two indoor samples. The lab reports *Aspergillus/Penicillium* levels outdoors at 100 spores per cubic meter of air (spores/m^3) and indoors at 200 and 300 (spores/m^3). In most cases, the investigator will consider these indoor levels to be elevated and most likely suggest that there is mold growth inside of the building even in the absence of visual observations to support this theory. However, a study by Eudey et al., 1995 (cited in "Bioaerosols Assessment and Control"), states that detectable differences between samples are likely to be in 10-fold multiplicative steps (e.g., 100 versus 1000). Therefore, there is no difference between the indoor and outdoor levels used in this example. In most cases, sampling data will only provide a small piece of the puzzle and must be combined with other data to determine the actual conditions within a building, or be considered reliable when used for litigation purposes.

Wall Cavity Samples

A number of investigators will collect air samples from the inside of a wall cavity by drilling a small hole into the wall, inserting a plastic tubing and attaching a special adaptor to a particulate air sampling cassette. Air is then pulled from the wall cavity into the sampling cassette. Some investigators will collect wall cavity samples using an aggressive method (i.e., pounding on the wall to disturb the spores). Like other sampling methods, wall cavity samples are best used as a piece of the investigative process and should not be relied upon alone to provide conclusive evidence that mold exists. Wall cavity samples have a number of disadvantages that include: lack of baseline comparison; lack of direct visual evidence inside of the wall cavity; a limited collection range; and the risk of incorporation of debris into the sample. A lack of baseline comparison is a major disadvantage associated with wall cavity sampling. Some investigators will try to compare results to the outdoors; however, most wall cavity environments do not have a direct or active communication with outdoor spaces. In other words, changes in outdoor levels do not directly correlate to changes in wall cavity levels. Another disadvantage is the lack of visual evidence inside of the wall cavity. Wall cavity samples can be impacted by the level of dirt and/or construction debris contained in the wall cavity. During the construction process, it is not uncommon for workers to deposit trash (including food and beverages) into wall cavities prior to closing the wall. This debris can create false positives as it may contain high levels of spores. In addition, because wall cavities are filled with dirt, debris and drywall dust (from drilling the hole), additional particulate matter is pulled into the cassette. As the amount of particulate matter increases in the cassette, the ability of the laboratory to accurately process the sample will decrease. Another limitation is that wall cavity samples can only pull air from the area immediately around the plastic tubing. If the tubing is inserted into the wall several inches from a mold colony there is an increasing probability of producing a false negative as airborne fungal spores may not be captured during sampling.

Culture Samples

Culture or viable samples are also used during a mold investigation. The most commonly used culture sample is collected by placing a culture plate containing a growth media into a multiple-hole impactor. The most commonly used impactors have 400 holes machined into the sampler and is commonly referred to as an Andersen sampler. Air enters the Andersen sampler and is passed over the plate allowing the airborne fungal spores to impact and stick to the culture media. After sampling, the culture plate is placed in an incubator set at a controlled temperature and humidity for seven to ten days to allow the mold spores to germinate and develop into a mature colony. A laboratory analyst can then determine the mold species based on the appearance of the colony. The advantage of culturable samples is that they will provide identification down to the species level. Some disadvantages include: a long turnaround time of seven to ten days; some spores (e.g., *Stachybotrys)* may not culture well and may not be detected by this method; this method will not detect spores that are inactive (dead); different mold species require different growth media; and high airborne spore concentrations or long sample times can negatively impact the samples by increasing the risk of two or more spores occupying the same hole in the sampler. Along with these specific disadvantages, culture samples also have the same general disadvantages (e.g., high sample variation) described for other air samples.

Polymerase Chain Reaction

Polymerase Chain Reaction (PCR) is a DNA-based test that can be used to assess mold levels in indoor environments. PCR sampling is conducted by pulling air through a filter cassette. Mold spores, hyphal fragments, and potentially free floating DNA can become trapped on the surface of the filter. Upon arrival to the laboratory, the analyst will remove the filter from the cassette and place it into a special solution to release the DNA from any mold cells trapped on the filter. The DNA is separated from the rest of the cellular material. DNA from a single mold spore cannot be detected directly due to the small quantity present in the sample. Therefore, the laboratory will use a PCR to make copies of specific DNA regions of the mold DNA. Copies are made by creating conditions for repeated DNA replication. In addition to the mold DNA, the lab will add DNA nucleotides (building blocks), primers (starter sections of DNA that target specific sections of the mold DNA), a buffer solution, and the polymerase enzyme that is responsible for building DNA copy. After a number of repeated cycles, the sample will contain enough copies of the target sites to allow the DNA to be detected by laboratory instrumentation. The regions currently used for laboratory analysis are species specific. Therefore, the lab can add primers for specific species like *Stachybotrys chartatum* and *Aspergillus fumigatus*. If DNA copies of these species are produced, the lab will know that these particular molds were present in the sample. The process can be quantified by adding specific markers to the copied DNA. These markers are commonly fluorescent and the intensity will be read by special laboratory instrumentation. The instrument will estimate the number of copies made based on the intensity of the fluorescence and estimate the number of cells present in the original sample. Some of the advantages of PCR sampling include: fast turnaround times, as samples can be processed in a few hours; accurate speciation in less time than culture samples; and collection of large sample volumes. The major disadvantages would be: the cost of sample analysis (~$150 to $400); the potential for free DNA to be detected in the sample resulting in false positives; and the propensity of PCR reactions to be highly sensitive to contamination, resulting in false positives and negatives. It should be noted that PCR has been researched extensively by the United States EPA and is the basis for their Environmental Relative Moldiness Index (ERMI), which will be discussed later in this chapter.

4.4 Surface Sampling

Surface sampling is a method commonly used to characterize mold growth in indoor environments. Surface sampling can be collected by several different methods and includes tape lift, swab (wipe), bulk and dust sampling. Surface samples can be analyzed by direct microscopy, culture or PCR depending on the collection method. Surface samples can be used by investigators as a method to confirm mold growth and determine what type or species of mold is growing on the surface. Surface samples cannot be used by an investigator to determine if an occupant has or is being exposed to mold and cannot be used to estimate airborne mold levels.

Tape Lift Samples

Tape lift samples are collected by placing a clear piece of cellophane tape over an area of suspected mold growth. The tape is then placed onto a clean microscope slide or inside a clean zip lock bag and sent to the lab for direct microscopic examination. The advantages of collecting tape lifts include: sampling supplies can be obtained at any grocery store; collection of samples does not require much training; and samples have a short turnaround time. Major disadvantages include not being able to culture the samples and the potential for high densities of mold particles on the slide decreasing the ability of the analyst to read the most concentrated areas of the slide.

Swab Samples

Swab or wipe samples are collected using a cotton swab to wipe a given area of suspect mold growth. Upon wiping the area with the swab, mold spores and mycelia will become trapped on the cotton swab. The swab is then placed in a buffer solution to provide a more stable environment for the spores and hyphae during transport to a lab. Upon arrival at the lab, the swab will be removed from the buffer and the mold spores and hyphae are removed from the swab and suspended in a liquid buffer solution. The sample can then be analyzed by direct microscopy, culture or PCR. The advantages of a swab sample include the ability to reach into small, tight spaces to collect samples and the ability of the investigator to choose several different analytical methods. A major disadvantage is the recovery of mold spores and hyphae from the swab itself. If the investigator is interested in quantifying the number of spores per sample, there can be an underestimation of the counts.

Bulk Samples

Bulk sampling is collected by removing a piece of building material with suspect mold growth. The entire piece of material is then submitted directly to the lab. The laboratory can then wash the mold colony from the building material. The sample can then be analyzed by direct microscopic exam, culture or PCR. Bulk sampling has the advantage of allowing the investigator the ability to select different analytical methods with an improved recovery over that of a swab sample. The major disadvantage is that the samples are destructive and it may not be possible to collect a bulk sample in all cases.

Dust Samples

Many investigators collect settled dust samples to provide an indication of molds that were previously airborne. Samples are collected by vacuuming an area of flooring or personal items with a filter cassette and vacuum pump. Investigators have different methods of collecting the samples. Some prefer to collect the samples from a given area and others prefer to collect a sample that will produce visible dust collection on the filter in the cassette. Because the laboratory reports are reported in spores or colony forming units per gram of dust, it is preferable to collect a visible sample. Collecting a visible sample also aids in the interpretation of the sample as published studies investigating typical dust-borne mold levels have used a count per gram system. The advantage of collecting a dust sample is that an investigator may be able to detect mold spores that may not have been collected in air samples. This data may sometimes be useful in determining if mold spores from a specific growth site have been disseminated to other areas of the building. Major disadvantages include: the lack of a definitive baseline for comparison; possibility of collected spores being tracked in from outside of the home; and an unknown impact from cleaning habits. While there are a number of publications that have studied typical dust-borne mold levels in buildings with and without mold growth, the reported levels vary greatly between studies. If the investigator collects the sample from high traffic areas of the carpet, it will be likely that a number of the mold types sampled were tracked into the building from outdoors. Lastly, because it is possible for mold spores to remain viable and intact for long periods of time, the investigator will need to use other visual observations such as visible signs of water damage or mold to conclude that the results in fact reflect contamination. An example of this is if an investigator was to collect samples in two homes—one home is 12 years old and is rarely vacuumed whereas the second home is only two years old and is vacuumed every week.

Spore accumulations in the first home will likely be greater due to the length of time that the spores have been collecting into the carpet and the fact that the spore loads are not removed by regular vacuuming. Another possible complication to the interpretation of dust samples is the presence of pets, children and the type of outdoor environment (e.g., rural versus urban), as these factors may influence the spore loads in the dust. However, studies have not yet been conducted to assess the exact impact of each of these factors on dust-borne spore levels in an indoor environment.

Mycotoxin Sampling

Mycotoxins are secondary metabolites produced by fungi. Mycotoxins are small organic molecules that are non-volatile and can remain intact in the environment for extended periods of time. Mycotoxins are typically excreted by the mold colony; however, research has demonstrated that mycotoxins can be found inside of mold spores. Mycotoxins may play an important role in reducing the number of competing organisms on the growth substrate. The kinds and amounts of toxin a mold will produce depends on a number of factors including: mold species and strain; the substrate on which the mold is growing; the presence of other organisms; temperature and pH, to name a few. Therefore, it is not appropriate to assume that just because a species of mold known to produce mycotoxins is identified growing in a building that mycotoxins are also present. Several commercial labs do offer analytical services for mycotoxin detection. Samples can be collected by air (on a filter cassette), bulk, swab, and dust sampling. It should be noted that the current analytical methods typically require a minimum of 100,000 spores to achieve a detectable level of mycotoxins. This can be very difficult to achieve in most indoor environments without collecting long-term air samples. Once a sample is collected and sent to the lab there are two common methods used by commercial labs for analysis. The most commonly used method is high performance liquid chromatography (HPLC). Commercial analysis is available for ten to twenty of the more commonly isolated mycotoxins through HPLC. The second method utilizes antibody columns and can analyze seven to ten of the more commonly isolated mycotoxins.

4.5 Data Interpretation Consideration

Data interpretation remains one of the most controversial areas among mold investigators, especially when it concerns determining potential health impacts. There are very few published guidance documents to aid in data interpretation. An example of a common interpretation issue involves the current recommendations for interpreting air data, which states that indoor levels and types of molds should be similar to that of the outdoor air. If an investigator collects a sample indoors that has

200 spores of *Aspergillus/Penicillium*-like spores per cubic meter of air and none were collected in the outdoor samples, the assumption might be that the air inside of the building has abnormal levels of *Aspergillus/Penicillium*-like spores. However, it is possible that at some point prior to sampling, the outdoor levels of *Aspergillus/Penicillium*-like spores were 300 spores per cubic meter of air. As very little information exists concerning communication rates between indoor and outdoor environments, it is possible that the higher levels observed inside of the building were a result of higher outdoor levels several hours before the sampling event. As previously discussed, investigators often fail to consider that air sampling only provides information concerning conditions existing at the time of sampling. Very few investigators take into account sampling conditions outdoors, variation between samples, seasonal or daily variation and regional levels. A competent investigator will always use sampling data to supplement a visual inspection and not solely rely on the sampling data to determine the condition of an indoor environment.

A. Laboratory Selection

In addition to the consideration of environmental conditions presented above, investigators must also understand the nuances of the laboratory reports. The American Industrial Hygiene Association (AIHA) recommends that investigators use accredited labs. The AIHA has developed the Environmental Microbiology Laboratory Accreditation Program (EMLAP) to ensure quality in the laboratory services. Labs that participate in the program are required to analyze samples to determine the lab's proficiency. Labs can obtain accreditation for culturable fungi, bacteria, and fungal direct exam. A laboratory is considered proficient if the laboratory receives a passing score in two of three consecutive rounds of samples. A passing score is achieved when the laboratory receives a minimum score of 85 percent for the associated sample. There are three rounds of samples per year; therefore, at a minimum it will take a lab one year to gain accreditation. Currently there are nearly 100 EMLAP-accredited labs in the United States and Canada. Although all of these labs have passed the accreditation process, each lab will have very different counting and reporting methods. The accreditation process only grades labs on their ability to accurately identify mold and does not provide a standard analytical method for the lab to follow. Laboratory analytical techniques vary from lab to lab. Some labs will use 400X magnification on the microscope, others 600X and others 1000X. Each of these factors will have an influence on the reported results. In addition to magnification, labs will differ on the percentage of a slide they will actually observe under the microscope. Some labs will observe 100 percent, others 50 percent and still others 25 percent or less. All of these factors impact the variability of the counts and the sensitivity of the sampling method.

B. Measuring Units

Most laboratories will report the data in some type of standard unit. Particulate air samples are commonly reported in spores per cubic meter of air (spores/m^3); culturable air samples are reported in colony forming units per cubic meter of air (CFU/m^3); PCR air samples are typically reported as cells per cubic meter of air (cells/m^3); tape samples are commonly reported as spores per square centimeter (spores/cm^2); swab samples are reported as spores, CFU, or cells per square centimeter depending on the analytical method used; bulk samples are reported as spores, CFU, or cells per gram of material depending on analytical method used; and dust samples are reported as spores, CFU, or cells per gram of dust. In addition to these units, labs will also develop internal scales for interpretation of surface samples. These scales can also significantly vary from lab to lab. An example of this is where Lab A has established that one to ten spores is called "rare," ten to 100 spores is "few," 100 to 500 is "many," and more than 500 is "loaded." Lab B, however, may use the same terms but indicate one to 100 is "rare" and 100 to 500 is "few," etc. Some labs will also include their opinion concerning what they are viewing, such as "mold growth present," "normal trapping," or "mold growth near." These added descriptions can be helpful in interpreting the data as the microscopist has more than likely observed some spore-producing structures or other structures that have led him to this conclusion. However, the investigator should be cautioned that the microscopist is basing this conclusion solely on the sample, and conclusions such as "mold growth near" may not be supported by observations made in the building.

When viewing a laboratory report, the investigator will also be provided with several other pieces of data other than the counts in the standard units provided above. Most labs will also provide information concerning the actual counts (raw counts) observed by the analyst, the detection limit or limit of detection, the amount of background debris, sample volume or area, and any laboratory comments. Of these items, the limit of detection is probably the most crucial for an investigator. As described above, laboratories may use different magnification and count a different percentage of the slide when conducting the analysis. These two factors will influence the calculations used by the lab to determine the counts reported per cubic meter (m^3) and detection limit. Also influencing the limit of detection is the amount of sample collected. While manufacturers of air sampling cassettes typically have recommended air flow rates and sample volumes, the final determination is typically made by the investigator. For example, an Air-O-Cell™ cassette has a manufacturer recommended flow rate of 15 liters of air per minute for a time period of one to ten minutes, for a total volume of 15-150 liters of air. If Investigator A collects a sample of 15 liters of air and Investigator B collects a sample of 150 liters of air and sends it to the same lab for analysis, there would still be a difference in the detection limit between the samples. The standard reporting unit of one cubic meter is equivalent to one thousand liters of air. Therefore, Investigator A collected 0.015 m^3 and Investigator B collected 0.15 m^3. For the lab to convert the raw counts to counts/m^3 they will need to multiply each spore detected on Investigator A's slide by 66.6 ($1\ m^3 \div 0.015\ m^3 = 66.6$) and Investigator B's slide by 6.66 ($1\ m^3 \div 0.15\ m^3 = 6.66$). The detection limit for Investigator A's sample will be reported as 67 (rounded up), and 7 (rounded up) for Investigator B's sample. If a lab only counts a fraction of the slide or uses a higher magnification, there will be additional calculations that will impact the limit of detection. It is important to note that just because a lab does not enter a value into the lab report for a given mold, does not mean that mold was not present. It only means that the number of spores per cubic meter of air was below the detection limit for the analytical method used.

C. Background Debris

In addition to the detection limit, an investigator should also be aware of the level of background debris. As the level of particulate material accumulates on the slide, it becomes more likely the mold spores will be covered and not observable through the microscope. Therefore, as the background debris increases so does the probability that the reported counts underestimate the actual results. While increasing the sample time may increase the sensitivity of the analytical method (lowering the detection limit), it may at the same time reduce the accuracy of the analysis. The same principle holds true for other forms of mold samples such as swab and dust samples. An investigator may be inclined to collect a large amount of dust in a sample to decrease the detection limit of their sample; however, the additional accumulation of dust will require additional dilutions of the sample for effective analytical analysis.

D. Standardized Interpretation of Data

There have been attempts to standardize or develop data interpretation software. There are currently companies that will use "proprietary" software to standardize or score laboratory data. While these products may aid some inexperienced investigators, it is important to thoroughly review the limitations section of the report, because such software typically is not designed for all sampling locations.

The EPA has developed a method using PCR to determine if a building has abnormal mold levels. The index was developed based on dust samples collected from homes across the U.S. High index scores alone cannot be used to conclude that mold is growing inside of a building, but simply to indicate that there is a greater chance of the building having a mold problem than homes with low ERMI scores. Under the EPA method, a single composite dust sample is collected from a home. The sample is then analyzed by PCR for 36 different fungal species divided into two groups. Group I are those typically found in water-damaged homes and Group II are those commonly found in all homes. The laboratory will report the PCR data as cells per gram or cells per milligram of dust. The data is then log-transformed (e.g., 72,844 cells per mg = 4.9) and the sum of group 2 is subtracted from the sum of group 1. Results of -10 to -4 are considered level 1 and indicates a building having the lowest likelihood of having a mold problem. Results of -4 to 0 is level 2 indicates a building having a lower likelihood of having a mold problem, 0 to 5 is a level 3 and indicates a building having a greater likelihood of having a mold problem and 5 to 20 is a level 4 building having the greatest likelihood of having a mold problem. The EPA has also developed an American Relative Moldiness Index (ARMI) that is similar to the ERMI but uses a 13 mold panel instead of 36. One of the goals of the EPA is to use this method to monitor childhood exposures to mold as a part of field studies, in order to establish whether a relationship exists between molds encountered in indoor environments and asthma-related health problems. Research is ongoing so it has not yet been established that this method is useful in monitoring or determining human mold exposures.

E. Determining Human Exposure to Mold

Investigators are commonly asked to use sampling to determine a person's level of exposure to mold. It is very important to recognize that the determination as to whether someone has had a significant exposure to mold is a complex problem that typically requires a number of different experts. This determination is based on four basic principles: 1) is there a source of the mold, 2) is the occupant coming into contact with the mold, 3) how much mold (dose) is the occupant coming into contact with, and 4) what is the occupant's response to that dose? Most individuals that conduct mold investigations attempt to characterize the environment for purposes of repair or remediation of the mold. Therefore, most mold investigations and sampling events are insufficient to establish the dose of mold to which a person may have been exposed. Texts such as "Bioaerosols Assessment and Control" (American Conference of Governmental Industrial Hygienists, 1999) and "Field Guide for the Determination of Biological Contaminants in Environmental Samples, Second Edition" (American Industrial Hygiene Association, 2005) provide information concerning how to determine the appropriate number of samples for an investigation. For example, to estimate average inhalation exposure (ACGIH, 1999) it is suggested that duplicate samples be collected ≥3 times a day for ≥3 consecutive representative days. Therefore, if an investigator is attempting to determine if a person is being exposed to mold or mycotoxins, it is essential that they collect the appropriate samples to 1) determine that mold is present, 2) determine what species of mold is present, 3) determine whether mycotoxins are being produced (if toxins are thought to be an issue), and 4) determine what level of mold or toxins the occupants were exposed to.

4.6 Current Guidance Documents

With the exception of Texas, mold has been relatively unregulated. There are no license or certification requirements, there are no governmental sampling standards or protocols, and there are no set safe and unsafe levels for data interpretation. Therefore, many investigators rely on guidance documents or texts to conduct mold investigations and interpret sampling data. A number of guidance documents have already been presented in the chapter; however, a more comprehensive list of the commonly used documents is presented below. It should be noted that this list does not include all documents on mold or mold sampling, but only the most commonly used resources.

- Bioaerosols Assessment and Control (ACGIH, 1999)
- Field Guide for the Determination of Biological Contaminants in Environmental Samples, Second Edition (AIHA, 2005)
- Assessment, Remediation, and Post-Remediation Verification of Mold in Buildings (AIHA, 2004)
- Report of Microbial Growth Task Force (AIHA, 2001)
- Mold Remediation in Schools and Commercial Buildings (USEPA, 2001)
- Guidelines on Assessment and Remediation of Fungi in Indoor Environments (New York City Department of Health, 2002)
- Fungal Contamination in Public Buildings: A Guide to Recognition and Management (Health Canada, 2004)
- IICRC S520 Standard and Reference Guide for Professional Mold Remediation (Institute of Inspection Cleaning and Restoration Certification, 2003)
- Standard Guide for Readily Observable Mold and Conditions Conducive to Mold in Commercial Buildings: Baseline Survey Process (ASTM International, 2006)
- Fungal Contamination A Manual for Investigation, Remediation and Control (BECi, 2005)
- Texas Mold Assessment and Remediation Rules (Texas Department of State Health Services, 2007)

Part II

Chapter 5

An Overview of Toxic Mold Litigation in Arizona

Dennis I. Wilenchik, Esq.

Synopsis

5.1 Introduction

Although mold issues had become a darling of plaintiff's lawyers, the phenomenon has, in Arizona, been relatively short-lived as these kinds of cases do not appear to now hold the attention of most lawyers who previously considered them a major threat to homebuilders. The public hysteria and phobias concerning mold claims appears to have been contained to a large degree, based on the passage of time since the issue became highly publicized. The reasons may be myriad for this, including a severe downturn in the housing markets, which made the previously cash-rich companies reluctant to pay any claims or be able to settle with their own funds before their insurance kicked in. In addition, insurance carriers have become increasingly reluctant either to cover such claims, with specific exclusions, or to pay any such claims, defending particularly any health-related claims attendant to repair demands. Given the difficult causal nexus necessary to prove these kinds of injury claims, the dubious state of the scientific proof of mold-related injuries and the natural skepticism of juries, these are difficult and expensive claims to pursue for plaintiff's lawyers, having very questionable results. Thus, although mold claims enjoyed a well-publicized shelf life, over the last few years in Arizona, they have become almost non-existent.

Although mold can certainly be found in dry climates like Arizona, to the average juror it is not an intuitive conclusion. A study conducted by University of Arizona researchers found mold in 64 percent of samples taken from homes in Tucson, Arizona, alone.[1] Although only 0.2 percent of samples collected nationwide in the study contained the well-publicized toxic mold, *Stachybotrys chartarum*, also known as "black mold," which took hold of the public imagination for a time, the study's findings also indicate that a majority of homes have some form of mold within them.[2] It would seem that most people would become immune to the effects of mold, given its frequency, or so the defense argument would proceed. The same study found that "[w]indowsills were the worst places for mold, testing positive 88 percent of the time. Refrigerator seals ranked second (84 percent), then areas below kitchen sinks (83 percent) and air vents (82 percent)."[3] Therefore, it would seem clear that because mold is all around us in our environment, despite the best efforts to contain it, we are all continuously exposed to its effects.

Notwithstanding this, a case can still be made that highly concentrated exposure or ingestion can still be harmful to certain individuals who may be allergic, or more susceptible, to certain strains than others, or who may have heightened levels of immune deficiencies and who may be affected more than the average person. Because it is likely that the homebuilder/vendor takes the owner as she finds them, it will not likely be a viable defense to such claims that there was no actual prior notice of such heightened conditions or susceptibility. This will be a problem particularly where subsequent purchasers claim injury. In such situations, likely defenses will involve costly factual findings as to who caused the mold to form and exist, and whether it could have been found on a reasonable inspection prior to purchase.

As stated above, as a result of a large number of mold and water damage claims previously made in Arizona, insurance rates increased and insurers began to routinely exclude or severely limit mold coverage in homeowner's policies as well as in the comprehensive general liability policies of the builders and in specific environmental and mold exclusions. Although Texas and California have had higher numbers of mold claims, insurers doing business in Arizona reported that a high number of homeowners' claims related to mold and water damage caused insurance rates to increase.[4] "Of the 104 home-insurance companies that wrote new policies in Arizona, 92 posted rate increases [in 2001], and most of the increases exceeded 10 percent."[5] State Farm Insurance paid $11.6 million in Arizona in 2001 related to water damage alone.[6] As discussed below, mold is now typically excluded from insurance policies, except perhaps if it is resulting damage of an otherwise covered peril.

In addition, the State of Arizona has spent millions of dollars in an effort to clean up mold problems in several government buildings.[7] Although officials of the Arizona Department of Health have traditionally attempted to publicly downplay some of the more wild claims of mold-related injuries, the government spent roughly $5 million to assess and clean a Yuma, Arizona, high school alone, built a new elementary school in Northeast Phoenix at a cost of $5.5 million because cleaning up the old building was cost-prohibitive, and replaced the U.S. Geographical Survey's field center in Flagstaff at a cost of $4.7 million.[8] The latter structure actually had roots to NASA's Apollo space program.[9] Other noteworthy Arizona buildings and structures, including theatres, airports, courthouses, and water treatment plants, have been or now will routinely be cleaned or replaced because of severe mold problems.[10]

Although remediating a home from mold will not cost in the millions of dollars, and routine demands of total destruction and replacement are now rare, it could easily cost a homeowner many thousands of dollars to remediate a home and to certify its condition. Many homeowners still have legitimate concerns over "disclosure" issues after flooding and water damage. Potential mold disclosure still is a problem and results in a "safe rather than sorry" attitude in performing remediations and certifications to protect against non-disclosure and misrepresentation/fraud claims upon resale. The Arizona Department of Health Services has gone so far as to provide helpful tips on what to do if there is mold found in a home, suggesting general cleanup procedures and disinfection and providing resources to consult.[11]

It has been curious that, although mold has been around us since the beginning of time, it suddenly took on a life of its own, insofar as the notion of mold exposure litigation exploded in the course of the phenomenon described above. Television, print, and Internet coverage brought mold awareness into our consciousness. Large jury verdicts, including the $32 million *Ballard* jury verdict in Texas, [12] also helped fuel the fire, but, by contrast, subsequent reversals of many of these awards also equally dampened the interest in these highly costly, expert-driven cases. Many of these publicized cases involved bad faith insurance claims, or involved damage to the property itself and remediation efforts that were excessive or unrealistic. There were hardly any major personal injury type claims that took over the imagination of the public that resulted in actual jury verdicts that were rendered or upheld. In fact, creative efforts to establish causal relationships between mold exposure claimed in homes to any actual documented injury have never been favored, let alone persuasive, even if admissible, based on the documented "experiences" of the expert. For one thing, from a purely practical standpoint of convincing a jury, the limited and untested experiences of an expert who only sees patients complaining of mold exposures, for example, and whose patients, therefore, are seen to make similar complaints of its effects, are not highly scientific in nature and not very persuasive in proving any causal connection to a reasonable degree of medical probability.

This chapter attempts to address the state of toxic mold litigation in Arizona today.

5.2 Possible Explanations for Arizona's Mold Problems

In an article published by the *Phoenix Business Journal*, the Greenguard Environmental Institute said that, in terms of losses on insurance claims in comparison to insurance premiums, Arizona was one of the 10 worst states for mold contamination on both commercial and residential property.[13] According to the article, "many buildings and houses in dry climates develop mold because moisture is nurtured within walls and windows that are tightly sealed because of the hot climate."[14] The Arizona Insurance Information Association quickly refuted the article by explaining that mold is typically excluded from insurance policies, except if it is the result of a covered peril.[15]

Mold requires wet or humid conditions to initiate and maintain growth. In determining the source of leaks and water intrusion, homeowners or inspectors should look at several places. Obviously, common suspects are inadequate or improper window or roof flashing and defective windows or surrounds. Blocked weep screed openings at the base of exterior stucco or around windows due to sunscreens are also typical places to find mold. Reducing moisture in a home may include fixing leaks and seepage, using exhaust fans in kitchens and bathrooms, limiting the use of humidifiers or swamp coolers, and using air conditioners.[16] Although mold growth is impossible in dry conditions, many factors have increased the number of occurrences in Arizona homes, schools, and office buildings, including the pace of construction, the construction materials used, Arizona's extreme swing in temperatures, and homeowner maintenance (or lack thereof).

A. The Pace of Construction in Arizona

Some people may blame the existence of mold awareness on Arizona's frantic pace of construction that boomed and recently has busted. Building permits in Phoenix in 2004 hit 60,873, up an astonishing 27.5 percent from 2003.[17] However, building permits in Phoenix in 2007 were down to only 31,172, which was 27 percent less than the number of permits in 2006 and continues to drop.[18] The large influx of residents into Arizona is another reason. In 1990, the Census Bureau estimated that there were 3,665,228 people living in Arizona.[19] Ten years later, in 2000, the Census Bureau estimated that there were 5,130,632 residents.[20] The difference represents an increase of nearly 40 percent and the Census Bureau expects continued population growth in Arizona at alarming rates.[21] Although building permits have rapidly declined recently, homebuilders are still building homes, and will continue to do so with the expected influx of new residents, and when the market comes back. One analyst predicts that there will be 47,000 building permits in Phoenix in 2012, which would match the pre-boom levels.[22]

The frantic pace of construction in the past has led some critics to claim that homes were poorly constructed and not as carefully inspected as they should have been. Although the majority of homes in Arizona are well built, given the government inspections required at critical stages, the fact is that homes remain one of the few manufactured items constructed outdoors and in uncontrolled conditions that vary widely. Construction quality, however, does not vary greatly among homebuilders despite popular misconceptions, given the common subcontractor pool available. Constructing affordable houses fast is a key to success in an ultra-competitive market, but some people maintain that the demands of speed, affordability and quality are not always compatible.[23]

Some disreputable builders may try to cut corners, but it is rare given the nature of construction practice in general, which is mostly guided by the same cadre of subcontractors that work for numerous builders. In some instances, cutting corners could eventually lead to a mold problem. For example, in the past, some builders chose not to flash properly and wrap waterproofing paper properly around windows.[24] Although the cost to install such waterproofing paper may have been only around $150 per house, builders faced an astronomical bill when problems arose after the fact.[25] Repair estimates can exceed over $118,000 per home to repair defects including leaking windows and roofs, and various related stucco problems.[26]

Unskilled and untrained workers may also compound construction problems. Overall, the construction industry added an additional 8,100 jobs between November 2002 and November 2003.[27] That number has likely decreased substantially given the current state of the housing market. Notwithstanding, given the large number of changing workers in the construction industry, it is hard to imagine that all are highly qualified. Even if a homebuilder uses waterproofing paper, if an untrained worker does not know how to properly install the paper, the house may later encounter problems.[28]

Roofing is another area where there is often shoddy or sloppy work, due to the fact that there are limited inspections, and the roof is not easily seen. In addition, lack of compaction of sewer and plumbing trenches and underground plumbing leaks may contribute to water intrusion.

B. Building Materials Used in Arizona

Any place where water intrudes is a possible source of mold growth. All it takes is 24 to 48 hours before mold begins to grow on building materials. Mold often enters a home through floodwaters, leaks, the outdoor environment (soil, dust, and dirt) through building materials at the time of construction, and the misuse of toilets and showers. Therefore, homebuilders must build homes that manage moisture effectively.

The National Association of Homebuilders recommends that builders should (1) use quality building products, especially with respect to siding, shingles, windows, and pipes; (2) carefully install roofs and windows and make sure that roofs and windows are properly flashed; (3) reduce the possibility of condensation on cold surfaces by adding proper insulation; (4) make sure that rainwater drains away from the building through proper landscaping and adequate downspouts; (5) make sure that building materials like wallboard are dry at the time of installation; (6) make sure that HVAC systems are properly designed and working; and (7) make sure that moisture-generating activities like showers, dryers, and cooking appliances are vented to the outside.[29]

Although the Western one-coat stucco system used through much of Arizona is popular with homebuilders, the system is not without its share of problems. Arizona's stucco system is typically designed to allow for moisture in hairline stucco cracks to drain to the outside environment over a membrane and down through to weep screeds that allow the water to evacuate. However, where moisture infiltrates the interior wall cavity through tears or voids in the underlying membrane and encounters wood, cellulose, or insulation fiber, various mold problems may arise in wall cavities. Insulation may reduce the ability of water to drain to the outside environment, reducing the rate at which the wall dries. Thin stucco systems can also crack excessively, allowing water to seep into the walls.[30]

Arizona homebuilders often use different materials than their counterparts in other portions of the country, making it difficult to readily compare various mold studies. In drier regions such as Arizona and Nevada, air conditioning is utilized more than evaporative coolers, walls are ventilated differently, and homebuilders use different insulation. Therefore, building interiors are generally cooler than the exterior for most of the year. In Phoenix and Tucson, vapor barriers in roofing are generally not necessary because stucco is a cladding system designed to absorb some moisture. Due to negative pressure, mold spores trapped in walls may be drawn throughout the home via the air conditioning.

Materials used may also contribute to the mold problem. For example, paper backed gypsum board, the use of insulation and wall-to-wall carpets may bring about mold growth.[31] Additionally, modern airtight construction may contribute to the problem. "Beginning in the 1970s, spurred by the energy crisis, architects started to design more airtight buildings that retain heat or air conditioning increasing energy efficiency. However, when airtight buildings with poor ventilation have water leaks, 'they trap high humidity and become hothouses for passing mold spores.'"[32] Homeowners renovating older homes can also create a more airtight environment by installing low-e windows, designed to keep out heat during the summer and in during the winter.

C. Arizona's Warm Temperatures

Arizona's warm temperatures, which incubate and help mold flourish, can also contribute to the growth of mold. Average monthly temperatures in Phoenix, Arizona, range from 54°F in January and December to 93°F in July, and Phoenix's average high temperature reaches a scorching 104°F in July.[33] Temperatures are also warm in Tucson, Arizona, where average monthly temperatures range from 54°F in January and December to 89°F in July.[34] In addition, Arizona's "dry heat" may contribute to the growth of mold. Phoenix averages just 8.29 inches of precipitation a year.[35] Although mold is not limited to warm climates, these temperatures might add to the growth of mold in Arizona.

Because of Arizona's warm temperatures, governmental and regional standards regarding mold from other climate zones may not be relevant. For example, New York has a completely different climate than Arizona, so the well-publicized New York City "Guidelines on Assessment and Remediation of Fungi in Indoor Environments"[36] should be limited to New York City or, at most, the Northeastern portion of the United States. Sanctioned guidelines specific for Arizona are not currently available, and many mold remediation specialists choose to create their own protocol.

D. Homeowners' Contribution to the Mold Problem

In addition, homeowners can contribute to mold intrusion and growth. This is especially true if a homeowner fails to undertake maintenance such as caulking and filling cracks. In addition, alterations to grading and drainage plans and overwatering of lands may cause excess moisture to develop under slabs and migrate through slab cracks. Certain homebuilders take it upon themselves to educate homeowners about such proper maintenance. "By providing homeowners with information about the relationship between proper maintenance and mold growth, homeowners will better understand their environment and their own obligations. An information disclosure statement should be given to homeowners before the sale and should be incorporated by reference into each sales agreement."[37] The information disclosure statement should include the following information: (1) mold growth is possible even where there is no moisture; (2) potential moisture sources include water in the air-conditioning unit and refrigerator drip pans, showers, bathtubs, sinks, and pipe leaks; (3) controlling and preventing moisture is possible if leaking pipes are promptly fixed and sinks and bathtubs are checked for standing water or signs of mold; and (4) a waiver of liability for mold growth caused by the homeowner's failure to follow the builder's recommendations.[38]

Homeowners often create mold growth situations by introducing excessive water to the stem walls. In Arizona, this typically plays out in several ways. First, homeowners may introduce excessive water to the stem walls by disrupting or disturbing the drainage plan for the property. In designing homes, homebuilders routinely engineer drainage troughs designed to carry water, especially during a rainstorm. Arizona homebuilders will provide the original homeowners with warnings not to disturb those features. Nevertheless, homeowners will often disturb these troughs by installing swimming pools and landscape features. Large lot spaces and the popularity of swimming pools contribute to a situation where engineered drainage and grading plans are sometimes disturbed, which causes water to run towards or pool up around a home. Second, homeowners may plant vegetation too close to a home, which might introduce excessive water to a stem wall. Placing plants and trees next to a home may cause the stem walls and foundation to be subject to an excessive amount of water from sprinkler and irrigation systems. If a home is not designed to handle this excessive amount of water, the homeowner may face mold growth.

Under Arizona law, a plaintiff generally is required to mitigate damages, and to not voluntarily incur them. Specifically, a plaintiff cannot recover damages that a plaintiff should have foreseen or that he could have avoided by reasonable effort without undue risk, expense, or humiliation.[39] A homeowner should have to accept an offer by the homebuilder to address water intrusion. Homeowners should also be required to cease activities noted in the previous paragraph, as well as fix known leaks.

5.3 Typical Claims Asserted by Plaintiffs in Arizona

Mold litigation is a relatively new phenomenon and there is not much reported case law in Arizona or other states on it, beyond insurance coverage issues, particularly because it has gone out of vogue in the last few years. Plaintiffs will typically assert claims based on both tort law (negligence) and contract law (warranty) when filing an action. Often, plaintiffs will attempt to assert other claims, such as strict liability and fraud, but these claims have had little success in Arizona.

A. Introduction

The Arizona Supreme Court held in *Woodward v. Chirco Const. Co.*[40] that plaintiffs can bring an action in both contract and tort law for damages related to "defects" in construction.[41] The Arizona Supreme Court explained the difference between contract and tort claims by announcing that "if a fireplace collapses, the purchaser can sue in contract for the cost of remedying the structural defects and sue in tort for damage to personal property or personal injury caused by the collapse. Each claim will stand or fail on its own; a distinct statute of limitation applies to each."[42]

In *Hayden Business Condominium Association v. Pegasus Development Corp.*,[43] the Arizona Court of Appeals clearly defined damages to the structure by stating that carpeting and landscaping are not personal property that are separate from the property. Thus, Arizona law is clear that, in order to bring suit under an implied warranty theory, discussed *infra*, there must be damage to the structure of the house. If a homeowner intends to bring suit in negligence, she must show personal injury or property damage separate from the structure of the house.

The Statute of Repose, A.R.S. § 12-552, sets a limit on the time a plaintiff may bring an action against "a person who develops or develops and sells real property, or performs or furnishes the design, specifications, surveying, planning, supervision, testing, construction or observation of construction of an improvement to real property" to eight years from the date of substantial completion.[44] If, however, the injury occurred during the eighth year, or was not discovered until the eighth year, a plaintiff has an additional year in which to bring the action.[45] Under no circumstances may an action commence where more than nine years has passed since substantial completion of the structure. The Statute applies to claims that are contract-based, such as those arising under an express warranty or of workmanship and habitability, but not to personal injury or death actions.[46] In addition, the Statute of Repose does not shorten a separate warranty provision in an express warranty.[47] However, most homebuilder warranties do not last eight or nine years.

The eight-year period commences upon the substantial completion of the building. The substantial completion date is the first of: (1) the time when the property is first used by the owner or occupant; (2) the date the property is first available for use according to the contract or agreement; or (3) the time of the final inspection by a governmental body.[48]

There is no debate whether the separate breach of contract limitation period set forth in A.R.S. § 12-548 applies to implied warranty claims, so as to trump the Statute of Repose. The Statute of Repose makes it clear that it applies regardless of any other statute of limitations. However, an area of unresolved concern is whether a repair made under the express or implied warranty establishes a new base for the running of a breach of contract or negligence statute of limitation on the repair that may exceed or extend the Statute of Repose. This problem frequently arises in settlement negotiations in older homes approaching the period of repose. As to the limitation period for implied warranty claims, it would seem that an implied warranty is a claim that is based in contract, although a creation of law, and, therefore, may be governed by the six-year limitation.[49] There is no known authority other than Registrar of Contractor rules that might apply that extends the Statute of Repose by a repair.

Regarding existing structures, buyers and sellers of homes usually have no special duties to one another, and their interests are by nature conflicting and adverse.[50] Sellers must disclose latent defects that they are aware of, but it is often difficult to prove knowledge.[51] The seller's common law duty to disclose defects generally applies only to matters uniquely within the seller's knowledge that could not be known by the buyer's exercise of reasonable due diligence.[52] The interests of a seller's broker are also in conflict with the buyer's interests, as they must exercise reasonable due care and diligence to effect a sale to the principal's best advantage.[53] Brokers must also disclose only to their clients information they possess pertaining to the transaction involved.[54]

Before you consider filing suit, it is important to identify and investigate the responsible parties. Likely responsible parties include the seller of the home (if a resale), homebuilders who are also vendors, subcontractors, architects, engineers, developers, landscapers, real estate brokers, inspectors, remediation companies, city inspectors, and intervening contractors. As discovery progresses, you may be able to identify additional responsible parties who may have contributed. Indeed, shortly after the Arizona Court of Appeals held that a homebuilder must also be a vendor for any implied warranty to apply, the Arizona Supreme Court (en banc) vacated the Court of Appeals decision and found such privity to be unnecessary.[55] Amending a complaint in Arizona is fairly routine, especially at the initial stages of a lawsuit, and it should not be too difficult to amend the complaint to add additional defendants. Defendants will notice non-parties potentially at fault, and the Plaintiff will have to analyze the nature of the allegation carefully to add such a non-party to the complaint or else risk suffering that percentage of fault due to the negligence of the non-party if the claim is for personal property loss or personal injury.

B. Negligence

Claims made in mold cases may include negligence for injury or personal property damage only based on the economic loss rule. Typical grounds for recovery under theories of negligence include negligent construction of property, negligent supervision, negligent maintenance, negligent design/maintenance/installation of heating/air conditioning systems, negligent hiring/supervision of contractors or maintenance workers, negligent maintenance or repair, and negligent misrepresentations. Negligence claims are typically brought to recover personal injury damages dealing with anything from rhinisitus to aggravation of asthma to lung disorders. For a plaintiff to succeed on a negligence claim, she must prove four elements: (1) duty; (2) breach of duty; (3) causation; (4) and damages.

In proving breach of duty, a plaintiff is required to show a standard of care violated by the builder through the testimony of another builder. Testimony from an engineer or architect will not suffice.[56] It would be prudent to look into applicable building codes, plans, and specifications to find deviations. In Arizona, homebuilders typically hire subcontractors to construct homes. Thus, mold injury claims generally involve active negligence by a subcontractor and not the homebuilder. Plaintiffs must allege that builders are liable for negligent independent selection, hiring, and supervision of subcontractors, who are alleged to have actually caused the mold problem by negligent construction. Plaintiffs who claim that the homebuilder or general contractor negligently supervised its subcontractors must introduce testimony from an expert homebuilder to establish the requisite standard of care.[57] However, as noted below, general contractors are commonly not liable for negligent acts of their independent subcontractors.

Causation is a major problem for plaintiffs to overcome. Plaintiffs must show that the defendant's failure to follow the applicable standard of care proximately resulted in injury. Because there is little established support showing a link between exposure to even allegedly toxic molds, like *Stachybotrys chartarum*, and permanent injury, plaintiffs may have a difficult time proving causation in personal injury cases. Even assuming that a plaintiff has damaged personal property, the burden still remains on the plaintiff to prove the defendant's negligence.[58]

Plaintiffs bringing suit against homebuilders in negligence must claim either personal injury or personal property damage. In *Nastri v. Wood Bros. Homes, Inc.*,[59] the Arizona Court of Appeals decided that a plaintiff could not maintain an action under a negligence theory against a homebuilder without property damage or personal injury.[60] In that case, the plaintiff's tort claim failed because the damage in the case involved structural defects to the property; plaintiff did not have any personal injury or damage to personal property.[61]

General contractors are typically not liable for the negligent acts of their independent subcontractors. Arizona homebuilders are ordinarily general contractors, and construct homes through the use of various specialist subcontractors. Under the Restatement of Agency, subcontractors retained by a general contractor are "independent contractors."[62] In *Wiggs v. City of Phoenix*,[63] the Arizona Supreme Court held that while an employer is liable for the negligence of its employees under the doctrine of respondeat superior, an employer is usually not liable for the negligence of an independent contractor.[64] In the *Wiggs* ruling, the Arizona Supreme Court expressly noted that Arizona follows the general rule that a general contractor is not liable for the acts of an independent contractor, in the absence of a recognized exception to that general rule.[65] The Supreme Court found that the City of Phoenix *could* be liable for the torts of an independent contractor related to work on a public roadway, because the city had a "non-delegable duty" to maintain the roadway.[66] The "non-delegable duty" exception is recognized in the Restatement of Torts, but neither the Restatement nor Arizona statutes nor case law have found that the duties of a general contractor constructing a home cannot properly be delegated to subcontractors.

Courts in Arizona and in other jurisdictions have found non-delegable duties in "inherently dangerous" activities. For example, in *Ft. Lowell-NSS Ltd. Partnership v. Kelly*,[67] the Arizona Supreme Court found a landowner liable for injuries to the employee of an independent contractor who received severe electrical shock while demonstrating an electronic security system. Additionally, the mere existence of a contract between a general contractor and a subcontractor does not create a non-delegable duty.[68] Finally, in explaining the non-delegable exception, courts in other jurisdictions have held that even where a house fire resulted in death, a general contractor/employer is still not liable for the negligent acts of its subcontractors.[69]

C. Implied Warranty of Habitability

Under the implied warranty of habitability or workmanship, a home must be reasonably suited for its intended use.[70] The implied warranty of habitability and fitness of a house arises from the contractual relationship between the homebuilder and purchaser, although it is a creation of law based on public policy.[71] The purpose of the implied warranty of habitability and workmanlike performance is to rectify latent and defective design, workmanship or construction within the Statute of Repose, A.R.S. §12-552.[72] The implied warranty of habitability and workmanlike performance was judicially created to ensure that construction is done in a workmanlike manner, and the implied warranty provides homeowners, including those who do not have privity of contract with the homebuilder, with an important guarantee that their homes are habitable.[73] The implied warranty may not extend to subsequent purchasers of commercial property.[74] However, in *Highland Village v. Bradbury & Stamm*, the Arizona Court of Appeals appears to limit this rule by allowing assignments of contractual rights in the commercial property context.[75]

In *Nastri*, the Arizona Court of Appeals found that the attempted disclaimer of the implied warranty of habitability was void against public policy as to innocent subsequent purchasers.[76] The court did not comment on a knowing and fully agreed-upon waiver. When the plaintiff is a subsequent purchaser rather than the original homeowner, the burden is placed on the subsequent homeowner to demonstrate that the builder-vendor caused the defect and that the action was brought within the appropriate timeframe prescribed by A.R.S. § 12-552.[77] In addition, the plaintiff must show not only that the defect originated with the builder-vendor, but also that the defect was latent, as discussed *infra*. The builder-vendor can claim that the defects are not attributable to it, that the defects are the result of ordinary wear and tear or age, that the plaintiff discovered the defects within the applicable statute of limitations, and that the plaintiff made substantial changes to the building that resulted in the problem.[78]

The implied warranty of habitability only applies to "latent defects which become manifest after the subsequent owner's purchase and which were not discoverable had a reasonable inspection of the structure been made prior to purchase."[79] In other words, the implied warranty of habitability does not apply where the purchaser could have discovered the defect through reasonable inspection.[80] Regarding latent defects, if the seller of real property fails to disclose a defect known to the seller or fails to give an appropriate opportunity to discover the facts, the doctrine of *caveat emptor* no longer applies and the vendor is subject to tort liability for nondisclosure.[81] Even though a potential home purchaser is afforded a certain number of days to conduct an inspection, the seller cannot withhold information about the presence of mold if the mold is a latent defect. The standard form contract used by realtors affords the buyer a certain number of days to conduct any type of inspection she desires. If a home inspector fails to find mold during the inspection and mold is present, the home purchaser may have an action against the home inspector, but home inspectors typically have in their contract a release from liability.

The implied warranty of habitability is limited by the reasonable lifespan of the item in question. In the past, Arizona courts have found that 12 years was not an unreasonable period of time for an implied warranty of habitability and workmanship to exist for stucco.[82] The Arizona Legislature responded in 1989 by enacting the Statute of Repose (A.R.S. § 12-552), which prevents plaintiffs from bringing any contract-based claims arising from the construction of a home more than eight years (or nine years) after "substantial completion." As noted *supra*, A.R.S. § 12-

552 sets a bright line rule that all construction defect claims must be brought either eight or nine years after the substantial completion of the home, no matter the "reasonable lifespan" of an item. For example, even if stucco is designed to last between 30 and 50 years, A.R.S. § 12-552 limits a construction defect claim to either eight or nine years, depending on when the homeowner discovered the defect.

In discussing mold claims in particular, some critics point out that "water intrusion is likely to occur because of defects in housing components that should last longer than eight years—components such as the roof, plumbing and stucco. The damage from defects in these components could occur well after the Statute of Limitations expires, but years before the end of the expected lifespan of the components. Nevertheless, homeowners cannot recover under the implied warranty in such situations."[83] A.R.S. § 12-552 acts to prevent homebuilders from being indefinitely liable for the failure of components in a home. Homebuilders are no longer eternal insurers of a home.

Note that actions brought under the implied warranty of habitability arise out of a contract and therefore fall within A.R.S. § 12-341.01, providing for attorneys' fees and costs.[84]

D. Breach of Contract or Breach of Express Warranty

In some instances, a plaintiff might be able to bring a mold claim because of a breach of an express warranty in a sales contract, lease, or advertisement. These cases will turn on specific language contained in a contract or warranty. In addition, express warranties are usually less than two years and contracts are limited by A.R.S. § 12-548, which provides a six-year Statute of Limitations. Finally, breach of contract claims generally require privity, which is not always present in homebuilding actions.

E. Landlord/Tenant Issues

The Arizona Residential Landlord Tenant Act (A.R.S. § 33-1301 *et seq.*) ("ARLTA") has several provisions that may be applicable in mold cases.

First, A.R.S. § 33-1341 provides that a tenant: (a) must comply with the building codes materially affecting health and safety; (b) must keep the premises clean and safe; must dispose all ashes, rubbish, garbage, and other waste; (c) must keep all the plumbing fixtures clean; and (d) must use all electrical, plumbing, sanitary, heating, ventilating, air-conditioning, and other facilities and appliances reasonably. Tenants should take care to be reasonable when they have reported mold or mildew damage, and they must allow the landlord an opportunity to inspect the unit. If the tenant is unreasonable with respect to allowing access to the apartment for the repairs or remediation, he may be deemed to not have mitigated his damages under A.R.S. §§ 33-1305, 33-1341, or 33-1343. Furthermore, if a tenant alleges that moving out of the unit could mitigate his damages, and the opportunity to move out arose, the tenant would be required to take that opportunity.

However, there are similar provisions in the Arizona Residential Landlord Tenant Act that would hold a landlord accountable for her actions (or inactions). Specifically, under A.R.S. § 33-1324, a landlord shall: (a) comply with the building codes materially affecting health and safety; (b) make all repairs and do whatever is necessary to put and keep the premises in a fit and habitable condition; (c) keep all common areas of the premises in a clean and safe condition; (d) maintain in good and safe working order and condition all electrical, plumbing, sanitary, heating, ventilating, air-conditioning and other facilities and appliances; (e) provide and maintain appropriate receptacles; (f) supply running water and reasonable amounts of hot water at all times; and (g) reasonable heat and reasonable air-conditioning or cooling where such units are installed and offered, when required by seasonal weather conditions.

A tenant has various remedies against the landlord in the event of a mold problem. For example, under A.R.S. § 33-1361, a tenant may claim damages or terminate the lease after giving the landlord notice and an opportunity to repair. A tenant must give the landlord ten days to cure a breach of the lease and five days to cure a breach of the ARLTA affecting health or safety. Damages may include the reduced rental value of the premises, injury to personal property, medical expenses resulting from illness caused by the defects, mental distress, and even lost profits in a business carried on in the premises.

Under A.R.S. § 33-1363, a tenant may make the repairs himself and deduct the cost from next month's rent. The amount is limited to the greater of $300 or ½ month's rent, and the tenant must use a licensed contractor and get a mechanic's lien waiver. Furthermore, the tenant must give the landlord ten days written notice before obtaining repairs.

Under A.R.S. § 33-1365, the tenant may raise the landlord's default as a defense if the landlord sues to terminate the lease. Under A.R.S. § 33-1367, if a landlord ousts a tenant unlawfully, the tenant may terminate the lease and recover damages equal to the greater of two months' rent or twice actual damages. Under A.R.S. § 33-1368, either party may terminate the lease if the other has materially breached the ARLTA provisions affecting health or safety, and the non-breaching party must give the breaching party five days to cure. Finally, under A.R.S. § 33-1381, a landlord may not raise rent, reduce services, or terminate a tenancy in retaliation for a tenant's complaining to the government about code-violations or complaining to the landlord about violations of his legal duties.

The ARLTA does not apply to commercial, industrial, farms, and other non-dwelling tenancies. If a lease exists, you should determine the responsibilities of the parties to the lease. A.R.S. § 33-321 provides that "[a] tenant shall exercise diligence to maintain the premises in as good condition as when he took possession, ordinary wear and tear excepted." Pursuant to A.R.S. § 33-343, "[t]he lessee of a building which, without fault or neglect on the part of the lessee, is destroyed or so injured by the elements or any other cause as to be untenantable or unfit for occupancy, is not liable thereafter to pay rent to the lessor or owner unless expressly provided by written agreement, and the lessee may thereupon quit and surrender possession of the premises."

There are several possible causes of action by a tenant against a landlord. Both A.R.S. § 33-343 and § 33-1366 permit a tenant to terminate a lease under certain situations. Additionally, a tenant can allege a constructive eviction. In *Steward Title v. Pribbeno*,[85] the Court of Appeals held that a marginally functioning air conditioner was not sufficient for a constructive eviction action. However, a severe mold problem may be sufficient. Finally, a tenant can also bring an action based in negligence. A landlord may be liable only if she knows or has reason to know of the defect.[86] However, a landlord is under no duty to warn a tenant of a condition which he reasonably believes the tenant will discover, or of the extent of risk involved in the obvious condition, unless he should realize that the tenant is unlikely to appreciate it.[87]

F. Other Potential Causes of Action and Homeowner Complaints

Arizona does not recognize strict liability or product liability in the context of homebuilding.[88] Strict liability and product liability are claims that do not require fault on the part of the defendant, and are typically reserved for hazardous and dangerous activities, manufacturing product defects, and product design defects. Although the seller of a "product" in a defective condition is usually liable in strict liability, policy reasons do not justify characterizing homes or homebuilding materials as "products."[89]

In addition, no reported Arizona case has addressed damages for emotional distress or lost wages in a construction defect or mold case, although if physical injury could be established in a negligence case, it is theoretically possible. Other jurisdictions considering such claims have denied recovery.[90] In any event, allegations of emotional and mental distress are not compensable unless based on some continuing, non-temporal physical injury, which might be difficult for a plaintiff to prove.[91] If an Arizona homebuilder is faced with an emotional distress claim, it could argue that contracts for the purchase of homes or real property are not considered the type of contract that would cause emotional distress as a foreseeable damage from its breach.[92]

In other jurisdictions, plaintiffs have brought actions based on improper appraisal,[93] breach of contract,[94] breach of duty of good faith and fair dealing,[95] civil rights violations,[96] deceptive trade practices,[97] fraud,[98] consumer fraud,[99] infliction of emotional distress,[100] and libel and slander.[101] Whether any of these potential causes of action would stand in Arizona is certainly debatable.

G. Damages

In Arizona, the measure of damages for a construction defect claim is either the cost of repair or, in the situation where repairs are economically wasteful, the diminution in value. The measure of damages does not contemplate damages for emotional distress.[102] Arizona law requires that damages be awarded only when the Plaintiff has met its burden of proving the amount of its damages with reasonable certainty.[103] "An award of damages cannot be based on conjecture or speculation."[104] Property damage valuation will likely require the services of a professional or expert appraiser. If an insurance company is involved, it will generally hire an appraiser to value the property that was affected. If the property has been completely destroyed so that it is of no further use and has no salvage value, the measure of damages can be set at the fair market value of the property immediately before its loss. If the property can be repaired, the amount of damages can be set at the amount it costs to repair the property, plus the loss of its use by the owner, if any. If the cost to repair the property exceeds the fair market value of the property before loss, the damages can be limited to the fair market value. In addition to the cost to repair or replace, plus loss of use, interest and loss of profits may also be added as elements of damages.

Certain building materials may be able to be cleaned, including floors, carpets, and certain hard surfaces. However, certain materials may not be salvageable. With respect to personal property items, depending upon the item, you may be able to salvage some items. If you are unsure what to do, or if the item is expensive or of sentimental value, you may wish to consult a specialist. Specialists in furniture repair/restoration, painting, art restoration and conservation, carpet and rug cleaning, water damage, and fire/water restoration are commonly listed in phone books. Be sure to ask for and check references and to look for affiliation with professional organizations.

Homeowners are also unable to recover "stigma" damages related to their home. Homeowners often complain that once they have encountered a mold problem, they are unable to sell their home for full value, or even at all. A plaintiff should not be entitled to "stigma" damages if a home is truly remediated and certified to be free of mold. Arizona case law has long established that the cost to repair is the proper measure of damage, unless the repair is economically wasteful or involves complete destruction.[105]

Diminution in value has only been recognized in Arizona as an issue when permanent and calculable physical damage to chattels has occurred.[106] Furthermore, diminution in value is only applicable when physical damage has occurred, and the relief to be awarded is the cost of repair or replacement not to exceed the amount of diminution in value.[107] Stigma damages are not compensable because "[a]n award of damages cannot be based on conjecture or speculation."[108] In any event, most new home construction contracts in Arizona have express limitations on the measure of damages contemplated, and include repair or replacement as the sole agreed-upon measure of damages.

Plaintiffs may also seek damages for personal injuries, including current medical damages, future medical damages, and pain and suffering. The science of mold injuries can be controversial. Certain claims might be easier to prove such as skin problems, rashes, burning sensations, irritation (eyes, ears, nose throat, lungs), difficulty breathing, upper respiratory tract infections, and cold and flu-like symptoms. Other claims may be more difficult to prove such as impacts on nervous, urinary, reproductive, digestive, and vascular systems. Plaintiffs may also seek damages for emotional distress, but allegations of emotional distress require some continuing, non-temporal physical injury.[109]

Depending on the claims brought, a plaintiff may seek punitive damages and lost wages. Plaintiffs may also be able to seek consequential damages such as relocation costs and damages for the cost of remediation.

Note that actions brought under the implied warranty of habitability arise out of a contract and therefore fall within A.R.S. § 12-341.01, providing for attorneys' fees and costs.[110] In addition, as discussed below, under A.R.S. § 12-1364, the prevailing party may recover attorneys' fees in dwelling actions.

Note also that remediation work is often performed on an emergency basis. However, pursuant to ER 3.4, "[a] lawyer shall not (a) unlawfully obstruct another party's access to evidence or unlawfully alter, destroy or conceal a document or other material having potential evidentiary value. A lawyer shall not counsel or assist another person to do any such act." If at all possible, provide notice to the other side of the remediation that will take place. Put the notice in writing to avoid later disputes.

Finally, note that homebuilders typically exclude the ability of a homeowner to recover consequential, special, and punitive damages in their standard purchase contracts.

5.4 Construction Legislation in Arizona

A. HB 2620 (2002), SB 1311 (2004), and SB 1374 (2006): Purchaser Dwelling Action; Opportunity to Repair

Pursuant to A.R.S. § 12-1361 *et seq.*, which was enacted and subsequently amended by HB 2620, SB 1311, and SB 1374, the homebuilder/seller now has the statutory right to make an offer to repair a property before the purchaser can file a "dwelling action" or else there are severe consequences.

"Dwelling actions" are defined as "any action brought by a purchaser against the seller of a dwelling arising out of or related to the design, construction, condition or sale of the dwelling" and would encompass mold actions.[111] The heart of House Bill 2620's changes can be found in A.R.S. 12-1363, entitled "notice and opportunity to repair." Purchasers must provide the seller the basis of the action by certified mail 90 days before filing the action.[112] SB 1374 amended A.R.S. § 12-1363 to further define the "reasonable detail" that is required to be provided. "Reasonable detail" now is defined as "a detailed and itemized list that describes each alleged defect and the location that each alleged defect has been observed by the purchaser in each dwelling that is the subject of the notice."[113]

However, A.R.S. § 12-1361 *et seq.* do not apply where the alleged defects involve "an immediate threat to the life or safety of persons occupying or visiting the dwelling."[114] Mold can arguably pose an immediate threat to safety or life, rendering this statute inapplicable. In addition, many contracts with homebuilders include alternative dispute provisions and even jury trial waivers. The standard form real estate contracts also may include such provisions. Therefore, many mold actions may not even be litigated in court.

Assuming that A.R.S. § 12-1361 *et seq.* applies, after the seller receives notice, the seller is able to inspect the dwelling unit or units to determine the nature and cause of the alleged defects and to assess possible repairs and replacements.[115] This inspection period provides the seller an opportunity to inspect the property for mold. Naturally, the purchaser must make her dwelling available to the seller for inspection, and the statute provides that the purchaser must comply within ten days after the seller makes a request for inspection.[116] In inspecting the unit, the seller is allowed to use "reasonable measures, including testing, to determine the nature and cause of the alleged defects and the nature and extent of any repairs or replacements necessary to remedy the alleged defects."[117] The seller is also required to return the premises to their pre-testing condition.[118] In this situation, a seller may want to bring a mold specialist or remediator to the premises in order to thoroughly investigate the claim.

Sixty days after the purchaser provides notice, the seller must respond to the purchaser's notice by certified mail.[119] In his response, the seller may offer to repair or replace the defects, to have the alleged defects repaired or replaced at the seller's expense, or provide the purchaser monetary compensation.[120] If the seller offers a solution to the problem, the seller must describe in detail what she plans to do and provide a reasonable completion date.[121] A mold remediator may wish to describe his services at this time. Where the Complaint has not yet been filed, if the seller does not respond to the purchaser's notice within 60 days, the purchaser can file her action without waiting for the expiration of the 90-day period.[122]

Within 20 days after receipt of the seller's response, the purchaser must respond by either accepting or rejecting the seller's offer by certified mail.[123] The purchaser may also include a counteroffer.[124] If the purchaser rejects the seller's offer, he must state the basis for his rejection.[125] The seller then has ten days within which to make her best and final offer by certified mail.[126]

In the event that the purchaser files an action, the statute provides that certain facts are inadmissible in court, including the purchaser's notice and all good-faith responses, counteroffers and final offers made by the purchaser and seller.[127] Other relevant provisions of A.R.S. § 12-1363 include allowing the purchaser to amend the original notice[128] and the tolling of the Statute of Limitations.[129]

A.R.S. § 12-1364 provides that "[i]n any contested dwelling action, the court shall award the successful party reasonable attorney fees, reasonable expert witness fees and taxable costs." A.R.S. § 12-1364 also incorporates a version of Rule 68 of the Arizona Rules of Civil Procedure regarding offers of judgment. If the purchaser rejects the seller's best offer and the final judgment is even less favorable to the purchaser than the seller's offer, the court deems that the seller is the successful party and is entitled to attorney fees, expert fees, and taxable costs.[130] Under A.R.S. § 12-1365, written contracts for the sale of newly constructed homes must provide specific language stating that the purchaser has the right to file an action with the Arizona Registrar of Contractors. Finally, A.R.S. § 12-1361 *et seq.* does not apply to personal injury claims, claims for damage to property other than a dwelling, common law fraud claims, claims where the sale contract contains commercially reasonable alternative dispute resolution procedures, and claims solely seeking recovery of monies expended for repairs to alleged defects already repaired by the purchaser.[131]

B. A.R.S. § 12-2602

Additionally, A.R.S. § 12-2602 requires that a certification that expert testimony be filed at the time of the Complaint, if the action is against a licensed professional such as a homebuilder. Specifically, A.R.S. § 12-2602(A) requires a certification as to whether or not expert opinion testimony will be required to prove a standard of care. This certification is required at the time the claim is filed. In addition, under A.R.S. § 12-2602(B), the claimant is required to provide a preliminary expert opinion with the initial disclosure statement that includes certain information including the expert's qualifications, the factual basis for the claim, and the licensed professional's acts, errors, or omissions that may violate the applicable standard of care. Failure to comply with this statute may result in the dismissal of a claim without prejudice, pursuant to A.R.S. § 12-2602(F).

5.5 Reported Mold Case Law in Arizona

The majority of Arizona cases discussing mold damage revolve around insurance issues. In *Cooper v. American Family Mut. Ins. Co.*,[132] decided by the Federal District Court in Arizona, the insured brought an action against the insurance carrier to recover for mold damage caused by a plumbing leak, which also damaged drywall and flooring.[133] The court, on cross-motions for summary judgment, held that the homeowner's insurance policy did not cover mold damage.[134] The relevant provision in the insurance policy stated that mold loss was not covered "regardless of any other cause or event contributing concurrently or in any sequence to the loss."[135] Another provision of the policy denied coverage for "smog, rust, corrosion, frost, condensation, *mold*, wet or dry rot."[136]

In *Liristis v. American Family Mut. Ins. Co.*,[137] the Arizona Court of Appeals held that the insurance policy *covered* mold damage, including the cost of removal or repair of the damage. Interestingly enough, the defendant was the same as in the *Cooper* case noted *supra*, and the insured had the same insurance exclusions.[138] In *Liristis*, plaintiffs claimed that a fire (and the water used to extinguish the fire) caused their mold problems.[139] The court found that the insurance policy distinguished between mold damage and loss caused by mold, and did not exclude mold damage caused by a covered event like fire.[140] If the mold resulted from the fire, then the cost of removing the mold was not a loss separate from or caused by the mold itself.[141] In reversing the granting of plaintiff's motion for summary judgment, the court remanded back to the trial court to determine whether some or all of the mold damage was caused by the fire and the water used to extinguish it.[142] It is difficult to distinguish *Cooper* and *Liristis* other than to say that they were decided by different courts.

In a third insurance coverage case, an Arizona jury awarded $4.25 million in a homeowner's claim against the insurer for its bad faith refusal to cover mold remediation. In *Hatley v. Century Nat'l Co.*,[143] a doctor advised plaintiffs to search their home for mold after the doctor found mold spores in plaintiffs' son's lungs. Plaintiffs filed a claim with their insurance company after discovering mold in the kitchen and bathroom. The insurer denied coverage claiming that the mold was caused by a preexisting condition and that the policy excluded mold under an exclusion. The jury awarded plaintiffs $244,000 in compensatory damages and $4 million in punitive damages.

In a fourth insurance coverage case, the Arizona District Court held that there was no evil intent to support a punitive damages claim in a bad faith case. In *Holy Trinity Greek Orthodox Church v. Church Mutual Insurance Company*,[144] the Arizona District Court did not feel that punitive damages were justified where the insurance company allegedly: (1) withheld testing results that were produced by its experts and/or did not timely share them with its insured; (2) hid from its insured the potential life-threatening situations concerning the use of the air conditioning unit and resulting moisture flowing from the ground into the facility that could result in the increased development in mold spores; (3) failed to advise of the threat of asbestos; and (4) advised the insured that the facility was safe when the insurer had information in its possession that indicated the possibility of mold.

In a case that did not involve insurance coverage, *Kari Kilian v. Gleneagles*, CV2000-014108, a Maricopa County jury awarded plaintiff the sum of $100,000 for her alleged personal injuries and property damage at an apartment complex. In a separate bench trial in District Court involving separate defendants, the Court found that there was insufficient evidence of an association between neuropsychiatric symptoms and the presence of mold.[145] The District Court excluded plaintiff's expert testimony, and her claim thus failed. *Id.* The case was then appealed to the Ninth Circuit, which held (1) that the testimony of three of plaintiff's expert witnesses was properly excluded as not scientifically valid, (2) that plaintiff failed to prove causation, precluding recovery, and (3) that attorneys' fees could properly be awarded in suit brought under the ARLTA.[146]

5.6 Admissibility of Expert Witness Testimony in Arizona

State courts in Arizona follow the *Frye* standard regarding the admissibility of scientific evidence. Under the *Frye* standard, the court considers whether the methodology employed by an expert is "generally accepted" within the scientific community. [147] Arizona's courts have made certain limited exceptions to the *Frye* standard "when a qualified witness offers relevant testimony or conclusions based on experience and observation about human behavior for the purpose of explaining that behavior."[148] This exception is further limited to opinions which are based on a qualified expert's own research, observations, and experience, as well as the research of others with which she is familiar.[149] Therefore, pursuant to *Frye*, an expert relying upon others' theories and methods will need to show that those theories have been generally accepted in the scientific community.

In Arizona, *Frye* hearings are required before the admission of expert testimony that relies on new or novel scientific tests or techniques.[150] *Frye* hearings are only necessary when an opposing party makes a timely request supported by evidence that the community does not generally accept an expert's technique or method. Thereafter, expert testimony is admissible only if the proponent of the expert testimony can demonstrate that the expert's methodology is generally accepted in his particular field.[151] *Frye* hearings are often conducted before trial in order to timely resolve the general acceptance issue.[152] Although there are no published Arizona *Frye* cases dealing with the admissibility of expert evidence regarding mold, Arizona courts have applied *Frye* to a number of other areas.[153]

It could be argued that expert testimony regarding mold must pass the *Frye* standard in order to be admissible, particularly as to its effect on the health of individuals. The Arizona Supreme Court has stated *in dicta* that an expert's opinion, which is nothing more than *ipse dixit* or an unsupported assertion, should not be allowed.[154] "The court's obligation to exclude unproven and potentially misleading scientific evidence is 'especially sensitive in cases where the plaintiff claims that exposure to a toxic substance caused his injury, [because a] jury may blindly accept an expert's opinion that conforms with their underlying fears of toxic substances without carefully understanding or examining the basis for that opinion.'"[155] Rule 702 of the Arizona Rules of Evidence allows an expert to testify regarding scientific, technical, or other specialized knowledge if it "will assist the trier of fact to understand the evidence or to determine a fact in issue." In toxic mold cases, the trial court could exclude expert testimony that is unproven or misleading because it will not assist the trier of fact but rather will cloud the trier of fact's judgment. Specifically, the court could exclude expert testimony regarding a causal link between exposure to toxic mold and human health consequences because recent scientific publications have "concluded that indoor airborne levels of microorganisms are only weakly correlated with human disease or building-related symptoms and that a causal relationship has not been established between these complaints and indoor exposures to [*Stachybotrys*] *chartarum*."[156]

5.7 Conclusion

Few would dispute that a mold problem exists today, particularly in states with warmer climates like Arizona. Even though mold has existed since the beginning of time, only recently has it been brought to our attention through the mainstream media, although it appears that the media is not discussing mold as much as it did a few years ago. Although we may not know the full consequences of exposure to mold, particularly in the long run, one thing is for certain: mold claims are becoming ever more prevalent, especially claims for property damage. For many people, their homes represent their largest investment. Unfortunately, many homeowners are disappointed once they discover that their dream home has a mold problem, and they quickly look to the homebuilder or the seller of the home for relief. However, homeowners are also responsible for their mold problems by such things as not properly maintaining their homes, by constructing swimming pools and tracking water into the home, or by adding vegetation or water features. In any event, the state of the science regarding mold is evolving quickly. No doubt, a response by the Arizona Legislature and the Arizona courts will follow and shape the future of mold law in Arizona in the next several years. The Arizona Legislature has already acted to pass laws related to construction defects in recent years, and the Arizona courts have also acted recently by publishing several decisions regarding insurance issues related to mold coverage. Although we do not know exactly what the future holds for toxic mold law in Arizona, we do know that this problem will not quietly disappear. As long as people discover mold in their homes, they will seek to recover at least for their property damages.

Endnotes

1. Kerry Fehr-Snyder, *Sneeze and Wheeze: Molds Make Themselves Right at Home*, ARIZONA REPUBLIC, Mar. 10, 2003, at A1.

2. Kelly A. Reynolds, Ph.D., research microbiologist, University of Arizona, Tucson; Jordan S. Josephson, M.D., director, New York Nasal and Sinus Center, and attending physician, Lenox Hill Hospital, New York City; March 10, 2003, presentation, American Academy of Allergy, Asthma and Immunology annual meeting, Denver.

3. *Sneeze and Wheeze: Molds Make Themselves Right at Home*, *supra* note 1.

4. Catherine Burrough, *Insurance Premiums for Homeowners Rising*, ARIZONA REPUBLIC, Oct. 26, 2003, at H10; Christine L. Romero, *Arizona Insurance Rates for Autos, Homes Soar*, ARIZONA REPUBLIC, Mar. 27, 2002 at A1.

5. *Insurance Premiums for Homeowners Rising*, *supra* note 1.

6. *Arizona Insurance Rates for Autos, Homes Soar*, *supra* note 1.

7. Kerry Fehr-Snyder, *Mold Removal Costs Soar*, ARIZONA REPUBLIC, July 27 2001, at A1.

8. *Id.*

9. *Id.*

10. *Id.*

11. *Mold in my Home: What do I do?*, available at http://www.azdhs.gov/phs/oeh/invsurv/air_qual/mold_contents.htm.

12. *Ballard v. Fire Ins. Exchange*, 2001 WL 883550 (Tex. Dist. Ct. 2001) *aff'd in part, rev'd in part sub nom. Allison v. Fire Ins. Exchange*, 98 S.W.3d 227 (Tex. App. 2002) (affirmed $4,006,320.72 of the $32 million award and remanded the case for further calculations).

13. *Group says Arizona one of the worst states for mold contamination*, PHOENIX BUSINESS JOURNAL, July 10, 2006.

14. *Id.*

15. *Mold not nearly the problem in Arizona that report suggests,* PHOENIX BUSINESS JOURNAL, July 21, 2006., available at http://www.bizjournals.com/phoenix/stories/200607/24/editorial4.html?t=printable.

16. Star Lawrence, *Researchers Divided on Toxic Mold*, available at http://my.webmd.com/content/Article/73/89002,htm?printing=true.

17. Glen Creno et al., "Home building, prices soared in 2004," Arizona Republic, January 27, 2005.

18. Catherine Reagor, "Permits may fall, but rebound on horizon," Arizona Republic, January 27, 2008.

19. U.S. Census Bureau data for 1990, available at http://factfinder.census.gov/servlet/BasicFactsTable?_lang=en&_vt_name=DEC_1990_STF1_DP1&_geo_id=04000US04.

20. U.S. Census Bureau data for 2000, available at http://factfinder.census.gov/servlet/BasicFactsTable?_lang=en&_vt_name=DEC_2000_SF1_U_DP1&_geo_id=04000US04.

21. By 2030, the Census expects Arizona to be the 10th most populous state with a population of over 10.7 million people. U.S. Census Bureau data available at http://www.census.gov/population/projections/PressTab1.xls

22. Catherine Reagor, "Permits may fall, but rebound on horizon," Arizona Republic, January 27, 2008.

23. Craig Harris et al., *Construction Quality Varies Widely*, ARIZONA REPUBLIC, Nov. 20, 2001, at A1.

24. *Id.*

25. *Id.*

26. *Id.*

27. Jonathan J. Higuera, *Jobless Rate in State Falls as Economy Makes Gains*, ARIZONA REPUBLIC, Dec. 19, 2003, at D1.

28. Harris et al., *supra* note 23.

29. National Association of Homebuilders, A BUILDER'S GUIDE TO HANDLING MOLD CLAIMS AND LITIGATION, 3 (2001).

30. Harris et al., *supra* note 23.

31. Joseph Lstiburek, Ph.D., P.Eng., et al., *Mold: Causes, Health Effects and Clean-Up*, 2 (2002) available at http://www.eere.energy.gov/buildings/building_america/pdfs/db/35012.pdf.

32. Thelma Jarman-Felstiner, *Mold is Gold: But, Will it be the Next Asbestos?* 30 PEPP. L. REV. 529, 535 (2003) citing Andy Dworkin, Mold Leaves a Trail of Victims, Lawsuits, THE OREGONIAN, Aug. 19, 2001, at A1, available at 2001 WL3611638. *But see, Blame Moisture, Not Airtight Construction*, SACRAMENTO BUSINESS JOURNAL, July 15, 2002, available at http://www.bizjournals.com/sacramento/stories/2002/07/15/editorial3.html?t=printable (Moisture problems are related to poor construction of building components and the failure of a building system. Airtight buildings will prevent the infiltration of outdoor mold particles, but will trap mold contaminants if an indoor mold source exists).

33. http://www.weather.com/outlook/travel/climatology/monthly/USAZ0166?from=search.

34. http://www.weather.com/outlook/travel/climatology/monthly/USAZ0247?from=search.

35. http://www.weather.com/outlook/travel/climatology/monthly/USAZ0166?from=search.

36. These guidelines are available at http://www.ci.nyc.ny.us/html/doh/html/epi/moldrpt1.html.

37. National Association of Homebuilders, *supra* note 29, at 4.

38. *Id.*

39. *See*, *Coury Bros. Ranches, Inc. v. Ellsworth*, 103 Ariz. 515, 518-520, 446 P.2d 458, 461-463 (1968) (When pasture renter became aware of the fact that certain acreage contracted for would not be available for pasturing, it became the renter's duty to make a reasonable effort to prevent losses).

40. *Woodward v. Chirco Constr. Co., Inc.*, 141 Ariz. 514, 687 P.2d 1269 (1984).

41. *Woodward*, 141 Ariz. at 516, 687 P.2d at 1271.

42. *Id.*

43. 209 Ariz. 511, 105 P.3d 157 (App. 2005).

44. A.R.S. § 12-552(A).

45. A.R.S. § 12-552(B).

46. A.R.S. § 12-552(C), (D); *see also*, *Evans Withycombe, Inc. v. Western Innovations, Inc.*, 215 Ariz. 237, 159 P.3d 547 (App. 2006) (Statute of Repose for contract actions in connection with construction defect. A.R.S. § 12-552, barred third-party action brought by a contractor that had been timely sued by homeowners but had waited two years to file a third-party action against the subcontractors). Notwithstanding, the holding in *Evans Withycombe* did not bar third-party claims for common-law indemnity.

47. A.R.S. § 12-552(D).

48. A.R.S. § 12-552(E).

49. *Woodward v. Chirco Constr. Co., Inc.*, 141 Ariz. 514, 516, 687 P.2d 1269, 1271 (1984)

50. *Oldenburger v. Del Webb Devel. Co.*, 159 Ariz. 129, 133, 765 P.2d 531, 535 (App. 1988).

51. *S. Develop Corp. v. Pima Capital Management Co.*, 201 Ariz. 10, 17, 31 P.3d 123, 130 (App. 2001).

52. *Hill v. Jones*, 151 Ariz. 81, 85, 725 P.2d 1115, 1119 (App. 1986).

53. *See*, *Haldiman v. Gosnell Devel. Corp.*, 155 Ariz. 585, 589, 748 P.2d 1209, 1213 (App. 1987); *Vivian Arnold Realty Co. v. McCormick*, 19 Ariz. App. 289, 293, 506 P.2d 1074, 1078 (1973).

54. *Jennings v. Lee*, 105 Ariz. 167, 173, 461 P.2d 161, 167 (1969).

55. *Lofts at Fillmore Condominium Association v. Reliance Commercial Construction, Inc.*, 190 P.3d 733 (2008) *vacating Lofts at Fillmore Condominium Association v. Reliance Commercial Construction, Inc.*, 189 P.3d 426 (App. Div. 1 2007).

56. *See, e.g.*, *Woodward v. Chirco Constr. Co., Inc.*, 141 Ariz. 520, 521-23, 687 P.2d 1276-78 (App. 1984) (trial court properly dismissed homeowners' negligence claim since no construction expert testified it was standard practice in the community to obtain a soil test prior to new construction).

57. *Id.*

58. *Payne v. M. Greenberg Constr.*, 130 Ariz. 338, 347, 636 P.2d 116, 125 (App. 1981).

59. *Nastri v. Wood Bros. Homes, Inc.*, 142 Ariz. 439, 690 P.2d 158 (App. 1984).

60. *Nastri*, 142 Ariz. at 444-45, 690 P.2d at 163-64.

61. *Id.*

62. The Restatement (Third) of Agency § 7.07 helps to delineate when workers are independent contractors. In pertinent part, § 7.07 states:

> (2) An employee acts within the scope of employment when performing work assigned by the employer or engaging in a course of conduct subject to the employer's control. An employee's act is not within the scope of employment when it occurs within an independent course of conduct not intended by the employee to serve any purpose of the employer.
> (3) For purposes of this section,
> (a) an employee is an agent whose principal controls or has the right to control the manner and means of the agent's performance of work, and
> (b) the fact that work is performed gratuitously does not relieve a principal of liability.

63. *Wiggs v. City of Phoenix*, 198 Ariz. 367, 10 P.3d 625 (2000).

64. *Wiggs*, 198 Ariz. at 369, 10 P.3d at 627.

65. *Id.*

66. *Wiggs*, 198 Ariz. at 369-70, 10 P.3d at 627-28.

67. 166 Ariz. 96, 800 P.2d 962 (1990).

68. *See e.g., Carrasquillo v. Holiday Carpet Service, Inc.*, 615 So.2d 862, 863 (Fla. App. 1993) ("the mere existence of a contract does not create vicarious liability as to third persons for the negligent acts of the independent contractor. There *must* be a nondelegable duty").

69. In *McGinnis v. Jim Walter Homes, Inc.*, 800 So.2d 140 (Ala. 2001), homeowners brought a negligence action against the contractor, electrical subcontractor, and electrical supplier seeking damages resulting from a fire in their home that killed their daughter. Citing to *Knight v. Burns, Kirkley & Williams Constr. Co.*, 331 So. 2d 651, 655 (Ala. 1976), the Alabama Supreme Court held that a general contractor is not liable for the alleged negligence of an independent contractor. *Id.* at 146. *See also, Rivera v. Goodenough*, 162 P.2d 498 (Cal. App. 1945) (a general contractor building a warehouse was not liable for the negligent acts of subcontractor installing trusses to support roof of the warehouse); *Hall v. Richardson Homes, Inc.*, 309 S.E.2d 825, 829 (Ga. App. 1983) (any negligence on the part of the subcontractor was not imputable to the homebuilder because the unrebutted evidence showed that septic tank system was installed by an independent subcontractor); *Miltz v. Borroughs-Shelving*, 497 A.2d 516 (N.J. App. 1985) (the general contractor was not liable for subcontractor's negligence in the installation of stairs, as there was no proof that the general contractor engaged an incompetent subcontractor or that installing the stairs was an inherently dangerous activity).

70. *Nastri v. Wood Bros. Homes, Inc.*, 142 Ariz. 439, 444, 690 P.2d 158, 163 (App. 1984) ("Rather, we find the test...that the home be reasonably suited for its intended use consistent with the Arizona decisions").

71. *Woodward v. Chirco Constr. Co., Inc.*, 141 Ariz. 514, 516, 687 P.2d 1269, 1271 (1984). *See also, Dillig v. Fisher*, 142 Ariz. 47, 50, 688 P.2d 693, 696 (App. 1984) (the rationale underlying the implied warranty of habitability supports its application where a completed structure, which has never been occupied by anyone, is placed for sale, even if the house was originally constructed for the builder's personal use and was the only house constructed by him in the state).

72. *Woodward*, 141 Ariz. at 516, 687 P.2d at 1271; *Richards v. Powercraft Homes, Inc.*, 139 Ariz. 242, 245, 678 P.2d 427, 430 (1984).

73. *Woodward*, 141 Ariz. at 516, 687 P.2d at 1271; *Richards*, 139 Ariz. at 245, 678 P.2d at 430; *Columbia Western Corp. v. Vela*, 122 Ariz. 28, 33, 592 P.2d 1299 (App. 1979).

74. *Hayden Business Condominium Association v. Pegasus Development Corp.*, 209 Ariz. 511, 105 P.3d 157 (App. 2005) (also citing to cases in other jurisdictions which hold that the implied warranty does not extend to commercial construction).

75. 195 P.3d 184 (Ariz. App. 2008).

76. *Nastri*, 142 Ariz. at 441-42, 690 P.2d at 160-61. *See also, Sheibels v. Estes Homes*, 161 Ariz. 403, 404, 778 P.2d 1299, 1300 (App. 1989) (builder's implied warranty of habitability and workmanship extends to subsequent purchasers).

77. *Richards v. Powercraft Homes, Inc.*, 139 Ariz. 242, 245, 678 P.2d 427, 430 (1984).

78. *Id.*

79. *Richards*, 139 Ariz. at 246, 678 P.2d at 431.

80. *See, Hershey v. Rich Rosen Const. Co.*, 169 Ariz. 110, 114, 817 P.2d 55, 59 (App. 1991) (reasonable inspection of residence need not include inspection by expert or professional home inspection service to scrutinize house for internal defects prior to purchase, but implied warranty will be voided for lack of reasonable inspection only if defect could have been discovered during inspection made by an average purchaser).

81. *S. Develop. Corp. v. Pima Capital Management Co.*, 201 Ariz. 10, 17, 31 P.3d 123, 130 (App. 2001).

82. *Hershey*, 169 Ariz. at 116, 817 P.2d at 61.

83. Mike Bischoff, *Theories of Toxic Mold Liability Facing Arizona Homebuilders*, 34 Ariz.St.L.J. 681, 700 (2002).

84. *Dillig v. Fisher*, 142 Ariz. 47, 51, 688 P.2d 693, 697 (App. 1984).

85. 129 Ariz. 15, 628 P.2d 52 (App. 1981).

86. *Shirkey v. Crain & Associates*, 129 Ariz. 128, 629 P.2d 95 (App. 1981).

87. *Piccola v. Woddall*, 186 Ariz. 307, 921 P.2d 710 (App. 1996).

88. *Nastri v. Wood Bros. Homes, Inc.*, 142 Ariz. 439, 445, 690 P.2d 158, 164 (App. 1984).

89. *Menendez v. Paddock Pool Const. Co.*, 172 Ariz. 258, 267, 836 P.2d 968, 977 (App. 1991) (swimming pool was not a "product" because swimming pool had not been shown to be standard model constructed, assembled, or manufactured by mass-production process).

90. *See, Hall v. Lovell Regency Homes*, 121 Md. App. 1, 708 A.2d 344 (App. 1998) (damages for mental anguish caused by living in a less than defect-free house were subsumed in the proper measure of damages for a property damage claim).

91. *See e.g., DeStories v. City of Phoenix*, 154 Ariz. 604, 606, 744 P.2d 705, 707 (App. 1987) (a subcontractor's employees could not recover for mental anguish upon learning of their exposure to asbestos absent physical injury, illness, or other physical consequences).

92. *See, Erlich v. Menezes*, 87 Cal. Rptr.2d 886, 981 P.2d 978 (1999), *Hall*, 121 Md. App. 1, 708 A.2d 344.

93. *Allison v. Fire Ins. Exchange*, 98 S.W.3d 227 (Tex. App. 2002).

94. *Centex-Rooney Const. Co., Inc. v. Martin County*, 706 So.2d 20 (Fla. App. 1997).

95. *Allison*, 98 S.W.3d 227.

96. *Greene v. Plano, I.S.D.*, F.Supp. 2d 615 (E.D. Tex. 2002).

97. *RCDI Const., Inc. v. Space/Architecture Planning & Interiors, P.A.*, 29 Fed. Appx. 120 (4th Cir. 2002); *See also, Allison*, 98 S.W.3d 227.

98. *Allison*, 98 S.W.3d 227.

99. *Amica Mut. Ins. Co. v. Henderson*, 2003 WL 21196261 (N.D.Ill. 2003).

100. *Id.*

101. *Reedy v. Webb*, 2002 WL 3168023 (Tex. App. 2002).

102. *See e.g., Dixon v. City of Phoenix*, 173 Ariz. 612, 618-19, 845 P.2d 1107, 1113-14 (App. 1992).

103. *Walter v. Simmons*, 169 Ariz. 229, 236, 818 P.2d 214, 221 (App. 1991); *Gilmore v. Cohen*, 95 Ariz. 34, 36, 386 P.2d 81, 82 (1963); *Short v. Riley*, 150 Ariz. 583, 586, 724 P.2d 1252, 1255 (App. 1986).

104. *Walter v. Simmons*, 169 Ariz. at 236, 818 P.2d at 221.

105. *Fairway Builders, Inc. v. Malouf Towers Rental Co., Inc.*, 124 Ariz. 242, 253, 603 P.2d 513, 524 (App. 1979) (the measure of damages for breach of a construction contract is the cost of repair. Only where such an award would result in economic waste is the proper measure of damages the difference between the value of the building as designed and the building as constructed).

106. *See e.g., Max of Switzerland, Inc. v. Allright Corp. of Delaware*, 187 Ariz. 496, 499, 930 P.2d 1010, 1013 (App. 1997) ("In Arizona, property damage claims for a negligently damaged vehicle include compensation for the cost of repair, residual diminution in fair market value, and loss of use").

107. *State v. Brockell*, 187 Ariz. 226, 228, 928 P.2d 650 (App. 1996); *Blanton & Co. v. Transamerica Title Ins. Co.*, 24 Ariz.App. 185, 188, 536 P.2d 1077, 1080 (1975); *A.I.D. Ins. Services v. Riley*, 25 Ariz.App. 132, 135-136, 541 P.2d 595, 598-599 (1975).

108. *Walter v. Simmons*, 169 Ariz. 229, 236, 818 P.2d 214, 221 (App. 1991) (Arizona law requires that damages be awarded only when the Plaintiff has met its burden of proving the amount of damages with reasonable certainty).

109. *See e.g., Dixon v. City of Phoenix*, 173 Ariz. 612, 618-19, 845 P.2d 1107, 1113-14 (App. 1992).

110. *See Dillig v. Fisher*, 142 Ariz. 47, 51, 688 P.2d 693, 697 (App. 1984).

111. A.R.S. § 12-1361(4).

112. A.R.S. § 12-1363(A).

113. A.R.S. § 12-1363(A).

114. A.R.S. § 12-1362(A).

115. A.R.S. § 12-1363(B).

116. *Id.*

117. *Id.*

118. *Id.*

119. A.R.S. § 12-1363(C).

120. *Id.*

121. *Id.*

122. A.R.S. § 12-1363(D).

123. A.R.S. § 12-1363(E).

124. *Id.*

125. *Id.*

126. *Id.*

127. A.R.S. § 12-1363(F).

128. A.R.S. § 12-1363(I).

129. A.R.S. § 12-1363(J).

130. A.R.S. § 12-1364.

131. A.R.S. § 12-1366.

132. *Cooper v. American Family Mut. Ins. Co.*, 184 F.Supp.2d 960 (D. Ariz. 2002).

133. *Id.* at 961

134. *Id.* The District Court specifically held that (1) the mold exclusion in the homeowners' insurance policy applied even if the covered water event was the efficient proximate cause of the mold damage; (2) damages caused by mycotoxins did not fall within the resulting loss provision; and (3) the supplementary coverage provision covering "pollutant" clean-up and removal did not modify the policy's mold exclusion.

135. *Id.* at 962.

136. *Id.* (emphasis added).

137. *Liristis v. American Family Mut. Ins. Co.*, 204 Ariz. 140, 61 P.3d 22 (App. 2002).

138. *Liristis*, 204 Ariz. at 142, 61 P.3d at 24.

139. *Liristis,* 204 Ariz. at 141, 61 P.3d at 23.

140. *Liristis*, 204 Ariz. at 144, 61 P.3d at 26.

141. *Id.*

142. *Liristis*, 204 Ariz. at 145, 61 P.3d at 27.

143. CV 2000-006713 (Ariz.Super. Nov. 2001).

144. 476 F.Supp.2d 1135 (D.Ariz. 2007).

145. *Kilian v. Equity Residential Trust*, 2004 WL 3606894 (D. Ariz. 2004).

146. *Kilian v. Equity Residential Properties Trust*, 2006 WL 1876907 (9th Cir. 2006).

147. *Frye v. United States*, 293 F. 1013, 1014 (D.C. Cir. 1923).

148. *Logerquist v. McVey*, 196 Ariz. 470, 480, 1 P.3d 113, 123 (2000). In *Logerquist*, the expert testified that the patient had repressed memories of childhood sexual abuse for purposes of a medical malpractice action against a pediatrician. *Logerquist*, 196 Ariz. at 475-76, 1 P.3d at 118-19. Note, however, that the Arizona Court of Appeals stated in *Lohmeier v. Hammer*, 214 Ariz. 57, 71, 148 P.3d 101, 115 (App. Div. 1 2006) that "the time may have come for the Arizona Supreme Court to reconsider *Logerquist*." To date, the Arizona Supreme Court has not reconsidered *Logerquist*.

149. *Logerquist*, 196 Ariz. at 481, 1 P.3d at 124.

150. *State ex rel. Romley v. Fields*, 201 Ariz. 321, 325, 35 P.3d 82, 86 (App. 2001).

151. *Id.*

152. *Id.*

153. *See e.g., id.* ("In Arizona, *Frye* has usually been applied in cases involving the results of physical scientific tests. *See, e.g., Valdez*, 91 Ariz. at 277-79, 371 P.2d at 896-98 (polygraph evidence); *Scales v. City Court*, 122 Ariz. 231, 234-35, 594 P.2d 97, 100-01 (1979) (breathalyzer); *State v. Gortarez*, 141

Ariz. 254, 262-66, 686 P.2d 1224, 1232-36 (1984) ("voiceprint" evidence); *State v. Superior Court (Blake)*, 149 Ariz. 269, 277-80, 718 P.2d 171, 179-82 (1986) (horizontal gaze nystagmus testing); *State v. Beaty*, 158 Ariz. 232, 241-42, 762 P.2d 519, 528-29 (1988) (phosphoglucomutase (PGM) blood grouping); *State v. Velasco*, 165 Ariz. 480, 486-87, 799 P.2d 821, 827-28 (1990) (silica gel blood alcohol test); *State v. Bible*, 175 Ariz. 549, 576-82, 858 P.2d 1152, 1179-85 (1993) (DNA evidence). However, *Frye* has also been applied to determine the basic reliability of techniques not necessarily involving 'hard' science. *See State v. Mena*, 128 Ariz. 226, 231-32, 624 P.2d 1274, 1279-80 (1981) (hypnotically refreshed testimony). In a variety of other situations, however, *Frye* has been found inapplicable. *See, e.g., State v. Roscoe*, 145 Ariz. 212, 219, 700 P.2d 1312, 1319 (1984) (dog tracking); *Baroldy v. Ortho Pharm. Corp.*, 157 Ariz. 574, 581-83, 760 P.2d 574, 581-83 (App. 1988) (scientific hypothesis of causation); *State v. Richards*, 166 Ariz. 576, 577-79, 804 P.2d 109, 110-12 (App. 1990) (bite mark comparison); *State v. Varela*, 178 Ariz. 319, 325-26, 873 P.2d 657, 663-64 (App. 1993) (general characteristics of child sexual abuse victims)").

154. *Logerquist*, 196 Ariz. at 482, 1 P.3d at 125.

155. *Lofgren v. Motorola*, 1998 WL 299925 (Ariz.Super. 1998), at 11 citing *Whiting v. Boston Edison Co.*, 891 F.Supp. 12, 24 (D.Mass.1995).

156. American College of Occupational and Environmental Medicine, *Adverse Human Health Effects Associated with Molds in the Indoor Environment* (2002) available at http://www.acoem.org/position/statements.asp?CATA_ID=52. citing Tobin RS, et al. Significance of fungi in indoor air: report of a working group. *Can J Public Health.* 1987; 78: S1-S32; Menzies D, Bourbeau J. Building-related illnesses. *N Engl J Med.* 1997; 337: 1524-31.; Fung F, Clark R, Williams S. *Stachybotrys*, a mycotoxin-producing fungus of increasing toxicologic importance. *J Toxicol Clin Toxicol.* 1998; 36: 79-86; Robbins CA, et al. Health effects of mycotoxins in indoor air: a critical review. *Appl Occup Environ Hyg.* 2000; 15: 773-84; Sudakin DL. *Stachybotrys chartarum*: current knowledge of its role in disease. *MedGenMed.* 2000; E11; Page EH, Trout DB. The role of *Stachybotrys* mycotoxins in buildings related illness. *Am Ind Hyg Assoc J.* 2001; 62: 644-8; Terr Al. *Stachybotrys*: relevance to human disease. *Ann Allergy Asthma Immunol.* 2001; 87: 57-63; Burge HA. Fungi: toxic killers or unavoidable nuisances? *Ann Allergy Asthma Immunol.* 2001; 87: 52-56.

Chapter 6

An Overview of Toxic Mold Litigation in California

Eric S. Fisher, Esq. and Ryan C. Grelecki, Esq.

Synopsis

6.1 Introduction

The landmark case in California toxic mold litigation, *Mazza v. Schurtz*, saw plaintiffs awarded nearly $3 million for personal injuries sustained due to toxic mold in the apartment.[1] Since that time plaintiffs have consistently realized settlements in excess of $1 million. In 2006, plaintiffs obtained the largest settlement involving a single-family home of over $26 million, based on severe injuries sustained by a child from moldy lumber used to build the home.

This continued rise of toxic mold litigation has had, and will likely continue to have, an impact on the insurance industry. In fact, in 2001, a California jury awarded a plaintiff homeowner $18.5 million against his insurer for the insurance carrier's bad faith denial of his mold claim.[2]

Although plaintiffs have received large jury awards and settlements, California defendants are not left without hope in toxic mold litigation. In fact, in 2006, defendant sellers successfully defeated plaintiff buyers' causes of action for negligence, fraud, breach of contract, and negligent misrepresentation related to mold discovered in a condominium.

6.2 California Mold Legislation

The Toxic Mold Protection Act of 2001 (the "Act")[3] requires property owners to disclose the known presence of mold to prospective or existing residents if the presence is in excess of accepted levels. The Act makes the presence of mold on a property a mandatory disclosure for all sellers and lessors in California.[4] Under the Act, the California Department of Public Health must take charge of: (1) adopting "permissible exposure limits" for mold in indoor environments; (2) developing standards for mold identification and remediation efforts; and (3) developing guidelines for determining what constitutes mold infestation.

6.3 Potential Causes Of Action

In a California mold case, a plaintiff may be entitled to relief under numerous causes of action. Several of the more common counts are: (1) negligence; (2) breach of fiduciary duty; (3) strict liability; (4) breach of warranty; (5) constructive eviction; and (6) violations of Business and Professions Code Section 17200.

A. Negligence

Negligence is the most common cause of action in California mold cases.[5] In order to prevail on a claim of negligence, the plaintiff must prove: (1) a duty of care was owed by the defendant to the plaintiff; (2) which was breached due to a failure to exercise ordinary or reasonable care that a person of ordinary prudence would use under similar circumstances; (3) resulting in injury to the plaintiff; and (4) that breach was the proximate cause of the injury, damage, or loss.[6] This cause of action is commonly asserted in actions against builders, general contractors, design professionals, and subcontractors for alleged negligence in the performance of their duties.[7]

A seller or transferor of commercial or industrial real property has an affirmative duty to provide written disclosure to prospective buyers, as soon as practicable, before the transfer of title, when the seller or transferor knows of the presence of mold that affects the unit or building.[8] The mold must either exceed permissible exposure limits or pose a health threat pursuant to the California Department of Public Health's guidelines.[9] The duty exists as to mold which is visible, invisible or hidden.[10] The California Health and Safety Code provides for certain circumstances under which these duties are lessened or excused.[11]

Commercial and industrial landlords also have an affirmative duty to provide written disclosure of affected units to prospective and current tenants, as soon as practicable, when the landlord knows that visible, invisible or hidden mold is present and affects the units or the building.[12] Again, the mold must either exceed permissible exposure limits or pose a health threat pursuant to the California Department of Public Health's guidelines; and the California Health and Safety Code provides for certain circumstances under which these duties are lessened or excused.[13]

The California Health and Safety Code places the same responsibilities on public entities which own, lease or operate buildings[14] and residential landlords.[15] Residential landlords also have a duty to provide a written disclosure to prospective tenants of the potential health risks and the health impact that may result from exposure to mold, through the distribution of a consumer-oriented booklet prior to the execution of a rental or lease agreement.[16]

B. Breach of Fiduciary Duty

The board of directors of a condominium association stands as a fiduciary to its members and owes such a duty to them.[17] Accordingly, members of a condominium association could assert a claim for breach of fiduciary duty against the board of directors for breaching its fiduciary duty with respect to execution of managerial responsibilities as they relate to information regarding mold.

C. Strict Liability

If the manufacturer of mass-produced homes caused or created a defect in the property, which has proximately caused the homeowner harm, the homeowner can sue under a strict liability theory.[18] The homeowner has the burden of proving that: the builder was involved in the mass production of housing, a defect in the house exists, damages were proximately caused by the defect and the defendant caused or created the defect.[19] The plaintiff is not required to prove that the defendant failed to follow the standard of care of similar builders in the community.[20] The theory does not apply to subcontractors, design professionals or commercial property.[21] If a cause of action is established against the manufacturer, then presumably all involved in the chain of distribution may be sued under Section 402A of the Restatement 2d Torts for products liability.[22]

D. Breach of Warranty

A landlord has a statutory duty to maintain and repair residential premises and a tenant's remedies, in the event a landlord breaches that duty, have been modified by the common-law implied warranty of habitability.[23] This judicially created warranty is implied in every lease or rental of a residential dwelling unit. In addition, where the seller, at the time of the sale, has reason to know any particular purpose for which the goods are required, and that the buyer is relying on the seller's skill or judgment to select or furnish suitable goods, there is an implied warranty that the goods shall be fit for that purpose.[24] There is an implied warranty of quality and fitness in the sale of a newly constructed building.[25]

E. Constructive Eviction

Where there is a substantial and material interference with the tenant's beneficial use and enjoyment of the premises, even though the tenant is not actually deprived of occupancy, a constructive eviction may exist.[26] A constructive eviction occurs when the acts or omissions of a landlord, or any disturbance or interference with the tenant's possession by the landlord, or at her procurement, or by one acting under her authority, renders the premises, or a substantial portion thereof, unfit for the purposes for which they were demised or has the effect of depriving the tenant of the beneficial enjoyment or use of the premises for a substantial period of time if the tenant vacates the premises within a reasonable time.[27]

F. Violation of Business and Professions Code Section 17200

California Business and Professions Code Section 17200 ("Section 17200") defines and prohibits unfair competition in the State of California.[28] Actions to enjoin an unfair business practice or for restitution of money or property acquired through an unfair business practice may be brought by "any person who has suffered injury in fact and has lost money or property as a result of the unfair competition."[29] To state a cause of action under Section 17200, it is only necessary to show that members of the public are likely to be deceived,[30] which is determined based on a "reasonable consumer standard."[31]

6.4 Damages

In 2001, in *Mazza*, a jury found an apartment owner, the property managers, and general partners liable for injuries caused by mold exposure and awarded the plaintiffs $2.7 million for such injuries.[32] In addition to seeking compensation for bodily injury and property damage, the plaintiffs were successful in arguing that mold contamination resulted in the loss of personal property beyond the area exposed to water damage.[33]

A. Personal Injury Claims

Plaintiffs in mold litigation may be entitled to:

- Past and future physical pain and mental suffering and emotional distress;

- Past and future medical expenses;
- Past and future loss of earnings and earning capacity;
- Future medical monitoring;
- Loss of life's pleasures and enjoyment;
- Spousal derivative claim for loss of consortium; or
- Prejudgment interest, if provided under local law for personal injury or negligence claims.[34]

B. Property Damage Claims

Plaintiffs in mold litigation may be entitled to:

- Benefits payable under plaintiff's insurance policy;
- Consequential damages as a result of breach of contract;
- Attorney fees, penalties, interest and costs as a result of any consumer protection claim for statutory damages (attorney fees may also be recoverable under breach of contract alone);
- Costs of suit, prejudgment and post judgment interest, as is recoverable irrespective of a consumer protection statutory claim;
- If negligent performance of a contract is pleaded or a third-party claim for tort proven, damages for emotional distress may be recoverable;
- Where appropriate, equitable relief by way of abatement or injunction for public nuisance or medical monitoring may be obtained; or
- Punitive damages in a third-party tort claim for property damage or, in either a first-party or third-party claim, in a subsequent bad faith action against insurance carrier(s).[35]

6.5 Statutes Of Limitations

In *Miller v. Lakeside Village Condominium Association*,[36] the California Court of Appeal held that the statute of limitations for personal injury began to run when a plaintiff suffered allergic reactions to mold, for which she sought medical advice and treatment.[37] The Court of Appeal held that it did not matter that plaintiffs' symptoms worsened, and that she was diagnosed with greater injuries.[38] The fact that the medical condition may not have been diagnosed correctly does not delay the running of the statute of limitations.[39] The Court of Appeal concluded that her earlier injuries, which manifested into more serious injuries, constituted actual and appreciable harm.[40] Moreover, the Court of Appeal concluded that to hold otherwise would disregard the rule against splitting a cause of action.[41]

In contrast to the short limitations period for personal injuries, recently increased from one year to two years,[42] California Code of Civil Procedure § 337.15 provides for a ten-year statute of limitations (from the time of substantial completion of the project) to a homeowner's cause of action for the underlying defective condition that caused the fungal contamination. In addition, California Code of Civil Procedure 338 provides for a three-year limitation period to commence an action for negligence arising from damage to real property. Thus, a homeowner who discovers a roof leak has up to three years to file suit (provided suit is filed within ten years of substantial completion of the project) but has only two years to sue for exposure to toxic fungus that grew because of that leak.

6.6 Admissibility Of Scientific Evidence Or Expert Testimony

California follows the *Kelly/Frye* standard.[43] Most mold cases in California are filed in state court. Thus, *Kelly/Frye*, rather than *Daubert*, applies. In California, under the *Kelly/Frye* standard, new scientific evidence is admissible only on a showing of scientific reliability, demonstrated by substantial agreement and consensus in the scientific community. Under the *Kelly/Frye* standard, the proponent of evidence derived from a new scientific methodology must satisfy three prongs: (1) whether the new technique has gained general acceptance in the relevant scientific community; (2) whether the expert testifying to that effect is qualified to do so; and (3) if the correct scientific procedures were used in the particular case.[44] The *Kelly/Frye* standard only applies in "new" areas of law and science.[45] It does not apply where an opinion is based upon commonly used statistical formulas.[46] If the focus of expertise is a new area, plaintiff will have to demonstrate that the new scientific method can be shown to be reliable, that the witness is qualified as an expert in the field and that the theory or method was implemented according to proper scientific procedures.[47] Moreover, in determining that plaintiff's mold expert was qualified to provide testimony, the California Court of Appeal held that, "[i]n California, neither a mold expert nor a mold abatement expert is required to be certified or licensed."[48]

6.7 Insurance Coverage Issues

In California, when determining whether coverage exists under an all-risk insurance policy where the loss could be attributed to an excluded risk and a covered risk, courts utilize the efficient proximate cause doctrine established in *Garvey v. State Farm Fire & Casualty Co.*[49] Under the efficient proximate cause doctrine, where a loss is caused by some combination of a covered risk and an excluded risk, the loss is covered only if the covered risk was the efficient proximate cause of the loss.[50]

In *De Bruyn v. Superior Court*, an insured homeowner brought an action against his insurer based on the insurer's denial of a claim for mold damage which resulted from a toilet that overflowed while the insured was on vacation.[51]

The policy at issue specifically excluded loss resulting from mold and loss resulting from mold created by water damage.[52] Applying the efficient proximate cause doctrine, the court found that the policy "'plainly and precisely communicate[s] an excluded risk' to a reasonable insured."[53]

In *Benavides v. State Farm General Ins. Co.*, plaintiff's insurance policy excluded mold, unless a covered peril was the predominant cause of the mold.[54] Although the jury found that there was no coverage under the policy, it did find that the insurer negligently investigated plaintiff's claim. Accordingly, the court had to determine if, absent coverage, an insurer could be held liable in tort for negligently investigating plaintiff's insurance claim.[55] Although the relationship between insured and insurer is contractual, tort liability will lie against an insurer for breach of the implied covenant of good faith and fair dealing.[56] Because plaintiff's cause of action was for negligence and not for breach of the implied covenant of good faith and fair dealing, and the relationship between the insurer and the insured did not give rise to a tort claim, the court found that there was no tort liability on the insurer's part for negligent investigation of plaintiff's first-party insurance claim.[57]

As discussed above, in *Anderson v. Allstate Ins. Co.*, a California jury awarded a plaintiff homeowner $18.5 million against his insurer for the insurance carrier's breach of the implied covenant of good faith and fair dealing based on the insurer's denial of his mold claim.[58] The court found that the actions of the insurer showed that it had maintained an inflexible position as to the insured's claim, which went beyond a genuine dispute over coverage, establishing bad faith on the part of the insured.[59]

Endnotes

1. *Mazza v. Schurtz et al.,* Sacramento Superior Court No. 00AS04795 (November 7, 2001).

2. *See Anderson v. Allstate Insurance Co.*, Nos. 01-15415, 01-15246, 01-15330, D.C. No. CV-00-00907-PAN, *Anderson v. Allstate Insurance Co.* 45 Fed. App'x 754 (9th Circ. 2002).

3. Cal. Health & Safety Code §§ 26100 to 26156.

4. *See id.*

5. Robertson IV, Alexander. *Mold: An Emerging Construction Defect*, GP Solo April/May 2001 at 44, 44.

6. *See* California Jury Instructions, BAJI No. 3.00 & 3.01.

7. Robertson, *supra* note 3, at 45.

8. Cal. Health & Safety Code § 26140(a).

9. *Id.*

10. *Id.*

11. *Id.* at § 26140(b)-(d).

12. *Id.* at § 26141(a).

13. *Id.* at § 26141(c)-(e).

14. *Id.* at § 26146.

15. *Id.* at § 26147.

16. *Id.* at § 26148.

17. *See Raven's Cove Townhomes, Inc. v. Knuppe Development Co.*, 171 Cal. Rptr. 334 (Cal. Ct. App. 1981).

18. *See Avner v. Longridge Estates*, 77 Cal. Rptr. 633 (Cal. Ct. App. 1969).

19. Robertson, *supra* note 3, at 45.

20. *Id.*

21. *Id.*

22. 26 COA 2d 529.

23. Miller & Starr, 7 Cal. Real Est. § 19:120 (3d ed.).

24. *See* California Jury Instructions, BAJI No. 9.55.

25. *Id.*, citing *Pollard v. Saxe and Yolles Dev. Co.*, 115 Cal. Rptr. 648, 651 (Cal. Ct. App. 1974).

26. Miller & Starr, 7 Cal. Real Est. § 19:157 (3d ed.), citing *Stoiber v. Honeychuck*, 101 Cal. App. 3d 903, 925-926, 162 Cal. Rptr. 194. Cal Ct. App. (1980).

27. *Id.*

28. Section 17200 states: "As used in this chapter, unfair competition shall mean and include any unlawful, unfair or fraudulent business act or practice and unfair, deceptive, untrue or misleading advertising and any act prohibited by Chapter 1 (commencing with Section 17500) of Part 3 of Division 7 of the Business and Professions Code."

29. Cal. Bus. and Prof. Code §§ 17203, 17204.

30. *Comm. on Children's Television, Inc. v. Gen. Foods Corp.*, 35 Cal. 3d 197, 211 (1983), superceded by statute on another ground, as stated in *Californians for Disability Rights v. Mervyn's, LLC* (39 Cal. 4th 223, 46 Cal. Rptr. 3d 57 (2006)); *Aron v. U-Haul Co. of California*, 143 Cal. App. 4th 796. 49 Cal. Rptr. 3d 555 (Cal. Ct. App. 2006); *Schnall v. Hertz Corp.*, 78 Cal. App. 4th 1144. 93 Cal. Rptr. 2d 439 (Cal. Ct. App. 2000).

31. *Aron*, 49 Cal. Rptr. 3d at 562.

32. *Mazza v. Schurtz et al.*, Sacramento Superior Court No. 00AS04795 (Nov. 7, 2001).

33. *Id. See also El Escorial Owners' Ass'n v. DLC Plastering, Inc.*, 154 Cal. App. 4th 1337. 65 Cal. Rptr. 3d 524 (Cal. Ct. App. 2007), as modified on denial of reh'g (Oct. 3, 2007), review denied (Dec. 19, 2007).

34. Robertson, *supra* note 3, at 49-50; 26 COA 2d 529 (2008).

35. *Id.*

36. *Miller v. Lakeside Village Condominium Assn.*, 1 Cal. App. 4th 1611. 2 Cal. Rptr. 2d 796 (Cal. Ct. App. 1991).

37. *Id.* 2 Cal. Rptr. 2d at 803.

38. *Id.*

39. *Id.*

40. *Id.* 2 Cal. Rptr. 2d at 804

41. *Id.*

42. Cal. Code Civ. Proc., former § 340, subd. (3); see now § 335.1, added by Stats. 2002, ch. 448, § 2 (extends personal injury limitations period to two years).

43. *People v. Kelly*, 17 Cal. 3d, 549 P.2d 1240 (1976).

44. *People v. Roybal*, 19 Cal. 4th 481, 966 P.2d 521 (1998).

45. *See Texaco Producing, Inc. v. County of Kern*, 66 Cal. App. 4th 1029, 78 Cal. Rptr. 2d 433 (Cal. Ct. App. 1998).

46. *Id.*

47. *See Kelly*, 549 P.2d 1240.

48. *Walker v. Allstate Ins. Co.*, B176719, 2005 WL 2995231 (Cal. Ct. App. Nov. 9, 2005). *Garvey v. State Farm & Cas. Co.* 48 Cal. 3d 395.

49. 770 P.2d 704 (Cal. 1989).

50. *Id.*

51. *De Bruyn v. Superior Court*, 158 Cal. App. 4th 1213, 70 Cal. Rptr. 3d 652 (Cal. Ct. App. 2008), review denied (Apr. 16, 2008).

52. *Id.* at 658.

53. *Id.* at 660 (citing *Julian v. Hartford Underwriters Ins. Co.*, 35 Cal. 4th 747, 110 P.3d 903 (Cal. 2005)).

54. *Benavides v. State Farm Gen. Ins. Co.*, 136 Cal. App. 4th 1241, 39 Cal. Rptr. 3d 650 (Cal. Ct. App. 2006).

55. *Id.* at 654.

56. *Id.*

57. *Id.* at 658.

58. *Anderson*, 45 Fed. App'x 754.

59. *Id.*

Chapter 7

An Overview of Toxic Mold Litigation in Delaware

Douglas F. Schleicher, Esq. and Julie Beddingfield, Esq.

Synopsis

7.1 Introduction

Delaware courts and regulatory authorities have taken a relatively proactive role in addressing the perceived public health threats posed by mold exposure. For example, an entire apartment complex was condemned by the Town of Elsmere, Delaware, causing the eviction of over 600 residents.[1] The Delaware Supreme court has also upheld a combined award of over $1 million dollars against a

Delaware landlord for mold-related personal injury claims.[2] This chapter will review these and other matters.

7.2 State and Local Enforcement Authority

Delaware has not enacted legislation specifically addressing mold. In addition, the Delaware Department of Natural Resources and Environmental Control ("DDEC") has not promulgated any specific regulations governing permissible mold exposure or remediation requirements. Notwithstanding the forgoing, there are several governmental bodies which have enforcement authority relating to the presence of mold.

A. Delaware State Housing Authority

Pursuant to the Delaware State Housing Code ("Code"), the Delaware State Housing Authority ("Housing Authority") has broad authority to respond to "unsanitary" conditions existing in residential structures. As part of this broad power grant, the legislature has provided the Housing Authority with the power to examine and survey property in the state with respect to unsanitary conditions. If such conditions are identified, the Housing Authority can then order the alleged condition to be abated or removed. If the landowner refuses, the Housing Authority has the ability to abate the condition itself and file a tax lien on the property for its response costs. The landowner may be found guilty of a misdemeanor punishable by a maximum penalty of $1,000 and 30 days in jail. The Housing Authority also has the statutory authority to declare the premises to be "unfit for human habitation" and instigate condemnation or eviction proceedings. The Code specifically permits counties and municipalities to enforce its provisions.

B. Local Cities and Municipalities

In addition to providing a broad grant of authority to the Housing Authority, the Code, or variations thereof, have been adopted by county, town and other municipal governments. Most of these local enactments provide local code officers with entry, inspection and abatement powers, including condemnation authority.

There are a number of examples of mold-related enforcement actions at the local level. For example, as noted above, in the Fall of 2002, the Town of Elsmere, Delaware, condemned a large apartment complex and required the eviction of the current tenants. Elsmere's purported authority for this action was based on both the Code and the local housing code. The town enforcement officer made a formal determination that mold on the premises rendered it unfit for human occupancy.

7.3 Private Rights of Action

A. Contractual Claims for Economic Loss

The specific terms of a contract will govern any contract claim. Provisions relating to safety or cleanliness may apply to mold-related claims. Absent a provision pertaining to mold or sanitation, certain types of claims can be expected.

1. Implied warranty of habitability (residential)

Unlike many other American jurisdictions, Delaware has not historically recognized an implied warranty of habitability in real estate leases.[3] Therefore, absent express contract language to the contrary, there is no implied contractual duty to provide safe and sanitary premises. Possibly to counteract this perceived problem, the legislature enacted the Delaware Landlord Tenant Code ("LTC") in 1972. The LTC comprehensively governs the relationship of landlords and tenants. The LTC explicitly provides a private right of action to either party injured by a violation of a lease agreement or the LTC.[4]

Relevant portions of the LTC require that landlords provide a rental unit that does not endanger the health, welfare or safety of the tenants or occupants. Landlords also are required to keep all common areas in a clean and sanitary condition. If a landlord fails to remedy violations of these provisions, the LTC provides the following potential remedies to the tenant:

- ability to terminate the lease;
- ability to remedy the problem and deduct relevant costs from outstanding rent; and
- keep two-thirds of rent accruing during the time of the violation (available only in limited cases).[5]

To date, there have not been any published cases involving mold in which a plaintiff has based its claim on the LTC's private right of action. There are several open issues regarding the remedy provisions of the LTC which have yet to be litigated. In *Brown v. Robyn Realty Co.*, the Delaware Superior Court construed a since-repealed version of the LTC and held that: 1) the LTC provides a statutory right of action for general "damages," not limited to the remedies listed in the statute; and 2) the duties found in the LTC are "engrafted" into all residential leases and can provide the basis for a residential tenant's claim for breach of contract.[6] In addition, the Court noted that the rent abatement provisions might apply retroactively.[7]

It is unclear whether the specific remedies in the current version of the LTC are exclusive. Landlords may be able to argue successfully that the remedies are exclusive because the legislature repealed the private right of action for general "damages" following the *Brown* decision. This is important because the new LTC requires that tenants prove actual or written notice of the unsanitary condition.

2. Warranty of habitability (commercial leases)

Commercial leases are normally assumed by courts to be the result of arms-length negotiations between parties with roughly equal bargaining power. Accordingly, many jurisdictions are unwilling to read a warranty of habitability into commercial leases. However, in one unreported decision involving a commercial lessee, a Delaware trial court noted that "[a] tenant has a right to claim breach of implied warranty of habitability as a defense or counterclaim."[8]

The original 1972 version of the LTC covered both commercial and residential leases.[9] However, during the 1996 revisions, the legislature explicitly exempted commercial leases from its coverage.

In light of the foregoing, commercial tenants should seek affirmative representations, warranties and covenants from the landlord regarding the sanitary condition of their space and other common areas of the building. In addition, they should consider identifying in the lease specific remedies that would be available in the case of a breach.

3. Implied warranty of construction in a skillful and workmanlike manner

Under Delaware law, construction contractors are deemed to provide an implied warranty that construction was performed in a reasonably workmanlike manner and that the finished product is fit for the purpose intended.[10] This warranty is based in contract law and results in regular contract damages in the case of a breach.

B. Torts

Tort claims can arise in a number of different contexts, such as landlord/tenant and premises liability matters. Entities such as design professionals (e.g., architects and engineers) and contractors may be targeted in property damage suits based on allegedly defective construction or design of buildings or HVAC systems.

1. Negligence (premises liability)

In *New Haverford Partnership v. Stroot*, two separate plaintiffs, Elizabeth Stroot and Joletta Watson, sought redress for bodily injury that they suffered as tenants of the defendant's apartment complex.[11] Ms. Stroot was a 33-year-old graduate student with a prior history of asthma and allergies that required hospital visits and previous medical attention.[12] In May of 1994, she was hospitalized because she could not breathe.[13] The hospitalization coincided with the collapse of her bathroom ceiling, which exposed growing mold of various kinds.[14] Ms. Watson had recurring mold in her bathroom.[15] Watson testified that she experienced fatigue, sinus problems, headaches, chest pains and body aches which dissipated roughly six months after she moved from defendant's property.[16]

The plaintiffs pursued three different theories of tort liability: negligence due to defendant's failure to maintain a safe and sanitary condition in the apartments; negligence *per se*, for violating the New Castle County Code; and negligence *per se* for violating the LTC.[17] The jury verdict form indicated that the jury found for the plaintiffs on all three of their theories, awarding one plaintiff $1,000,000 and the other $40,000.[18]

On appeal, the defendant argued that plaintiffs' ordinary negligence claim was cut off by Delaware's enactment of the LTC.[19] The court disagreed noting that there was nothing in the LTC that suggested the legislature intended to cut off a plaintiff's common law tort claims.[20] The court also noted that the plaintiffs could look to the LTC as a basis for establishing that the landlord owed a duty of care to its tenants to provide a safe and sanitary rental unit.[21] The defendant also argued that the opinions of the plaintiffs' four different medical experts were deficient and should not have been presented to the jury, due to faulty protocols, insufficiency of corroborating data and inadequate rebuttal of the defendant's alternative explanations of the injuries.[22] The Supreme Court held that the trial court has flexibility to evaluate the applicable *Daubert* factors under the circumstances presented in each case, and that the trial court had not abused its discretion.[23]

2. Professional negligence

Professional negligence claims may arise against architects or engineers for personal injuries related to the alleged improper design or supervision relating to a building, its HVAC system, the building envelope or other features.[24] There are no reported Delaware decisions discussing the merits of a claim for professional liability for personal injury or property damage from mold. However, the Supreme Court of Delaware has generally recognized that architects and engineers have a duty to provide design services in accordance with the ordinary skill of their profession.[25] This duty extends to unrelated third parties and is not dependant on privity of contract.[26]

3. Strict products liability

In addition to targeting the entities that own, manage, design or construct buildings, tort plaintiffs have also targeted manufacturers of exterior cladding systems using strict product liability theories.[27] However, Delaware does not recognize a common law right of action for strict products liability based on the sale of defective goods under Section 402A of the Restatement (Second) of Torts (1965).[28]

4. Negligent misrepresentation (professional)

Mold litigation often involves finger pointing between contractors and professionals with respect to responsibility for the specific conditions leading to mold growth. Contractors may allege defects in the designs of the professionals associated with the project. This can be done via claims based on the Restatement (Second) of Torts §552 arguing that the design professional's plans and specifications incorporated "negligent misrepresentations." In order to state a claim for negligent misrepresentation a contractor must show misrepresentation of a material fact; that the defendant either knows it is a misrepresentation, makes it without knowledge of its truth or falsity, or makes the representation under circumstances in which it ought to know of its falsity; that the defendant must intend the representation to induce another to act on the misrepresentation; and that the contractor suffered an injury acting in justifiable reliance on the misrepresentation.[29]

At this time, there are no reported cases in Delaware involving a contractor's claims of negligent misrepresentation against a design professional related to mold. However, a contractor will be provided with an opportunity to prove these claims even if they are based on strictly economic loss.[30]

5. Implied warranty of fitness for intended purpose (professionals)

Although a contractor's action for negligent misrepresentation against an architect is not precluded by the economic loss doctrine under Delaware law, design professionals may be insulated from claims that they impliedly warrant that their plans and specifications will result in a structure reasonably fit for its intended purpose.[31] Therefore, in the absence of any express warranties in contract, owners may be limited to suing contractors and indirectly accessing the professional by way of the contractor's own third-party negligent misrepresentation claim for errors or omissions.

6. Negligent workmanship/construction

Contractors and construction managers are likely to be targeted directly by owners in property damage claims related to mold and moisture conditions. Delaware courts generally recognize several different theories of redress against contractors for construction defects, including an action for "negligent workmanship."[32] In at least one unpublished opinion, a Delaware court awarded the plaintiff property owner $5,220.00 in damages from the contractor for negligence in supervising and performing its contracted work, and breach of express and implied warranties, related to faulty construction of a shower that resulted in mold and water damage.[33]

7. Fraudulent misrepresentation (sale of property)

Fraudulent misrepresentation is actionable if the following is shown: 1) a representation is made; 2) with knowledge of its falsity or recklessness as to whether it is true or false; 3) with the intent to induce the plaintiff to act or to refrain from acting; 4) plaintiff acts or fails to act in justifiable reliance on the representation; and 5) the resulting injury was proximately caused by the reliance.[34] The tort of fraudulent concealment has the same elements as fraudulent misrepresentation, except that with concealment the party intentionally conceals, rather than affirmatively misrepresents, the material fact.[35] While concealment may be fraudulent, mere silence is not sufficient in the absence of a duty to speak.[36] Normally, fraudulent concealment is not actionable unless there is active conduct.

A real estate broker, in addition to a seller, can be liable for the torts of fraudulent non-disclosure.[37] In *Lock v. Schreppler*, the court refused to dispose of the plaintiff's claim and held that a broker had an affirmative duty to disclose all relevant information regarding a known termite infestation once the broker had raised the subject in discussions with the purchasers.[38]

8. Negligent misrepresentation (sale of property)

To successfully claim negligent misrepresentation, the plaintiff must prove: 1) a pecuniary duty to provide accurate information; 2) the provision of false information; 3) the failure to exercise reasonable care in obtaining or communicating the information; and 4) pecuniary loss to a party acting in justifiable reliance on the misrepresentation.[39] Unlike intentional misrepresentation, the speaker need not know her words are untrue, but must have failed to make a reasonable investigation of their truth.

9. Innocent misrepresentation (sale of property)

An innocent misrepresentation is actionable if it is material to and the basis of a transaction, and the purchaser is justified in relying on the misrepresentation.[40] However, the remedy for an innocent misrepresentation is rescission, not monetary damages for tort recovery. *Id.*

Endnotes

1. *See Elsmere Park Club L.P. v. Town of Elsmere,* 542 F.3d 412 (C.A.3 Del. 2008).

2. *See New Haverford Partnership v. Stroot*, 772 A.2d 792 (Del. Spr. Ct. 2001).

3. *See Leech v. Husbands*, 152 A. 729 (Del. Spr. Ct. 1930). *See also Brandt v. Yeager*, 199 A.2d 768 (Del. Spr. Ct. 1964).

4. Del. Code Ann. tit. 25 §5117 (2002).

5. Del. Code Ann. tit. 25 §§ 5306-5308 (2002).

6. 367 A.2d 183 (Del. Super. Ct. 1976).

7. *Id* at 190.

8. *See Groves v. E&H, Inc.*, No. 79C-JN-7, 1981 WL 376978 (Del. Super. Sept. 18, 1981) citing *Pugh v. Holmes*, 384 A.2d 1234 (Pa. Spr. Ct.) (Pennsylvania case establishing implied warranty of habitability in residential leases).

9. *See Hand v. Davis*, 87C-OC-6, 1990 WL 96583 (Del. Super. Ct. June 8, 1990).

10. *Bougourd v. Village Gardens Homes, Inc.*, No. CIV.A.0006-136, 2002 WL 32072790 (Del. Com. Pl. Dec 31, 2002). *See also Smith v. Berwin Builders, Inc.*, 287 A.2d 693 (Del. Super. 1972).

11. 772 A.2d 792.

12. *Id.* at 795.

13. *Id.* at 796.

14. *Id.*

15. *Id.*

16. *Id.*

17. *Id.* at 797.

18. *Id.* Each award was reduced by 22 percent by the court, based on a finding of contributory negligence. *Id.*

19. *Id.* at 797-98.

20. *Id.*

21. *Id.* at 798.

22. *Id.*

23. *Id.* at 798-99.

24. *See Bonnette, et al. v. Tunica-Biloxi Indians*, No. 02-919, 2003 WL 21229282 (La. Ct. App. May, 28, 2003) (several groups of plaintiffs filed suit against construction defendants, including an architect and an engineering firm, for personal injuries from alleged mold exposure at a casino and its related child care facility).

25. *Seiler v. Levitz Furniture Company of Eastern Region, Inc.*, 367 A.2d 999 (Del. Spr. Ct. 1976).

26. *Id.* at 1007 (tenant of building was able to maintain suit against architect in negligence after suffering property damage from two floods).

27. *See Gropper, et al. v. STO Corporation, et al.*, 552 S.E.2d 118 (Ga. App. 2001) (homeowners filed suit against builder, stucco subcontractor and stucco manufacturer asserting claims of strict products liability for mold-related personal injuries and property damage due to use of synthetic stucco product on the exterior of their home).

28. *See Cline v. Prowler Industries of Maryland, Inc.*, 418 A.2d 968 (Del. 1980) (Supreme Court of Delaware held that the Uniform Commercial Code pre-empted strict products liability theory in Delaware).

29. *See Guardian Construction Co. v. Tetra Tech Richardson, Inc.*, 583 A.2d 1378 (Del. Super. 1990); *Counsel of Dorset Condominium Apartments v. Dorset Apartments*, Civ. A. No. 90C-10-269, 1992 WL 240444 (Del. Super Aug. 26, 1992).

30. S*ee id.* (economic loss doctrine not applicable to negligent misrepresentation claims based on §552 of the Restatement (Second) of Torts).

31. *See, e.g., Grotto Pizza, Inc. v. Endecon, Inc.*, No. CIV. A. 96C-01-031, 1997 WL 366904 (Del. Super. Mar. 26, 1997).

32. *See Oliver B. Cannon & Sons, Inc., v. Dorr-Oliver Inc.*, 312 A.2d 322, 325 (Del. Super. 1973).

33. *Healy v. Silverhill Construction, Inc.*, CA. No. 06-03-030, 2009 WL 295391 (Del. Com. Pl. 2009).

34. *Stephenson v. Capano*, 462 A.2d 1069, 1074 (Del. 1999).

35. *Lock v. Schreppler*, 426 A.2d 856, 860 (Del. Super. 1981).

36. *The Marcom Group v. Redgo Properties, Inc.*, No. CIV.A. 96C-11-002JOH, 1998 WL 278368 (Del. Super. Apr. 15, 1998).

37. *See Lock*, 426 A.2d at 860.

38. *Id.* at 861.

39. *Durnam v. Manallo*, No. 2002-10-309, 2004 WL 326924 (Del. Com. Pl. Jan. 15, 2004).

40. *Norton v. Poplos,* 443 A.2d 1 (Del. 1982).

Chapter 8

An Overview of Toxic Mold Litigation in Florida

David B. Weinstein, Esq. and Kimberly S. Mello, Esq.

Synopsis

8.1 Introduction

Florida's warm, humid climate provides ideal conditions for molds to grow. Increased public awareness of the potential dangers of mold has undoubtedly helped fuel mold-related litigation throughout the country, including Florida. Mold-related lawsuits in Florida range from single-plaintiff cases to class actions, and, in some cases, have resulted in multi-million dollar settlements or jury verdicts.

While the number of mold cases has diminished in recent years (perhaps due to the mold exclusions in insurance policies) significant cases remain in Florida.

As in other states, trial and appellate courts in Florida have wrestled with, among other things, the admissibility of expert testimony,[1] class certification issues,[2] and workers' compensation immunity[3] in mold cases. The Florida Legislature has also enacted the Construction Defect Law and Mold-Related Services statutes, each of which potentially impacts mold-related litigation in this state.[4] This chapter will discuss the current status of Florida law on these and other issues, as well as the key legislation impacting mold-related claims.

8.2 Personal Injury Claims

Plaintiffs asserting personal injury claims for mold exposure rely on various theories of liability, including negligence, intentional torts[5] such as fraud and misrepresentation, and violations of the Florida Building Code.[6] Negligence, which is one of the most common theories pleaded in mold-related personal injury claims, can be premised on multiple grounds, including the following:

- negligent design of a building, which has allowed water to intrude with resulting mold growth;
- negligent monitoring of indoor air quality;
- negligent construction of a building, which has allowed water to intrude with resulting mold growth;[7] and
- negligent failure to maintain premises.[8]

One of the primary hurdles plaintiffs must overcome in establishing liability in mold cases is demonstrating that their injuries were, in fact, caused by mold exposure. Such proof necessarily requires expert testimony.[9] However, because "existing scientific evidence on the health effects of mold is not fully accepted," expert witnesses in mold cases may have difficulty satisfying the existing standards for admissibility of expert testimony.[10] In Florida, which follows the *Frye* standard, expert testimony is admissible only if the scientific principles underlying the evidence have gained general acceptance in the relevant scientific community.[11] To date, no Florida appellate court has addressed the admissibility of expert testimony in personal injury mold-related litigation.[12] Other jurisdictions addressing this issue have, however, reached varying results.[13] In addition to the challenges to the admissibility of expert testimony, plaintiffs can be subject to a variety of affirmative defenses, including statute of limitations, failure to mitigate damages, and comparative negligence.[14]

Unlike other states,[15] there is no reported appellate decision in Florida reviewing a judgment in favor of a plaintiff in a personal injury mold claim. This may be due, in part, to pre-trial mediation,[16] which is often successful in resolving such cases.

8.3 Workers' Compensation Claims

In Florida, workers' compensation is a statutory substitute for common law rights and liabilities, and is typically an employee's exclusive remedy against an employer for accidental workplace injury or death, with certain limited exceptions.[17] Thus, an employee who claims that he was exposed to mold in the workplace will likely be limited to the compensation afforded under Florida's Workers' Compensation Act (the "Act"). Section 440.02(1) expressly addresses employees' claims brought as a result of mold exposure and provides, in relevant part, as follows:

> An injury or disease caused by exposure to a toxic substance, including, but not limited to, fungus or mold, is not an injury by accident arising out of the employment unless there is clear and convincing evidence establishing that exposure to the specific substance involved, at the levels to which the employee was exposed, can cause the injury or disease sustained by the employee.[18]

This heightened "clear and convincing" causation standard is a difficult standard for claimants to meet, particularly because the level of exposure required to cause injury or disease is the subject of scientific debate and there are no regulatory standards in Florida establishing an unsafe exposure level.

Given this difficult standard, employees may attempt to avoid the Act by claiming that the employer engaged in conduct sufficient to satisfy one of the limited exceptions to workers' compensation immunity. However, the exceptions are also difficult to prove. Of these, the intentional tort exception is most often raised by employees.[19] In 2003, the legislature amended the intentional tort exception to require that it be proved by "clear and convincing evidence."[20] Moreover, the exception requires a showing that "[t]he employer engaged in conduct that the employer knew, based on prior similar accidents or on explicit warnings specifically identifying a known danger, was virtually certain to result in injury or death to the employee."[21]

To date, there are no known reported appellate decisions where a claimant has successfully avoided an employer's workers' compensation immunity for mold-related injuries based on the employer's intentional conduct. In fact, the only decision to address this issue predates the more stringent requirements adopted in the 2003 amendments.[22] In that case, the appellate court affirmed the trial court's conclusion that the intentional tort exception did not apply.[23] According to the court, evidence demonstrating that "the agencies were made aware of the problems with the air quality in the building, that they did little to remedy the situation other than to clean and replace air conditioning filters, and that they were less than candid with the employees about the extent of the problems or the risks they posed" would, at most, only establish that the agencies negligently exposed employees to an increased risk.[24] Thus, based on the Act and case law, compensation for mold-related injuries is an uphill battle for Florida employees.

8.4 Class Actions

Mold-related class actions have been brought by home buyers against home builders,[25] lessees against apartment building owners,[26] insureds against insurance companies,[27] parents on behalf of their children against School Boards,[28] and employees against their employers for injuries suffered due to exposure to toxic mold in the workplace.[29] Parties seeking class certification must satisfy the four prerequisites of Florida Rule of Civil Procedure 1.220(a): (1) the members of the class must be so numerous that joinder of each member is impracticable (the "numerosity" requirement);[30] (2) common questions of law or fact predominate (the "commonality" requirement);[31] (3) the claims of the class representative are typical of the claims of the class members (the "typicality" requirement);[32] and (4) the representative party can fairly and adequately represent the interests of each member of the class (the "adequacy" requirement).[33] Some examples of Florida class actions for mold-related claims are discussed below.

A. Class Certification Denied

In *Welcome v. Arvida Community Sales, Inc.*, the plaintiff filed a class action complaint against the defendants,[34] seeking damage on behalf of herself and 300 others similarly situated for defects in homes purchased on James Island, in Duval County, Florida.[35] In Count I, the plaintiff sought damages resulting from building code violations under section 553.84 of the Florida Statutes. In Count II, the plaintiff asserted a claim based on nondisclosure of material defects. The trial court denied certification on the grounds that the plaintiff was unable to meet the prerequisites and the appellate court affirmed.

In denying certification, the trial court relied on, among other things, the following: (a) the plaintiff's proposed class definition was problematic, and would prevent certain plaintiffs from being able to opt-out in a timely manner; (b) an analysis of whether there was "economic waste" would have to be undertaken as to each individual home, thus defeating the plaintiff's contention of typicality; and (c) there was no commonality because (i) different legal standards, including applicable defenses, would apply to different class members because of the two potentially applicable versions of section 553.84; (ii) purchase agreements signed by the putative class members differed in significant ways; (iii) section 558.04, Florida Statutes, effective May 27, 2003, which required the defendants to be given notice and an opportunity to cure any defect with the home before filing legal action, would not apply to all class members; (iv) the affirmative defenses, including waiver, estoppel, and failure to mitigate damages, were individualized; (v) damages would have to be established on a case by case basis; and (vi) the defendants' duties to disclose would vary from house to house.

According to the court, the overabundance of individual issues would destroy cohesion and overwhelm common issues. Finally, due to the enormous amount of individualized proof that would be required to support the claims and the defendants' defenses, the prosecution of the lawsuit as a class action would be unmanageable and would not be "superior" to individual suits. Thus, the court concluded that the homeowners should pursue their claims as separate lawsuits.

B. Class Certification Granted

In *Henriques v. Archstone-Smith Operating Trust*, filed in 2002, the trial court certified a mold-related class action brought by current and former residents of the 452-unit Harbour House South apartment complex in Miami.[36] The plaintiffs alleged that their personal injury and property damage claims arose from mold contamination caused by a faulty air-conditioning system. The plaintiffs sought damages for (a) negligence; (b) breach of lease agreements; (c) breach of the statutory warranty of habitability; and (d) violations of Florida's deceptive and unfair trade practices act. Additional plaintiffs subsequently filed related class actions.[37]

In granting certification, the court first determined that the four elements of Florida Rule of Civil Procedure 1.220(a) had been established. Next, the judge ruled that the requirements of Rule 1.220(b) were satisfied because (a) the defendant had acted or refused to act on grounds generally applicable to all the class members because it did not test for mold post-remediation and did not warn new or prospective tenants about the mold remediation or contamination; and (b) there were questions of law and fact common to the class because the HVAC system caused common problems to all members.[38]

The defendants argued unsuccessfully that individual issues predominated because not all class members had signed the same lease agreement: some had signed a "mold addendum" and/or a "construction addendum" to their lease. The court rejected this argument, finding that the "mold addendum" was simply a form letter to the residents that was not binding on the parties, and that the "construction addendum," although binding, was not relevant to the issues before the court. The court also rejected the defendants' argument that the individual questions characteristic of personal injury claims predominated over common questions because there was a common issue of causation before the court, i.e., one contaminated building caused by a shared HVAC system.[39]

In late 2003, the class action was settled. Under the settlement terms, Archstone-Smith was required to remediate the mold-contaminated apartments and pay (a) for temporary housing; (b) attorneys' fees and expenses; (c) 100 percent of each class member's personal property damages; (d) 65 percent of each tenant's rent obligation; (e) $3000 of each class member's aggravated damages; and (f) 2.5 times the amount of actual medical expenses for certain medical conditions. The settlement amount of approximately $25 million was in addition to the $38 million that Archstone-Smith was to pay to remediate the mold contamination in the building. In addition, under the settlement, the plaintiffs could pursue any personal injury claims that they were unable to settle through mediation.[40]

Archstone-Smith Trust also filed a mold-related construction defect suit in Miami-Dade Circuit Court against the architect, engineering firm, and air conditioning contractor that had worked on the Harbour House apartment complex, seeking over $30 million in damages.[41]

8.5 Property Damage and Building Defect Claims

As with personal injury claims, plaintiffs asserting mold-related property damage claims also rely on various theories of liability, including breach of contract, negligence, intentional torts[42] such as fraud and misrepresentation, and violations of the Florida Building Code.[43] Significant Florida decisions are discussed below.

The leading Florida case on property damage claims related to mold growth involved the Martin County Courthouse. In that case, the county sued Centex-Rooney, the construction manager, and others, for breach of contract because of defective construction, which led to water intrusion, high humidity, and mold growth.[44]

The problems for the defendants began shortly after the building was occupied in December of 1988, when employees began complaining about the mold growth and the county began receiving health complaints from building occupants and visitors. Within four years after initial occupancy, 25 percent of the occupants had evacuated the buildings for health reasons.[45] By December of 1992, the courthouse advisory committee voted to evacuate because they did not believe they could, "in good faith and good conscience, ask the County's employees, the litigants, the attorneys and the general public to enter these buildings under the existing conditions."[46]

Subsequently, the remediation efforts revealed more mold and water damage than originally anticipated, as well as numerous other hidden and dangerous electrical and structural defects in the buildings.[47] Consequently, the repairs took over three years to complete and were still underway at the time of trial. At trial, the jury returned a verdict against Centex-Rooney in the amount of $11,550,000, which was reduced by $2,750,000, the amount of the county's prior settlements.[48] The court awarded prejudgment interest from December 12, 1988, the date of substantial completion, through June 18, 1996, resulting in a final judgment of over $14 million.[49]

On appeal, the court found that the county had presented sufficient evidence to meet its burden of proving that Centex-Rooney's breach of contract was a substantial factor in causing the county's extensive damages.[50] The county demonstrated that the construction defects resulted in significant mold growth, including two highly unusual toxic molds, which were linked to health hazards. These defects resulted in the need for extensive and costly remediation. In addition, the appellate court rejected Centex-Rooney's argument that scientific principles underlying the county's expert testimony—studies linking exposure to toxic molds found in the buildings with health risks—did not meet the *Frye* test. According to the court, "the County met its burden under *Frye* of proving by a preponderance of the evidence that the basic underlying principles of scientific evidence were sufficiently tested and accepted by the relevant scientific community."[51]

Finally, the court found that the county had presented sufficient evidence to support its damages claim. The court noted that in a breach of contract case, a measure of damages is the reasonable cost of performing construction and repairs in conformance with the original contract requirements, plus relocation and financing costs and additional engineering and architectural fees necessary to accomplish the reconstruction.[52] Here, "[t]he County's unrefuted evidence of its actual costs to remediate, redesign, and reconstruct the buildings as well as relocate and finance, reduced by the costs for upgrades and improvements, established a sufficient basis to determine damages as of the date of the breach."[53]

More recently, in 2006, a development company, CC-Aventura, Inc., and a senior living community manager, Classic Residence Management Limited Partnership, filed a $100 million dollar federal lawsuit against the general contractor, architect, and subcontractors who took part in the design and construction of a luxury senior living community.[54] According to the plaintiffs, extensive water damage and mold growth was discovered in 2004 after the first residents moved into the facility. The residents were ultimately required to relocate to other facilities so that the plaintiffs could investigate and correct the deficiencies in the facility. The damages sought by the plaintiffs include expenses and other losses incurred as a result of the construction and design defects, such as property damage resulting from water intrusion, investigation costs, remediation, redesign, and repairs; costs incurred to relocate residents and provide alternative comparable facilities; and business interruption costs. As of the date of this chapter, the litigation is ongoing.

Defendants confronted with a mold-related property damage tort claim, like those discussed in this section, should, of course, raise all available defenses, including the economic loss rule. Under Florida law, the economic loss rule "bars a negligence action to recover solely economic damages only in circumstances where the parties are either in contractual privity or the defendant is a manufacturer or distributor of a product, and no established exception to the application of the rule applies."[55] Thus, a plaintiff in contractual privity with a defendant in a mold-related case involving solely economic losses may be barred from recovering damages if the defendant has committed no breach of duty apart from a breach of contract. Claims for purely economic damages also may be precluded based on traditional tort principles.[56]

8.6 Florida's Construction Defect Law

Florida's Construction Defect Law, enacted in 2003 and codified at sections 558.001 through 558.005 of the Florida Statutes, provides an alternative method to resolve construction disputes, with the goal of protecting the rights of property owners while reducing the need for litigation.[57] Under Florida's Construction Defect Law, most property owners claiming damage to or loss of real or personal property resulting from an alleged construction defect must provide the allegedly responsible parties with (a) written notice of the defect; and (b) an opportunity to resolve the claim or repair the defect before filing suit.[58] Moreover, the procedures set forth in the Construction Defect Law supersede any conflicting provisions of an arbitration clause in the parties' contract for the sale, design, construction, or remodeling of real property.[59]

A. Application

"Claimants" required to give notice of defects under Florida's Construction Defect Law include property owners (subsequent purchasers and associations fall within this definition) asserting claims for damages against a contractor, subcontractor, supplier, or design professional concerning a construction defect, or subsequent owners who assert claims for indemnification for such damages.[60] Contractors,[61] subcontractors,[62] suppliers,[63] and design professionals[64] are specifically excluded from the definition of claimants.[65]

"Construction defects" covered by the Construction Defect Law include deficiencies in, or arising out of, the "design, specifications, surveying, planning, supervision, observation of construction, or construction, repair, alteration, or remodeling of real property" resulting from (a) defective material, products, or components used in the construction or remodeling; (b) violation of applicable building codes; (c) design malpractice; or (d) failure to employ workmanlike construction methods.[66] The Construction Defect Law, however, does not apply to personal injury claims.[67]

B. Procedure

1. Service of the notice of claim

Under Florida's Construction Defect Law, a claimant must serve a written notice of claim on the allegedly responsible contractor, subcontractor, supplier, or design professional before filing a civil action or arbitration proceeding.[68] If the alleged construction defect arises from work performed under a contract, however, the claimant must serve the written notice of claim on the person with whom the claimant contracted.[69]

Claimants are encouraged to serve the notice of claim within 15 days after discovering the alleged defect.[70] Failure to serve the notice of claim within the 15-day window is not fatal to a claimant's ability to file an action; however, the notice must be served (a) at least 60 days before filing any action; or (b) at least 120 days before filing an action involving an association representing more than 20 parcels.[71] The notice of claim must (a) be in writing; (b) refer to chapter 558 of the Florida Statutes; (c) "describe the claim in reasonable detail sufficient to determine the general nature of each alleged construction defect"; and (d) describe "the damage or loss resulting from the defect, if known."[72]

If a claimant files an action for property damage or loss resulting from an alleged construction defect without first complying with the notice requirements, a party to the action may move to abate (i.e., suspend) the action, without prejudice, and the action may not proceed until the claimant has complied with those requirements.[73] After the recipient receives a notice of claim, the recipient and the claimant may alter the notice of claim process by a mutual written agreement.[74]

Serving the notice of claim tolls the statute of limitations to the later of (a) 90 or 120 days, as applicable, after receipt of the notice of claim; or (b) 30 days after the end of the repair period stated in an offer made by the recipient of the notice of claim if the claimant has accepted the offer.[75] In addition, the parties may stipulate to an extension of the repair period, during which time the statute of limitations is tolled.[76]

2. Procedure following receipt of the notice of claim

Within 30 days after receiving the notice of claim (or within 50 days after receiving the notice of claim involving an association representing more than 20 parcels), the claim recipient has the right (but is not required) to perform a reasonable inspection of the property or each unit subject to the claim in order to assess each alleged construction defect.[77] In addition, within ten days after receipt of the claim, the claim recipient can notify those that it believes are responsible for the defect.[78]

If the claim recipient wants to perform an inspection, the claimant is required to provide reasonable access to the property for this purpose during normal working hours.[79] The inspection may include destructive testing, if the claimant and the claim recipient agree to it.[80] If, however, a claimant fails or refuses to agree to destructive testing, the claimant will not have a claim for any damages that "could have been avoided or mitigated had destructive testing been allowed when requested and had a feasible remedy been promptly implemented."[81]

Within 45 days after receiving the claimant's notice of claim (or within 75 days after receiving a copy of the notice of claim involving an association representing more than 20 parcels), each claim recipient must serve a written response to the claimant.[82] In the response, the claim recipient must (a) offer to remedy the defect at no cost to the claimant; (b) offer to settle for a monetary payment; (c) offer to settle based on a combination of repairs and monetary payment; (d) dispute the claim; or (e) state that a monetary payment, including insurance proceeds, if any, will be determined by the recipient's insurer within 30 days after notification to the insurer.[83]

If the claim recipient disputes the claim within the allocated time period, the claimant may commence litigation without further notice.[84] If, however, the recipient's timely response offers to repair the defect or settle the claim, the claimant must accept or reject the proposal within 45 days after receiving the offer.[85] After rejecting an offer, the claimant may litigate without further notice. If, however, a claimant sues before responding to an offer, the court must abate the claimant's action upon a timely motion until the claimant responds.[86]

If the claimant accepts an offer to repair a defect, the claimant must provide the claim recipient with reasonable access to the claimant's property in order to repair the defect.[87] If the defect is timely repaired, no suit can be filed.[88] However, absent reasonable delays outside the claim recipient's control, if the repairs are not made or payment is not received within the agreed time or in the agreed manner, the claimant may file suit without further notice.[89]

3. Effect on litigation

The Construction Defect Law is clearly meant to promote settlement of disputes without the need to resort to litigation. It, however, may create practical difficulties for both claimants and parties allegedly responsible for construction defects. In particular, the statute requires that actions be taken within certain narrow time frames. Consequently, parties may have difficulty obtaining independent advice and conducting thorough inspections within the designated time frames.

In addition, the Construction Defect Law provides that, upon request, a claimant and the claim recipient have a "mutual duty to exchange all available discoverable evidence relating to the construction defects," including, but not limited to, expert reports,[90] videotapes, photographs, and information received from persons to whom the recipient forwarded the notice of claim, and videotapes.[91] Thus, if subsequent litigation results, the court may impose sanctions on any party who failed to provide such evidence.[92]

8.7 Insurance Coverage

The issue of whether mold-related property damages or personal injuries are covered under various insurance policies has been frequently litigated. Florida courts generally have found that commercial general liability ("CGL") policies do not provide coverage for damages caused by faulty workmanship.[93] However, in 2007, the Florida Supreme Court held that a subcontractor's faulty workmanship that was not intended or expected by the contractor could constitute "property damage" covered by a CGL policy.[94]

Historically, insurance policies cover damages from a "covered peril." For example, in *Fisher v. Certain Interested Underwriters at Lloyds*,[95] the court held that mold damage to personal property was covered under the homeowner's policy because it constituted a "direct physical loss" caused by a "named peril" in the policy (i.e., a leaking water pipe). The court stated as follows:

> "direct loss" is loss proximately caused by the peril insured against, and the term "proximate cause" as applied in insurance cases has essentially the same meaning as it does in negligence cases, except that in insurance cases, the element of foreseeableness or anticipation of the injury as the result of the peril insured against is not required....Thus, in a suit on a policy insuring for "direct loss" caused by the named peril, a proper definition of proximate cause would be 'that cause which in a natural and continuous sequence unbroken by any new and intervening cause, produces a loss, and without which the loss would not have occurred.'[96]

Significantly, the court also noted that had the insurer wanted to exclude mold damage from the policy, it could have easily done so.[97]

Due to the sharp rise in mold-related insurance claims between 2000 and 2003, the insurance industry adopted a universal mold exclusion that has been included in nearly all property and liability policies since 2003.[98] Such mold exclusions in policies will likely curtail mold-related insurance litigation in the future.[99]

8.8 Florida Mold Legislation

In 2007, Florida enacted sections 468.84 through 468.8423 of the Florida Statutes, entitled "Mold-Related Services," which will take effect on July 1, 2010. The purpose of this legislation is to "prevent damage to real and personal property, to avert economic injury to the residents of the state, and to regulate persons and companies that hold themselves out to the public as qualified to perform mold-related services."[100]

Before the enactment of these statutes, the Florida Senate recognized the "heightened awareness regarding mold and mold-related issues," including "a variety of media accounts detailing homeowners' problems with persons holding themselves out as mold remediators and using unorthodox methods and charging exorbitant sums for testing,"[101] which are issues that have surfaced in recent Florida cases.[102] The Mold-Related Services statutes should help relieve these concerns by establishing standards to which mold assessors and remediators must adhere, and imposing penalties on individuals and companies who fail to comply with those standards. Key provisions of the Mold-Related Services statutes are highlighted below.

A. Application

Florida's Mold-Related Services statutes will apply to mold assessors and mold remediators. "Mold assessors" are defined as persons performing or directly supervising "the physical sampling and detailed evaluation of data obtained from a building history and inspection to formulate an initial hypothesis about the origin, identity, location, and extent of amplification of mold growth of greater than 10 square feet."[103] "Mold remediators" are persons engaging in the "removal, cleaning, sanitizing, demolition, or other treatment, including preventive activities, of mold or mold-contaminated matter of greater than 10 square feet that was not purposefully grown at that location."[104] Numerous types of "persons" are specifically excluded from the statute's operation.[105]

B. Licensing, Fees, and Additional Requirements

To become licensed as a mold assessor or remediator, a person must: (a) be of good moral character; (b) meet the educational requirements set forth in the Mold-Related Services statutes; and (c) take a licensure examination.[106] Continuing education requirements are necessary in order to maintain an active license.[107] Partnerships or corporations offering mold assessment or remediation services to the public are required to obtain a certificate of authorization, which must be renewed every two years.[108] Florida's Department of Business and Professional Regulation is permitted to establish fees for application, examination, reexamination, licensing and renewal, inactive status application, reactivation of inactive licenses, application for continuing education providers, and delinquency, as long as those fees do not exceed certain statutory caps.[109]

In addition to being licensed, mold assessors must maintain general liability and errors and omissions insurance coverage in an amount of not less than $1,000,000.[110] Mold remediators must maintain a general liability insurance policy (a) in an amount not less than $1,000,000; and (b) including specific coverage for mold-related claims.[111]

Contracts entered into for mold assessment or remediation services are required to be in a document or electronic record that is signed or otherwise authenticated by the parties.[112] Mold assessors and remediators are not required to provide estimates in those contracts.[113]

C. Prohibitions and Penalties

Mold assessors and remediators, companies employing them, and any company controlled by a company that also has a financial interest in a company employing a mold assessor or remediator are prohibited from, among other things, the following:

- Performing or offering to perform any mold assessment or remediation unless the mold assessors or remediators have documented training in water, mold, and respiratory protection;
- Performing or offering to perform any mold assessment or remediation unless they have complied with the Mold-Related Services statutes;
- Using the name or title "certified mold assessor," "registered mold assessor," "licensed mold assessor," "mold assessor," "professional mold assessor," "certified mold remediator," "registered mold remediator," "licensed mold remediator," "mold remediator," or "professional mold remediator," or any combination thereof unless they have complied with the Mold-Related Services statutes;
- Performing or offering to perform any mold remediation to a structure on which the mold assessors or the mold assessors' company provided a mold assessment within the last 12 months; or performing or offering to perform any mold assessment to a structure on which the mold remediators or the mold remediators' company provided a mold remediation within the last 12 months; or
- Inspecting for a fee any property in which the mold assessors, remediators, or assessors' or remediators' company has any financial or transfer interest.[114]

The first violation of any of these provisions is a misdemeanor of the second degree.[115] The second and third violations of any of these provisions is a misdemeanor of the first degree and a felony of the third degree, respectively.[116] The statutes also allow the Department of Business and Professional Regulation to impose penalties, including placing a mold assessor or remediator on probation; restricting the scope of her practice; or denying, revoking, or suspending a license. The numerous grounds for such disciplinary action are specifically listed in the statute, and include, for instance, violating any of the Mold-Related Services statutes or taking any actions constituting general grounds for discipline for businesses and professions;[117] attempting to procure a license to practice mold assessment or mold remediation by bribery or fraudulent misrepresentations; engaging in fraud, deceit, negligence, incompetency, or misconduct in the practice of mold assessment or mold remediation; or practicing with a revoked, suspended, inactive, or delinquent license.[118]

8.9 Conclusion

Because Florida's climate is ideal for mold growth, Florida courts will undoubtedly continue to be confronted with the myriad of issues involved in mold-related litigation. However, relatively recent changes in Florida's Construction Defect Law, the fact that most insurers no longer provide coverage for mold-related damages, and the ongoing scientific debate regarding the health effects of mold exposure will likely impact the number of lawsuits filed in the future, and in some circumstances, will encourage parties to reach an early resolution of mold-related disputes.

Endnotes

1. *Centex-Rooney Constr. Co. v. Martin County,* 706 So. 2d 20 (Fla. 4th DCA 1997), *rev. denied,* 718 So. 2d 1233 (Fla. 1998).

2. *Archstone-Smith Operating Trust v. Henriques*, 865 So. 2d 503 (Fla. 3d DCA 2004), *app. vol. dismissed.*

3. *McClanahan v. State,* 854 So. 2d 793 (Fla. 2d DCA 2003).

4. Sections 468.84-468.8423 of the Florida Statutes (Mold-Related Services statutes); Sections 558.001-558.005 of the Florida Statutes (Construction Defect Law).

5. *McClanahan*, 854 So. 2d at 795.

6. *Pulte Home Corp. v. Smith,* 823 So. 2d 305 (Fla. 2d DCA 2002) (plaintiffs sought damages for personal injuries and property damage caused by toxic mold that allegedly resulted from failure to comply with minimum building codes); § 553.84, Fla. Stat. (providing for statutory civil action for persons aggrieved by violations of the Florida Building Code).

7. *See, e.g., Schornberg v. Panorama Custom Home Builders*, 972 So. 2d 243 (Fla. 2d DCA 2007) (plaintiffs asserted a personal injury claim on behalf of their minor daughter who allegedly suffered allergic and upper respiratory reactions to unsafe and unsanitary conditions created in the home by bacteria and mold due to defective construction).

8. *See, e.g., Kolnick v. Fountainview Ass'n, Inc. #2*, 737 So. 2d 1192 (Fla. 3d DCA 1999) (plaintiff filed a personal injury action against defendant alleging negligence for its failure to maintain the roof on the building, resulting in water intrusion in his apartment that caused mold and mildew growth, which purportedly caused personal injuries).

9. *See Frye v. U.S.*, 293 F. 1013 (D.C. Cir. 1923). Florida follows the *Frye* standard regarding admissibility of expert testimony rather than the standard in *Daubert v. Merrell Dow Pharmaceuticals, Inc.*, 509 U.S. 579, 592-93 (1993). *Marsh v. Valyou,* 977 So. 2d 543, 547 (Fla. 2007). There has been an ongoing debate as to which test, *Daubert* or *Frye*, imposes the more stringent requirements for admissibility of expert testimony. *See, e.g., Berry v. CSX Transp.*, 709 So. 2d 552, 570, n.16 (Fla. 1st DCA 1998) ("[i]t is yet a matter of debate whether the *Daubert* test...will be more liberal and allow more expert testimony than the *Frye* requirement").

10. Reid S. Hooper, *Got Mold? Improving Plaintiffs' Toxic Mold Causation Problems with the Introduction of DNA and Mycotoxin Extraction Testing*, 42 Valpraiso U. L. Rev. 585, 589 (2008).

11. In 2008 and 2009, both the Florida House of Representatives and Florida Senate introduced bills adopting the *Daubert* standard in Florida. Fla. S.B. 1448, § 5 (2008); Fla. H.B. 645, § 5 (2008); Fla. S.B. 1220 (2009); Fla. H.B. 661 (2009). *See also Marsh*, 997 So. 2d at 554 (Anstead, J., concurring) (stating that Florida should adopt the *Daubert* standard). However, by the conclusion of the regular legislative session, the bills had failed to make it out of their respective committees. In order to be reconsidered, the bills will have to be reintroduced at a subsequent legislative session.

12. In *Centex-Rooney Construction Co. v. Martin County*, 706 So. 2d 20 (Fla. 4th DCA 1997), discussed in this chapter, the court held that expert tes-

timony finding a causal connection between the construction defects and mold growth in the building was admissible. While the case only involved property damages, it does, at least, provide some insight on the admissibility of expert testimony in mold-related claims under Florida law.

13. *See, e.g., New Haverford P'ship v. Stroot*, 772 A.2d 792 (Del. 2001) (admitting expert testimony regarding excessive mold in apartment building and causation of tenants' health problems); *Mondelli v. Kendel Homes Corp.*, 631 N.W.2d 846 (Neb. 2001) (reversing and remanding for a new trial on the issues of causation and damages due to, in part, district court's abuse of discretion in excluding testimony of mold experts); *see also Jazairi v. Royal Oaks Apt. Ass'n, L.P.*, 217 Fed. App'x 895 (11th Cir. 2007) (affirming trial court's striking of affidavit of mold expert because expert relied too heavily on temporal proximity and anecdotal evidence); *Roche v. Lincoln Prop. Co.*, 175 Fed. App'x 597 (4th Cir. 2006) (affirming trial court's finding that mold expert's testimony was unreliable because the expert could not determine that the types of mold in the apartment caused the injuries); *Herzner v. Fischer Attached Homes, Ltd.*, 2008 WL 2004473 (Ohio Ct. App. May 12, 2008) (affirming trial court's exclusion of expert testimony because (a) no tests were performed to determine whether the mold spores at issue were producing mycotoxins to which the plaintiff was exposed; and (b) there was no evidence that the expert's testing methods or "mold illness" theory had been sufficiently peer reviewed or supported by scientific literature); *Brandt v. Rokeby Realty Co.*, 2006 WL 1942314 (Del. Super. Ct. July 7, 2006) (affirming trial court's ruling that expert testimony was admissible).

14. *See Kolnick,* 737 So. 2d at 1193; § 768.81, Fla. Stat. If plaintiffs allege an intentional tort, the comparative negligence statute will not apply. § 768.81(4)(b), Fla. Stat.

15. *See, e.g., Allison v. Fire Ins. Exch.*, 98 S.W.3d 227 (Tex. App. 2002) ($32 million award to homeowner reduced to $4 million on appeal).

16. *See* § 44.102, Fla. Stat. (2007).

17. *See* § 440.11(1), Fla. Stat. (2003). The employer's immunity also extends to fellow employees, unless they act "with willful and wanton disregard or unprovoked physical aggression or with gross negligence when such acts result in injury or death or such acts proximately cause such injury or death." *Id.* at § 440.11(1)(b)(2). The immunity does not apply to employees of the same employer, "when each is operating in the furtherance of the employer's business but they are assigned primarily to unrelated works within private or public employment." *Id.*

18. The portion of the statute regarding fungus or mold became effective July 15, 2003, and applies to accidents occurring after the July 15, 2003 effective date. *See, e.g., Fla. Cmty. Health Center v. Ross*, 590 So. 2d 1037 (Fla. 1st DCA 1991) (noting that substantive statutory amendments did not apply to earlier injuries).

19. *Id.* at § 440.11(1)(a)-(b). The exceptions include the following: (1) the employer fails to pay for compensation benefits; (2) the employer commits an intentional tort against the employee, causing the employee's injury; or (3) the employer intentionally exposes the employee to a condition that was virtually certain to cause injury, but misrepresented or deliberately concealed the danger so as to prevent the employee from exercising informed judgment about whether to perform the work, and the employee was not aware of the risk because the danger was not apparent. *Id.*

20. *Id.* at § 440.11(1)(b). The 2003 amendment providing for the "clear and convincing evidence" standard became effective on October 1, 2003, and applies to accidents occurring after that effective date. *See, e.g., The Bombay Co. v. Bakerman, 961 So. 2d 259, 262 n.3 (Fla. 2007) (noting that 2003 amendment to section 440.11(1)(b)(2) does not apply retroactively).* For cases involving injuries that occurred before October 1, 2003, an employer would receive immunity from suit as long as it did not (1) exhibit a "deliberate intent to injure" or (2) engage in conduct that a reasonable person would view as "substantially certain to result in injury or death" to the employee. *Turner v. PCR, Inc.*, 754 So. 2d 683 (Fla. 2000). This was "evaluated under an objective standard." *Id.*

21. § 440.11(1)(b), Fla. Stat.; *see also Pendergrass v. R.D. Michaels, Inc.*, 936 So. 2d 684, 689 n.1 (Fla. 4th DCA 2006), *rev. denied*, 969 So. 2d 1014 (Fla. 2007).

22. *McClanahan v. State*, 854 So. 2d 793 (Fla. 2d DCA 2003).

23. *Id.*

24. *Id.* at 796.

25. *Pulte Home Corp. v. Smith*, 823 So. 2d 305 (Fla. 2d DCA 2002).

26. *Henriques v. Archstone-Smith Operating Trust*, No. 3D03-403 (Fla. 3d DCA Feb. 7, 2003), *app. vol. dismissed.*

27. *See, e.g., Guy v. Allstate Floridian Ins. Co.*, 216 Fed. App'x 953 (11th Cir. 2007) (denial of class certification upheld where common issues did not predominate), *see supra* n.22.

28. *See Taylor v. Sanders*, Civ. No. 03-0883-CA-WCM (Fla. Cir. Ct. Feb. 11. 2003) (complaint).

29. *See, e.g., Moore v. The School Bd. of Lee County, Fla.*, No. 03-4548 (Fla. Cir. Ct. 2003) (complaint).

30. Fla. R. Civ. P. 1.220(a)(1).

31. Fla. R. Civ. P. 1.220(a)(2).

32. Fla. R. Civ. P. 1.220(a)(3).

33. Fla. R. Civ. P. 1.220(a)(4); *see Earnest v. Amoco Oil Co.,* 859 So. 2d 1255, 1258 (Fla. 1st DCA 2003).

34. The defendants were as follows: St. Joe Residential Acquisitions, Inc., the developer of James Island, which sold the home to the plaintiff; Arvida West Florida Contracting, Inc., the builder of the subject homes; and Arvida Community Sales, Inc., the real estate broker who marketed the James Island homes.

35. *See Welcome v. Arvida Cmty. Sales, Inc.*, 2004 WL 2340249 (Fla. Cir. Ct. Sept. 13, 2004) (plaintiff who sought class certification on behalf of homeowners who had construction defects related to mold contamination failed to establish that she met any of the four prerequisites), *aff'd,* 903 So. 2d 942 (Fla. 1st DCA 2005); *see also Guy v. Allstate Floridian Ins. Co.*, 216 Fed. App'x 953 (11th Cir. 2007) (class action seeking recovery of mold remediation benefits under homeowners policy did not meet requirements of commonality, typicality, and superiority).

36. *Henriques v. Archstone-Smith Operating Trust*, No. 02-21697 CA 02 (Fla. Cir. Ct. Jan. 6, 2003) (order granting class certification).

37. *See Santos v. Archstone-Smith Operating Trust*, No. 03-3940-CA-01 (Fla. Cir. Ct. filed Feb. 13, 2003); *Semidey v. Archstone-Smith Operating Trust*, No. 03-13232-CA-01 (Fla. Cir. Ct. filed June 9, 2003); *Bercovits v. Archstone-Smith Operating Trust*, No. 04-14668-CA-01 (Fla. Cir. Ct. filed July 6, 2004).

38. *See Henriques, supra* n.36.

39. *Id.*

40. *Henriques v. Archstone-Smith Operating Trust,* No. 02-21697 CA 06 (Fla. Cir. Ct. Aug. 26, 2003) (class settlement agreement).

41. *See Archstone-Smith Operating Trust v. Zyscovich Inc.*, No. 2003-12450-CA-01, (Fla. Cir. Ct. filed May 27, 2003).

42. *Id.*

43. *Pulte Home Corp. v. Smith,* 823 So. 2d 305 (Fla. 2d DCA 2002) (plaintiffs sought damages for personal injuries and property damage caused by toxic mold that allegedly resulted from failure to comply with minimum building codes); *see also Mann v. Island Resorts Dev., Inc.*, 2008 U.S. Dist. LEXIS 102721 (N.D. Fla. Dec. 19, 2008). § 553.84, Fla. Stat. (provides for statutory civil action for persons aggrieved by violations of the Florida Building Code).

44. *Centex-Rooney Constr. Co. v. Martin Co.*, 706 So. 2d 20 (Fla. 4th DCA 1997), *rev. dismissed*, 718 So. 2d 1233 (Fla. 1998).

45. *Id.* at 24.

46. *Id.*

47. *Id.*

48. *Id.* at 25. Prior to trial, the County settled with all defendants except Centex-Rooney and its sureties.

49. *Id.*

50. *Id.*

51. *Id.* at 26.

52. *Id.* at 27.

53. *Id.* at 28.

54. *CC-Aventura, Inc. v. Weitz Co., LLC*, No. 1:06-CV-21598-PCH (S.D. Fla. filed June 22, 2006).

55. *Indemnity Ins. Co. of N. America v. American Aviation, Inc.*, 891 So. 2d 532, 534 (Fla. 2004); *see also Mann v. Island Resorts Dev. Inc.*, 2008 U.S. Dist. LEXIS 102725 (N.D. Fla. Dec. 19, 2008) (economic loss rule did not apply to negligence claim against developer for drainage problems causing mold damage because case did not involve product that damages itself and parties did not enjoy privity of contract).

56. *Indemnity Ins.*, 891 So. 2d at 534; *Monroe v. Sarasota County Sch. Bd.*, 746 So. 2d 530, 534 (Fla. 2d DCA 1999).

57. §§ 558.001, 558.002(1), 558.003 (2008), Fla. Stat.

58. *Id.* at §§ 558.002(1), 558.003.

59. *Id.* at § 558.004(14).

60. *Id.* at § 558.002(3).

61. "Contractors" are defined as persons "legally engaged in the business of designing, developing, constructing, manufacturing, repairing, or remodeling real property." *Id.* at § 558.002(5).

62. A "subcontractor" is defined as a person "who is a contractor who performs labor and supplies material on behalf of another contractor in the construction or remodeling of real property." *Id.* at § 558.002(9).

63. A "supplier" is a person "who provides only materials, equipment, or other supplies for the construction or remodeling of real property." *Id.* at § 558.002(10).

64. A "design professional" is defined as a person who is "licensed in [Florida] as an architect, interior designer, landscape architect, engineer, or surveyor." *Id.* at § 558.002(6).

65. *Id.* at § 558.002(3).

66. *Id.* at § 558.002(4).

67. *Id.* at § 558.002(1).

68. *Id.* at § 558.004(1).

69. *Id.*

70. *Id.*

71. *Id.*

72. *Id.*

73. *Id.* at § 558.003.

74. *Id.* at § 558.005(3).

75. *Id.* at § 558.004(10).

76. *Id.*

77. *Id.* at § 558.004(2).

78. *Id.* at § 558.004(3). This notice must identify the specific defect for which the claim recipient believes the contractor, subcontractor, supplier, or design professional is responsible. *Id.* Those potentially liable have 15 days (or 30 days, in the case of a notice involving an association representing more than 20 parcels) to (a) inspect the property; and (b) serve a written response. *Id.* at § 558.004(4). The response must include a written report describing (a) the scope of the inspection; (b) the findings and results of the inspection; (c) a statement of whether they are willing to repair the property or whether they dispute the claim; (d) any repairs they are willing to make; and (e) a timetable for completing those repairs. *Id.*

79. *Id.* at § 558.004(2).

80. *Id.* The procedure for requesting destructive testing is specifically set forth in the statute.

81. *Id.*

82. *Id.* at § 558.004(5).

83. *Id.*

84. *Id.* at § 558.004(6).

85. *Id.* at § 558.004(7).

86. *Id.*

87. *Id.* at § 558.004(8).

88. *Id.*

89. *Id.*

90. *Id.* at § 558.004(15). Expert reports exchanged may not be used in subsequent litigation unless the expert, or a person affiliated with the expert, testifies as a witness or the report is relied upon by an expert testifying on behalf of the party for whom the report was prepared. *Id.*

91. *Id.*

92. *Id.*

93. *See LaMarche v. Shelby Mut. Ins. Co.*, 390 So. 2d 325 (Fla. 1980) (finding subcontractor's faulty workmanship that was not intended or expected by the contractor could constitute "property damage" covered by CGL policy).

94. *United States Fire Ins. Co. v. J.S.U.B., Inc.*, 979 So. 2d 871, 883 (Fla. 2007).

95. *Fisher v. Certain Interested Underwriters at Lloyds*, 930 So. 2d 756 (Fla. 4th DCA 2006).

96. *Id.* at 759, quoting *Fed. Ins. Co. v. Bock*, 382 S.W.2d 305, 307 (Tex. App. 1964).

97. *Id.*

98. D. Dybdahl, *Managing Mold Related Risks, After the Mold Exclusions Become Effective*, available at: http://www.erraonline.org/moldrisks.pdf.

99. *See, e.g., Empire Indem. Ins. Co. v. Winsett*, 2009 U.S. App. LEXIS 9719 (11th Cir. May 4, 2009) (holding that insurer's duty to defend and indemnify in connection renters' mold-related property damages and bodily injuries was not triggered because policy plainly excluded coverage for mold); *Church of the Palms–Presbyterian (USA), Inc. v. Cincinnati Ins. Co.*, 404 F. Supp. 2d 1339 (M.D. Fla. 2005), *aff'd*, 189 Fed. App'x 932 (11th Cir. 2006)

(holding that fungus exclusion in an all risk policy precluded coverage for losses directly or indirectly caused by fungus).

100. § 468.84, Fla. Stat. (2008).

101. Florida Senate, Committee on Regulated Industries, Interim Project Report 2004-158 (Dec. 2003).

102. *See, e.g., Kodsky v. Dept. of Fin. Servs.*, 972 So. 2d 999 (Fla. 4th DCA 2008); *Chodorow v. Moore*, 947 So. 2d 577 (Fla. 4th DCA 2007); *Drew v. Mobile USA Ins. Co.*, 920 So. 2d 832 (Fla. 4th DCA 2006); *Cotton States Mut. Ins. v. D'Alto*, 879 So. 2d 67 (Fla. 1st DCA 2004).

103. § 468.8411(3), (4), Fla. Stat. (2008).

104. *Id.* at § 468.8411(5), (6).

105. *Id.* at § 468.841.

106. *Id.* at §§ 468.8413(1), (2), 468.8414.

107. *Id.* at § 468.8416.

108. *Id.* at § 468.8418.

109. *Id.* at § 468.8412(1).

110. *Id.* at § 468.8421(1).

111. *Id.* at § 468.8421(2).

112. *Id.* at § 468.8422.

113. *Id.*

114. *Id.* at § 468.8419. In addition, mold assessors may not (a) accept any compensation, inducement, or reward from a mold remediator or mold remediator's company for referring any business to the mold remediator or the mold remediator's company; or (b) offer any compensation, inducement, or reward to a mold remediator or mold remediator's company for referring any business from the mold remediator or the mold remediator's company. *Id.* Reciprocally, mold remediators and their companies may not accept or offer referral fees from mold assessors. *Id.* Furthermore, mold assessors may

not accept an engagement to make an omission of the assessment or conduct an assessment in which the assessment itself, or the fee payable for the assessment, is contingent upon the conclusions of the assessment. *Id.*

115. *Id.* at § 468.8419(3)(a).

116. *Id.* at § 468.8419(3)(b), (c).

117. *See id.* at § 455.227(1).

118. *Id.* at § 468.842.

Chapter 9

An Overview of Toxic Mold Litigation in Georgia

Ernest L. Greer, Esq., Richard J. Valladares, Esq., and Ryan C. Grelecki, Esq.

Synopsis

9.1 Introduction

Mold-related litigation persists in the State of Georgia. On July 8, 2008, in *Slutzkin v. Fahandeza,* a Georgia Superior Court jury awarded $404,000 to plaintiff home buyers, and against a defendant home seller, based upon allegations that the home seller concealed mold infestation in the subject residence.[1] Although the Plaintiffs' complaint in *Slutzkin* stated, "[p]laintiffs have suffered damages in an amount estimated to be not less than $150,000," the jury awarded the plaintiff a total of $90,000 for their fraud claim, $200,000 for defendant's negligence and $111,000 in attorneys' fees. The plaintiff homebuyers in *Slutzkin* never physically moved into the property, having discovered the mold infestation prior to the move-in date, and, therefore, no personal injury claims were made in that case or contemplated within the $404,000 jury award.

Mold-related litigation in Georgia, however, is not simply confined to property damage claims. For example, on June 4, 2007, a Georgia jury awarded $33,500 to a plaintiff tenant for claims that mold exposure in her apartment caused flu-like symptoms in her two children, ages 2 and 4.[2]

Thus, mold litigation not only exists in the State of Georgia, but such claims appear to have sympathetic appeal to Georgia juries.

9.2 Potential Causes of Action

Toxic mold lawsuits in Georgia are often filed against construction professionals and premised upon traditional claims of negligence, breach of contract, breach of implied warranties, misrepresentation and fraud. However, there do exist certain mold-related claims unique to the jurisdiction of Georgia which have increased the scope of potential mold-related defendants and causes of action. For example, Georgia plaintiffs have sued real estate brokers and landlords based on specific statutorily imposed duties under the Georgia Brokerage Relationships in Real Estate Transactions Act and upon violations of the Georgia Landlord and Tenant Act. Below is a discussion of some of the potential defendants and causes of action that have been, or may be, included in a mold litigation in Georgia.

A. Tort Claims

1. Sellers of real estate

As in the *Slutzkin* case discussed above, a classic mold-related tort claim often concerns allegations that a seller of real estate concealed the existence of mold on or in the subject real property, or concealed some other defect that ultimately caused or resulted in mold growth on, or in, the subject real property. Classic examples of mold-related causative defects are leaking pipes, water intrusion in basements, or malfunctioning HVAC systems.

Merely identifying a leaky pipe or moldy basement subsequent to purchase that was unknown to a buyer, however, is, in and of itself, insufficient to attach liability to a seller of real estate. This is because Georgia adheres to the doctrine of *caveat emptor*, which is commonly referred to as "buyer beware." Under this doctrine, a property developer or home builder that has sold a property to another is generally not liable for damages resulting from defects that could have been discovered through a reasonable inspection by the buyer.[3] This is so even if the defect constitutes a violation of building codes.[4] Accordingly, the onus is on the real estate purchaser to fully inspect the property, prior to purchase, for any existing defects. This question, of whether a purchaser has exercised reasonable diligence in inspecting real property, is usually one that is reserved for a jury.[5]

An exception to the *caveat emptor* doctrine in Georgia exists where the plaintiff alleges fraud or deceit by the developer or builder. Proof of such fraud by the seller with respect to mold issues, however, imposes a heavy burden on plaintiffs. A *prima facie* case of fraud and deceit in Georgia requires proof of: (1) a false representation made by defendant; (2) scienter; (3) an intention to induce plaintiff to act or refrain from acting in reliance by plaintiff; (4) justifiable reliance by plaintiff; and (5) damage to plaintiff.[6]

In mold-related litigation, specifically against builder-sellers, plaintiffs will often frame their fraud claim as a cause of action for "passive concealment." Passive concealment is a category of fraud that constitutes an exception to the rule of *caveat emptor*[7] and places upon the builder-seller a duty to disclose in situations where he has special knowledge of a latent construction defect and is aware that the buyer is acting under a misapprehension as to important facts that would affect the buyer's decision.[8] Thus, if a builder-seller of real estate knows of a construction defect in the property of which the purchaser is ignorant, and which would likely influence the purchase decision, he has a duty to disclose such knowledge to the purchaser.[9] Similar to fraud claims, in cases of passive concealment by the builder-seller of defective realty, the buyer must prove that the builder-seller's concealment of the defect was an act of fraud, that the defect could not have been discovered by the buyer in the exercise of due diligence, and that the builder-seller was aware of the problems but did not make a disclosure.[10] It is important to note, however, that the doctrine of "passive concealment" is limited to controversies between residential homeowners and residential builder/sellers.[11]

Regardless of whether the plaintiff asserts a claim for fraud or passive concealment, in both cases a plaintiff is forced early on to elect between seeking to rescind the contract or affirm the contract and claim damages for its breach.[12]

2. Real estate agents or brokers

In addition to the real estate seller, the real estate agent or broker may also be liable for non-disclosure of known mold-related defects or contamination.

The duties of Georgia real estate agents are, in part, governed by the Brokerage Relationships in Real Estate Transactions Act (BRRETA), which provides that a broker must timely disclose to buyers:

> [a]ll adverse material facts pertaining to the physical condition of the property and improvements located thereon including but not limited to material defects in the property, environmental contamination, and facts required by statute or regulation to be disclosed which are actually known by the broker which could not be discovered by a reasonably diligent inspection of the property by the buyer.[13]

Georgia courts have held that BRRETA-mandated disclosures include disclosure of all known mold-related defects or contamination. Mold contamination is considered as a "material defect" or "environmental contamination" under BRRETA. Indeed, in *Asuamah v. Haley*, the Georgia Court of Appeals directly held that BRRETA imposed an obligation on a real estate broker to disclose to a potential buyer a mold report that was in the broker's possession.[14]

3. Architects, designers or general contractors

Architects, designers and general contractors often confront mold-related lawsuits based upon a plaintiff's negligence theory for defective construction. A negligent construction claim arises not from a breach of contract claim but from breach of a duty implied by law to perform the work in accordance with industry standards.[15] This cause of action arises in tort and is separate and apart from any claim for breach of contract.[16]

In such cases, plaintiffs assert that the construction professional did not perform the work in accordance with the applicable standard of care, which ultimately caused mold growth and resulted in property damage or physical injury. Indeed, "the law imposes upon the professional builder and others performing skilled services, the obligation to exercise a reasonable degree of care, skill and ability, which can be shown as that degree of care and skill which, under similar conditions and like surrounding circumstances, is ordinarily employed by others of the same profession."[17] It is well established that plaintiffs in a negligent construction case must establish the applicable standard of care through the introduction of expert testimony.[18]

The scope of potential plaintiffs and defendants in a negligent construction case in Georgia is broad. Unlike most jurisdictions, in Georgia, a project foreman or other supervisor on a construction project, who is personally involved in the construction on a daily basis, may be personally exposed to liability for negligent construction which the foreman or supervisor supervised or directed on behalf of a construction company or corporation.[19] This is because in Georgia, an officer of a corporation who takes part in the commission of a tort by the corporation has been held to be personally liable if he specifically directed or participated in the negligent construction or repairs. [20] Moreover, in Georgia, a negligent construction claim does not rest solely on privity of contract, and, therefore, the construction professional or company may have to defend against negligent construction claims brought by a subsequent purchaser of a home or some other unknown, but foreseeable, third party.[21]

As a general rule, damages for defective construction, whether those damages are the result of a breach of contract or negligence of the contractor, are determined by measuring the cost of repairing or restoring the damage, unless the cost of repair is disproportionate to the property's probable loss of value.[22] Where demanded by the facts of a case, courts have determined damages in such cases by measuring the diminution in value of the property after the injury occurred.[23] "Thus, under Georgia law, the cost of repair and diminution in value are alternative, although oftentimes interchangeable, measures of damages in negligent construction cases."[24]

B. Breach of Contract

In addition to the scope of work and date for substantial completion, the terms of a construction contract often contemplate the method for performance and specifications for materials. Work not adhering to those contract terms, that ultimately causes mold contamination, may expose a contractor to a lawsuit for breach of contract. A *prima facie* breach of contract case requires the plaintiff to prove: (1) a valid and enforceable contract; (2) that the plaintiff performed all conditions precedent to the defendant's performance; and (3) that defendant breached the contract by failing to perform in accordance with the terms of the contract.

C. Breach of Implied Warranties

1. Implied warranty of good workmanship

In addition to the express terms of a construction or repair contract, implied in every construction or repair contract is the requirement to perform such work in a fit and workmanlike manner. This contract duty is breached if the builder fails to exercise a reasonable degree of care, skill, and ability under similar conditions and like surrounding circumstances as is ordinarily employed by others in the same profession.[25] A breach of the implied warranty of good workmanship may constitute a breach of contract for which a plaintiff may recover damages.[26]

2. Implied warranty of habitability

Under Georgia law, a landlord has a duty to a tenant to "keep the premises in repair."[27] The failure to repair defects in a premises that results in water intrusion, or some other condition that causes mold damage, may expose a landlord to liability.

When a landlord is notified by the tenant that the premises is out of repair, it becomes her duty to inspect and investigate, so as to make such repairs as the safety of the tenant requires.[28] If, after such notice of the defects, she fails to make the requisite repairs within a reasonable time, she is chargeable with notice of all defects which a proper inspection would have disclosed.[29] Therefore, even where the landlord never actually discovered the defect, if the landlord undertakes to inspect the property, she then has a duty to repair any unsafe conditions which should have been discovered during the inspection.[30] Moreover, once a landlord has notice of a defect, she is deemed to have constructive knowledge of all other defects which would have been discovered in repairing the first defect.[31]

It has been also held in Georgia that a tenant's equal knowledge of a defective condition does not necessarily bar recovery where a factual issue exists as to whether the tenant had no alternative but to assume the risk and encounter the dangerous condition.[32] This is often referred to as the "necessity rule." For example, in *Thompson v. Crownover*, a tenant's knowledge of a defective heater did not bar recovery because a question of fact existed in that case under the "necessity rule."[33]

9.3 Class Actions

In the context of multi-family dwellings or office buildings, a defendant property owner, landlord or maintenance company may risk exposure to a mold-litigation class action lawsuit. Indeed, the term "sick building syndrome" is defined by the Environmental Protection Agency (EPA) to describe those situations in which multiple building occupants experience acute health and comfort effects that appear to be linked to time spent in a building, but no specific illness or cause can be identified. Although the EPA recognizes that such complaints may be localized in a particular room or zone, it also acknowledges that the complaints are sometimes widespread throughout the building. Moreover, the EPA recognizes that causes of, or contributing factors to, sick building syndrome could be biological contaminants such as bacteria, molds, pollen, and viruses. In cases of sick building syndrome, numerous plaintiffs experience similar symptoms all from the same causative factor, which in turn, leads to consideration for certification of class action lawsuit.

In Georgia, a class of plaintiffs may be certified when the requirements of O.C.G.A. § 9-11-23 are met.[34] These requirements are that:

> (1) the members of the class are so numerous that it is impracticable to bring them all before the court; (2) the questions of fact and law common to the class members predominate over any individual questions; (3) the named plaintiff's claims are typical of those of the class members; (4) the named plaintiff and counsel will adequately represent the interests of the class; and (5) a class action better serves the interests of achieving a fair and efficient adjudication of the controversy.[35]

No class of mold plaintiffs has yet been certified in the State of Georgia. Moreover, although Georgia does not have legislation which explicitly pertains to toxic mold claims, in May 2007, the Georgia legislature passed a law which banned class actions for claims arising out of damage caused by exposure to asbestos and silica.[36]

9.4 Potential Defenses

Mold lawsuits filed in Georgia may also give rise to the assertion of unique defenses by mold litigation defendants, such as the defense that certain statutory preconditions to suit against a builder, which are enumerated in Georgia's Right to Repair statute, were not satisfied. Below is a discussion of some of the potential defenses that have been, or may be, asserted by a mold litigation defendant in Georgia.

A. Statute of Limitations

Regardless of whether a mold-litigation defendant is faced with claims based on fraud, negligence or for breach of contract, the first defensive tactic is to determine whether the plaintiff has filed the complaint within the applicable statute of limitations period. A plaintiff's failure to satisfy the statute of limitations period will bar the action.

The statute of limitations applicable to a plaintiff's claim for damage to real property, including, but not limited to, negligent construction, breach of warranty and negligent misrepresentation, is governed by O.C.G.A. § 9-3-30(a) which states that "[a]ll action for trespass upon or damage to realty shall be brought within four years after the right of action accrues." The statute of limitations applicable to a plaintiff's claim for breach of a construction contract is governed by O.C.G.A. § 9-3-24 and states that "[a]ll actions upon simple contracts in writing shall be brought within six years after the same became due and payable." The six-year statute of limitations period under O.C.G.A. § 9-3-24, not the four-year statute of limitations period under O.C.G.A. § 9-3-30, applies to all claims for breach of a contract arising out of a construction contract.[37]

The statute of limitations period for personal injury claims is governed by O.C.G.A. § 9-3-33, which states that, "[a]ctions for injuries to the person shall be brought within two years after the right of action accrues...." The scope of the application of O.C.G.A. § 9-3-33 is determined by the nature of the injury sustained as opposed to the legal theory underlying the claim for relief.[38] Indeed, Georgia follows a specialized rule for determining the limitation period applicable to personal injury claims regardless of the underlying liability theory:

> The more commonly accepted [rule] would seem to be that an action to recover for personal injuries is, in essence, a personal injury action, and, regardless of whether it is based upon an alleged breach of an implied warranty or is based upon an alleged tort, the limitations statute governing actions for personal injury is controlling.[39]

Although determination of the applicable statute of limitations period in a mold case may not be problematical, determination of the date of the accrual of the action may be a particularly difficult analysis. For example, mold defects are often hidden or latent, and mold-related injuries often go undiagnosed for long periods of time. As a result, the statute of limitations analysis in mold cases requires an understanding of whether the "discovery rule" will apply to a particular claim. In Georgia, courts have differentiated the applicability of the discovery rule depending on whether the plaintiff's claim is one for personal injury or property damage.

In *King v. Seitzingers, Inc.*, a plaintiff was diagnosed with lead poisoning and later was told that it had resulted from his exposure to lead fumes at his workplace years earlier.[40] The plaintiff filed suit more than two years after being informed of his diagnosis, but within two years of being told of the causal connection between the diagnosis and his workplace exposure.[41] The Court of Appeals in *King* held that it was a "logical extension of the existing Georgia law" to adopt the rule that the plaintiff's cause of action would not accrue and the statute of limitations would not run against him until he knew or through the exercise of reasonable diligence should have discovered not only the nature of his injury, but also the causal link between the injury and the alleged negligent conduct of the defendant.[42]

Conversely, in Georgia, if a plaintiff seeks recovery for property damage as opposed to personal injury, courts have refused to apply the discovery rule.[43] Therefore, a mold-litigation defendant must cautiously evaluate statute of limitations accrual issues, including the potential application of the discovery rule.

B. Statute of Repose

A statute of limitations sets forth the period within which an action must be commenced based on the accrual of the action. A statute of repose, however, bars a cause of action after a certain period of time regardless of when the action accrues. This is significant to certain mold-litigation defendants because they are certain that they will not be sued for claims on older projects after the expiration of a certain period of time, regardless of accrual issues, including even the discovery rule.

Pursuant to O.C.G.A. § 9-3-51, actions to recover damages against architects, engineers, and contractors for a "deficiency in…[the] design…or construction of an improvement to real property" must be brought within eight years.[44] This eight-year period begins to run "upon substantial completion of an improvement to real property"[45] regardless of whether the damage has actually occurred or been discovered.[46] An improvement is substantially complete "when construction [is] sufficiently completed, in accordance with the contract…so that the owner could occupy the project for the use for which it was intended."[47] Moreover, the substantial completion date triggers the time period for the statute of repose, even if the claimant did not own the property at that time.[48]

C. Spoliation

Upon the discovery of mold in or on any property, the first reaction of the discovering individual is usually to remove the affected material and have it destroyed. However, a plaintiff's removal or destruction of mold-contaminated building product may act to provide a defense to a mold defendant.

"Spoliation" refers to the destruction of, or failure to preserve, evidence necessary to a contemplated or pending litigation.[49] Such destruction creates a presumption that the evidence would have been harmful to the spoliator.[50] When key evidence is destroyed, exclusion of that evidence or dismissal of the case may be warranted.[51] The party moving for such a sanction must show that the opposing party destroyed or failed to preserve evidence necessary to contemplated or pending litigation.[52]

To determine whether the evidence should be excluded or the case dismissed the court must consider:

> (1) whether the defendant was prejudiced as a result of the destruction of the evidence; (2) whether the prejudice could be cured; (3) the practical importance of the evidence; (4) whether the plaintiff acted in good or bad faith; and (5) the potential for abuse if expert testimony about the evidence was not excluded.[53]

With regard to the fourth factor, the court must weigh the degree of the spoliator's culpability against the prejudice to the opposing party.[54]

Even when a defendant successfully proves spoliation by the plaintiff, the remedy of a dismissal or exclusion of evidence is not mandated as a matter of law, and the court may consider alternative sanctions.[55] Dismissal is the most severe sanction,[56] and is typically "reserve[d] for cases where a party has maliciously destroyed relevant evidence with the sole purpose of precluding an adversary from examining that relevant evidence."[57]

D. Right to Repair

A homeowner's discovery of negligently performed construction work that may cause, or has caused, mold growth does not necessarily mean the homeowner has an immediate right to file a lawsuit. Indeed, to reduce the need for litigation resulting from construction disputes while still protecting the rights of homeowners, the Georgia legislature passed the Right to Repair Act (the "Repair Act") in 2004.[58] Under the Repair Act, the Georgia legislature established an alternative dispute resolution mechanism by which homeowners are required to send a notice of claim to contractors believed to be responsible for particular construction defects prior to filing suit. The contractor is then given the opportunity to resolve the dispute without being forced into litigation.

Under the Repair Act, a claimant must send written notice of a claim to the responsible contractor at least 90 days prior to initiating an action against the contractor. If a claimant fails to provide the requisite notice, any action filed will be stayed until the claimant complies with the requirements of the Repair Act. The notice must include a description of the defect and the results of the defect, as well as evidence depicting the nature and cause of the defect.

Thirty days after service of a notice, the contractor must serve upon the claimant, and any other contractor that received the notice, a written response that either offers to settle the claim through payments or repairs or proposes to inspect the dwelling with the alleged defect. If a contractor rejects the claim and will not remedy the defect or fails to respond within the requisite time, the claimant may initiate litigation without further notice. Any contractor that fails to respond according to the Repair Act waives the right to contest the sufficiency of the notice.

If the contractor offers to settle and the claimant rejects the offer, the claimant must provide written notice of the rejection, including reasons for rejection. If the contractor proposes an inspection, within 30 days of receiving the proposal, the claimant must provide the contractor prompt and reasonable access to the dwelling with the alleged defect. The contractor must begin and diligently pursue completion of the inspection within the 30-day period after delivery of its written proposal of inspection. Inspection should be completed in that same period, if reasonable, or a reasonable time thereafter.

Within 14 days of completion of the inspection, the contractor must serve a claimant with a written offer to remedy, settle or reject the original claim. If the claimant accepts an offer to remedy or settle, and the contractor does not repair the defect or make the promised payment, the claimant may initiate litigation without further notice. A claimant may also use the contractor's offer and claimant's acceptance to create a rebuttable presumption of a binding and valid settlement agreement the court should enforce. If the contractor rejects the claim after inspection or fails to serve a written offer, again, the claimant may initiate litigation without further notice. If the contractor rejects the claim, it must provide all known reasons for rejection.

If the claimant rejects the contractor's offer, upon receipt of the rejection and reasons for such rejection, the contractor may make a supplemental offer within 15 days of receiving the rejection. If the claimant rejects the supplemental offer, again, written notice must be served on the contractor. If the claimant rejects a reasonable offer or supplemental offer, or does not permit repair under an accepted offer, the claimant may not recover anything above the fair market value of the offer or actual cost of the repairs or the amount of the monetary settlement. The claimant must serve the contractor with written notice of the acceptance of an offer within 30 days of receipt of the offer. If no response is served within the 30 days, the offer is deemed accepted.

If an applicable limitations period would expire during the process required by the Repair Act, the claimant may file an action, which will be immediately stayed until completion of the process. The Repair Act does not revive a statute of limitations period which has expired prior to the date claimant's notice of claim is served and will not extend any applicable statute of repose. The claimant and contractor may alter the notice of claim procedure, after the initial notice of claim, by written mutual agreement.

If a claimant discovers an additional defect after sending the initial notice of claim to the contractor, the claimant cannot allege that defect in an action until the contractor is given notice of claim of that defect and an opportunity to resolve the claim as provided under the Repair Act. If, after compliance with the Repair Act, an action is filed and an additional defect is discovered during the pendency of that action, such a defect may be added as a supplemental or additional claim in the action, if failure to do so would prejudice either the claimant's or the contractor's legal rights. Still, the claimant must provide the contractor with notice of the additional claim and an opportunity to resolve it. The action will be stayed until completion of the claim process, unless the parties agree otherwise.

9.5 Damages and the Economic Loss Doctrine

The calculation of damage in a toxic mold case under Georgia law is dictated by the nature of the claims asserted. As discussed above, mold claims may be based upon property damage or personal injury, or both.

"[D]amages are intended to place the injured party, as nearly as possible, in the same position they would have been if the injury had never occurred."[59] Breach of contract and tort cases carry dissimilar measures of damages (e.g., the availability of the recovery of consequential damages). Analyzing the correct measure of damages in a toxic mold case against a contractor or builder, therefore, may be complicated where the plaintiff sues under both a breach of contract and a negligence theory.

"Damages recoverable for a breach of contract are such as arise naturally and according to the usual course of things from such breach and such as the parties contemplated, when the contract was made, as the probable result of its breach."[60] "[W]here the action is for breach of contract only, the difference between the value of the house as finished and the value of the house as it should have been finished (e.g., the benefit of the bargain), is a proper measure of damages...."[61] This measure is often referred to as the "diminution of value" analysis.

In Georgia diminution of value is one "but...by no means the exclusive measure" of damages in a construction case.[62] Indeed, "[a]s a general rule, damages for defective construction, whether those damages are the result of breach of contract or negligence of the contractor, are determined by measuring the cost of repairing or restoring the damage, unless the cost of repair is disproportionate to the property's probable loss of value."[63] Thus, generally, the proper measure of damages for defective workmanship would be the cost of repair of the defect when claiming negligent construction, as well as when claiming breach of contract.[64] Accordingly, under Georgia law, cost of repair and diminution in value are alternative, although often times interchangeable, measures of damages in negligent construction and breach of contract cases.[65] An injured party may choose to present his case using either or both methods of measuring damages, depending on his particular circumstances.[66]

The plaintiff bears the burden of producing evidence supporting a claim for damages under either method.[67] The defendant has the burden to present all contradictory evidence challenging the reasonableness or proportionality of those damages and "where appropriate, evidence of an alternative measure of damages for the jury's consideration." [68]

It is often the case that a plaintiff may assert a mold-related claim based upon the failure of a component part of the residence, i.e., a defective HVAC system which results in mold growth. In such cases, the component part manufacturer may invoke the economic loss rule to constrain the scope of plaintiff's plea for damages.

The economic loss rule provides that absent personal injury or damage to property *other than to the allegedly defective product itself* an action in negligence does not lie and any such cause of action may be brought only as a contract warranty action.[69] The rationale underlying this rule is that when a defective product has resulted in the loss of the value or use of the product itself, or the cost of repairing it, the plaintiff is merely suing for the benefit of her bargain.[70] The theory underlying the economic loss rule is that "a contracting party who suffers purely economic losses must seek his remedy in contract and not in tort[,]" and "a plaintiff can recover in tort only those economic losses resulting from injury to his person or damage to his property."[71]

9.6 Admissibility of Scientific Evidence or Expert Testimony

Regardless of whether a mold case involves claims for personal injury or property damage, the plaintiff bears the burden of proving causation through expert testimony, that is, that the mold was caused by the defect in construction or component part and that the property has been adversely affected by the presence of mold, or that the physical injury was caused by mold exposure.

The admissibility of expert testimony in civil actions in Georgia is governed by O.C.G.A. § 24-9-67.1.[72] Section (f) provides that the courts *may* use certain U.S. Supreme Court case law as well as other Federal case law as a guideline toward determining the admissibility of expert testimony in Georgia.[73]

One of the leading Supreme Court cases on this issue is *Daubert*. Under *Daubert*, trial courts have a flexible standard for determining whether or not to admit an expert's testimony.[74] The expert must give an opinion that would assist the trier of fact in understanding the evidence or determining a fact at issue.[75] The expert may rely on hypothetical questions or evidence brought into evidence by another witness.[76] The testimony must be based on sufficient facts or data of a type reasonably relied upon by experts in the particular field in forming opinions or inferences on the subject.[77] The expert's testimony must be the product of reliable principles and methods, and the witness must apply the principles and methods reliably to the facts of the case.[78]

Because there is little guidance by way of comprehensive generally accepted standards for the safe level of mold exposure or indoor air quality, from the EPA or otherwise, most cases turn on whether the expert testimony proffered by plaintiff is sufficient to show dangerous mold exposure levels and causation.

9.7 Georgia Mold Legislation

Georgia has not enacted any legislation or agency regulations regarding toxic mold. The legislature did propose resolutions H.R. 52 and S.R. 22 in 2003. These resolutions proposed the creation of toxic mold study committees. Neither resolution was ever passed.

9.8 Insurance Coverage

A. First-Party Property Coverage

A property owner that experiences mold contamination will immediately look for remediation and replacement costs to be covered under a first-party property insurance policy. Property policies are generally divided up into two categories: (1) a "specified peril" policy, which will only respond to mold contamination claims if such contamination was caused by a peril or cause specified in the policy; or (2) an "all risk" policy, which may respond to a mold contamination claim, unless the specific cause of the mold contamination is expressly excluded by the policy language.

It is often the case that property policies will expressly exclude coverage for damage caused by failure of the property owner to maintain the property in good condition. Such exclusions can include claims based on corrosion, deterioration or wear and tear. Others may even expressly exclude claims for damage caused by mold. Thus, a policyholder must identify the cause of the mold growth, and determine whether that cause is covered or excluded by the first-party property policy.

B. Third-Party Liability Coverage

When a property owner or construction company is faced with a third-party claim for property damage or bodily injury, she will often turn to her third-party comprehensive general liability policy to determine whether her insurance company is bound to provide for a defense and indemnification for that claim.

A third-party liability policy typically pays for those sums that the insured becomes legally obligated to pay for bodily injury and property damage, absent an applicable exclusion in the policy.

C. Absolute Pollution Exclusion

Prior to some insurers inserting mold-specific exclusions in their policies, the most common defense asserted by an insurer to comprehensive general liability coverage for third-party mold claims rested on the "pollution exclusion."

To counteract the increase in claims for pollution liability, the insurance industry implemented an "absolute-pollution exclusion" clause ("the exclusion") in most of its policies, beginning in 1986.[79] The exclusion, usually disclaims policy coverage for bodily injury or property damage arising out of the actual, alleged or threatened discharge, dispersal, seepage, migration, release or escape of pollutants at or from any premises, site or location which is or was at any time owned or occupied by, or rented or loaned to, any insured.[80] The word "pollutants" in this definition has caused the greatest amount of litigation in insurance disputes.

Under Georgia law, an insurance company must clearly and distinctly define any exclusions to coverage under an insurance contract.[81] In the event of a dispute, a court must construe any ambiguous language in favor of the insured and against the insurer.[82] Georgia courts have not yet considered whether toxic mold is a pollutant under the CGL exclusion.

Older CGL policies used different terminology in the exclusion, resulting in some additional case law. These policies stated that the "...exclusion does not apply if such discharge, dispersal, release, or escape is sudden or accidental."[83] Georgia courts have long held that the term "sudden" is ambiguous, and, therefore, should be defined as unexpected for the purposes of insurance contracts.[84] Any contract containing such a provision must be considered in a light most favorable to the insured and would not preclude coverage under the exclusion.[85] Because some insurance contracts still contain this older language, parties considering litigation should review the contract terms carefully. Courts in Georgia enforce insurance exclusions strictly, absent some ambiguous terminology in the contract.

D. Bad Faith Claims

Once the insured establishes coverage under an insurance policy, refusal by the insurance company within 60 days of demand may subject the insurer to liability for the amount owed plus a penalty and any attorneys' fees required to collect the payment.[86] For such a penalty to apply, the insured must prove that the insurance company acted in bad faith.[87] In other words, the burden is on the insured to prove bad faith on the part of the insurer.[88] Georgia law defines bad-faith failure to pay as a "frivolous and unfounded refusal to pay a claim."[89]

A bad faith complaint will fail if the insurer has any reasonable grounds to contest the claim.[90] "Reasonable grounds" includes any reasonable question of law or disputed question of fact.[91] Applying Georgia statutes and decision, the Fifth Circuit held that there could not be bad faith when the amount of loss by the insured was in controversy.[92] The presence of a factual dispute, such as whether the insured is entitled to the amount sought or whether a person lives in the house under which she was claiming insurance coverage, overcomes an assertion of bad faith.[93] Additionally, even if there is doubtful question of law, the insurer has a complete defense against bad faith penalties.[94] The insurer cannot, however, assert the question of law after denying coverage on other grounds.[95]

Endnotes

1. *See Slutzkin v. Fahandeza,* Superior Court of Cobb County, Docket No. 05-1-7168-34.

2. *See Wilson v. Crane-Williams*, Superior Court of DeKalb County, Docket No. 06CV2806.

3. *See Florence v. Knight,* 217 Ga. App. 799, 800, 459 S.E.2d 436 (a home builder was not liable for damages resulting from negligent construction defects which were discoverable upon reasonable inspection by the home buyer).

4. *Id.*

5. *Akins v. Couch*, 271 Ga. 276, 278, 518 S.E.2d 674 (1999)

6. *Rhone v. Bolden*, 270 Ga. App. 712, 719, 608 S.E.2d 22 (2004).

7. *Wilhite v. Mays*, 140 Ga. App. 816, 817-818, 232 S.E.2d 141 (1976), *aff'd*, 239 Ga. 31, 235 S.E.2d 532 (1977).

8. *Id.* at 818.

9. *See Smalls v. Blueprint Development, Inc.,* 230 Ga. App. 556, 557, 497 S.E.2d 54 (1998).

10. *Ben Farmer Realty Co. v. Woodard*, 212 Ga. App. 74, 76, 441 S.E.2d 421 (1994).

11. *Toys 'R' Us v. Atlanta Economic Development Corp.*, 195 Ga. App. 195, 198, 393 S.E.2d 44 (1990); *see also Holmes v. Worthey,* 159 Ga. App. 262, 282 S.E.2d 919 (1981), *aff'd*, *Worthey v. Holmes*, 249 Ga. 104, 287 S.E.2d 9 (1982).

12. *Fussell v. Carl E. Jones Develpoment Co.*, 207 Ga. App. 521, 428 S.E.2d 426 (1993).

13. *See* OCGA § 10-6A-1 *et seq.*; OCGA § 10-6A-14 (b).

14. 2008-GA-A0717.006, 666 S.E.2d 426 (2008).

15. *Fussell*, 207 Ga. App. at 522 (citing *Hudgins v. Bacon*, 171 Ga. App. 856, 859-860, 321 SE2d 359 (1984) and *Howell v. Ayers*, 129 Ga. App. 899, 900, 202 SE2d 189 (1973)).

16. *Id.* (citing *Sam Finley, Inc. v. Barnes*, 156 Ga. App. 802, 275 SE2d 380 (1980)).

17. *Wilson v. Brighton Homes, Inc.*, 204 Ga. App. 677, 420 S.E.2d 360 (1992).

18. *See Newberry v. D.R. Horton, Inc.*, 215 Ga. App. 858, 452 S.E.2d 560 (citing *Coursey Bldg. Assoc. v. Baker*, 165 Ga. App. 521, 301 SE2d 688 (1983) and *Hudgins*, 171 Ga. App. at 856).

19. *Cherry v. Ward*, 204 Ga. App. 833, 420 S.E.2d 763 (1992).

20. *Jennings v. Smith*, 226 Ga. App. 765, 487 S.E.2d 362 (1997).

21. *Stancliff v. Brown & Webb Builders, Inc.*, 254 Ga. App. 224, 561 S.E.2d 438 (2002).

22. *Hall v. Chastain*, 246 Ga. 782, 784, 273 S.E.2d 12 (1980); *Central R&B Co. v. Murray*, 93 Ga. 256, 257, 20 S.E. 129 (1894); *Empire Mills Co. v. Burrell Engineering & Constr. Co.*, 18 Ga. App. 253, 256, 89 S.E. 530 (1916).

23. *See Harrison v. Kiser*, 79 Ga. 588, 4 S.E. 320 (1887); *Ryland Group v. Daley*, 245 Ga. App. 496, 537 S.E.2d 732 (2000) (damages measured by diminution in value where defects are permanent); *Mercer v. J&M Transportation Co.*, 103 Ga. App. 141, 118 SE2d 716 (1961) (measuring damages by diminution in value where restoration would require construction of entirely new home).

24. *John Thurmond & Associates, Inc. v. Kennedy*, 284 Ga. 469, 471, 668 S.E.2d 666 (2008).

25. *See Holmes*, 159 Ga. App. 262; *Rosenheimer v. Tidal Constr. Co.*, 250 Ga. App. 145, 550 S.E.2d 698 (2001).

26. *Howell v. Ayers*, 129 Ga. App. 899, 202 S.E.2d 189 (1973).

27. OCGA § 44-7-13.

28. *Mathis v. Gazan*, 51 Ga. App. 805, 806, 181 S.E. 503 (1935).

29. *Id.*

30. *Home Owners Loan Corp. v. Brazzeal*, 62 Ga. App. 683, 692, 9 S.E.2d 773 (1940).

31. *Carpet Central, Inc. v. Johnson*, 222 Ga. App. 26, 27, 473 S.E.2d 569 (1996).

32. *See Fitzgerald v. Storer Cable Communications*, 213 Ga. App. 872, 874, 446 S.E.2d 755 (1994); *Grier v. Jeffco Mgmt. Co.*, 176 Ga. App. 158, 335 S.E.2d 408 (1985); *Hull v. Mass. Mut. Life Ins. Co.*, 142 Ga. App. 269, 235 S.E.2d 601 (1977); *Phelps v. Consolidated Equities Corp.*, 133 Ga. App. 189, 193, 210 S.E.2d 337 (1974).

33. 259 Ga. 126, 129-30, 381 S.E.2d 283 (1989).

34. O.C.G.A. § 9-11-23.

35. *Life Ins. Co. of Georgia v. Meeks*, 274 Ga. App. 212, 215, 617 S.E.2d 179 (2005).

36. O.C.G.A. § 51-14-7(c).

37. *Costrini v. Hansen Architects*, P.C., 247 Ga. App. 136, 136-37, 543 S.E.2d 760 (2000).

38. *Daniel v. American Optical Corp.*, 251 Ga. 166, 167, 304 S.E.2d 383 (1983).

39. *Gropper v. STO Corp.*, 250 Ga. App. 820, 822, 552 S.E.2d 118 (2001) (citing *Adair v. Baker Bros., Inc.*, 185 Ga. App. 807, 808, 366 S.E.2d 164 (1988)).

40. 160 Ga. App. 318, 287 S.E.2d 252 (1981).

41. *Id.*

42. *Id.*

43. *See Griffin v. Kangaroo, Inc.*, 208 Ga. App. 190, 430 S.E.2d 82 (1993).

44. O.C.G.A. § 9-3-51. The only exception is for injury to property or person which occurs during the seventh or eighth year after substantial completion of the improvement. § 9-3-51(b). In that case, the injured party must bring the claim within two years. *Id.* However, the claim may never be brought more than ten years after substantial completion of the improvement. *Id.*

45. *Benning Constr. Co. v. Lakeshore Plaza Enters.*, 240 Ga. 426, 428, 241 S.E.2d 184 (1977).

46. *Hanna v. McWilliams*, 213 Ga. App. 648, 651, 446 S.E.2d 741 (1994).

47. O.C.G.A. § 9-3-50(2).

48. *Colormatch Exteriors, Inc. v. Hickey*, 275 Ga. 249, 252, 569 S.E.2d 495 (2002).

49. *Bridgestone/Firestone North American Tire, LLC v. Campbell*, 258 Ga. App. 767, 768, 574 S.E.2d 923 (2003).

50. *Glynn Plymouth, Inc. v. Davis*, 120 Ga. App. 475, 482, 170 S.E.2d 848 (1969).

51. *Id.*

52. *Strickland v. CMCR Investments,* 279 Ga. 112, 115 n.7, 610 S.E.2d 71 (2005); *Ga. Bd. of Dentistry v. Pence,* 223 Ga. App. 603, 608, 478 S.E.2d 437 (1996).

53. *Bridgestone/Firestone*, at 768-69.

54. *Id.* at 770.

55. *Id.* at 771.

56. *Id.*

57. *Chapman v. Auto Owners Insurance Company*, 220 Ga. App. 539, 542, 469 S.E.2d 783, 785-86 (1996) (quoting *Northern Assurance Co. v. Ware*, 145 F.R.D. 281 (D. Me. 1993)).

58. *See* O.C.G.A. § 8-2-35, et. seq.

59. *John Thurmond & Assocs.*, 284 Ga. at 469.

60. *See* OCGA § 13-6-2.

61. *Kennedy v. John Thurmond & Assocs., Inc.*, 286 Ga. App. 642, 644-45, 649 S.E.2d 762 (2008).

62. *Id.*

63. *John Thurmond & Assocs.*, 284 Ga. at 470.

64. *Kennedy*, 286 Ga. App. at 644-45.

65. *John Thurmond & Assocs.*, 284 Ga. at 471.

66. *Id.* at 471.

67. *Id.*

68. *Id.*

69. *See Long v. Jim Letts Oldsmobile, Inc.*, 135 Ga. App. 293, 295, 217 S.E.2d 602 (1975).

70. *Vulcan Materials Co. v. Driltech, Inc.*, 251 Ga. 383, 387, 306 S.E.2d 253 (1983).

71. *City of Cairo v. Hightower Consulting Engineers, Inc.*, 278 Ga. App. 721, 728, 629 S.E.2d 518 (2006) (quoting *Gen. Elec. Co. v. Lowe's Home Centers*, 279 Ga. 77, 78, 608 S.E.2d 636 (2005)).

72. O.C.G.A. § 24-9-67.1 (2005).

73. *Id.*

74. *Hamilton-King v. HNTB Georgia, Inc.*, 296 Ga. App. 864, 676 S.E.2d 287 (2009).

75. *Id.*

76. *Ga. Dep't of Transp. v. Baldwin*, 292 Ga. App. 816, 820-24, 665 S.E.2d 898, 904 (2008).

77. O.C.G.A. § 24-9-67.1.

78. O.C.G.A. § 24-9-67.1. *See Gianotti v. Beleza Hair Salon, Inc.*, 296 Ga. App. 636, 638-39, 675 S.E.2d 544, 547 (2009) (holding that the trial court had not abused its discretion in excluding expert testimony when the expert used a different heat source, a different product, and a different medium, glass instead of hair).

79. 9 Ga. Jur. *Environmental Law* § 16:3 (2008).

80. Commercial General Liability Coverage Form CG 00 01 10 01 § I (2) (f) (ISO Properties, Inc. 2000).

81. *Hurst v. Grange Mut. Cas. Co.*, 266 Ga. 712, 716, 470 S.E.2d 659 (1996).

82. O.C.G.A. § 13-2-2 (5) (1964).

83. *Claussen v. Aetna Cas. & Sur. Co.*, 259 Ga. 333, 334, 380 S.E.2d 686 (1989).

84. *Id.* at 334.

85. *See State Farm Fire & Cas. Co. v. Walnut Avenue Partners, LLC.*, 296 Ga. App. 648, 649-51, 675 S.E.2d 534 (2009).

86. O.C.G.A. § 33-4-6 (2001).

87. *Id.*

88. *Cincinnati Ins. Co. v. Kastner*, 233 Ga. App. 594, 595-96, 504 S.E.2d 496 (1998).

89. *United Services Auto Ass'n v. Carroll*, 226 Ga. App. 144, 148, 486 S.E.2d 613, 616 (1997) (citing *Dixie Constr. Prods. v. WMH, Inc.*, 179 Ga. App. 658, 347 S.E.2d 303 (1986)).

90. *Swyters v. Motorola Employees Credit Union*, 244 Ga. App. 356, 358, 535 S.E.2d 508, 510 (2000) (citing *Canal Ins. Co. v. Savannah Bank & Trust Co.*, 181 Ga. App. 520, 352 S.E.2d 835 (1987).

91. *American Family Life Assur. Co. of Columbus, Ga. v. U.S. Fire Co.*, 885 F.2d 826, 834 (11th Cir. 1989). This case involved application of Ga. Code. Ann. § 13-6-11, which has since been held to not apply to insurance bad-faith claims; however, the courts have applied the same reasoning to § 33-4-6 despite not allowing for specific § 13-6-11 recovery. *See Colonial Oil Indus., Inc. v. Underwriters Subscribing To Policy Nos. T031504670 and T031504671*, 910 F. Supp. 655, 656 (S.D. Ga. 1995).

92. *Aetna Ins. Co. of Hartford, Conn. v. Taylor*, 86 F.2d 225, 227 (5th Cir. 1936).

93. *Moon v. Mercury Ins. Co. of Ga.*, 253 Ga. App. 506, 508-09, 559 S.E.2d 532 (2002).

94. *Georgia Farm Bureau Mut. Ins. Co. v. Jackson*, 240 Ga. App. 127, 130, 522 S.E.2d 716 (1999) (holding that the question of law was not in doubt at the time the insurer refused to pay; therefore, even if it was a valid question of law, the insurer could not use that as a defense against bad faith.).

95. *Id.*

Chapter 10

An Overview of Toxic Mold Litigation in Illinois

Edward Eshoo, Jr., Esq.

Synopsis

10.1 Introduction

Illinois is no stranger to mold litigation. An ever increasing number of mold-related personal injury and property damage lawsuits are being filed in Illinois against property insurers, building product manufacturers, contractors, mold abatement companies, indoor air quality professionals as well as owners and sellers of real property. Even Michael Jordan, arguably Illinois' most famous resident over the past 20 years, has joined the parade of litigants.[1] This chapter will examine legal issues confronting mold litigants in Illinois.

10.2 First-Party Property Insurance Coverage

A first-party property insurance policy typically provides coverage for physical loss or damage to the insured's covered property caused by a covered cause of loss. Insurers traditionally have covered mold damage if it is the result of a covered peril.[2] However, in *DeVore v. American Family Mutual Insurance Co.,*[3] an Illinois appellate court rejected the distinction between mold that results from an otherwise covered peril and mold that results from some other source or event. The policy language in that case excluded coverage for losses "resulting directly or indirectly from or caused by...mold...regardless of any other cause or event contributing concurrently or in any sequence to the loss." The appellate court concluded that this language clearly and unambiguously indicated that a loss from mold from any cause at any time is excluded.

The Illinois Department of Insurance has issued a bulletin advising as follows:

> All personal and commercial property policies that provide coverage for the perils of fire or lightning (pursuant to Class 3 (a) of Section 4 of the Illinois Insurance Code) must cover mold, fungus, etc. that results from a covered fire or lightning loss. If there is water damage and mold following a covered fire or lightning loss, the total of all damages is subject to the full policy limit.[4]

The Illinois Department of Insurance's position is based on the 165-line, 1943 New York Standard Fire Policy (SFP). Illinois has adopted the SFP by statute. All fire insurance policies written in the State of Illinois must conform to the requirements of the SFP.[5] As such, the SFP sets forth minimum fire insurance coverage upon which an insured can rely under any fire insurance policy issued in the State of Illinois. The SFP guarantees a minimum level of coverage that supersedes any attempt to limit coverage to less than the statutory minimum. A fire insurance policy may not provide less coverage than that set forth in the SFP. Stated differently, a fire insurance policy must provide coverage in conformity with or in excess of the SFP. The SFP thus prohibits the use in fire insurance policies of limitations, conditions, or exclusions not expressly authorized.[6]

The SFP provides coverage for all direct loss by fire and lightning.[7] The perils not covered include such things as loss caused by enemy attack, invasion, insurrection, rebellion, revolution, and civil war.[8] The SFP neither limits nor excludes coverage for mold damage. Thus, under the SFP, water damage and mold damage resulting from a covered fire or lightning loss is covered.

There have been a number of legal challenges outside of Illinois involving first-party property insurance coverage for mold damage. The issues in many of these cases involved: (a) whether mold spores constitute physical loss or damage, as required by the insuring agreement for most first-party property insurance policies; (b) whether coverage for mold damage is barred by the exclusions for (1) loss caused by rust, corrosion, mold, wet or dry rot, or (2) loss caused by the discharge, dispersal, seepage, migration, release, or escape of pollutants, which term is usually defined to include any solid, liquid, gaseous or thermal irritant or contaminant; and (c) whether coverage is afforded for water and mold damage which ensues from faulty, inadequate, or defective workmanship, construction, or maintenance. This author submits that, under Illinois law, mold spores constitute physical loss or damage.[9] This author submits that, under Illinois law, neither the "pollution" exclusion nor the "mold" exclusion should be a bar to coverage for mold damage.[10] This author also submits that, under Illinois law, water and mold damage which ensue from faulty, inadequate, or defective workmanship, construction, or maintenance is covered.

In *Board of Education of Township High School District No. 211 v. International Insurance Co.,*[11] the applicable policies provided coverage for "all risks of physical loss or damage to all real or personal property of every kind or description wherever located occurring the period of this insurance." The issues were whether the presence of friable asbestos-containing building materials and asbestos fibers constituted physical loss or damage to covered property and whether such physical loss or damage occurred during the period the policies were in effect. The appellate court concluded that asbestos fiber contamination in plaintiffs' schools constituted physical loss or damage. The appellate court also concluded that the insureds' claim for asbestos removal costs incurred during the policy period "triggered" coverage. In reaching this conclusion, the appellate court applied the "equitable continuous trigger." Under that trigger, asbestos property damage is deemed an ongoing, continuous process, triggering every policy in effect during the period beginning with the installation of the friable, fiber-releasing asbestos materials and ending when those materials are removed or contained. In deciding to apply an equitable continuous trigger, the appellate court was persuaded by the analysis in *United States Gypsum Co. v. Admiral Insurance Co.,*[12] i.e., that property damage, whether from the presence of airborne asbestos fibers or settled fibers subject to reentrainment, occurs over a span of time and cannot be linked to or confined to different policy periods and that the difficulty in determining precisely when the damage occurred or in following its progress or proliferation is exacerbated by the interchangeable nature of the fibers and that their release occurs on a continuing basis.

Determining when property damage from airborne mold spores occurs is equally difficult for the same reasons: the interchangeable nature of the spores and the fact that their release occurs on a continuing basis. *The Board of Education of Township High School District No. 211* case supports not only the position that mold spore contamination constitutes physical loss or damage,[13] but also the adoption of the equitable continuous trigger to determine the timing of mold damage for coverage purpose, beginning with the initial water event that caused the ensuing mold damage and ending when the moldy building materials are removed.

The Illinois Supreme Court, in *American States Insurance Co. v. Koloms*,[14] concluded that the "pollution" exclusion applies only to injury or damage caused by traditional environmental pollution, i.e., industrial discharge of toxic waste into the environment.[15] Accordingly, even if it is considered a "pollutant," neither mold growth nor the discharge, dispersal, migration, release, or escape of mold spores in a contained or indoor environment constitutes the type of traditional environmental pollution contemplated by the exclusion.

Illinois courts adhere to the rule of insurance contract construction known as "*noscitur a sociis*," which requires that language be construed in accordance with the words which are associated with it.[16] The term "mold" in the typical "mold" exclusion is surrounded by types of loss (rust, corrosion, wet or dry rot) that occur naturally over a period of time. As such, the intent of the mold exclusion is to bar coverage for mold which occurs gradually, and which is not associated with a fortuitous event. This also is the interpretation advanced by the Illinois Department of Insurance on its website, as well as in response to inquiries made by insureds.[17] Interpreting the mold exclusion in the manner above is not only consistent with, but is also required by, the well-established rule of insurance contract construction in Illinois that "[p]rovisions in insurance policies that limit or exclude coverage are to be construed liberally in favor of the insured."[18] Under this canon of insurance contract construction, even if a particular limiting or exclusionary phrase or term is capable of being interpreted in the manner sought by the insurer, where another interpretation favorable to the insured reasonably can be made, that construction must be applied. Interpreting the mold exclusion liberally in favor of insureds thus results in the conclusion that mold damage which originates from a covered peril is not excluded.

In addition to the "mold" and "pollution" exclusions, many, if not most, first-party property insurance policies exclude loss or damage caused by faulty, inadequate, or defective: (1) workmanship, repair, construction, renovation, or remodeling; (2) materials used in repair, construction, renovation, or remodeling; or (3) maintenance. However, the "faulty, inadequate or defective" exclusion typically covers any "ensuing loss" not excluded or excepted by the policy. In *Board of Education of Maine Township High School District 207 v. International Insurance Co.*, the appellate court interpreted the ensuing loss exception as follows: "if a nonexcluded loss is caused by perils that either occur after an excluded peril or are causally related to an excluded peril, the nonexcluded loss will remain covered. Only the nonexcluded portion of the loss will be covered, however. The uncovered peril itself will not be covered." [19]

As an example, a roof leaks, with resultant interior water and mold damage. The roof was faultily maintained. Under the interpretation espoused by the appellate court in *Board of Education of Maine Township*, the leaking roof itself is not covered because of the "faulty maintenance" exclusion; however, the interior water and mold damage is covered as an "ensuing loss" because (a) the standard "water damage" exclusion does not preclude coverage for interior water damage caused by rain or melting ice or snow and (b) the mold damage is the result or consequence of a covered water peril.[20]

Although it did not involve application of an "ensuing loss" exception, *McGrath v. American Family Mutual Ins. Co.*,[21] is instructive on the issue of whether an exclusion for loss caused by construction defects excludes resulting water and mold damage. There, the insureds suffered loss from external water or moisture (rain, melting ice or snow, or ambient humidity) that had penetrated the exterior brick walls of their recently constructed home in Chicago. The insurer argued that any loss connected to or caused by a construction defect was excluded. The insureds, in contrast, argued that only losses directly related to the construction defect were excluded, such as the cost to correct the faulty brick walls. Because they sought only reimbursement for the loss resulting from the interior water damage (damaged drywall, insulation and the like), the insureds contended that the exclusion was not applicable.

The Illinois federal district court in *McGrath* concluded that while the plain language of the construction or design defects exclusion expressly excluded the cost to correct the construction defect, the extent of the exclusion to ancillary damage was ambiguous. The provision included no language that indicated that the exclusion extended to any loss resulting, however remotely, from construction or design defects, while other exclusions found in the policy did include such language. For example, the "latent or inherent defect" exclusion in the policy included specific language that excluded "loss caused directly or indirectly" by defects. Such language was notably absent in the construction or design defect exclusion. Thus, the district court read the exclusion narrowly against the insurer and found that the construction and design defects exclusion did not apply to loss from moisture intrusion that occurred as a result of construction or design defects. The district court also concluded that the latent or inherent defect exclusion did not apply to the insureds' loss, reasoning that a latent defect is a hidden defect other than a construction or design defect.

In Illinois, in addition to breach of contract, causes of action available to an insured against his property insurer in a mold damage case include: (1) negligence; (2) consumer fraud; (3) violation of section 155 of the Illinois Insurance Code; and (4) equitable relief, including injunctive and declaratory relief, as well as specific performance.

Negligence actions may be available to an insured in a mold damage case if the remediation goes sour. Because of the lack of regulatory or professional standards as to acceptable or unacceptable mold contamination levels, a "successful" remediation may be subject to dispute. However, common sense dictates that a "successful" remediation is one in which the insured is able to re-occupy her premises without health complaints or physical discomfort.

A negligence action may be available against the insurer after an unsuccessful remediation if the remediation contractor was acting as the insurer's agent. A principal-agent relationship can exist through a contract or guaranteed contractor program. It also can exist if the insurer (1) directed, supervised, and managed the remediation contractor, and exercised decision-making authority as to the scope of the mold remediation and (2) paid the remediation contractor directly.

Typical negligent acts or omissions on the part of a remediation contractor in cleaning, restoring, or remediating the insured premises and personal property include:

- failing to dry the insured premises;
- failing to take proper measures to protect the insured premises from continued water intrusion;
- failing to take reasonable steps to prevent or to inhibit the microbial growth in the insured premises;
- failing to warn the insured of the dangers and biohazards it left behind in the insured premises;
- failing to properly address the water damage and the dangerous microbial contamination that ensued;
- failing to complete the cleaning, restoration, and remediation of the insured premises;
- failing to restore the insured premises to its pre-loss condition;
- failing to perform the cleaning, restoration, and remediation services in a good and workmanlike manner;
- failing to perform the cleaning, restoration, and remediation services according to established guidelines or standards for fungal or mold problems; and
- neglecting, mistreating, and otherwise damaging the personal property and household goods and contents by, among other things, failing to take reasonable steps to clean it, failing to adequately store it, and otherwise failing to take steps to protect it from additional loss and damage.

A negligence action also may be available against the insurer after an unsuccessful remediation, if the insurer voluntarily undertook to direct, supervise, manage, and employ experts or specialists to inspect, assess, remediate, and contain the mold growth in the insured premises. Typical negligent acts or omissions on the part of the insurer include:

- allowing claim personnel who have no experience or training in mold to direct, supervise, manage, and employ an expert or specialist, such as a certified industrial hygienist, to inspect the insured premises to determine if there is mold growth in the insured premises;
- allowing claim personnel who have no experience or training in mold to direct, supervise, manage, and employ a remediation contractor to inspect, assess, remediate, and contain the mold growth in the insured premises;
- allowing claim personnel who have no experience or training in mold to exercise decision-making authority as to the scope of diagnostic testing, sampling, and investigation to be performed by the expert or specialist;
- allowing claim personnel who have no experience or training in mold to exercise decision-making authority as to what cleaning, restoration, remediation, repair, replacement or renovation or other services will or will not be performed by the remediation contractor;
- hiring a remediation contractor who is not qualified to inspect, assess, remediate, and contain the mold growth in the insured premises;
- failing to direct the remediation contractor to complete the cleaning, restoration, and remediation of the insured premises;
- failing to direct the remediation contractor to clean, restore, and remediate the insured's personal property and household goods and contents;
- failing to properly supervise the remediation contractor so as to ensure that its cleaning, restoration, and remediation of the insured premises was performed in a good and workmanlike manner;
- failing to properly supervise the remediation contractor so as to ensure that its cleaning, restoration, and remediation of the insured premises was performed according to established industry guidelines or standards;
- failing to direct that a final "clearance" test be conducted of the insured premises so as to ensure (1) that the remediation work has eliminated the mold growth in the insured premises and (2) that the insured premises is fit for human occupation;
- failing to direct the expert or specialist to collect samples of building materials and to analyze for mold content; and
- failing to direct the expert or specialist to collect samples of dust/debris from the personal property and household goods and contents in the insured premises and to analyze for mold content so as to determine if any remediation of the personal property and household goods and contents is necessary.

Amica Mutual Insurance Co. v. Henderson is a case which illustrates an insurer's, a remediation contractor's, and an environmental testing company's exposure arising out of an unsuccessful remediation. In that case, water and mold damage to plaintiff's home was discovered following a fire loss. Her homeowners insurer retained service companies to repair and to remediate the damage to her property. The repair and remediation work was performed negligently. As a result, water was able to seep into her home, causing toxic mold to grow and to spread throughout the home. Her homeowners insurer retained specialized service companies to perform investigations and microbial toxin testing at her property. The district court denied the environmental testing company's motion to dismiss. The district court concluded that the insured had sufficiently pleaded negligent conduct on the part of the environmental testing company (failing to tell the insured that the mold in the home could be toxic, that contact with the mold could be hazardous, that the remediation contractor's work did not isolate and contain the mold contamination, and allowing her and her family to reside in the home knowing the toxicity of the mold) and that this negligent conduct caused the insured and her children emotional distress.[22]

The Illinois Consumer Fraud and Deceptive Business Practices Act ("Consumer Fraud Act") states, in pertinent part, that "[u]nfair methods of competition and unfair or deceptive acts or practices, including but not limited to the use or employment of any deception, fraud, false pretense, false promise, misrepresentation or the concealment, suppression or omission of any material fact...are hereby declared unlawful."[23] The Consumer Fraud Act was intended to protect consumers against fraud, unfair methods of competition, and unfair or deceptive acts or practices in the conduct of trade or commerce.[24] The Consumer Fraud Act is to be broadly construed to prohibit deception or false promises. As Illinois courts have stated, "we perceive a clear mandate from the Illinois legislature that the courts of this State are to utilize the Consumer Fraud Act to the utmost degree in eradicating all forms of deceptive and unfair business practices and to grant appropriate remedies to defrauded consumers."[25] Because the Consumer Fraud Act was designed to provide broader protection for consumers than common law fraud, a plaintiff is not required to prove every element of common law fraud in order to recover. In order to state a claim for a violation of the Consumer Fraud Act, a plaintiff must allege the following: (1) a deceptive act or practice; (2) an intent by defendant that plaintiff rely on the deception; and (3) that the deception occurred in the course of conduct involving trade or commerce.[26]

Deceptive marketing practices are actionable as independent torts, provided the deceptive marketing or advertising actually deceives the insured.[27] In that regard, mold damage claims can be appropriate Consumer Fraud Act claims. For example, one insurer's marketing slogans are to get its insureds back to where they belong and to restore their lives to order following a loss.[28] Its failure to do so, particularly after an unsuccessful remediation where it directs, supervises, and manages the remediation contractor and exercises decision-making authority as to the scope of the remediation, could constitute a deceptive act or practice within the meaning of the Consumer Fraud Act.

Section 155 of the Illinois Insurance Code "provides an extracontractual remedy to policyholders whose insurer's refusal to recognize liability and pay a claim under a policy is vexatious and unreasonable."[29] Section 155 allows as part of the taxable costs in an action reasonable attorney fees and an amount not to exceed $60,000.[30]

Examples of vexatious and unreasonable conduct on the part of the insurer include: (a) refusing to pay, despite knowledge that it was liable and knowledge that its refusal would result in serious damage to the insured; (b) failing to adequately investigate a claim; (c) denial of the claim without adequate supporting evidence; (d) failing to evaluate a claim objectively; and (e) interpreting policy provisions in an unreasonable manner.[31]

The question of vexatious and unreasonable conduct within the meaning of section 155 is a factual one, which must be based upon an assessment of the totality of the circumstances, including: (a) the insurer's attitude; (b) whether an insured was forced to file suit to recover; and (c) if an insured was deprived of the use of his property.[32]

Vexatious and unreasonable conduct on the part of an insurer in a mold damage claim—which, if proven, should constitute a violation of section 155—includes:

- failing to promptly contact the insured once the loss is reported;
- failing to pay the insured amounts due under the insurance policy within 40 days of the loss, which constitutes an unreasonable delay in paying her claim as a matter of law, in violation of the regulations promulgated by the Illinois Director of Insurance within section 919.80(d)(7)(A) of Part 919 of Title 50 of the Illinois Administrative Code;[33]
- failing to advise the insured in writing within 75 days from the date the loss was reported of the reason for the delay in not resolving his claim, in violation of the regulations promulgated by the Illinois Director of Insurance within section 919.80(d)(7)(B) of Part 919 of the Illinois Administrative Code;[34]
- failing to provide the insured with a reasonable written explanation for the delay in resolving her claim, in violation of the regulations promulgated by the Illinois Director of Insurance within Part 919 of the Illinois Administrative Code;[35]

- adjusting the claim contrary to and in violation of its own internal water and mold adjusting policies, practices and procedures;
- adjusting the claim contrary to and in violation of its own internal property claims handling policies, practices and procedures;
- assigning claim representatives to adjust the claim who are untrained and inexperienced in mold, and who make numerous misrepresentations to the insured, in violation of section 154.6 of the Illinois Insurance Code;[36]
- not attempting in good faith to effectuate a prompt, fair, and equitable settlement of the claim, a claim in which liability is reasonably clear, in violation of section 154.6 of the Illinois Insurance Code and the regulations promulgated by the Illinois Director of Insurance within section 919.50 of Part 919 of the Illinois Administrative Code;[37]
- without proper cause, wrongfully and knowingly refusing to reimburse the insured for certain losses, and delaying payment on other losses which it acknowledges are covered under the insurance policy, such losses including additional living expenses and other structural repairs, in violation of section 919.50 of Part 919 of the Illinois Administrative Code;[38]
- forcing the insured to retain legal counsel to investigate his claim and to file a lawsuit to recover the benefits that should have been immediately forthcoming under the insurance policy;
- failing to acknowledge, with reasonable promptness, pertinent communications with respect to the claim, in violation of the regulations promulgated by the Illinois Director of Insurance within section 919.40 of Part 919 of the Illinois Administrative Code;[39]
- failing to provide the insured with reports prepared by experts, despite repeated requests for the same;
- willfully refusing to undertake coverage obligations to protect the insured, instead undertaking a continuous effort to conceal material information from the insured, to procrastinate and to delay at every turn, and acting to maximize its own financial interest at the expense and to the financial demise of the insured;
- refusing to pay the insured's claim without conducting a full, fair and prompt investigation based on all available information, in violation of section 154.6 of the Illinois Insurance Code;[40]
- denying the insured's claim without adequate supporting evidence;
- denying the insured's claim based on an unreasonable and erroneous interpretation of its own insurance policy provisions;[41] and
- denying the insured's claim knowing that it was liable and that there was no bona fide or genuine dispute as to coverage for the water damage and mold damage.[42]

The construction of an insurance contract is a proper subject of inquiry in a declaratory judgment action.[43] Declaratory relief is thus appropriate in a mold damage case if there is a dispute over coverage. Specific performance may be appropriate in a mold damage case if the insurer fails to honor specific agreements made with its insured, such as agreeing to pay for the following items: (a) the cost to pack, to move, and to store the personal property and household goods and contents inside the insured premises while the insured premises is being remediated and reconstructed; (b) the cost to clean the insured's clothing; (c) the cost of the mold remediation work to be performed at the insured premises; (d) the cost to reconstruct the interior of the insured premises following the completion of the mold remediation work; and (e) all of the increased living expenses necessarily incurred by the insured while the insured premises is inhabitable and unfit for human occupation.[44]

Some Illinois courts have recognized that injunctive relief is appropriate in a mold damage case if the insurer is threatening to cut-off the insureds' additional living expenses prior to the completion of remediation and reconstruction (such as rent and rental furniture if the insured is required to move out of the insured dwelling) and the insureds are financially unable to pay these expenses themselves.[45] In *Lumberman's Mutual Casualty Co. v. Sykes*,[46] however, an Illinois appellate court concluded that the trial court abused its discretion in issuing an injunction requiring Lumberman's to pay Sykes' additional living expenses that she incurred due to being unable to stay in her home after the discovery of toxic mold growth. The appellate court reasoned that Sykes had an adequate remedy at law in the form of monetary damages which were readily and precisely calculable. The *Sykes* decision is also significant because of the appellate court's finding that Lumberman's was estopped from raising the defense of noncoverage for mold damage because of certain representations and assurances of coverage it had made to Sykes.

10.3 Residential Real Property Disclosure Act

The Illinois Residential Real Property Disclosure Act (the "Act") requires sellers of residential real estate to provide potential buyers with a written disclosure of material defects and other conditions of the property. Included in the report are such items as flooding or recurring leakage, asbestos, termites, underground tanks and, in some realtor disclosure reports, mold.[47] The Act provides that a seller is not liable for any inaccuracy, omission or error in the report if: (1) she had no knowledge of such error, inaccuracy or omission; (2) she had a reasonable belief that such error, inaccuracy, or omission was correct; or (3) the error, inaccuracy, or omission is based on information provided by a public agency or licensed professional, and the seller had no knowledge of such error, inaccuracy, or omission.[48] Sellers that knowingly violate this Act and fail to truthfully complete the disclosure report shall be liable for actual damages, court costs, and reasonable attorney fees.[49]

Claims against a seller of residential real estate for violation of the Act, fraudulent misrepresentation, and negligent misrepresentation in failing to disclose known material defects in the property resulting in water infiltration and ensuing mold damage may not be covered under the seller's homeowners liability insurance coverage, as was the case in *Allstate Insurance Co. v. Lane.*[50] In that case, the buyers sought rescission of a real estate contract and damages because the home they purchased from the sellers had been damaged by extensive water infiltration before the closing. The buyers alleged that the sellers replaced most of the windows in the house; but, because of improper installation, the windows leaked and rainwater entered the house. The buyers claimed that the sellers knew of the water infiltration when they discovered damaged plaster, bubbling in the wallpaper, and puddling in the basement during heavy rains, but misrepresented the same when they signed a residential real property disclosure report stating that they were not aware of either recurring leaks in the basement, material defects in walls or floors, or leaks or material defects in the roof, ceiling or chimney. The sellers' Allstate Family Liability insurance policy provided that "Allstate will pay damages which an insured person becomes legally obligated to pay because of bodily injury or property damage arising from an occurrence to which this policy applies, and is covered by this part of the policy." The appellate court concluded that Allstate was not obligated either to defend or to indemnify the sellers in the underlying lawsuit because the buyers' claims did not arise from an "occurrence" within the meaning of the Allstate policy. The appellate court reasoned that the actual accident or occurrence was the faulty installation of windows and water infiltration, leading to the structural deterioration of the house. The buyers' claim pertained to the nondisclosure of the damage, not to the damage itself. Accordingly, the underlying claims were outside the scope of the Allstate policy.

10.4 Personal Injury and Property Damage Claims

In Illinois, the success of a mold-related property damage tort claim requires pleading around the economic loss doctrine. First enunciated in Illinois in 1982 by the Supreme Court in *Moorman Manufacturing Co. v. National Tank Co.*,[51] the doctrine precludes the recovery in tort of *purely* economic losses, i.e., economic losses unaccompanied by property damage or personal injury resulting from a sudden, calamitous, or dangerous event.

Toxic contamination of a building itself, other parts of a building, and the building contents is damage to "other property," as seen in *Board of Education of*

City of Chicago v. A, C and S, Inc.[52] There, the issue was whether the plaintiffs, 34 school districts, had sufficiently pleaded negligence and strict liability causes of action to recover the removal and repair costs of asbestos-containing material (ACM) in their buildings from various defendants involved at some level of the manufacturing and distribution chain of ACM. The linchpin for both of these causes of action was whether the complaints sufficiently alleged that asbestos had caused damage to other property or injury to persons so as to fall within a tort claim, as opposed to a contract cause of action. The defendants contended that plaintiffs only suffered economic loss, which is recoverable in contract and not in tort. They argued that there was alleged only a risk of harm to people and no actual harm was pleaded. Further, they argued that no property damage was alleged in the complaint.

The Illinois Supreme Court disagreed, holding that the complaints alleged sufficient facts to establish tort actions under the principles established in *Moorman.* The complaints alleged that friable asbestos existed in plaintiffs' buildings and that asbestos had been released throughout the schools. The Court stated that "it would be incongruous to argue there is no damage to other property when a harmful element exists throughout a building or an area of a building which by law must be corrected and at trial may be proven to exist at unacceptably dangerous levels."[53] Relying on cases in which courts had found that asbestos fibers may contaminate a building sufficiently to allege damage to property, the Court concluded that the complaints alleged damage to property because the buildings were contaminated with a toxic substance which rendered them unsafe for their normal use.

A, C & S, Inc. is not limited to asbestos contamination. In *American United Logistics, Inc. v. Catellus Development Corp.*,[54] the Seventh Circuit Court of Appeals concluded that recovery for contamination is not barred by the economic loss doctrine if the contamination is hazardous or unreasonably dangerous. Accordingly, this author submits that, under *A, C & S, Inc.* and *American United Logistics, Inc.*, if the toxic microbial contamination inside a dwelling or building is hazardous or unreasonably dangerous, i.e., the toxic microbial contamination poses a serious health risk to the occupants, then all losses caused by the contamination, including economic losses, are recoverable.

In *Murfield Village-Vernon Hills, LLC v. Reinke*,[55] it was alleged that wet or saturated insulation or carpentry materials were negligently installed during construction of a home, which led to the growth of unacceptably high levels of mold and bacteria. While the growth of the mold and bacteria occurred gradually, the appellate court nonetheless concluded that its manifestation was "sudden and calamitous," damaging the homeowners' personal property and requiring them to flee their home or experience the likelihood of personal injury. Because the occurrence was sufficiently sudden and calamitous to place it under the exception to the economic loss rule for property damage resulting from a sudden or dangerous occurrence, the appellate court allowed recovery in tort for the loss to the homeowners' personal property. However, as to the damages accruing from the loss of the home, the appellate court barred recovery in tort, reasoning that it was a "classic" economic loss. This author submits that the *Reinke* decision is inconsistent with *Moorman* and its progeny, which establish that a tort claim which alleges economic loss in *combination* with non-economic loss (personal injury or property damage) is not barred by the economic loss doctrine.[56]

The premise behind the economic loss doctrine is that tort law is appropriately suited for personal injury or property damage resulting from a sudden or dangerous occurrence, whereas, contract and warranty law are appropriately suited for loss relating to a purchaser's disappointed expectations when a defect renders a product (which can be a home under Illinois law) inferior or unable adequately to perform its intended function. With respect to warranty law, the Illinois Supreme Court held in *Peterson v. Hubschman Construction Co.*[57] that, in the sale of a new house by a builder-vendor, there is an implied warranty of habitability which will support an action against the builder-vendor by the original purchaser.[58] To establish a cause of action for breach of the implied warranty of habitability, the plaintiff must plead and prove that the home had a latent defect caused by improper design, material, or workmanship in its construction which rendered the property unsuitable for use as a home. A latent defect "is one which, in the circumstances of the case, would not have been discovered by the exercise of ordinary and reasonable care."[59] The remedy for breach of the implied warranty of habitability is rescission, if the defects were discovered before the conveyance to the purchasers had been completed, or damages measured by the cost of correcting the defective conditions.[60]

Since *Peterson*, the implied warranty of habitability has been extended by Illinois courts to include: (1) actions against a developer-vendor of a new condominium;[61] (2) actions against a builder or developer-vendor by subsequent purchasers, provided the latent defects manifest themselves within a reasonable time after the purchase of the home;[62] (3) actions against subcontractors of a builder-vendor where the builder-vendor has been dissolved as an entity and is insolvent;[63] (4) actions by subsequent purchasers against builders that construct significant structural additions to an existing residence;[64] and (5) actions against a developer/seller for latent defects in improved land.[65]

A. Standard for Admissibility of Experts

The success of a mold-related personal injury claim usually comes down to the admissibility of expert testimony with respect to causation of illness and injury by mold. In Illinois, the admissibility is governed by what is known as the *Frye*[66] standard, which standard dictates that scientific evidence is admissible at trial only if the methodology or scientific principle upon which the opinion is based is sufficiently established to have gained general acceptance in the particular field in which it belongs. In this context, "general acceptance" does not mean universal acceptance, and it does not require that the methodology in question be accepted by unanimity, consensus, or even a majority of experts. Instead, it is sufficient that the underlying method used to generate an expert's opinion is reasonably relied upon by experts in the relevant field. Significantly, the *Frye* test applies only to "new" or "novel" scientific methodologies.[67] There is no reported appellate decision in Illinois regarding the admissibility of expert medical testimony in mold-related personal injury cases.

B. Statutes of Limitations and Repose

In Illinois, any mold-related personal injury or property damage action, whether based upon tort, contract, or otherwise,[68] arising out of an act or omission in the design, planning, supervision, observation, or management of construction, or construction of an improvement to real property, must be commenced within four years from the time the person bringing the action knew or should reasonably have known of such act or omission.[69] Additionally, any mold-related personal injury or property damage action not brought with ten years of an act or omission in the design, planning, supervision, observation, or management of construction, or construction of an improvement to real property is barred, unless the act or omission is discovered prior to the expiration of the ten-year period of repose, in which case the action must be brought within four years from the date of discovery.[70]

The limitation and repose periods articulated above do not apply to bar any action against a defendant who has expressly warranted or promised the improvement to real property for a longer period.[71] However, many new construction contracts expressly disclaim the implied warranty of habitability or limit the period of its express warranty to one year from the date of closing. A disclaimer is a bar to the cause of action for breach of the implied warranty of habitability if: (1) it references the implied warranty of habitability by name; (2) it is a conspicuous provision which fully discloses the consequences of its inclusion; and (3) the agreement of the parties in fact included the disclaimer.[72]

10.5 Third-Party Liability Insurance

A third-party liability insurance policy provides coverage for the insured's legal liability to another arising from claims resulting in "bodily injury" or "property damage" that occur during the policy period. Liability coverage issues involving mold-related bodily injury or property damage caused by water or moisture intrusion resulting from faulty workmanship or defective construction include whether the "bodily injury" or "property damage" was caused by an "occurrence" and whether the injury or damage occurred during the policy period.

"Occurrence" is typically defined in liability insurance policies as "an accident, including continuous or repeated exposure to substantially the same general harmful conditions." The term "accident" is usually an undefined term. The dictionary definition of "accident" is "an event or condition occurring by chance or arising from unknown or remote causes."[73] Black's Law Dictionary defines "accident" as follows: "The word 'accident,' in accident policies, means an event which takes place without one's foresight or expectation. A result, though unexpected, is not an accident; the means or cause must be accidental."[74]

Illinois courts have concluded that damage caused by faulty workmanship or defective construction standing alone is not an "occurrence."[75] While faulty workmanship or defective construction standing along may not be an occurrence under a liability policy, an accident caused by faulty workmanship or defective construction is a covered occurrence. Stated otherwise, although a liability policy may not provide coverage for faulty workmanship that damages only the resulting work product, if faulty workmanship causes bodily injury or property damage to something other than the insured's work product, an unintended and unexpected event has occurred, and coverage exists.[76]

Not only must there by an "occurrence," general liability insurance policies require that bodily injury or property damage occur during the policy period. Simply stated, the insurance policy in effect at the time injury or damage occurs is the policy that "triggers" coverage, even if a claim is not made until after the policy expires. *The Board of Education* of *Township High School District No. 211 v. International Insurance Co.*, discussed previously, supports adoption of the equitable continuous trigger to determine the timing of mold damage resulting from water intrusion caused by faulty workmanship or defective construction, beginning with the initial water event that caused the ensuing mold damage and ending when the moldy building materials are removed.

10.6 Mold Legislation

In June 2003, the 93rd General Assembly of the State of Illinois passed House Joint Resolution 12. This Resolution created the Joint Task Force on Mold in Indoor Environments. In creating this Joint Task Force, the General Assembly recognized that:

- The presence of mold in indoor environments presents a public health risk to the citizens of Illinois;

- Mold in schools, places of employment, and homes has been shown to adversely affect the health of Illinois' children and senior citizens; and
- The adverse health effects of exposure to molds on the general population and the specific effects of mold on certain subpopulations, including infants, children, the elderly, pregnant women, asthmatics, allergic individuals, immune-comprised individuals, and others are resulting in illness and increased medical costs.

The purpose of the Joint Task Force is "examining the mold issue in Illinois and making recommendations to the General Assembly pertaining to regulation of mold in indoor environments in Illinois."

In February, 2004, the 93rd General Assembly of the State of Illinois introduced the Toxic and Pathogenic Mold Protection Act (the "Toxic Mold Act"). The Toxic Mold Act, which has yet to become law, requires the Illinois Department of Public Health to: (1) consider adopting permissible exposure limits for molds; (2) adopt standards for reducing the occurrence of mold contamination in indoor environments; (3) adopt mold identification guidelines; and (4) develop mold abatement standards. The Toxic Mold Act also requires a seller of residential, commercial, or industrial real property to disclose to prospective buyers the existence of mold in the indoor environment. Finally, the Toxic Mold Act authorizes enforcement of the Illinois Department of Public Health's standards and guidelines by local health authorities and others.

In December, 2004, the Joint Task Force issued its final report of "Mold in Indoor Environments." The report summarized the activities of the Task Force and made various recommendations, including (1) that parties providing mold remediation services in residential, public, and commercial buildings in Illinois be required to register with the Illinois Department of Public Health and provide proof of financial responsibility and (2) that laboratories performing tests to confirm mold contamination be certified by the American Industrial Hygiene Association using nationally recognized accreditation standards set by the Environmental Microbiology Laboratory Accreditation Program.

The 95th General Assembly of the State of Illinois enacted the Mold Remediation Registration Act ("Registration Act"), effective January 1, 2008[77]. The General Assembly found that:

(1) Excessive indoor dampness in buildings is a widespread problem that warrants action at the local, State, and national levels.

(2) Because of the public's concern about the possible public health effects of exposure to mold in buildings, as well as the effects on workers per-

forming remediation work, and the costs of remediation for the property owner, there is a need to identify parties performing mold remediation in the State.

(3) Because there is a need to reduce moisture that fosters mold formation in buildings, the State should review current State building codes to ensure that they do not foster mold.

(4) Parties providing mold remediation services in residential, public, and commercial buildings in Illinois should be required to register with the State and provide proof of financial responsibility.

(5) Laboratories performing tests to confirm mold contamination in buildings should be certified by the American Industrial Hygiene Association using nationally recognized accreditation standards set under the Environmental Microbiology Laboratory Accreditation Program.

Section 15 of the Registration Act requires the Department of Public Health to "report to the Environment and Energy Committees of the House of Representatives and the Senate, on an annual basis, concerning the implementation of any federal regulations that establish: (1) scientific evidence concerning any health effects associated with fungi, bacteria, and their byproducts in indoor environments including any indoor air quality standard; and (2) standards for the training, certification, and licensing of parties providing mold remediation services in residential, public, and commercial buildings."

Section 20 of the Registration Act also authorizes the Department of Public Health to "adopt rules, under the Illinois Administrative Procedure Act, to implement a program establishing procedures for parties that provide mold remediation services to register with the State and provide evidence of financial responsibility."

Endnotes

1. *Michael and Juanita Jordan v. STO Corporation, et al.*, Circuit Court of Cook County, Illinois No. 04 L 3097. The essence of the lawsuit is that the STO exterior insulation and finish system ("EIFS") cladding applied to the Jordans' home failed to provide for the collection and redirection of foreseeable water that intrudes behind the cladding; instead, the EIFS traps water between the cladding, the structural components, and interior finishes of building walls and, as a consequence, results in deterioration to structural components, ensuing damage to interior finishes and other building com-

ponents, and the growth and proliferation of toxic microbial contamination throughout the home. The complaint seeks to recover the cost to remove and to replace the EIFS cladding under contract and warranty theories.

2. According to the National Association of Mutual Insurance Companies, "[w]hen it comes to the insurance industry, mold is not part of the standard insurance policy and is covered only if it's a direct result of a covered peril" (www.moldupdate.com). MoldUpdate.com, which is owned and operated by the National Association of Mutual Insurance Companies, is a site where those interested in the issue of mold can come for current news, education, scientific links, litigation updates, state legislation, and matters of mold as it relates to the insurance industry.

3. 338 Ill. App. 3d 266 (2008).

4. *See* Illinois Department of Insurance Bulletin CB#2002-07, dated December 5, 2002.

5. 215 ILL. COMP. STAT. 5/397 (2006); 50 Ill Adm. Code § 2301.100 (effective March 17, 1961).

6. *Lundquist v. Allstate Insurance Co.*, 314 Ill.App.3d 240 (2000).

7. Standard Fire Policy, Insuring Clause.

8. Standard Fire Policy, Lines 14-24.

9. Mold contamination has been held to constitute a "physical" loss despite the fact that mold spores may not be tangible or perceptible by the naked eye. See *Sullivan v. Standard Fire Insurance Co.*, 2008 WL 361141 (Del. Supr. August 29, 2007); *Fisher v. Certain Interested Underwriters*, 930 So.2d 756 (4th DCA Fla. 2006); *Prudential Property Casualty Insurance Co. v. Lillard-Roberts*, 2002 WL 31495830 (D.Or. June 18, 2002); *Columbiaknit, Inc. v. Affiliated FM Insurance Co.*, 1999 WL 619100 (D.Or. August 4, 1999).

10. In *Wallis v. Country Mutual Insurance Co.*, 309 Ill.App.3d 566, 570 (2000), the appellate court articulated the respective burdens of proof in a lawsuit for an insurer's failure to pay a claim under an all-risk insurance policy. The insured's burden is to establish (1) that a loss occurred, (2) that the loss resulted from a fortuitous event, and (3) that an all-risk policy covering the insured property was in effect at the time of loss. Once an insured establishes a *prima facie* case, the burden then shifts to the insurer to show that the loss resulted from a peril expressly excluded from coverage.

11. 308 Ill. App. 3d 597 (1999).

12. 268 Ill. App. 3d 598 (1994).

13. A variety of contaminating conditions have been held to constitute physical loss of or damage to property. *See, e.g., Matzner v. Seaco Insurance Co.,* *1*998 WL 566658 (Mass.Super. Aug. 12, 1998) (carbon monoxide contamination); *Sentinel Mgmt. Co. v. Hew Hampshire Insurance Co.,* 563 N.W.2d 296 (Minn. App. 1997) (asbestos contamination); *Farmers Insurance Co. of Oregon v. Trutunich,* 858 P.2d 1332 (1993) (odors from illegal methamphetamine cooking); *Western Fire Insurance Co. v. First Presbyterian Church,* 437 P.2d 52 (Colo. 1968) (gasoline accumulation).

14. 177 Ill.2d 473 (1997).

15. *See also Kim v. State Farm Fire and Casualty Co.,* 312 Ill.App.3d 770 (2000).

16. *Hardware Wholesaler, Inc. v. Heath,* 10 Ill.App.3d 337, 343 (1973). *See also Black's Law Dictionary* 1660 (6th ed. 1990).

17. "Illinois Insurance Facts Mold Facts and Homeowners Insurance," dated December, 2002 *at* http://www.ins.state.il.us/HomeInsurance/Mold.htm.

18. *Allstate Insurance Co. v. Davenport,* 309 Ill.App.3d 750, 754 (1999) (construing the term "continuously" under an "any occupation" disability provision of an automobile insurance policy liberally in favor of the insured).

19. 292 Ill.App.3d 14, 21 (1997).

20. This is the interpretation advanced by the Property Loss Research Bureau ("PLRB"), which is a recognized resource in the insurance industry for *insurers* in interpreting policy provisions. *See* PLRB Question & Answer Reference Service 146.1, "Interior Water Damage" (July, 1996). *See also Phillips v. United Services Automobile Association,* 146 S.W.3d 629 (Tenn. Ct. App. 2004); *Arnold v. Cincinnati Insurance Co.,* 276 Wis.2d 762 (Wis. App. 2004); *Eckstein v. Cincinnati Insurance Co.,* 469 F.Supp.2d 444 (W.D. Ky. 2007); *Dawson Farms, L.L.C. v. Millers Mutual Fire Insurance Co.,* 794 So.2d 949 (La. App. 2001); *Buscher v. Economy Premier Assurance Co.,* 2006 WL 268781 (D. Minn. February 1, 2006); *Smith v. Westfield Insurance Co.,* 2007 WL 1740816 (E.D. Pa. June 15, 2007); *Tento International, Inc. v. State Farm Fire and Casualty Co.,* 222 F.3d 660 (9th Cir. 2000); and *Blaine Construction Corp. v. Insurance Co. of North America,* 171 F.3d 343 (6th Cir. 1999).

21. 2008 U.S. Dist. Lexis 35725 (N.D. Ill.).

22. No. 02 C 5193, 2003 WL 21196261 (N.D. Ill. May 15, 2003).

23. 815 ILL. COMP. STAT. 505/2 (2006).

24. *Washington Courte Condominium Association-Four v. Washington-Golf Corp.*, 267 Ill.App.3d 790 (1994).

25. *American Buyers Club of Mt. Vernon, Illinois, Inc. v. Honecker,* 46 Ill.App.3d 252, 257 (1977).

26. *Connick v. Suzuki Motor Co. Ltd.*, 174 Ill.2d. 482, 501 (1977); *Siegel v. Levy Organization Development Co., Inc.*, 153 Ill.2d 534 (1997).

27. *See Shannon v. Boise Cascade Corp.*, 208 Ill.2d 517 (2004). In that case, homeowners failed to establish that a composite siding manufacturer's deceptive advertising was a proximate cause of their damages under the Consumer Fraud Act because there was no allegation that the homeowners were actually deceived by the manufacturer's allegedly deceptive advertising, or that product literature had deceived a particular builder, architect, or contractor, resulting in installation of defective siding on the homes. *See also Commonwealth Insurance Co. v. Stone Container Corp.*, No. 99 C 8471, 2001 WL 477151 (N.D. Ill. May 3, 2001) and *Industrial Enclosure Corp. v. Northern Insurance Corp. of New York,* No. 97 C 6850, 1998 WL 852845 (N.D. Ill. Nov. 30, 1998).

28. This is the Farmers Insurance Group marketing slogan, which is set forth in its website materials at http://www.farmersinsurance.com/.

29. *Cramer v. Insurance Exchange Agency,* 174 Ill.2d 513, 516 (1996); *see also Richardson v. Illinois Power Co.*, 217 Ill.App.3d 708, 715 (1991) ("The legislature intended to provide a remedy to an insured who encounters unnecessary difficulties when an insurer withholds policy benefits."); *Myrda v. Coronet Insurance Co.*, 221 Ill.App.3d 482, 491 (1991) ("[S]ection 155 of the Code is intended to aid the insured and to encourage insurers from profiting by their superior financial positions while delaying in the payment of contractual obligations."); *McGee v. State Farm Fire and Casualty Co.*, 315 Ill.App.3d 673, 681 (2000) ("The attorney fees, costs, and limited penalty provisions of section 155 are intended to make suits by policyholders economically feasible and punish insurance companies for misconduct.").

30. 215 ILL.COMP.STAT. 5/155 (2006).

31. *Emerson v. American Bankers Insurance Co.*, 223 Ill.App.3d 929, 936 (1992).

32. *Mohr v. Dix Mutual Country Fire Insurance Co.*, 143 Ill.App.3d 989, 998-99 (1986).

33. 50 Ill. Adm. Code §919.50. Illinois administrative rules and regulations have the force and effect of law. *See Comito v. Police Board of City of Chicago*, 317 Ill.App.3d 677, 691 (2000). Section 919.20(b) states that the purpose of Part 919 of the Department of Insurance Regulations "is to set forth minimum standards for the investigation and disposition of claims arising under contracts and certificates issued to residents of Illinois." 50 Ill. Adm. Code §919.20(b).

34. 50 Ill. Adm. Code §919.80(d)(7)(B).

35. 50 Ill. Adm. Code §919.

36. 215 ILL. COMP. STAT. 5/154.6(a) (2006).

37. 215 ILL. COMP. STAT. 5/154.6(d) (2006); 50 Ill. Adm. Code §919.50(a)(1).

38. 50 Ill. Adm. Code §919.50(a)(1). *See also Millers Mutual Insurance Association of Ill. v. House*, 286 Ill.App.3d 378 (1997).

39. 50 Ill. Adm. Code §919.40.

40. 215 ILL. COMP. STAT. 5/154.6(h) (2006).

41. *Industrial Enclosure Corp. v. Northern Insurance Corp. of New York,* 1998 WL 852845 (N.D. Ill. November 25, 1998); *Mobil Oil Corp. v. Maryland Casualty Co.,* 288 Ill. App. 3d 743 (1997). *See also Aguilera v. Pacific Insurance Co., Ltd.,* 1996 WL 14043 (N.D. Ill. January 11, 1996).

42. Although sections 154.5 and 154.6 of the Illinois Insurance Code and Part 919 of Title 50 of the Illinois Administrative Code do not provide a basis for a private cause of action, they nevertheless are part of the *totality of the circumstances* that the court can consider in determining whether an insurer acted unreasonably and vexatiously in its handling of the insured's claim. (*See, e.g., Mathis v. Lumbermen's Mutual Casualty Co.,* 354 Ill. App. 3d 854, 860 (5th Dist. 2004) ("While the violation of section 919.80(d)(8)(C) [of Part 919 of the Illinois Administrative Code] does not provide a basis for a private cause of action, the violation of the regulation is a fact that a court

can consider in determining whether an insurer waived a time limitation provision when enforcement of the provision would be unjust, inequitable, and unconscionable.").) In that regard, courts regularly admit in insurance "bad faith" actions evidence of an insurer's violation of a state's unfair insurance claims practices act and insurance regulations. *See Certainteed Corp. v. Fed. Insurance Co.*, 913 F. Supp. 351, 360-61 (E.D. Pa. 1995); *Spray Gould & Bowers v. Associated International Insurance Co.*, 84 Cal. Rptr. 2d 552, 557-559 (Cal. App. 1999); *Ingalls v. Paul Revere Life Insurance Group.*, 561 N.W.2d 273, 281-82 (N.D. 1997).

43. *Farmers Automobile Insurance Association v. Janusick,* 30 Ill.App.2d 352 (1961).

44. *See, e.g., New Park Forest Associates II v. Rogers Enterprises, Inc.*, 195 Ill. App.3d 757 (1990).

45. *Lamka v. Illinois Farmers Insurance Co.*, Circuit Court of Cook County, Illinois No. 02 CH 4388; *Cianci v. Safeco Insurance Co. of Illinois*, Circuit Court of Cook County, Illinois No. 02 CH 4670.

46. 384 Ill. App. 3d 207 (2008).

47. 765 ILL. COMP. STAT. 77/20 (2006).

48. 765 ILL. COMP. STAT. 77/35 (2006).

49. 765 ILL. COMP. STAT. 77/25 (2006).

50. 345 Ill. App. 3d 547 (2003).

51. 91 Ill.2d 69 (1982).

52. 131 Ill.2d 428 (1989).

53. *Id.* at 446.

54. 319 F.3d 921 (7th Cir. 2003).

55. 349 Ill. App. 3d 178 (2004).

56. *See In re Chicago Flood Litigation*, 176 Ill.2d 179, 201 (1997) ("Absent injury to a plaintiff's person or property, a claim presents an economic loss not recoverable in tort."); *Mars, Inc. v. Heritage Builders of Effingham, Inc.*, 327

Ill.App.3d 346,351 (2002) ("A plaintiff may still recover economic damages in tort when the plaintiff has sustained a personal injury or property damage as a result of a sudden or dangerous occurrence."); *Great Oak, L.L.C. v. Begley Co.*, 2003 WL 880994 (N.D. Ill. March 5, 2003) ("[T]he pleadings sufficiently allege damage to property to overcome the *Moorman* doctrine. Although it appears that the bulk of Plaintiff's damages are in the nature of economic losses, the complaint alleges damages to Plaintiff's property as well as clean up damages and future damages.") *See also Daanen & Janssen, Inc. v. Cedarapids, Inc.*, 216 Wis.2d 395, 573 N.W.2d 842, 845 (1998) ("The economic loss doctrine, however, does not bar a commercial purchaser's claim based on personal injury or damage to property other than the product, or economic loss claims that are alleged in combination with noneconomic losses.").

57. 76 Ill.2d 31 (1979).

58. The implied warranty of habitability also applies to all leases of residential real estate. *Glasoe v. Trinkle*, 107 Ill.2d 1 (1985). In order to assert a claim for a landlord's breach of the implied warranty of habitability, a tenant must show either that she gave notice of the alleged defect to the landlord or that the landlord had knowledge of the alleged defect. *Abram v. Lithman*, 150 Ill.App.3d 174 (1986). The remedy for a landlord's breach of the implied warranty is the deterioration in the benefits from the lease rather than for personal injuries or property damage. *Auburn v. Amoco Oil Co.*, 106 Ill. App.3d 60 (1982).

59. *Ollivier v. Alden, 262 Ill.App.3d 190, 197 (1994).*

60. *Park v. Sohn,* 89 Ill.2d 453 (1982).

61. *Tassan v. United Development Co.,* 88 Ill.App.3d 581 (1980).

62. *Redarowicz v. Ohlendorf,* 92 Ill.2d 171 (1982).

63. *Minton v. Richards Group of Chicago,* 116 Ill.App.3d 852 (1983). Where a Plaintiff timely files an action against a general contractor for faults or defects in construction, and the general contractor subsequently becomes insolvent allowing the Plaintiff to bring an action against a subcontractor for breach of implied warranty of habitability under *Minton*, the statute of limitations is triggered at the time that the Plaintiff knew or reasonably should have known of the general contractor's insolvency. *Dearlove Cove Condominiums v. Kin Construction Co., Inc.*, 180 Ill.App.3d 437 (1989).

64. *VonHoldt v. Barba & Barba Construction, Inc.*, 175 Ill.2d 426 (1997). In this case, the Illinois Supreme Court also held that the reasonable time for bringing a cause of action under the "reasonable time" standard of *Redarowicz* begins with the act or omission causing the defect rather than the date on which the subsequent purchaser takes title to the property.

65. *Overton v. Kingsbrooke Development, Inc.*, 338 Ill. App. 3d 321 (2003).

66. *Frye v. United States*, 293 F.1013 (D.C. Cir. 1923).

67. *Donaldson v. Central Illinois Public Service Co.*, 199 Ill.2d 63 (2002). In *In re commitment of Stephen E. Simons*, 213 Ill.2d 523 (2004), the Illinois Supreme Court adopted a dual standard of review with respect to the trial court's admission of expert scientific testimony. The decision as to whether an expert scientific witness is qualified to testify in a subject area, and whether the proffered testimony is relevant in a particular case, remains in the sound discretion of the trial court. The trial court's *Frye* analysis, however, is subject to *de novo* review. In conducting such *de novo* review, the reviewing court may consider not only the trial court record but also, where appropriate, sources outside the record, including legal and scientific articles, as well as court opinions from other jurisdictions.

68. Several Illinois courts have applied section 13-214 of the Illinois Code of Civil Procedure to actions against persons involved in construction-related activities based on allegations of the breach of the implied warranty of habitability. *See, e.g., Eickmeyer v. Blietz Organization, Inc.*, 284 Ill.App.3d 134 (1996); *Schleyhahn v. Cole*, 178 Ill.App.3d 111 (1989); *Zielinski v. Miller*, 277 Ill.App.3d 735 (1995).

69. 735 ILL. COMP. STAT. 5/13-214 (a) (2006).

70. 735 ILL. COMP. STAT. 5/13-214 (b) (2006). The time of accrual under this section governing a purchaser's suit against a builder to recover for latent defects in the purchaser's new house begins from the date the purchaser takes possession of the house. *See Andreoli v. John Henry Homes, Inc.*, 297 Ill.App.3d 151 (1998).

71. 735 ILL. COMP. STAT. 5/13-214 (d) (2006).

72. In *Board of Managers of Chestnut Hills Condominium Association v. Pasquinelli*, 354 Ill.App.3d 749 (2004), the disclaimer was found to be invalid because the record in the case did not show an effective waiver of the im-

plied warranty of habitability. There was no evidence that the builder-vendor called the purchasers' attention to the disclaimer provision, or instructed the purchasers to specifically initial the provision. The provision also failed to set forth the consequences of the waiver of the implied warranty of habitability. In *Board of Managers of the Village Centre Condominium Association, Inc. v. Wilmette Partners,* 198 Ill.2d 132 (2001), the disclaimer also was found to be invalid because it did not refer to the implied warranty of habitability by name. In *Breckenridge v. Cambridge Homes, Inc.*, 246 Ill.App.3d 810 (1993), the appellate court found the disclaimer to be valid because it was in a conspicuous location, in large-size and bold print, and in plain language. The Plaintiffs also initialed the disclaimer provision indicating that they had accepted its terms.

73. Webster's Third New International Dictionary of the English Language 11 (2002).

74. Black's Law Dictionary 15 (7th ed. 1999).

75. *American Fire & Casualty Co. v. Broeren Russo Construction, Inc.*, 54 F.Supp.2d 842 (C.D. Ill. 1999); *Bituminous Casualty Corp. v. Gust K. Newberg Construction Co.*, 218 Ill.App.3d 956 (1991).

76. *Pekin Insurance Co. v. Richard Marker Assoc., Inc.*, 289 Ill. App. 3d 819 (1997)

77. 410 ILL. COMP. STAT. 105/1 (2006).

Chapter 11

An Overview of Toxic Mold Litigation in Indiana

Abigail A. Clapp, Esq. and Matthew Levinstein

Synopsis

11.1 Introduction

Mold is resilient, causes property damage, and may affect our health—all issues that make mold perfect fodder for the media, and for lawyers. Mold-related litigation has spread across the country, quashing the belief that mold problems arise only in perpetually warm and humid regions. While researchers have not conclusively established causality between mold and bodily injury, evidence suggesting that mold causes bodily harm may increase attorney interest in mold-related litigation.

Much of Indiana's mold case law involves insurance. But, as more insurance companies exclude mold damage from their policies, contractors and property owners may see an increase in mold-related lawsuits.

Indiana lawyers should have an understanding of the causes of action and defenses that may apply to mold litigation under Indiana law. While Indiana's mold case law is undeveloped, it is likely that the following principles of Indiana law will apply in the mold context.

11.2 Potential Causes of Action

Plaintiffs may select from a variety of claims when filing a mold-related lawsuit. Such claims include, but are not limited to: negligence, breach of contract, breach of implied warranties, and fraud.[1] This chapter will focus on these four claims because they are the most applicable to litigation involving real property.

A. Negligence

A plaintiff must prove three elements to establish a *prima facie* case of negligence under Indiana law. First, plaintiff must establish that the defendant owes plaintiff a duty.[2] Second, the defendant must have breached that duty by engaging in conduct that falls below the applicable standard of care.[3] Finally, plaintiff must establish that the breach proximately caused an actual injury to the plaintiff.[4]

The precise scope of the duty owed by a defendant will vary depending upon the type of defendant, such as contractors, subcontractors, architects, supply manufacturers, and property owners. In many cases, plaintiffs will name defendants in more than one of these categories. Furthermore, given the recent abrogation of the doctrine of *caveat emptor* and the concept of privity under Indiana law, there are now more potential mold defendants for plaintiffs to sue.

1. Sellers of real estate

Until recently, the concept of *caveat emptor*, meaning "let the buyer beware," governed real property sales in Indiana. Under *caveat emptor*, if no special relationship existed between the buyer and the seller, the seller had no duty to disclose any information regarding the condition of the property.[5] But once the buyer inquired about a particular aspect of the property, a special relationship developed that obligated the seller to disclose any problems related to the buyer's inquiry.[6]

Indiana moved away from *caveat emptor* through case law and legislation. Under the more recent standard, a real estate broker is obliged to inform a potential buyer of known, latent defects in a property.[7] Thus, a professional seller of real estate will likely have the duty to inform a potential buyer about a property's latent mold damage. If the seller has recently remedied existing mold damage, it will be in the seller's best interest (or that of his real estate broker) to disclose such mold problems to the buyer given mold's propensity to recur.

Recently, Indiana passed a law requiring sellers of one- to four-unit residential properties to complete a Disclosure Form.[8] The Disclosure Form comprises a list of common household components and systems,[9] and requires sellers to affirmatively indicate which components or systems the house has and which, if any, are defective.[10] The seller must complete the Disclosure Form and the buyer must sign it before the seller can enforce the sale against the buyer.[11] One question on the Disclosure Form asks, "Have there been or are there any hazardous conditions on the property, such as...mold...?"[12]

The Disclosure Form provides that the information furnished is for "disclosure only and is not intended to be a part of any contract between the buyer and the owner,"[13] and Section 32-21-5-9 of the Indiana Code further states that the "disclosure form is not a warranty by the owner." Because the Disclosure Form is not part of the contract and is not a warranty, it appears that a buyer alleging that the seller failed to disclose latent defects can look to tort law for a remedy. Thus, the erosion of *caveat emptor* provides plaintiffs with at least two additional claims in the context of mold litigation: a potential negligence claim against a professional seller of real estate for failing to disclose known, latent defects, and a potential fraud claim against a seller for any intentional misrepresentations made on her Disclosure Form.

2. Builders

Home buyers often sue builders for construction defects that allow moisture or water to leak into a property, facilitating mold growth. Mold can damage a variety of housing components, such as the building envelope, windows, and roof.

Until recently, a builder owed no duty of care to an injured third party when an injury occurred after the property owner accepted the builder's work.[14] However, in *Peters v. Forster*, the Indiana Supreme Court in 2004 rejected the former "Acceptance Rule" in favor of the "Modern Rule" or "Foreseeability Doctrine."[15] Now, builders owe a duty of care to third parties not in privity with the builder even after the property owner accepts the builder's work where the work, if negligently completed, is reasonably certain to endanger such third parties.[16] The third-party plaintiff still must establish the elements of negligence before the builder is held liable.[17]

Indiana has two similar statutes upon which liability for certain types of defects may be based for new home builders and home improvement contractors.[18] The relevant portions of these acts provide for: (a) a two-year warranty that a new home or home improvement is free from material defects in workmanship; (2) a two-year warranty that a new home or home improvement is free from defects caused by the faulty installation of plumbing, electrical, heating, cooling, and ventilation systems; (3) a four-year warranty that a new home or home improvement is free from defects caused by defective materials or faulty workmanship for roofing work; and (4) a ten-year warranty that a new home or home improvement is free from major structural defects.[19]

B. Breach of Contract

Plaintiffs may also file breach of contract claims in the context of mold lawsuits. To prove a breach of contract, an Indiana plaintiff must prove that the defendant (1) damaged the plaintiff by (2) breaching (3) an existing, valid contract.[20] For instance, a property owner can sue for construction defects that cause mold growth when the presence of such defects constitutes a breach of the *express* contract between the builder and the owner.[21]

C. Breach of Implied Warranties

An Indiana plaintiff may also sue a defendant for breach of one or more of the following implied warranties: (1) good workmanship, (2) habitability, and (3) quiet enjoyment.

1. Implied warranty of good workmanship

An Indiana property owner may sue a builder for violation of the implied warranty of good workmanship. Under the common law, a builder has an "implied duty to do the work skillfully, carefully, and in a workmanlike manner."[22] Thus, a builder's failure to complete the work in a workmanlike manner "is a breach of contract as well as a tort."[23]

2. Implied warranty of habitability

Mold growth resulting from a building defect may affect a property's habitability. While *caveat emptor* previously applied to the sale of new homes, the Indiana Supreme Court discarded the concept in favor of an implied warranty of fitness for human habitation on new home sales.[24] The implied warranty of habitability was originally limited to new purchasers, but the Supreme Court eventually extended the warranty to include subsequent purchasers.[25] The Indiana Court of Appeals limited the warranty to "builder-vendors" shortly thereafter.[26]

Breaching the implied warranty of habitability "does not require that the dwelling be rendered totally uninhabitable.... Rather, breach of the warranty is established by proof of a defect of a nature which substantially impairs the enjoyment of the residence."[27]

Indiana law does not universally impose a warranty of habitability in a landlord-tenant relationship.[28] However, the warranty may derive from an express or implied agreement between the landlord and tenant.[29]

3. Implied warranty of quiet enjoyment

Landlord-tenant claims often implicate the implied warranty of quiet enjoyment. Among other things, the warranty protects a lessee's possessory interest in the use and enjoyment of the leased premises.[30] Thus, any act or omission by the landlord that affects the "beneficial use and enjoyment" of the property may constitute a breach of the warranty.[31]

If the landlord interferes with a tenant's possession *and* beneficial use and enjoyment of any part of the leased property, the tenant may withhold rent payments.[32] Or, if the landlord merely interferes with the tenant's use and enjoyment, but not with the tenant's possessory rights, the tenant may abandon the property and avoid fulfilling its lease obligations.[33]

D. Fraud

When property owners, builders, subcontractors, or real estate professionals intentionally[34] misrepresent the severity or existence of a mold-related defect, fraud claims will likely follow. Under Indiana law, "[t]o constitute a valid claim for fraud the party must prove there was a material misrepresentation of past or existing facts made with knowledge or reckless ignorance of its falsity, and the misrepresentation caused reliance to the detriment of the person relying upon it."[35] A buyer may sue a seller for fraud if he fails to accurately complete a Disclosure Form as required by IND. CODE § 32-21-5.[36]

The Indiana Deceptive Consumer Sales Act may provide an additional claim for a plaintiff who feels deceived by a property owner, builder, or real estate professional. According to the Act, any "seller, lessor, assignor, or other person who regularly engages in or solicits consumer transactions," who commits a "deceptive act," may be liable for up to three times the amount of actual damages suffered by the buyer.[37] The Act expressly includes the sale of real property as a "consumer transaction."[38]

E. Workers' Compensation

When an employee is exposed to mold at work, employers become susceptible to mold-related liability. Even though experts have not yet proved a direct, causal connection between mold exposure and bodily harm, employees may file workers' compensation claims alleging injuries from mold exposure in the workplace. Under Indiana's Workers' Compensation Statute, an employee entitled to compensation may not bring a common-law action for the same injury to obtain additional compensation.[39] But, the Workers' Compensation Act compensates for accidental employment-related injuries, when neither party intended for the injury to occur.[40] Thus, for injuries resulting from an employer's intentional torts, an employee can avoid the Workers' Compensation Statute's exclusivity of remedies provision.[41] An employer would therefore be wise to remediate any mold growth brought to its attention to avoid liability for intentional torts.

11.3 Class Actions

Mold litigation lawsuits often involve many similarly-situated plaintiffs. For example, home purchasers may file mold lawsuits against a common builder, and multiple tenants in a large apartment complex or commercial building may all experience mold growth problems and sue the property owner. In these situations, among others, plaintiffs may seek class certification. In Indiana, a plaintiff class must meet four criteria to be eligible for class certification: (a) the size of the class must make joinder impractical, (b) the class must share common questions of law or fact, (c) the claims or defenses of the representative party must be typical of the entire class, and (d) the representative party must adequately represent the class.[42]

11.4 Potential Defenses

A. Statute of Repose

A statute of limitations sets a time limit from the accrual of a cause of action within which a claimant must bring the cause of action.[43] A statute of repose sets a time limit from the occurrence of a real-world event—such as, for example, the completion of construction of a house—within which a claimant must bring a cause of action.[44] Indiana has a statute of repose for actions to recover for property damage or personal injury arising out of a "deficiency in the design, planning, supervision, construction, or observation of construction of an improvement to real property."[45]

Any Indiana plaintiff alleging such a deficiency must bring her action within ten years of "substantial completion of the improvement."[46] But, if the plaintiff alleges a design flaw, she must also file suit within 12 years of "the completion and submission of plans and specifications to the owner."[47] Thus, in the case of an alleged design flaw, if the designer submitted completed plans to the plaintiff more than two years before the "substantial completion" of the improvement, the plaintiff must bring the action within 12 years of the submission of the completed plans. Otherwise, the plaintiff must file suit within ten years of substantial completion of the improvement.

Manufacturers and sellers of fungible products that contractors subsequently use in an improvement project generally cannot take advantage of the real property improvement statute of repose.[48] "[C]ourts in Indiana treat an action against a manufacturer of a product as products liability actions even if the product ultimately becomes a part of an improvement to real estate."[49] The real estate improvement statute of repose protects only those entities that are "intimately involved in designing, planning, constructing, or supervising the construction of an improvement to a particular piece of real estate."[50]

Potential mold litigation plaintiffs should routinely inspect their properties for mold following an improvement project. Because mold growth is often a slow process, early detection will preclude an opposing party from asserting the Indiana real estate improvement statute of repose to preclude liability.

B. Spoliation of Evidence

Spoliation is "[t]he intentional destruction, mutilation, alteration, or concealment of evidence."[51] Toxic mold litigation presents unique spoliation concerns. Tenants of mold-infested properties usually want it removed immediately given the tendency of mold to redevelop if not properly remedied. However, a party removing mold from a property should not inadvertently destroy relevant evidence in its haste to remedy the problem. Instead, the party should give all other parties an opportunity to examine or take physical evidence from the property before destruction.

If a party destroys or otherwise fails to preserve relevant evidence for litigation, a court has broad discretion to remedy the situation.[52] A court may "order...that designated facts be taken as established, prohibit...the introduction of evidence, dismiss...all or any part of an action, render...a judgment by default against a disobedient party, and [require a disobedient party to] pay...reasonable expenses including attorney fees."[53] While Indiana law has not addressed how the spoliator's level of intent (for instance, negligent, reckless, or purposeful) bears on the severity of the sanction imposed by the court, we can assume that a higher degree of intent will increase the severity of the sanction.[54]

Due in part to the wide array of available remedies, Indiana courts do not generally recognize independent claims against tortfeasors for negligently or unintentionally destroying evidence.[55] Also, at least two Indiana courts have refused to recognize a spoliation cause of action against a third party against whom no other independent claim was brought.[56] However, Indiana may impose a common law duty to preserve evidence upon a third party against whom no other tort or contract claim exists, particularly when the third party is an insurance company.[57]

C. Contractual Provisions

The savvy mold litigation defendant will limit its potential liability through contract. While Indiana law generally prohibits a defendant from avoiding personal injury damages through contractual limitations of liability, the defendant may contract to limit its potential liability for property damage.[58] Because Indiana permits parties to make contracts "so long as they are knowingly and willingly made and free from fraud,"[59] Indiana courts have reason to uphold contractual damage limitations in mold litigation cases. On the other hand, Indiana courts have stated on several occasions that Indiana law generally disfavors limitation of remedies provisions, and that courts will therefore construe such provisions against a seller-defendant.[60]

11.5 Damages

A. Attorneys' Fees and Costs

In Indiana, as in many states, each party bears its own attorneys' fees and costs absent a statute, agreement, or stipulation to the contrary.[61] Indiana courts will enforce a contract clause allowing for recovery of attorneys' fees provided that the clause (i) does not violate law and (ii) is not contrary to public policy.[62]

If a plaintiff claims that a defendant violated the Indiana Deceptive Consumer Sales Act regarding the sale of real property, the plaintiff may *not* seek attorneys' fees and costs from the defendant under the statute.[63]

B. Cost of Repair versus Diminution of Value

For real property, the proper measure of damages depends upon whether the injury is permanent or temporary. "[I]f the injury is permanent, the measure of damages is the market value of the real estate before the injury, less the market value after the injury;...if the injury to real estate is not permanent, then the measure of damages is the cost of restoration."[64] While Indiana case law does not clearly define the difference between permanent and temporary injuries,[65] the overarching goal in awarding damages in Indiana appears to be to "fairly and adequately compensate an injured party for his loss."[66] Consistent with this goal, at least one Indiana court has defined a permanent injury as "one wherein the cost of restoration exceeds the market value of the building prior to the injury."[67]

C. Opportunity to Repair

"Right to cure" laws afford builders the opportunity to remedy construction defects before a party files a lawsuit. According to Indiana's Notice and Opportunity to Repair Statute, the person alleging the construction defect must provide written notice thereof to the builder at least 60 days prior to filing a lawsuit.[68]

The builder must respond in writing within 21 days of receiving written notice of the defect, and select one of the three following options:

(1) Propose to inspect the residence that is the subject of the claim and complete the inspection within a specified time frame. A response made under this subdivision must include the statement that the construction professional shall, based on the inspection, offer to remedy the defect, compromise by payment, or dispute the claim.

(2) Offer to compromise and settle the claim by monetary payment without inspection. A construction professional's offer under this subdivision may include, but is not limited to, an express offer to purchase the claimant's residence that is the subject of the claim and to pay the claimant's reasonable relocation costs.

(3) State that the construction professional disputes the claim and will neither remedy the construction defect nor compromise and settle the claim.[69]

D. Application of the Economic Loss Doctrine

Generally, under the economic loss doctrine, tort law does not provide a remedy for a product's failure to perform as expected.[70] Only when the defective product causes personal injury or damage to "other property" may a party recover in tort.[71] Until recently, Indiana struggled to define "other property."[72] Ultimately, the Indiana Supreme Court concluded that "other parts of a finished product damaged by components supplied to the seller by other manufacturers and imported into the seller's product" is not "other property."[73]

For example, suppose that a newly-built house has defective roofing, causing flooding and mold damage to the rest of the house. Under Indiana law, the rest of the house is not "other property," and a party may not recover in tort for property damage to the rest of the house. However, if the house already exists, and a contractor improperly installs a new roof, causing mold damage to the rest of the house, the rest of the house is "other property." Thus, in this case, the economic loss doctrine would not prevent a recovery in tort.

11.6 Admissibility of Expert Testimony

Experts have not yet agreed upon the extent of the causal relationship between mold and bodily injury. Because this dispute remains unsettled, expert testimony is often an integral part of mold-related litigation, particularly when the plaintiff alleges bodily injury. A particular expert's testimony is admissible when:

> (1) the subject of the inference to be drawn from the facts must be so distinctly related to some science, profession, business, or occupation as to be beyond the ken of laymen; and (2) the witness must have sufficient skill, knowledge, or experience in that field so as to make it appear that his opinion or inference will probably aid the trier in his search for the truth.[74]

Once qualified, the expert's testimony must be reliable for a court to admit it. Two general standards exist for the admissibility of scientific expert testimony: the *Frye*[75] test and the *Daubert*[76] test. According to *Frye v. United States*, the admissibility of expert testimony turns on whether the expert bases her testimony on scientific principles that are generally accepted in the relevant scientific community.[77] In *Daubert v. Merrell Dow Pharmaceuticals, Inc.*, the Supreme Court overturned *Frye*[78] and held that a trial court judge should examine the following four factors when determining whether expert testimony is reliable: (1) whether the technique or theory can and has been tested; (2) whether the technique or theory has been subjected to peer review and publication; (3) the known or potential rate of error; and (4) whether the technique or theory has gained general acceptance in the relevant scientific community (the *Frye* test).[79]

Indiana courts have developed their own standards for admitting expert testimony. Indiana Rules of Evidence 702, 703, and 104 control the admissibility of expert testimony. Pursuant to these rules, a trial court "must determine whether such evidence appears sufficiently valid or, in other words, trustworthy, to assist the trier of fact."[80] The trial court must assess "whether the reasoning or methodology underlying the testimony is scientifically valid and whether that reasoning or methodology properly can be applied to the facts in issue."[81] In performing these tasks, a court may consider the *Daubert* factors.[82]

11.7 Indiana Mold Legislation

While Indiana has several statutes that implicate mold-related issues, Indiana has not yet established mold exposure limits via statute or regulation. However, Indiana does require that all home inspection reports provided to potential buyers and sellers of real estate include a statement that the report does not address environmental hazards, including mold.[83] This requirement alerts potential buyers and sellers to the fact that mold may exist in the property, and that a standard home inspection does not address such concerns. Also, Indiana's State Department of Health may perform air quality inspections in "all public buildings and institutions that are occupied by an agency of state or local government."[84] Presumably, the state would assess mold when conducting an air quality inspection.

11.8 Insurance Coverage

Mold lawsuits frequently involve insurance companies. Claimants and insurance providers often disagree whether the claimant's comprehensive general liability (CGL) policy covers mold damage. Because most pending mold litigation claims involve policies written prior to the proliferation of mold-related lawsuits, insurance providers often deny coverage under the policy's absolute pollution exclusion provision. Now, insurance companies typically add mold-specific exclusion provisions to more recently issued policies.

A. Absolute Pollution Exclusion Provisions

Insurance providers commonly deny coverage for mold-related claims through traditional absolute pollution exclusion provisions. For example, an absolute pollution exclusion provision may bar insurance coverage for: "bodily injury or property damage arising out of the discharge, dispersal, release, or escape of smoke, vapors, soot, fumes, acids, alkalis, toxic chemicals, liquids or gases, waste materials or other irritants, contaminants or pollutants into or upon land, the atmosphere or any water course or body of water."[85]

Whether an absolute pollution exclusion provision will include mold will depend largely upon the language of the insurance policy. Insurance policies are subject to the same general principles of contract interpretation as other contracts.[86] Under Indiana law, courts will construe an ambiguity in an insurance policy against the insurance provider.[87] Courts adhere especially close to this maxim when interpreting a provision that excludes coverage.[88]

B. Mold-Specific Exclusion Provisions

Insurance companies now add mold-specific exclusion provisions to their policies to avoid the problems inherent in more general pollution exclusion provisions.[89] Because an insurance policy is a contract, and is subject to traditional principles of contract interpretation,[90] Indiana courts are likely to uphold mold-specific exclusions as long as the policies are unambiguous and not otherwise unconscionable.[91]

To date, the Indiana Department of Insurance has not provided any guidance to insurance carriers regarding mold exclusions for personal and commercial lines.

11.9 Conclusion

Although mold litigation is in its relative infancy in Indiana, the recent increase in the number of mold-related lawsuits suggests a potential burgeoning area of law. While Indiana's mold litigation case law is not well-established, many of Indiana's foundational legal concepts will likely apply in the mold litigation context.

Endnotes

1. *See, e.g.*, *Williams v. Younginer*, 851 N.E.2d 351 (Ind. Ct. App. 2006) (purchaser-plaintiff sued builder-defendant for, *inter alia*, breach of implied warranty of fitness of habitation, breach of implied warranty of workmanship, breach of contract, negligence, and fraud).

2. *Schmitt v. City of Evansville*, 868 N.E.2d 1127, 1128 (Ind. Ct. App. 2007).

3. *Id.*

4. *Id.*

5. *See, e.g.*, *Choung v. Iemma*, 708 N.E.2d 7, 14 (Ind. Ct. App. 1999).

6. *Id.* at 14 (citing *Thompson v. Best*, 478 N.E.2d 79, 84 (Ind. Ct. App. 1985)).

7. *Masick v. McColly Realtors, Inc.*, 858 N.E.2d 682, 692 (Ind. Ct. App. 2006).

8. Ind. Code Ann. §§ 32-21-5-1 to -13 (West 2008).

9. Ind. Real Estate Commission, State Form 46234, Seller's Residential Real Estate Sales Disclosure (2007), *available at* http://www.in.gov/icpr/webfile/formsdiv/46234.pdf.

10. *Id.*

11. Ind. Code § 32-21-5-10 (West 2008).

12. Ind. Real Estate Commission, *supra* note 9, at 2.

13. Ind. Real Estate Commission, *supra* note 9, at 1.

14. *Blake v. Calumet Constr. Corp.*, 674 N.E.2d 167, 170 (Ind. 1996) (*overruled by Peters v. Forster*, 804 N.E.2d 736 (Ind. 2004)).

15. *Peters*, 804 N.E.2d at 743.

16. *Bond v. Walsh & Kelly, Inc.*, 869 N.E.2d 1264, 1266 (Ind. Ct. App. 2007).

17. *Id.*

18. IND. CODE ANN. § 32-27-2 (West 2008) (New Home Construction Warranties); IND. CODE ANN. § 32-27-1 (West 2008) (Statutory Home Improvement Warranties).

19. IND. CODE ANN. § 32-27-2-8 (West 2008) (New Home Construction Warranties); IND. CODE ANN. § 32-27-1-12 (West 2008) (Statutory Home Improvement Warranties).

20. *Collins v. McKinney*, 871 N.E.2d 363, 370 (Ind. Ct. App. 2007) (citing *Breeding v. Kye's Inc.*, 831 N.E.2d 188, 191 (Ind. Ct. App. 2005)).

21. *See, e.g., Williams*, 851 N.E.2d 351 (reversing and remanding trial court's grant of defendant's motion for judgment on the evidence on plaintiff's breach of contract claim).

22. *Benge v. Miller*, 855 N.E.2d 716, 719 (Ind. Ct. App. 2006) (citing *INS Investigations Bureau, Inc. v. Lee*, 784 N.E.2d 566, 576 (Ind. Ct. App. 2003)).

23. *Id.* (citing *INS Investigations Bureau*, 784 N.E.2d at 576).

24. *Theis v. Heuer*, 280 N.E.2d 300, 303-07 (Ind. 1972).

25. *Barnes v. Mac Brown & Co., Inc.*, 342 N.E.2d 619, 620 (Ind. 1976).

26. *Vetor v. Shockey*, 414 N.E.2d 575, 577-78 (Ind. Ct. App. 1980).

27. *Wagner Constr. Co., Inc. v. Noonan*, 403 N.E.2d 1144, 1148 (Ind. Ct. App. 1980).

28. *Johnson v. Scandia Assocs., Inc.*, 717 N.E.2d 24, 30 (Ind. 1999).

29. *Id.*; *see, e.g., Geels v. Dunbar*, 812 N.E.2d 857, 861 (Ind. Ct. App. 2004) (holding that an implied warranty of habitability existed even absent an express warranty in lease agreement).

30. *Sigsbee v. Swathwood*, 419 N.E.2d 789, 797 n.8 (Ind. Ct. App. 1981).

31. *Vill. Commons, LLC v. Marion County Prosecutor's Office*, 882 N.E.2d 210, 217 (Ind. Ct. App. 2008) (citing *Sigsbee*, 419 N.E.2d at 795).

32. *Id.* at 216-17. This remedy is known as an actual eviction.

33. *Id.* at 217. This remedy is known as a constructive eviction.

34. Generally, Indiana does not recognize the tort of negligent misrepresentation. *See, e.g., Jim Barna Log Sys. Midwest, Inc. v. Gen. Cas. Ins. Co. of Wisc.*, 791 N.E.2d 816, 830 (Ind. Ct. App. 2003) (quoting *Darst v. Ill. Farmers Ins. Co.*, 716 N.E.2d 579, 584 (Ind. Ct. App. 1999)).

35. *Fimbel v. DeClark*, 695 N.E.2d 125, 127 (Ind. Ct. App. 1998) (citing *Adoptive Parents of M.L.V. & A.L.V. v. Wilkens*, 598 N.E.2d 1054, 1058 (Ind. 1992)).

36. *See supra* Part 1.2(A)(1).

37. Ind. Code Ann. §§ 24-5-0.5-2 to -12 (West 2008). The list of deceptive acts encompasses a broad range of activities. The deceptive act most relevant to mold-related litigation is representing that the property is "of a particular standard, quality, grade, style, or model" when it is not and when the seller knows or reasonably should know that it is not.

38. *Id.* at § 24-5-0.5-2(a)(1).

39. Ind. Code Ann. § 22-3-2-6 (West 2008); *see, e.g., Wine-Settergren v. Lamey*, 716 N.E.2d 381, 384 (Ind. 1999).

40. Ind. Code Ann. § 22-3-2-2 (West 2008).

41. *Williams v. Delta Steel Corp.*, 695 N.E.2d 633, 635 (Ind. Ct. App. 1998) (citing *Baker v. Westinghouse Elec. Corp.*, 637 N.E.2d 1271, 1274 (Ind. 1994)).

42. Ind. R. Trial P. 23(A).

43. *See, e.g., Havens v. Ritchey*, 582 N.E.2d 792, 794 n.1 (Ind. 1991). Generally "a cause of action accrues when the resultant damage of a negligent act is ascertainable or could be ascertained by due diligence." *Id.* (citing *Barnes v. A.H. Robins Co., Inc.*, 476 N.E.2d 84 (Ind. 1985)).

44. *See, e.g.*, Ind. Code Ann. § 32-30-1-5 (West 2008).

45. *Id.*

46. *Id.*

47. *Id.*

48. *See Grain Dealers Mut. Ins. Co., Inc. v. Chief Indus., Inc.*, 612 F.Supp. 1179, 1181 (N.D. Ind. 1985) (applying Indiana law).

49. *Id.* at 1182.

50. *Id.* at 1181.

51. *Blacks Law Dictionary* 1437 (8th ed. 2004).

52. *Gribben v. Wal-Mart Stores, Inc.*, 824 N.E.2d 349, 351 (Ind. 2005).

53. *Id.*

54. *See* DOUGLAS E. KRESSLER, SPOLIATION OF EVIDENCE, 36 Res Gestae 510, 512-13 (1993).

55. *Gribben,* 824 N.E.2d at 355.

56. *See, e.g., Glotzbach v. Froman*, 854 N.E.2d 337 (Ind. 2006) (declining to impose a common law duty to preserve evidence on the party that allegedly spoliated evidence, noting that no special relationship between the two parties existed).

57. *Thompson v. Owensby*, 704 N.E.2d 134, 137 (Ind. Ct. App. 1998) (permitting claim against defendant's liability insurer because "[l]iability insurance carriers are no strangers to litigation, and it strains credulity to posit…that a liability carrier could be unaware of the potential importance of physical evidence").

58. *McGraw-Edison Co. v. N.E. Rural Elec. Membership Corp.*, 678 N.E.2d 1120, 1123 n.5 (Ind. 1997) (citing IND. CODE ANN. § 26-1-2-719(3) (West 2008)). Section 26-1-2-719(3) provides: "Consequential damages may be limited or excluded unless the limitation or exclusion is unconscionable. Limitation of consequential damages for injury to the person in the case of consumer goods is prima facie unconscionable, but limitation of damages where the loss is commercial is not."

59. *Gen. Bargain Ctr. v. Am. Alarm Co., Inc.*, 430 N.E.2d 407, 411-12 (Ind. Ct. App. 1982).

60. *Hahn v. Ford Motor Co., Inc.*, 434 N.E.2d 943, 948 (Ind. Ct. App. 1982) (citing *Auto-Teria, Inc. v. Ahern*, 352 N.E.2d 774 (Ind. Ct. App. 1976)).

61. *Dempsey v. Carter,* 797 N.E.2d 268, 274–75 (Ind. Ct. App. 2003) (citing *Holliday v. Crooked Creek Vills. Homeowners Ass'n, Inc.*, 759 N.E.2d 1088, 1095 (Ind. Ct. App. 2001)).

62. *Id.* at 275.

63. IND. CODE ANN. § 24-5-0.5-4(a) (West 2008).

64. *Gen. Outdoor Adver. Co. v. LaSalle Realty Corp.*, 218 N.E.2d 141, 150 (Ind. Ct. App. 1966).

65. *Id.*

66. *Terra-Prods., Inc. v. Kraft Gen. Foods, Inc.*, 653 N.E.2d 89, 93 (Ind. Ct. App. 1995) (citing *Wiese-GMC, Inc. v. Wells,* 626 N.E.2d 595, 597 (Ind. Ct. App. 1993)).

67. *Gen. Outdoor Adver. Co.*, 218 N.E.2d at 151.

68. IND. CODE ANN. § 32-27-3-2(a) (West 2008).

69. *Id.* at § 32-27-3-2(b).

70. *Gunkel v. Renovations, Inc.*, 822 N.E.2d 150, 152 (Ind. 2005).

71. *Id.* at 153.

72. *Id.* at 154.

73. *Id.* at 156.

74. *Ind. v. Maudlin*, 416 N.E.2d 477, 481 (Ind. Ct. App. 1981).

75. *Frye v. U.S.*, 293 F. 1013 (D.C. Cir. 1923).

76. *Daubert v. Merrell Dow Pharm., Inc.*, 509 U.S. 579 (1993).

77. 293 F. at 1013.

78. While *Daubert* replaced *Frye* as the expert testimony admissibility standard at the federal level, *Frye* remains important for two reasons: (1) at the federal level, the *Frye* test is one of the four *Daubert* factors, and (2) state courts are free to adopt *Daubert*, *Frye*, or their own evidentiary standard.

79. 509 U.S. at 593-94.

80. *Shafer & Freeman Lakes Envtl. Conservation Corp. v. Stichnoth*, 877 N.E.2d 475, 484 (Ind. Ct. App. 2007) (citing *West v. Ind.*, 805 N.E.2d 909, 913 (Ind. Ct. App. 2004)).

81. *Id.* (citing *Lytle v. Ford Motor Co.*, 814 N.E.2d 301, 309 (Ind. Ct. App. 2004)).

82. *Id.* (citing *Steward v. Ind.*, 652 N.E.2d 490, 498 (Ind. 1995)).

83. IND. CODE ANN. § 25-20.2-2-7 (West 2008). The statute defines a "home inspection" as:

> a visual analysis for the purpose of providing a professional opinion of the condition of a residential dwelling and the dwelling's carports or garages, any reasonably accessible installed components, and the operation of the dwelling's systems, including any controls normally operated by the owner of the dwelling, for the following components:(1) Heating systems; (2) Cooling systems; (3) Electrical systems; (4) Plumbing systems; (5) Structural components; (6) Foundations; (7) Roof coverings; and (8) Exterior and interior components. (9) Any other site aspects that affect the residential dwelling.

84. IND. CODE ANN. § 16-19-3-7 (West 2008).

85. Gregory A. Goodman, *Insurance Triggers as Judicial Gatekeepers in Toxic Mold Litigation*, 57 VAND. L. REV. 241, 256 (2004) (citing *Leverence v. U.S. Fid. & Guar.*, 462 N.W.2d 218, 232 (Wis. Ct. App. 1990)).

86. *Eli Lilly & Co. v. Home Ins. Co.*, 482 N.E.2d 467, 470 (Ind. 1985).

87. *Am. States Ins. Co. v. Kiger*, 662 N.E.2d 945, 947 (Ind. 1996) (*citing Fid. & Deposit Co. of Md. v. Pettis Dry Goods Co.*, 190 N.E. 63 (Ind. 1934)).

88. *Id.* (citing *Asbury v. Ind. Union Mut. Ins. Co.*, 441 N.E.2d 232, 242 (Ind. Ct. App. 1982)).

89. *Goodman*, *supra* note 82 at 256 (citing Elizabeth Amon, *As Toxic Mold Suits Grow, Insurers Go,* NAT'L L. J., Oct. 21, 2002, at A-17).

90. *Eli Lilly & Co.*, 482 N.E.2d at 470.

91. *See, e.g., Sammons v. State Farm Fire & Cas. Co.*, No. 4:05-cv-0028-JDT-WGH, 2006 WL 1547102, 2006 U.S. Dist. LEXIS 36534 (S.D. Ind. June 2, 2006) (applying Indiana law).

Chapter 12

An Overview of Toxic Mold Litigation in Massachusetts

David M. Governo, Esq., Marianne E. Brown, Esq., and
Sarah E. O'Leary, Esq.

Synopsis

12.1 Introduction

Since the first edition of *Toxic Mold Litigation*, courts in Massachusetts have continued to struggle with the issues posed by mold claims. These mold claims may arise in a variety of different contexts: claims against governmental entities, counter claims in eviction actions, facility management, personal injury suits, real estate disputes between neighbors or agents and purchasers, contract claims against builders or developers and litigation concerning insurance coverage. In addition, recent mold litigation has arisen in the context of workplace disputes including entitlement to workers' compensation or retirement benefits. It is important for any attorney involved in mold litigation to become familiar with the many facets of prosecuting or defending the case including the unique issues of sampling, testing, analysis, remediation, potential health effects, building science and insurance coverage. The harsh effects of Massachusetts' four-season climate on building structures and the pervasiveness of moisture and humidity, make mold problems a fact of life in New England. Though the limited availability of insurance coverage for mold claims has probably kept the number of mold claims relatively low, there have been several significant mold decisions that form the current status of the law in Massachusetts.

In Massachusetts, common law causes of action for mold-related damages can be brought under theories of negligence, breach of contract, breach of warranty, and nuisance. Statutory claims can be brought pursuant to landlord-tenant and consumer protection laws.

12.2 Massachusetts Common Law Theories

The most common theories asserted by claimants for mold-related injuries are negligence, breach of contract, and breach of warranty.

A. Negligence

A claimant may assert claims for negligence, negligent trespass, and negligent misrepresentation as a result of excessive mold accumulation. Potential defendants include anyone who designs, owns, builds, renovates, repairs, or cleans buildings as well as real estate brokers and managers.

In a negligence action, a plaintiff must prove the existence of a duty owed by the defendant to the plaintiff, a breach of that duty, and actual harm proximately resulting from that breach of duty.[1] Causes of action relating to mold present substantial hurdles given the difficulty of proving a causal relationship between the alleged tortious conduct and mold-related injuries.

Whether a defendant owes a plaintiff a legal duty turns on the existence of a special legal relationship, and the foreseeability of the resulting harm if the duty owed is breached.[2] A plaintiff need not show the foreseeability of the particular harm, only harm of the same general character as the harm allegedly suffered.[3]

In mold claims, the foreseeability question arises in the context of the relationships between landlords and tenants, as well as contractors and property owners. In the latter instance, for example, a plaintiff must demonstrate it was foreseeable that the design, construction or maintenance of a building caused an accumulation of mold. Since mold-based claims are a relatively new phenomenon, a plaintiff may have difficulty proving that harm of this nature was foreseeable.

If the plaintiff does prove the existence of a duty, she must next demonstrate a breach of that duty. The standard used to determine a breach is whether the defendant employed the same level of care a reasonably prudent person skilled in the same trade would exercise under the same or similar circumstances.[4] The Center for Disease Control has stated that

> [m]olds are simple organisms that are found virtually everywhere, indoors and outdoors. The potential health effects of indoor mold are a growing concern. Mold can cause or worsen certain illnesses (e.g., some allergic and occupation-related diseases and infections in health care settings). However, no conclusive evidence exists that indoor mold is associated with a multitude of other health problems, such as pulmonary hemorrhage, memory loss, and lack of energy.[5]

Proving a deviation from accepted practices will require testimony from one or more expert witnesses depending upon the complexity of the defect or conduct which gave rise to the accumulation of mold.

Medical, environmental, and other expert testimony is also essential for a plaintiff to demonstrate the existence of a causal relationship between the defendant's conduct and the plaintiff's injuries or property damage. The proximate cause test requires a showing that (1) the defendant's conduct was a "but-for" cause of the injury, and (2) the defendant's conduct was a "substantial contributing legal factor" in bringing about the plaintiff's harm.[6]

In a claim for property damage, proving a connection between the defect (e.g., water infiltration) and resulting mold may not be all that difficult. The same cannot be said, however, in the personal injury context where the proof of causation is more complex.

Personal injury mold claims are similar to cases involving claims for lead poisoning in that, in both instances, the plaintiff must meet a two-tier proximate cause standard. That is, a plaintiff must show (1) the mold in the plaintiff was caused by the offending conduct, structure or defect, and (2) the plaintiff's mold exposure was the cause of the personal injuries alleged. The first tier for proving proximate cause is challenging because mold is ubiquitous and exists naturally in the environment. It is difficult, and perhaps impossible, in some instances, to identify all possible sources of mold which may have contributed to any mold present in the claimant's body. Indeed, mold identified in a person could be linked to mold in the home, business, school, soil, water, and air.

The second part of the equation, whether the mold to which the person was exposed caused the injuries alleged, poses just as challenging a question. Symptoms which claimants relate to "toxic" mold exposure are typically non-specific and subjective in nature. Potential health effects stemming from "toxic" mold exposure are not well known or documented medically or scientifically. The debate in these scientific fields continues, and there are few medical or scientific studies or other authorities upon which a claimant can rely to prove causation. Massachusetts courts have been willing to entertain claims for damages caused by mold but have required reputable expert testimony and strong proof of causation to establish a successful claim for recovery. In addition, the proponent of a mold claim must be able to demonstrate actual damages and show that other mold exposures did not cause his symptoms.

The pioneer mold trial in Massachusetts, which addressed the admissibility of expert testimony as well as causation issues, was litigated in Essex County in 2002.[7] The plaintiff claimed she experienced physical symptoms six weeks after moving into her one-bedroom condominium in 1995. She alleged property damage, real estate loss, and physical injuries including asthma and immune-system compromise due to the inhalation of toxic mold. In *Stevens,* the court denied the defendant's motion, *in limine,* to exclude the testimony of the plaintiff's mold expert, Eckardt Johanning, M.D., on the grounds that his anticipated testimony did not meet the standard set forth in *Daubert v. Merrell Dow Pharmaceuticals, Inc.*[8] Dr. Johanning testified at the trial as both a mold expert and as the plaintiff's treating physician. He opined that mold causes infections, allergies, and toxic reactions in humans. He testified that these three categories of effects of molds on humans are generally accepted by the medical community. He was not allowed to testify regarding the plaintiff's specific toxic encephalopathy. Dr. Johanning was permitted to testify, however, that the plaintiff's six-week exposure to mold in the subject premises was of sufficient duration for her to develop a sensitivity to mold. During the eight-day trial, the plaintiff's attorney argued that the defendant condominium trust knew the plaintiff's garden-level unit had a chronic wetness problem, but failed to remedy the water seepage into the condominium. In June of 2002, the jury returned a verdict for the plaintiff in the amount of $285,000 to which $264,326 in interest was added.

Whether a medical expert's anticipated testimony satisfied the *Daubert* standard was also considered by the Barnstable Superior Court in the case of *Liska v. Travelers Property Casualty Corp. et al.*[9] *Liska* was a declaratory judgment action involving insurance coverage in a property damage case. Ms. Liska sued her homeowners' insurers alleging her home was unlivable due to mold. She did not claim any personal injury. Since there were two possible sources of the mold in her home's ductwork, Ms. Liska had to prove the mold was caused by a covered event in order to prevail against her insurers.[10]

Prior to trial, a three-day evidentiary hearing on *motions in limine* was held, and the court determined that plaintiff's experts, Jeffrey Adams, Ph.D. and Eckardt Johanning, M.D., were qualified to render causation opinions vis-à-vis mold.[11] The defendants argued that Dr. Johanning's opinion was based upon an incomplete medical history since he never reviewed Ms. Liska's medical records. The defendants also argued Ms. Liska's work environment was contaminated with mold.[12] The court noted the arguments raised by the defendants were best left to rigorous cross-examination of Dr. Johanning at trial.[13] The court held that Dr. Johanning could testify that Ms. Liska was exposed to mold that led to an allergy hypersensitivity reaction. More important to the specific issue in this case, however, he was also allowed to testify about the timing of the commencement of her exposure to the mold.[14]

The case was tried, jury-waived, in September 2004.[15] The court ruled in favor of both insurance carriers because the mold in the ductwork of the house was not caused by a leaking hot water tank, but by a series of previous water and moisture events that were not covered losses under the policy.[16] The court noted that Dr. Johanning assumed that her symptoms began when the hot water tank leaked.[17] Plaintiff's own primary-care physician, however, testified that her respiratory and allergy problems began long before the event involving the leaking hot water tank.[18]

In its post-trial opinion, the court noted a difference between a loss that is caused by an excluded event, and a loss caused by a covered event that gives rise to damage, such as mold, which is specifically excluded under the policy.[19] The court noted that the failure of the hot water tank (and any resulting mold) was a covered event under the policy but that the leaking water tank was not the proximate cause of the mycotoxins in the ducts.[20] As a result, the plaintiff was unable to prevail against her insurers.

Another Massachusetts (Norfolk County) Superior Court judge afforded considerable deference to the opinions of Christine Oliver, M.D. in an action to close a courthouse in Dedham, Massachusetts.[21] In *Schmidt v. County of Norfolk*, the plaintiffs sought to have the courthouse closed on the grounds that it posed significant health risks to all those who entered the building.[22] One of the many problems was mold accumulation due to inadequate ventilation throughout the building.[23] The court noted Dr. Oliver's impressive credentials and experience in the field of occupational medicine.[24] She conducted an epidemiologic study among the courthouse employees, and those who spent any time at the courthouse (attorneys, clients, etc.), regarding their medical symptoms, and the extent to which the symptoms abated while they were away from the building.[25] The court issued a permanent injunction closing the courthouse based, in large measure, upon the testimony of Dr. Oliver.[26]

Defense counsel must consider using expert testimony to rebut proximate cause testimony by plaintiff's expert and, if applicable, to mitigate damages. Defense experts should stand prepared to discuss the duration of exposure and the level of toxicity of the mold to which the plaintiff was allegedly exposed. Other factors include pre-existing medical conditions, tobacco smoking, and other significant environmental exposures.

As to the question of damages, a plaintiff must demonstrate identifiable physical injuries which were caused or aggravated by exposure to mold. A plaintiff may only be awarded compensatory damages for medical expenses, lost earnings, lost earning capacity, pain and suffering, emotional distress, and loss of consortium once she demonstrates that mold caused the particular damages alleged.

These same issues concerning causation and the sufficiency of medical proof arose in the setting of whether a school's music teacher should be entitled to disability benefits when she alleged that mold in her workspace caused ongoing disability. The case was heard originally by an administrative magistrate for the Contributory Retirement Appeals Board. The Board denied benefits on the basis that it could not be established whether mold in the home or mold in the workplace were the cause of the injury. The case was appealed to the Superior Court which affirmed the denial of benefits. A second appeal of the case was heard by the Massachusetts Appeals Court which examined the evidence available to the administrative magistrate to determine whether the decision was supported by substantial evidence. The Appeals Court found that the evidence produced by the plaintiff, which included certifications of four physicians with respiratory specialties that she was disabled by her condition, was sufficient to demonstrate disability, but that her claim must be denied because such proof did not establish whether the disability was caused by mold in the workplace.

The Appeals Court held that the board's finding that mold in her workplace was not the proven cause of her disability must be given deference, where the facts fairly detracting from the plaintiff's claim of workplace injury were sufficient to show that the board's decision was not arbitrary and capricious. The court also stated that if the administrative magistrate had found in plaintiff's favor it would have also affirmed the award because the plaintiff had satisfied her burden of proof by providing adequate evidence of causation through opinions from four respiratory specialists supporting her claim. However, the board was not convinced that the plaintiff's disability stemmed from her workplace rather than from mold found in her home. It was the plaintiff's burden to demonstrate that her injuries were caused by mold in the workplace and there was no burden on the employer to prove that the injuries were caused by mold in the plaintiff's home and not the workplace.[27]

Issues of proving causation also derailed a plaintiff's novel claim that mold exposure due to the negligence of condominium trustees caused her daughter, Emilia, to develop an autism spectrum disorder. The court refused to qualify the plaintiff's experts and dismissed all claims for damages related to the child's diagnosis.[28] In *MacGregor v. Born*, the plaintiffs sued condominium trustees alleging that negligent maintenance of common areas in the building caused water leaks which led to mold contamination in their rental unit. The plaintiffs alleged that health problems and personal property damage caused them to move out of the unit. In addition, the plaintiff contended that her daughter's exposure to this mold during the time she lived in the condominium, between the age of 18 and 33 months, caused her to develop Pervasive Developmental Disorder (a milder condition on the spectrum of autism disorders). The trustees filed a *Daubert* motion to exclude the plaintiff's expert witness testimony on the subject, contending that it was speculative and unreliable. Because the theory that mold exposure can cause autism is not generally accepted in the scientific community, the trial judge was required to determine whether the plaintiff's theory has been subjected to peer review and publication, whether it can or has been tested and whether it has a known error rate.[29] The court must balance these factors to determine whether the testimony is sufficiently reliable to be introduced at trial.[30]

Dr. Eckhard Johanning and Dr. Martha Herbert, the plaintiffs' proposed experts, were deposed prior to trial. Dr. Johanning testified that his opinion was that mold was a plausible cause of Emilia's developmental disorder. He testified that he had done allergy testing on Emilia which was negative for molds but positive for cats. He had not done testing to determine what molds were present in the residential unit. On cross examination he agreed that his opinion was more properly characterized as a working hypothesis. The court held that a hypothesis is not competent evidence.

Dr. Herbert, a pediatric neurologist, testified that it was her opinion that the child's history was consistent with environmental sensitivity triggered by mold exposure.[31] Insofar as this theory is not generally accepted, the court analyzed whether her testimony met other indicia of scientific reliability.

Dr. Herbert had performed research in the field of autism and other neurodevelopmental disabilities. The case analyzes Dr. Herbert's opinion that mold can trigger an inflammatory process in the body that injures the brain and causes autism to develop. At her deposition, Dr. Herbert testified that she had considered and eliminated other possible causes of autism in the child and it was her opinion that the presence of mold triggered the child's environmental sensitivity leading to Pervasive Developmental Disorder. The court determined that while the process of elimination may be a reliable method of determining causation, for such a process to be reliable it is necessary to have a finite list of known potential causes and a reliable method of eliminating causes other than the one in issue. Because the causes of autism are not yet known or understood, there was no reliable method by which Dr. Herbert could eliminate all potential sources or causes of autism spectrum disorders which may have affected Emilia.

The court granted defendant's motion and excluded the plaintiffs' proposed expert testimony that mold exposure triggered Emilia's autism and struck all plaintiffs' claims for damages based on Emilia's autism. The plaintiffs' claims for other health effects and property damages to the condominium unit were allowed to survive for trial.

1. Claims of negligence

A claimant may also proceed under the theory of negligent trespass when, for example, the claim involves the flow of water onto property resulting in mold growth.[32] To succeed, the plaintiff must demonstrate that the trespassing water caused the mold growth on the subject property.[33] In *Espahbodi v. Town of Sudbury*, the plaintiff homeowner's property was bisected by a drainage easement held by the Town. Over the years, the house became increasingly musty and humid.[34] The wallpaper peeled, the kitchen floor tile cracked, the garage floor was damp, the basement was chronically wet, moss grew on two sides of the house, and wetlands were encroaching on the property's backyard.[35] A tenant in the property complained of excessive mold accumulation, and a state sanitary code violation notice was sent to the plaintiff.[36] The homeowner sued the town for nuisance, trespass, negligence, and diminution of the value of their property as the result of the town's negligent maintenance of the easement.[37] The court held that while there was evidence that the easement was negligently maintained, there was no evidence of a causal connection between the negligence and the moisture in the house, and further, there was not enough evidence to prove a diminution in value of the house, regardless of the cause.[38]

In February 2006, in the case of *Martino v. Banwake, LLC*, a Massachusetts (Middlesex County) Superior Court jury awarded a $133,000 trial verdict for water damage and resulting mold following building activity on adjacent property.[39] The Martino's sued the developer of a subdivision on adjacent property for negligently altering the contours of land and reshaping an existing ledge so as to channel water onto their property. The defendant also installed new utilities in a trench cut into rock along the private roadway leading to the plaintiffs' house. On one occasion the plaintiffs, who had not had water problems before construction, had 16,000 gallons of water in their basement. After the water was removed, severe mold damage followed. At trial, the plaintiffs presented the testimony of mold expert Martin Golden, who testified that the plaintiffs' home represented one of the worst infestations of mold he had ever seen. The plaintiff's expert testified regarding the damage caused by mold, his testing methods and the measures taken to remove the mold. He stated that mold would return to the plaintiff's basement whenever it got wet. The plaintiff's sought recovery for property damage, out of pocket costs, loss of possessions, mold removal and engineering designs to keep water out in the future. A jury found against the developer and awarded the plaintiff $146,000 for negligence and $3,000 in nuisance damages. The jury reduced the verdict by $16,000 for contributory negligence by the plaintiff homeowners. The jury found that the surveyor and site contractor were not negligent.

A plaintiff may also assert a claim for negligent misrepresentation. To prove misrepresentation, the plaintiff must show the defendant made a false statement of a material fact to induce the plaintiff to act, and that the plaintiff relied on the false statement to his detriment.[40] An action may lie even though the defendant did not know the falsity of the statement when made, if the truth of the matter was reasonably susceptible of actual knowledge.[41]

Misrepresentation allegations regarding mold contamination have been held sufficient to survive a Motion to Dismiss.[42] In *Manock v. Chamoun,* the condominium manager's motion to dismiss plaintiff's suit alleging that the defendant misrepresented the condition of mold contamination in premises was denied, and the plaintiff was permitted to amend her Complaint to add a claim against the defendant condominium association. However, prevailing on a misrepresentation claim at trial is more difficult. In *Delauri v. Niebrzydowski*, an Essex County jury issued a defense verdict in favor of a real estate agent accused of failing to disclose the presence of mold in a condominium unit prior to purchase.[43] The defendant real estate agent contended that he had no prior notice of the mold and first spotted it during the final pre-sale walkthrough of the property, at which time the realtor pointed out a spot on the wall to the plaintiff and stated that it looked like mold. The jury granted a defense verdict finding that the plaintiff would have purchased the property even if the presence of mold had been disclosed prior to the sale.

2. March 2009 plaintiffs' verdict: *Herman v. Sullivan*

Helen Herman and Christian Langlois v. Kevin Sullivan et al. Northeast Housing Court, Docket No. 05-CV-0047, was tried in Lawrence, Massachusetts from March 3 through March 13, 2009. The jury returned a verdict on all counts in the plaintiff/tenants' favor: negligence, breach of the implied warranty of habitability, breach of the covenant of quiet enjoyment under G.L. c. 186, § 14 and violation of the consumer protection statute, G.L. c. 93A with an advisory finding of knowing and willfulness. The Court took under advisement the plaintiffs' motion for triple damages under c. 93A. Also pending are plaintiffs' motion for costs and attorneys' fees under c. 93A and c. 186, § 14. The verdict reflected the large lost wage component of Ms. Herman's case. She had been a 27-year employee of the Transit Authority who was forced to retire because of her asthma. Ms. Herman developed asthma as a result of mold and chronic dampness caused by water intrusions and leaks in her rented residence. The defendants' credibility may have impacted the jury in a major way. None of the denials of liability made by the defendants were apparently believed. The defense physician was cross examined with a treatise deemed authoritative by plaintiff's expert physician pursuant to *Commonwealth v. Sneed.*[44] The treatise was *Dampness and Mold in the Indoor Environment: Implications for Asthma,*[45] which criticizes the earlier Institute of Medicine publication: *Damp Indoor Space and Health.* The verdict, before interest was $726,000. Interest of 44 percent, attorneys' fees, costs and maybe a punitive multiplier are expected to be added to the verdict.

3. Negligence per se

In Massachusetts, a violation of a statute or regulation does not constitute negligence *per se*; rather, such a violation is evidence of negligence.[46]

B. Breach of Contract

Mold-related breach of contract claims are typically commenced in cases between contractors and property owners, or in the landlord-tenant situation. The terms and conditions of the contract or lease determine the nature of the breach. One may also add other parties to the case depending upon the language of the contract. Indemnity provisions may also be included.

Contractual provisions limiting liability are enforceable in Massachusetts.[47] Whether a provision will be upheld is determined on a case-by-case basis by interpreting the contractual language employed.[48]

C. Breach of Express Warranty

Express warranties in contracts have been upheld by the courts in Massachusetts.[49] The standard of performance is determined by the promise allegedly made by defendant, rather than a standard set forth by law.[50]

Of note is that in *Albrecht v. Clifford*, the court strictly interpreted the express warranty to defeat the property owner's claim against the contractor.[51] The building contract guaranteed the fitness, *inter alia,* of the chimneys of defendant's new home for one year.[52] Several years thereafter, the owners learned of the defective installation of the chimneys.[53] The court ruled against the owners, noting that their failure to light the chimneys during the one-year express guaranty period was unreasonable.[54] The court ruled that the defective condition of the chimneys was "knowable" to the owners, that is, patent, and dismissed their action as time barred.[55]

In *Anthony's Pier Four, Inc. v. Crandall Dry Dock Engineers, Inc.*, the court recognized the potential for an oral express warranty beyond the actual language of the building contract.[56] The defendant designed and installed a dock to which the plaintiff moored his yacht/restaurant in 1968.[57] The ship sank in 1978.[58] The court determined that the plaintiff's claim for breach of express warranty did not accrue until the boat actually sank because that was the first time the plaintiff had notice of the defect.[59] The plaintiff swore that the defendant made an express warranty when he orally assured the plaintiff that extra pilings were not necessary because the existing plans were sufficient to hold the ship.[60] The defendant denied making such guarantees.[61] The court denied the defendant's motion for summary judgment and remanded the case to be determined on its merits.[62]

Express warranties made in the context of construction, remodeling or cleaning contracts may give rise to mold claims. Plaintiffs must be attentive to their obligation to assess for the emergence of mold or mildew and bring such claims within the guarantee period. Contractors and service providers should note that oral warranties may be sufficient to permit a case to survive summary judgment. It is essential for them to carefully draft their contracts to avoid potential liabilities.

D. Breach of Implied Warranty

1. Warranty of fitness

A person who enters into a contract to do work or to perform a service impliedly agrees to complete the job in a workmanlike manner and to use the skills a reasonably prudent person skilled in such work would exercise under the same or similar circumstances.[63] This theory has obvious implications in a mold case; however, a plaintiff must still prove it was the un-workmanlike conduct which caused the accumulation of mold.

2. Warranty of habitability

The Massachusetts Supreme Court only recently recognized a cause of action for breach of warranty of habitability in the sale of new homes.[64] The purpose of the law is to protect a consumer from latent defects.[65] This warranty cannot be waived by the buyer or disclaimed by the builder.[66]

To succeed on this claim, the plaintiff must demonstrate that: (1) she purchased a new house from the defendant; (2) the house contained a latent defect; (3) the defect manifested only after purchase; (4) the defect was caused by the builder's improper design, material, or workmanship; and (5) the defect created a substantial question of safety or made the house unfit for human habitation.[67]

A cause of action under this theory is ideal for a new homeowner who has a claim for mold growth. The claim must be brought within three years of the owner's knowledge of the defect and within the six-year statute of repose set forth at Mass. Gen. Laws ch. 260 § 2B.[68] However, a subsequent purchaser may not bring a warranty of habitability claim against the builder.[69] As a result it is important for real estate purchasers to make a complete inspection for any conditions which are likely to promote mold growth. Similarly, a warranty of habitability is not implied in the transfer of property from one owner to the next.[70]

Shortly after the *Albrecht* decision, the Massachusetts Supreme Judicial Court extended the implied warranty to latent defects in the sale of new condominiums in *Berish v. Bornstein*.[71] The case concerned defects in workmanship and construction which, among other things, led to the growth of mold in certain units. After nearly a decade of litigation in the lower courts, the Massachusetts Supreme Judicial Court heard the case.

In *Berish*, the court extended the implied warranty of habitability to an individual unit owner of a condominium, as well as to a condominium association bringing a claim for breach of the implied warranty of habitability "when there are *latent* defects in the common areas that implicate the habitability of individual units."[72] The court required the organization of unit owners "to demonstrate that (1) it is an organization of unit owners as defined by M.G.L., ch. 183A, § 1; (2) the common area of the condominium development contains a latent defect; (3) the latent defect manifested itself after construction of the common areas was substantially completed; (4) the defect was caused by the builder's improper design, material, or workmanship; and (5) the defect created a substantial question of safety as to one or more individual units, or made such units unfit for human habitation."[73] The Supreme Judicial Court further held that the common law "economic loss rule" limiting remedies in warranty claims to those specified in the contract, does not bar recovery for additional property damages caused by negligent defects in the construction of the premises which violate the implied warranty of habitability.[74]

Upon remand, the case was tried over four weeks in the Barnstable Superior Court to determine whether the property defects constituted a breach of the implied warranty of habitability.[75] The plaintiff argued that the contractor caused a mold condition by venting the bathroom exhaust into the attic and crawl spaces of the condominium unit rather than to the outdoors. The plaintiffs presented expert testimony from David Gordon, a certified industrial hygienist. Gordon initially tested six of the condominium units where there were complaints of odors and visible mold. He tested surface and air samples from each unit as well as the bathroom exhaust systems and HVAC exhaust vents. All six units tested contained mold.

Gordon testified that he found that air samples from the basement of one unit demonstrated mold colonies ten times higher than the minimum threshold and "somewhat significant."[76] Surface testing in the same unit demonstrated that *Cladosporium aureobasidium* molds, too numerous to count, were present. Gordon testified that this mold type causes odor but does not raise health concerns. Gordon also found a significant amount of *Penicillium* and some *Stachybotrys* which is considered a toxic mold. Gordon later returned to survey an additional 25 units. His final conclusion was that there was a probable mold contamination source in one or two of the 31 units he surveyed, generated by vapor from the bathrooms entering into the spaces of the attics and elevating humidity, dependent upon the number of showers taken on a daily basis.[77] On cross examination, Gordon agreed that the lack of regular HVAC maintenance could possibly be a cause of the mold.

At the trial's conclusion, the Superior Court found that the plaintiffs failed to prove that the mold was a threat to safety or had resulted in sickness by any occupant of the condominiums, and could not satisfy the fifth prong of the test established by the Supreme Judicial Court, that the defect created a substantial question of safety as to one or more individual units, or made such units unfit for human habitation. The court also found that the plaintiff failed to show a causal relationship between improper bathroom ventilation and mold as only two of 62 condominium units demonstrated problem levels of mold, which could alternatively have been caused by the lack of an HVAC maintenance program. The court concluded that the mold found in the bathroom exhaust fans did not rise to the level of a material breach stating that the implied warranty of habitability does not make the builder an insurer "against any and all defects in a home, impose on the builder an obligation to deliver a perfect house, or protect against mere defects in workmanship, minor or procedural violations of the applicable building codes, or defects that are trivial or aesthetic."[78] Not every sanitary code violation is a breach of the implied warranty of habitability.[79]

E. Nuisance and Negligent Maintenance

A claimant can also commence an action for a private nuisance for mold under certain circumstances. A private nuisance occurs when an owner of property creates, permits or maintains a condition or activity on property which creates a substantive or unreasonable interference with another owner's use and enjoyment of his property.[80] One who allows a nuisance to continue may be as liable as the person who created the initial nuisance.[81] The jury in the *Martino* case, described above, at Section 2.A.1, rendered a comparatively small verdict of $3,000 for nuisance, as compared to their verdict of $146,000 for negligence, in connection with the increased flow of water onto their land following the development of a subdivision on adjacent land.[82]

Negligent maintenance of property that, for example, brings about an accumulation of mold is a separate claim from a private nuisance.[83] The distinction may be relevant if a governmental body is a potential defendant. The Massachusetts Tort Claims Act, ch. 258, § 4, requires a claimant to present, in writing, her negligent maintenance claim within two years of the occurrence when seeking to sue a governmental entity. A failure to meet this statutory requisite is fatal to proceeding with a tort action. This presentment requirement, however, does not apply to claims for a private nuisance.[84] A claimant may proceed with a private nuisance claim against the government, commenced more than two years after the occurrence, subject, of course, to the three-year statute of limitations.[85] For an example of a nuisance and negligent maintenance mold case, see *Espahbodi v. Town of Sudbury*, discussed above in Section 2.A.1.

Allegations of negligent maintenance have survived motions for summary judgment where there is sufficient evidence to create a question of fact for the jury.[86] In *Patkin*, the defendant condominium trustees' motion for summary judgment was denied where the plaintiff presented evidence that water and mold growth originating from a common area resulted in mold infestation within plaintiff's condominium unit. The plaintiff claimed that the defendant's failure and refusal to remediate moisture and mold in the common areas caused interference with the unit's use and enjoyment. The plaintiff produced a report from Gordon Mycology Laboratory, Inc. stating that contamination was found in the hallway and wall cavity as well as five photographs showing the wall cavity contaminated with mold. Though the origin of the water and mold was thought to be a leaking washing machine in an adjacent unit, the court relied upon the condominium master deed which specified that wall cavities between units were common areas.

Negligent maintenance claims may also arise from more straightforward personal injury cases. In *Daniels v. Circle Furniture*, the jury issued a defense verdict at the conclusion of trial.[87] The plaintiff alleged she fell on a stairway as a result of slippery mold resulting in significant personal injuries. The plaintiff provided photographs of mold to support her claims that the defendant was negligent in maintaining the furniture store. The defendant successfully proved, however, that the plaintiff fell because her shoe was not properly strapped on.

12.3 Massachusetts Statutory Claims

The landlord-tenant and consumer protection statutes have wide application and significant consequences in mold cases, the most important being the ability to recover attorneys' fees, costs, and sometimes punitive damages.

A. Landlord-Tenant Laws

1. Quiet enjoyment

Massachusetts General Laws, ch. 186, §14 codifies a tenant's common law rights to the quiet enjoyment of the premises.[88] A finding of liability under this statute requires a showing of negligence by the landlord.[89] Violation of the sanitary code alone is not sufficient, since the landlord must have notice of the violation.[90] Under ch. 186, § 14, a landlord can be liable for actual and consequential damages, or three months' rent, whichever is greater. The case of *Curtis v. Surrette*, sets forth a good example of how to calculate damages and fees under the quiet enjoyment statute.[91]

What gives this statute and the reprisal and consumer protection law discussed below their impact is the ability to recover attorneys' fees and costs. Even a claim with insignificant actual damages, resulting in a minimum recovery of three months' rent, can be greatly enhanced by an award of fees and costs.

2. Warranty of habitability

Another Massachusetts landlord-tenant statute, the warranty of habitability, encompasses both common and statutory law. The landmark case of *Boston Housing Authority v. Hemingway* held that an implied warranty of habitability existed in a lease of residential properties.[92] Every landlord warrants to its tenants that the premises will be delivered and maintained in a habitable condition.[93] In *Crowell v. McCaffrey*, the court extended the warranty to encompass liability for personal injuries caused by a breach.[94]

Separate from the common law is the statutory version of the warranty of habitability, M.G.L., ch. 239, § 8A. Proof that the premises is in violation of the state sanitary code creates a presumption that entitles the tenant to a defense against an eviction for the non-payment of rent. Tenants can withhold rents or initiate sanitary code enforcement proceedings against landlords who refused to remedy code violations.[95] If the tenant is entitled to relief, he can offset his rent, or recover the difference of the value of the apartment as warranted and the rental value in its defective condition.[96]

Attorneys' fees and costs, however, are not available under the warranty of habitability. Additionally, duplicative recoveries under the quiet enjoyment statute and warranty of habitability statute are also not allowed.[97] Since the remedy for a breach of the warranty of habitability is not as extensive as the remedy under quiet enjoyment statute, the habitability claim may not be of great value to a plaintiff. When used as an alternative in the event that negligence actions are susceptible to summary judgment, however, the warranty of habitability has significant consequences and should not be ignored.

Massachusetts courts considering habitability claims by tenants have found that the presence of mold in a rental unit does not violate the implied warranty of habitability where the level of mold does not exceed that found in similar residential settings. In *Avalon Oaks v. King*, the counterclaim of a tenant being evicted was dismissed.[98] The Superior Court Appellate Division held that mold in the apartment did not breach the implied warranty of habitability. A landlord does have a duty under the State Sanitary Code to maintain structural elements so they are free of chronic dampness, defined as "the regular and/or periodic appearance of moisture, water, mold or fungi."[99] Though mold was present in the HVAC system and the bathroom tub and tile area, the plaintiff presented no evidence that the mold was "regular" or "periodic." The court held that the typical levels of airborne mold and visible mold commonly found in residential units does not rise to the level of a breach of the warranty of habitability.[100]

3. Reprisal statutes

There are also Massachusetts landlord-tenant statutes that provide relief for a tenant when a landlord retaliates against her for reporting code violations, such as excessive mold growth.

Pursuant to M.G.L., ch. 186, § 18, any landlord who threatens a tenant for reporting violations is liable for one to three months' rent or actual damages, whichever is greater, including costs and attorneys' fees.[101] Additionally, ch. 239, § 2A creates a rebuttable presumption that an eviction is a reprisal against a tenant who has reported a code violation.[102] A landlord must take great care, therefore, before initiating eviction actions against a tenant who had reported mold accumulation in the premises.

B. Massachusetts Consumer Protection Law

The Massachusetts Consumer Protection Law, Chapter 93A, is a far-reaching statute which prohibits unfair acts in the context of trade or commerce. Under section 9 of the statute, if there is a willful violation of Chapter 93A, double or triple damages can be awarded. This is yet another Massachusetts statute that allows for the recovery of attorneys' fees and costs. Unlike the landlord-tenant statutes, however, Chapter 93A applies to anyone who is involved in a business transaction. It typically involves consumer transactions, such as those between a homeowner and a contractor, but can also include business to business transactions. A demand letter is a prerequisite to a lawsuit under section 9 of the statute.[103]

This statute is particularly important in mold cases since it potentially increases the typical recovery found in a tort action. Not only can a plaintiff recover attorneys' fees and costs under this law, he may also be entitled to multiple damages. In the personal injury context, attorneys' fees and costs can be extensive given the need for one or more expert opinions to succeed on the claims alleged. When punitive damages are awarded, recovery can be significant. The case of *Brossi v. Fisher* sets forth an analysis of Chapter 93A liability and calculation of damages in a landlord-tenant dispute where damages included mold accumulation.[104]

Chapter 93A also encompasses an insured's claim against her insurance company for "bad faith" in denying coverage or failing to timely respond to a mold infiltration claim. *See also* M.G.L., ch. 176D, § 3 for a description of unfair methods of competition and unfair and deceptive acts and practices in the insurance business.

12.4 Procedural Considerations

A. Statutes of Limitation

1. Negligence

Pursuant to M.G.L., ch. 260, § 2A, a person filing a claim for personal injuries must bring the claim three years from the date the claimant discovers the personal injury or property damage, and its cause. Under section 7 of the statute, a minor plaintiff has until three years from the date of his eighteenth birthday to file suit. These statutes begin to run when the claimant discovers or, in the exercise of reasonable diligence, should have discovered the harm.[105]

An exception to the three-year tort action limitation may exist if the tortious conduct is deemed continuous.[106] In a wrongful death case, *Freeman v. Massachusetts Institute of Technology*, a Massachusetts (Middlesex County) Superior Court judge recently addressed whether repeated flooding, resulting in the growth of mold over a seven-year period, constituted a "continuous tort" for purposes of the statute of limitations.[107] In *Freeman*, the plaintiff alleged that her apartment initially flooded in 1990.[108] Problems with flooding and the ensuing growth of mold, bacteria, and mildew continued through 1996.[109] In September of 1996, the city ordered the owner of the property to correct the cause of the flooding.[110]

In 1991, the plaintiff's son was diagnosed with severe bronchial asthma, with a strong allergic component.[111] His exposure to mold, and other allergens related to the flooding caused chronic inflammation of his lungs.[112] Two months after the

September 1996 flood, the child was hospitalized with a collapsed lung following a severe asthma attack.[113] The child subsequently died on July 30, 1997.[114]

The plaintiff presented her claim to the city on July 7, 1999.[115] In her presentment letter, the plaintiff claimed that the family only "recently" learned that the mold problem in the apartment had exacerbated her son's asthma.[116] The plaintiff filed her complaint on January 14, 2000.[117] The city filed a motion for summary judgment in which it argued that all claims relating back further than January 15, 1997, were time barred.[118]

The court stated that a continuous tort does not occur where conduct occurring prior to the statute of limitations continues to cause adverse effects or damages beyond the three-year limitation.[119] A continuous tort only tolls the statute of limitation where the *tortious act continues, not where the continuing effects of the initial tort continue*.[120] In *Cooper v. United States*, the court determined the cause of action accrued when it became apparent to the claimant that no medical treatment was forthcoming.[121]

The *Freeman* court went on to say that, if the problem with flooding was caused by the negligent design and installation of the sewer system, the conduct was not continuous throughout the tenancy, and the claims would be time barred.[122] If, on the other hand, the city's tortious conduct was in the nature of failing repeatedly to clear blockages from the sewers, such conduct could constitute a continuing tort, and these claims could be deemed timely.[123]

2. Breach of contract

Under M.G.L., ch. 260, § 2, a claim for breach of contract must be filed within six years after the cause of action accrues.

3. Breach of express warranty

The claimant must assert a claim for breach of express warranty under a breach of contract theory, and therefore, has six years from the accrual of the cause of action within which to file the claim.[124] Since the action does not sound in tort, the statute of repose (discussed at Section C below) does not apply.[125]

4. Breach of implied warranty

A claim for breach of an implied warranty is considered a tort which must be commenced within the three-year statute of limitations and the six-year statute of repose.[126]

5. Consumer bad faith statute

A claimant has four years within which to file a claim for breach of the consumer bad-faith statute. A claimant may still pursue a claim under ch. 93A even if the underlying tort action is barred by the three-year statute of limitations (assuming the ch. 93A claim is brought within the four-year time limitation).[127]

B. Claims Against the Government

Massachusetts General Laws, ch. 258 provides procedural limitations for claims brought against the Commonwealth of Massachusetts, its municipalities, counties, districts, and the officers and employees thereof. Under section 4 of the statute, a claimant must present, in writing, her claim within two years after the date upon which the cause of action arose. Failure to make a proper presentment of a claim could result in the dismissal of the claim by the court.[128]

Note that, in a claim for nuisance, the claimant need not present the claim under this statute.[129] According to section 10 of the statute, presentment is also not required for intentional torts and other limited actions by the government.

C. Statute of Repose

The Massachusetts statute of repose creates a second time limitation and is designed to protect those engaged in the construction industry. Massachusetts General Laws, ch. 260, § 2B sets forth time limitations in the context of torts arising from "improvements to real property." A tort claim for damages relating to "deficiency or neglect in the design, planning, construction or general administration of an improvement to real property" (not including a public agency) must be brought within three years after the cause of action accrues; however, such an action cannot be commenced more than six years after the earlier of the dates of:

- the opening of the improvement to use; or
- substantial completion of the improvement and the taking of possession for occupancy by the owner.

The same three-year limitation applies to a public agency; however, the six-year limitation applies to the earlier of the dates of:

- official acceptance of the project by the public agency;
- the opening of the real property to public use;
- the acceptance by the contractor of a final estimate prepared by the public agency pursuant to M.G.L., ch. 30, § 39G; or
- substantial completion of the work and the taking of possession for occupancy by the awarding authority.

The term "improvement" has been defined as "a permanent addition to or betterment of real property which enhances its capital value, and that involves the expenditure or labor or money and is designed to make the property more useful or valuable as distinguished from ordinary repairs."[130]

It is important to remember that the statute of repose protects against a specific category of actions as opposed to classes of people.[131] The statute of repose provides no protection to landlords and property owners, as well as many tradespeople who work on buildings or provide building materials. Parties protected by this statute include, *inter alia*, architects, engineers, and contractors. The statute may also bar claims against a manufacturer or supplier if the product is produced for a particular project and meets the specifications of an architect or engineer.[132] The court in *Snow v. Harnischfeger Corporation* stated that the statute of repose defines protected actors by reference to the acts protected under the statute.[133] The *Dighton v. Federal Pacific Electric Co.* court determined that a circuit switch manufacturer was not a protected party under the statute even though the circuits became a permanent part of the structure.[134] This case is also significant because the court ruled that a claim for contribution could not stand against an architect because the statute of repose barred the plaintiff's claims against the architect.[135]

The relation-back doctrine, set forth in Mass. R. Civ. P. 15(C), does not apply in cases in which the statute of repose applies.[136] In *Ferrera & Sons, Inc. v. Samuels & Hannan Construction*, for example, the plaintiff was precluded from amending its complaint to add additional parties, and the defendants were barred from bringing third-party claims for indemnification and contribution against the additional defendants after the six-year repose limitation had expired.[137]

It does not matter that the defect was not discovered, nor could it reasonably have been discovered within the six-year deadline under the repose statute. The statute of repose completely eliminates a cause of action after six years.[138] This includes claims for indemnification and contribution which can be brought within one year of a settlement or judgment in a non-construction context.

Unlike the statute of limitations, the statute of repose does *not* create an extension of time (i.e., three years from the date a minor claimant turns 18) within which a claim may be brought by a minor.[139]

This statute is significant in the context of mold because it could result in a cause of action for mold being barred after six years regardless of whether mold was present in the improvement to real property during the six-year period.

12.5 Insurance Considerations

By and large, the insurance industry in Massachusetts has been successful in limiting the proliferation of mold claims in Massachusetts. Many Massachusetts insurers have adopted limitations for mold in their homeowners' policies which exclude coverage for mold unless the condition resulted from a "covered peril," such as water damage from an accidental discharge or overflow of water, or windstorm. Some policies also include an endorsement with a separate limit for mold. Insurance coverage is clearly important to both plaintiffs and defendants, but plaintiffs especially need to consider this issue when deciding their litigation strategy.

A. Policy Coverage

Massachusetts permits insurers to limit mold coverage in property insurance policies.[140] Insurers writing homeowners and commercial property policies in the state are required to offer fungi and mold coverage of at least $10,000 for homeowners and $15,000 for commercial properties. The insured may opt to purchase this coverage of fungi and mold losses which result from an "otherwise covered peril." If the insured declines the fungi/mold endorsement, the insurer is not obligated to offer such coverage on subsequent renewals.[141] This change is likely to significantly limit the coverage available for mold claims and limit future mold litigation against insurers.

B. Claims Litigation

1. Homeowner's insurance

Insurers have been required to provide coverage of mold claims arising from covered perils. In the case of *Pride v. Latham*, the plaintiff homeowner made claims against her builder and homeowner's insurer concerning extensive mold growth caused by improperly installing a new bathroom shower and venting the bathroom fan into the attic crawl space rather than through the roof to the outside of the house.[142] She also alleged, as a separate cause of moisture build-up, leakage around the chimney which was unrelated to the contractor's work. Her insurer denied coverage and filed a motion for summary judgment seeking relief. The motion was granted as to any mold caused by the contractor's faulty workmanship but denied as to mold caused by the leaking chimney. The court found that the leakage around the chimney could be a distinct covered risk under the homeowner's policy and a discrete antecedent occurrence that is a covered risk that caused the otherwise excluded mold damage.[143] The motion for summary judgment by the contractor's commercial general liability insurer was denied on the ground that the policy's pollution and business risk exclusions are inapplicable.[144]

2. General liability policies

In the *Pride* case, the court held that the pollution and business risk exclusions in a general contractor's policy of commercial general liability insurance do not preclude coverage for mold damage caused by the negligence of the contractor. A motion for summary judgment by the contractor's commercial general liability insurer was denied on the ground that the policy's pollution and business risk exclusions are inapplicable where improper installation of a shower and venting fan in a bathroom caused mold growth.

On the other hand, in a case where homeowners alleged that a contractor's negligence while constructing an addition to their home allowed rainwater to enter the property leading to water damage and mold growth, the Essex County Superior Court found that coverage was excluded when the commercial general liability policy included a Fungi Exclusion Endorsement.[145] In *Arbella Protection Ins. Co. v. Arnold*, the homeowners sued a contractor, Twomey, alleging that his negligent failure to seal their property from the elements during construction caused property damage when water entered their home after severe rainstorms resulting in water damage and mold growth.[146] Ruling on a Motion for Declaratory Judgment by the insurer Arbella, the court held that there was no coverage for the Arnold's water and mold damage and found that Arbella had no obligation to defend and indemnify Twomey.

The homeowners argued that coverage should be allowed because the entering rainwater which caused the mold growth resulted from an antecedent negligent act of the contractor. Under Massachusetts law, if the insurance policy does not clearly and unambiguously exclude coverage for events caused by an antecedent negligent action which is a covered risk, courts will determine liability based on the train of events test.[147] The court rejected the Arnold's contention that the "train of events test" applied, finding that the Fungi Exclusion Endorsement was clearly and unambiguously made a part of the policy's general exclusion section via an advisory notice sent to all policy holders, and received by the contractor Twomey, Advisory Notice 31 AP 1094 (AN 1094), warning policyholders that the attached Fungi Exclusion Endorsement could change their policy's coverage.

Specifically, the court found that the renovation contractor's business' general liability policy excluded coverage for fungi or bacteria through a policy endorsement (CG 21670402 Fungi Exclusion Endorsement) and that the language of the exclusion was clearly and unambiguously made a part of the policy's general exclusion section. In finding that the exclusion was clear and unambiguous the court was persuaded by the fact that the information was provided in bold capital letters and stated that it would be "added to Paragraph 2., Exclusions of Section I—Coverage A—Bodily Injury and Property Damage Liability" where all other general exclusions of the policy were listed in the first section of the policy.

3. Disability insurance

The case of *Narducci v. Contributory Retirement Appeal Bd.* demonstrates the heavy burden of an employee seeking to establish a mold-related workplace disability claim. Narducci was a school music teacher requesting accidental disability pension benefits from the Massachusetts Teachers Retirement System.[148] The plaintiff alleged that she suffered mold-related occupational injuries after her workspace was moved into the basement of the school building. The case was heard originally by an administrative magistrate for the Contributory Retirement Appeals Board, who denied benefits on the basis that it could not be established as to whether claimant's injury was caused by mold in the home or mold in the workplace. The administrative magistrate's decision was affirmed by the Superior Court, the Massachusetts Appeals Court and the Supreme Judicial Court. In its decision, the Massachusetts Appeals Court thoroughly examined the evidence available to the administrative magistrate to determine whether the decision was supported by substantial evidence. The Appeals Court held that the board's finding that mold in her workplace was not the proven cause of her disability must be given deference, where the facts fairly detracting from the plaintiff's claim of workplace injury were sufficient to show that the board's decision was not arbitrary and capricious. It was the plaintiff's burden to demonstrate that her injuries were caused by mold in the workplace and there was no burden on the employer to prove that the injuries were caused by mold in the plaintiff's home and not the workplace mold.[149]

However, it should also be noted that the Appeals Court was impressed by the evidence produced by the plaintiff to demonstrate her disability, which included certifications of four physicians with respiratory specialties stating that Narducci was disabled by her condition. The court specifically noted that the physicians' opinions provided sufficient evidence to demonstrate the disability, and had the decision of the administrative magistrate been to grant disability benefits that it would have affirmed that decision as well.[150]

Endnotes

1. *Bacon v. Federal Kemper Life Assurance Co.*, 400 Mass. 850, 853, 512 N.E.2d 941, 943 (1987).

2. *Coughlin v. Titus & Bean Graphics, Inc.*, 54 Mass. App. Ct. 633, 639, 767 N.E.2d 106, 111 (2002) quoting *Irwin v. Ware*, 392 Mass. 745, 756, 467 N.E.2d 1292, 1300 (1984).

3. *Jorgensen v. Massachusetts Port Authority*, 905 F.2d 515, 523 (1st Cir. 1990) citing *In Re Sponatski*, 220 Mass. 526, 530-31, 108 N.E. 466-68 (1915).

4. *Klein v. Catalano*, 386 Mass. 701, 718, 437 N.E.2d 514, 525 (1982).

5. http://www.cdc.gov/mold/pib.htm.

6. *Jorgensen*, 905 F.2d at 524 citing *Tritsch v. Boston Edison Co.,* 363 Mass. 179, 182, 293 N.E.2d 264, 267 (1973); *Wallace v. Ludwig,* 292 Mass. 251, 254, 198 N.E. 159, 161 (1935).

7. *Stevens v. The Pirates Lane Condominium Trust*, No. 96-00403 (Mass. Super., filed February 27, 1996).

8. 509 U.S. 579 (1993). *See Stevens*, No. 96-0040, Memorandum and Order by Judge Agnes, Jr. (June 19, 2002).

9. 17 Mass. L. Rep. 352 (Mass. Super. Ct. 2004).

10. *Id.*

11. *Id.*

12. *Id.*

13. *Id.*

14. *Id.*

15. *Liska v. Travelers Property Casualty Corp., et al.,* 18 Mass. L. Rep. 644 (Mass. Super. Ct. 2004).

16. *Id.*

17. *Id.*

18. *Id.*

19. *Id. citing Hanover New England v. Smith,* 35 Mass. App. Ct. 417, 420-21, 621 N.E.2d 382, 383 (1993) (*citations omitted*).

20. *Id.*

21. *Schmidt v. County of Norfolk*, No. 02-00614, 2002 Mass. Super. LEXIS 327 (August 15, 2002). There is no mention in the opinion as to whether the defendant challenged Dr. Olliver's anticipated testimony under *Daubert*.

22. *Id.* at 3.

23. *Id.* at 8-9.

24. *Id.* at 14-15.

25. *Id.* at 15-16.

26. *Id.* at 44.

27. *Narducci v. Contributory Retirement Appeal Bd.*, 68 Mass. App. Ct. 127, 860 N.E.2d 943 (2007), *rev. denied*, 448 Mass. 1108, 864 N.E.2d 23 (2007).

28. *MacGregor v. Born*, 21 Mass. L. Rep. 353, Mass. Super. LEXIS 394 (03-1349, Norfolk Superior Court, August 17, 2006).

29. *See Commonwealth v. Lanigan*, 419 Mass. 15, 25, 641 N.E.2d 1342 (1994), citing *Daubert*, 509 U.S. at 593-94.

30. *Id.*, 419 Mass. at 24.

31. *Id* at 11.

32. *DeSanctis v. Lynn Water & Sewer Commission*, 423 Mass. 112, 118, 666 N.E.2d 1292, 1296 (1996).

33. *Id.*; *Espahbodi v. Town of Sudbury*, No. 94-4230, 1998 Mass. Super. LEXIS 436, at *25-*26 (August 4, 1998).

34. *Id.* at *14.

35. *Id.* at *14-*16.

36. *Id.* at *19.

37. *Id.* at *1.

38. *Id.* at *21-*26.

39. No. MIC V 2004-02698 (February 2006)

40. *Ravosa v. Zais*, 40 Mass. App. Ct. 47, 52, 661 N.E.2d 111, 116 (1996), *rev. denied*, 422 Mass. 1108, 664 N.E.2d 1198 (1996) (citations omitted).

41. *Acushnet Federal Credit Union v. Roderick*, 26 Mass. App. Ct. 604, 605, 530 N.E.2d 1243, 1244 (1988), citing *Yorke v. Taylor* 332 Mass. 368, 374, 124 N.E.2d. 912, 916 (1955). A plaintiff may also allege intentional misrepresentation, but it requires a higher burden of proof than negligent misrepresentation. The plaintiff would be required to show that the defendant made the claim knowing it was false for the purpose of inducing the plaintiffs to act. *See Barrett Associates v. Aronson*, 346 Mass. 150, 152, 190 N.E.2d 867, 868 (1963).

42. *Manock v. Chamoun,* No. 06-CV-00001, Northeast Housing Court (June 26, 2006).

43. ESCV 2003-01715 (September 2005).

44. 413 Mass. 387, 394-397 (1992).

45. Immunol Allergy Clin. N. Am. 20 (2008) 485-505.

46. *St. Germaine v. Pendergast*, 411 Mass. 615, 620, 584 N.E.2d 611, 614 (1992).

47. *Canal Electric Co. v. Westinghouse Electric Co.*, 973 F.2d 988, 990 (1st Cir. 1992).

48. *Id.* at 992.

49. *Albrecht v. Clifford,* 436 Mass. 706, 708, 767 N.E.2d 42, 44 (2002).

50. *Anthony's Pier Four, Inc. v. Crandall Dry Dock Engineers, Inc.*, 396 Mass. 818, 822, 489 N.E.2d 172, 175 (1986).

51. *Albrecht*, 436 Mass. at 718, 767 N.E.2d at 51.

52. *Id.* at 708, 767 N.E.2d at 44.

53. *Id.*

54. *Id.* at 715, 767 N.E.2d at 49-50.

55. *Id.*

56. *Anthony's Pier Four*, 396 Mass. at 828, 489 N.E.2d at 178.

57. *Id.* at 820, 489 N.E.2d at 174.

58. *Id.*

59. *Id.* at 825-26, 489 N.E.2d at 177.

60. *Id.* at 827, 489 N.E.2d at 177.

61. *Id.*

62. *Id.* at 829, 489 N.E.2d at 179.

63. *Klein*, 386 Mass. at 718, 437 N.E.2d at 525.

64. *Albrecht*, 436 Mass. at 710-11, 767 N.E.2d at 46-47 (2002).

65. *Id.* at 711, 767 N.E.2d at 47.

66. *Id.*

67. *Id.* at 711-12, 767 N.E.2d at 47.

68. *Id.* at 712, 767 N.E. 2d at 47.

69. *Berish v. Bornstein,* 437 Mass. 252, 263-64, 770 N.E.2d 961, 972 *(2002).*

70. *Solomon v. Birger,* 19 Mass. App. Ct. 634, 638, n.7, 477 N.E.2d 137, 141 n.7 (1985), *rev. denied*, 395 Mass. 1103, 481 N.E.2d 198 (1985).

71. *Berish*, 437 Mass. at 264-65, 770 N.E.2d at 973.

72. *Berish*, 437 Mass. at 265, 770 N.E.2d at 973-74 (emphasis added).

73. *Id. at 264.*

74. *Id.* at 268.

75. *Berish v. Bornstein*, 21 Mass. L. Rptr. 530 (2006).

76. *Id.*

77. *Id.*

78. *Id.* citing *Albrecht*, 436 Mass. at 711.

79. *Id.* citing, *McAllister v. Boston Housing Auth.*, 429 Mass. at 305 (1999).

80. *Murphy v. Town of Chatham*, 41 Mass. App. Ct. 821, 823, 676 N.E.2d 473, 475 (1996) (citations omitted).

81. *Id.* (citations omitted).

82. *Martino v. Banwake, LLC*, No. MIC V 2004-02698, Middlesex Superior Court (February 2006).

83. *Murphy*, 41 Mass. App. Ct. at 825, 676 N.E.2d at 476.

84. *Id.* at 825, 676 N.E.2d at 476-77.

85. *Id.* at 824, 676 N.E.2d at 476.

86. *Patkin v. Northside Condominium,* No. 03-CV-00046, Northeast Housing Court (June 26, 2006).

87. SUCV 2004-04827, Suffolk Superior Court (May 23, 2006).

88. *Al-Ziab v. Mourgis*, 424 Mass. 847, 850, 679 N.E.2d. 528, 529 (1997).

89. *Id.* at 850, 679 N.E.2d at 530.

90. *Id.* at 850-51, 679 N.E.2d at 529-30.

91. 49 Mass. App. Ct. 99, 104, 726 N.E.2d 967, 971 (2000).

92. 363 Mass. 184, 199, 293 N.E.2d 831, 843 (1973)

93. *Id.* at 199, 293 N.E.2d at 843.

94. 377 Mass. 443, 447, 386 N.E.2d 1256, 1259 (1979). *See also Simon v. Solomon*, 385 Mass. 91, 96, 431 N.E.2d 556, 561 (1982).

95. *Hemingway*, 363 Mass. at 199, 293 N.E.2d at 843.

96. *Id.* at 201-02, 293 N.E.2d at 844-45.

97. *Wolfberg v. Hunter*, 385 Mass. 390, 401, 432 N.E.2d 467, 474 (1982); *Darmetko v. Boston Housing Authority*, 378 Mass. 758, 761-62, 393 N.E.2d 395, 398 (1979).

98. 2007 Mass. App. Div. No. 174, 2007 Mass. App. Div. LEXIS 57 (2007).

99. 105 CMR § 410.020.

100. *Id.* at *8.

101. *Manzaro v. McCann*, 401 Mass. 880, 883, n. 3, 519 N.E.2d 1337, 1340, n. 3 (1988).

102. *Appelstein v. Quinn*, 361 Mass. 861, 281 N.E.2d 228, 229 (1972).

103. *Cassano v. Gogos*, 20 Mass. App. Ct. 348, 350, 480 N.E.2d 649, 651 (1985); *Spring v. Geriatric Authority of Holyoke*, 394 Mass. 274, 289, 475 N.E.2d 727, 736 (1985).

104. 1999 Mass. App. Div. 99 (1999).

105. *Riley v. Presnell,* 409 Mass. 239, 244, 565 N.E.2d 780, 785 (1991).

106. *Doe v. Blandford*, 402 Mass. 831, 839, 525 N.E.2d 403, 409 (1988) (citations omitted).

107. *Freeman v. Massachusetts Institute of Technology,* No. 00-0204, 2000 Mass. Super. LEXIS 311, at *7-*11 (August 14, 2000).

108. *Id.* at *2.

109. *Id.*

110. *Id.*

111. *Id.*

112. *Id.* at *2.

113. *Id.* at *3.

114. *Id.*

115. *Id.*

116. *Id.* at *3-*4.

117. *Id.* at *4.

118. The plaintiff was statutorily required to present her claim to the city within two years of the occurrence, hence, the defendant argued that all claims prior to the two-year period of the presentment letter should be dismissed. *Id.* at *5.

119. *Id.* at *5-*7.

120. *Id.,* citing *Maslauskas* v. *United States.*, 583 F. Supp. 349, 351 (D. Mass. 1984). *See also Cooper v. United States*, 442 F.2d 908, 911-12 (1971) (claim time barred because of the government's refusal to provide medical care was not continuous despite the claimant's repeated requests for medical attention).

121. *Cooper*, 442 F.2d at 912.

122. *Freeman*, 2000 Mass. Super. LEXIS 311, at *9-*10.

123. *Id.* at **11.*

124. *Anthony's Pier Four, Inc. v. Crandall Dry Dock Engineers, Inc.*, 396 Mass. 818, 822, 489 N.E.2d 172, 174 (1986). *See also, Burke v. Foremost Ins. Co.*, 2004 Mass. Super. LEXIS 621, 18 Mass. L. Rep. 625 (Mass. Super. Ct. 2004) (Mobile home owner's claims for breach of express warranties arising from mold in housing unit barred by statute of limitations.)

125. *Anthony's Pier Four*, 396 Mass. at 823, 489 N.E.2d at 175.

126. *Albrecht v. Clifford,* 436 Mass. 706, 712, 767 N.E.2d 42, 47 (2002). *See Burke v. Foremost Ins. Co.,* 2004 Mass. Super. LEXIS 621, 18 Mass. L. Rep. 625 (Mass. Super. Ct. 2004) (barring mobile home owner's implied warranty claims where the roof leak which caused the mold was discovered as early as 1992 and claim was not filed until 2003).

127. *Fine v. Huygens et al.,* 57 Mass. App. Ct. 397, 401, 783 N.E.2d 842, 846 (2003).

128. *Doe v. Blandford*, 402 Mass. 831, 839, 525 N.E.2d 403, 408 (1988)

129. *Murphy v. Town of Chatham*, 41 Mass. App. Ct. 821, 824-5, 676 N.E.2d 473, 476-7 (1996).

130. *Snow v. Harnischfeger Corporation*, 12 F.3d 1154, 1161 (1st Cir. 1993).

131. *Dighton v. Federal Pacific Electric Co.*, 399 Mass. 687, 695, 506 N.E.2d 509, 515 (1987) (citations omitted)

132. *Id.* at 1160; *Rosario v. M.D. Knowlton* Co., 54 Mass. App. Ct. 796, 801, 767 N.E.2d 1126, 1131 (2002).

133. 12 F.3d at 1160; *See also Dighton v. Federal Pacific Electric Co.*, 399 Mass. 687, 695, 506 N.E.2d 509, 515 (1987) (citations omitted).

134. *Dighton*, 399 Mass. at 699, 506 N.E.2d at 517.

135. *Id.* at 692-93, 506 N.E.2d at 513.

136. *Tindol v. Boston Housing Authority*, 396 Mass. 515, 518, 487 N.E.2d 488, 490 (1986), *Fine v. Huygens* 57 Mass. App. Ct. 397, 401, 783 N.E.2d 842, 846 (2003); *Ferrera & Sons, Inc. v. Samuels & Hannan Construction,* 21 Mass. App. Ct. 170, 172-173, 486 N.E.2d 58, 60 (1985).

137. *Ferrera*, 21 Mass. App. Ct. at 172-173, 486 N.E.2d at 60.

138. *Ferrera,* 21 Mass. App. Ct. at 173, and 486 N.E.2d at 60.

139. *Tindol v. Boston Housing Authority*, 396 Mass. 515, 518, 487 N.E.2d 488, 490 (1986).

140. M*assachusetts Division of Insurance Bulletin 2006-02* (Fungus/Mold Wet & Dry Rot Coverage Requirements) (January 31, 2006).

141. *Id.*

142. *Pride v. Latham, No. 04-CV-00059 and O5-CV-00105 (*Northeast Housing Court June 28, 2006).

143. *Id.*

144. *Id.*

145. *Arbella Protection Ins. Co. v. Arnold,* No. 06-1445 (August 15, 2007).

146. *Id.*

147. *Jussim v. Mass. Bay Ins. Co.*, 415 Mass. 24, 31, 610 N.E.2d 954 (1993).

148. 68 Mass. App. Ct. 127, 860 N.E.2d 943 (2007), *review denied*, 448 Mass. 1108, 864 N.E.2d 23 (2007)

149. *Id* at 137.

150. *Id.*

Chapter 13

An Overview of Toxic Mold Litigation in New Jersey

Patrick J. Perrone, Esq., Richard J. Valladares, Esq.
and Ashley Turner

Synopsis

13.1 Introduction

The optimistic assumption that mold litigation was an anomaly confined to a few geographic areas with continual warm, humid weather has all but been abandoned in light of the continued filing of mold-related claims across the nation. Mold spores are present everywhere, and although mold growth flourishes in locations with warm, humid weather, there are various other conditions that may cause indoor mold such as building envelope construction defects.

In addition, mold-related liability claims are no less contingent on specific weather conditions than they are on heightened publicity, rapid demand for new housing, and mounting interest from the plaintiffs' bar. The effect of these unconventional factors is readily apparent in New Jersey. New Jersey's population growth of approximately 78,000 people each year and the consequential demand for new housing and development combined with recent media hype has created an acute awareness of mold presence and mold-related personal injury and property damage allegations within New Jersey's general population. This acute awareness has resulted in a proliferation of mold-related claims in New Jersey. Although the epicenter of such claims is in the insurance arena, because of the fallout from the recent appearance of mold exclusions in insurance policies and the denial of insurance coverage for these claims, there is likely to be increased mold litigation against builders and property owners. Mold litigation is made even more likely due to the nationwide focus by plaintiffs' attorneys on recent allegations that serious bodily injury is caused by mold exposure.

Litigators serving their respective clients should be well-versed on relevant New Jersey legal principles which define applicable causes of action and offer defenses that may lessen the liability blow of a mold lawsuit. Although case law in the mold litigation context is not as well-developed in New Jersey as it is in other states (such as California and Florida), there is no reason to believe these general legal principles will not be wholly applicable to the mold phenomenon.

13.2 Potential Causes of Action

Mold-related lawsuits may encompass a variety of causes of action including, but not limited to, claims founded in negligence, breach of contract, breach of implied warranties, misrepresentation and fraud. These claims spring from the unique responsibilities associated with the construction, sale, operation, management, control, maintenance, and/or renovation of residential or commercial structures. Although these duties and responsibilities have not been fully defined by New Jersey courts in the mold context, the following sections identify the most probable application of New Jersey legal principles to the mold litigation phenomenon.

A. Negligence

As in any negligence action, there are four basic requirements to presenting a *prima facie* case of negligence. The plaintiff must show that the defendant owed a duty of care, that the defendant breached that duty, that the defendant's breach was the actual and proximate cause of the alleged property damage or bodily injury, and that there was actual property damage or bodily injury.[1] Although contractors, subcontractors, architects, building supply manufacturers, maintenance companies, and property owners all have unique duties to a homeowner or tenant, they will often be sued by the same plaintiff in the same case. Exemplifying the broad exposure to a wide array of professionals susceptible to mold litigation is a January 2003 lawsuit filed in Middlesex County, New Jersey. In that suit, home purchasers simultaneously sued previous homeowners, real estate agents, and home inspectors.[2] Specifically, plaintiffs alleged that the previous homeowners intentionally concealed water problems and other hazardous conditions on the disclosure statement; that the real estate agents knew of, and intentionally misrepresented, the true condition of the home; and that their home inspector provided inaccurate inspection findings.[3]

The typical array of potential defendants in a mold case may be further broadened by virtue of the fact that New Jersey courts have abandoned concepts such as privity[4] and *caveat emptor.*[5] The following sub-sections describe the nature of the duties imposed on a broad range of professionals.

1. Professional sellers of real estate

Historically, real estate purchases were governed by the doctrine of *caveat emptor* or "let the buyer beware." Under this doctrine, the sellers of real estate had no obligation to disclose defects unless otherwise agreed. Currently, state law varies concerning a seller's duty to disclose. Nevertheless, even in those states that follow *caveat emptor* and impose no duty to disclose patent defects, a seller is nonetheless required to disclose known latent defects.[6] Although real estate non-disclosure cases in New Jersey involve more conventional problems such as termite infestation, there appears to be no apparent reason these principles would be inapplicable in a mold case. In fact, mold may be as latent as termite damage, existing behind walls, in basements, or behind drop-ceilings.

Moreover, even in cases in which mold conditions have already been remediated, and the sellers might be tempted to keep that remedial information to themselves by arguing that the property is no longer in an allegedly "defective condition," such an option presents high risk to the non-disclosing seller if mold growth re-occurs (which is possible under certain conditions).

Disclosures by a professional seller of residential real estate should be carefully considered in New Jersey, since New Jersey courts reject the *caveat emptor* doctrine entirely, finding that the doctrine is inconsistent with modern home buying practices.[7] New Jersey courts have noted that the principal reasons for imposing on professional sellers a duty to disclose, relates to the difference in bargaining power between the professional seller of real estate and the purchaser of such housing, as well as the difference in access to information between the seller and the buyer.[8] Therefore, the explicit disclosure of discovered mold growth and prior mold remediation should be carefully considered by professional sellers of real property, since such conditions might be deemed a "material" defect by courts or juries.

Pending legislation should also be considered. Currently pending is a toxic mold bill which expressly requires the disclosure of the presence of mold by persons selling or leasing commercial or industrial property, public entities that own, lease or operate property, lessors of residential property, or lessees who know that mold is present in a property.[9] The mold must either exceed permissible exposure limits or pose a health risk, as defined by the Department of Health and Senior Services, for disclosure to be required. No disclosure is required if a mold hazard is remediated as described by the Department of Community Affairs' remediation standards. Unlike legislation in other states, there is no immunity provision in the New Jersey bill. Thus, although landlords may be required to divulge to prospective tenants the presence of any known mold, the landlord may nonetheless be liable in any action based on the presence of, or propensity for, mold growth in a building. A seller or lessor of residential housing must provide the purchaser or lessee with a mold hazard information pamphlet developed by the Department of Community Affairs before the purchaser or lessee is obligated under any contract to purchase or lease the residential property. Also, the Department of Community Affairs is required to keep a record of information regarding contracting for the removal of mold in a building or surrounding area. According to the bill, this record will be available to the public upon request.

Additionally, pending legislation in New Jersey, if passed, would require sellers of residential property containing less than five units to conduct a mold inspection prior to the closing.[10] Both the buyer and seller will be required to certify that they have reviewed the results of the inspection. Other legislation will require sellers to provide a mold hazard warning within the sale contract and will give buyers a ten-day period to conduct an inspection for the presence of mold.[11]

2. Builders

Builders are most commonly sued for construction defects causing moisture and water intrusion that fosters mold growth. Plaintiffs typically allege that such defects constitute a breach of the builder's implied duty to carry out its work in a reasonable and prudent manner. Common mold-related defects are those associated with the building envelope, roof, windows, venting, or plumbing. In New Jersey, a builder's duty may extend not only to parties in direct privity, but also to third parties who can establish that the builder's negligence was the proximate cause of their injuries (whether personal injury or property damage).[12]

New Jersey's "New Home Warranty and Builders' Registration Act" specifically protects new homeowners and is likely to apply to certain mold claims.[13] The New Home Warranty and Builders' Registration Act provides that a builder of a new home is liable to any owner thereof for any defect covered by the Act.[14] Warranty periods established by the Act are as follows: (1) one year from and after the warranty date, the dwelling shall be free from defects caused by faulty workmanship and defective materials due to noncompliance with the building standards as approved by the Commissioner of Community Affairs; (2) two years from and after the warranty date, the dwelling shall be free from defects caused by faulty installation of plumbing, electrical, heating and cooling systems, except in the case of appliances in which the manufacturers' warranty governs; and (3) ten years from and after the warranty date, the dwelling shall be free from major construction defects as defined in the Act.[15] Notwithstanding the existence of the Act, homeowners are not limited to submitting a claim under the New Home Warranty and Builders' Registration Act and are statutorily granted the right to pursue any remedy legally available to them.[16]

3. Subcontractor liability

A recurring question in the construction setting is whether an owner can file a claim against a subcontractor with whom it has no contract.[17] This is a significant issue in mold litigation since water intrusion problems are often identifiable and assignable to individual subcontractors (e.g., window installation, roofing installation, and flashing installation). In most jurisdictions, the lack of privity between an owner and a subcontractor impedes the pursuit of claims directly against subcontractors.[18] In light of this privity dilemma, jurisdictions that recognize an owner's right of recovery against a subcontractor rest liability not on contract principles, but on tort principles.

New Jersey appears to be one of the few jurisdictions that has held that a subcontractor may be held directly liable in tort to an owner or developer even in the absence of a direct contractual relationship. In *Juliano v. Gaston,* a New Jersey court permitted an owner to file a tort action against various subcontractors for failure to carry out their work with reasonable care and skill.[19] In *Gaston,* homeowners brought an action alleging they had been damaged by the negligent workmanship of two subcontractors involved in their home's construction.[20] The general allegations were that the work of these defendants "was done in a negligent, unworkmanlike manner, contrary to the standards of the industry and in all respects carelessly and improperly" and that "as the direct and proximate result thereof," the home was damaged and had to be repaired (at a significant cost).[21] Although the trial court granted summary judgment to the subcontractors, the New Jersey Appellate Court reversed and remanded.[22] In doing so, the New Jersey Appellate Court rejected the trial court's finding that the action was barred due to lack of privity between the parties, noting that the claim was based on the subcontractors' negligence and had no relation to the contract between the builder and the subcontractors.[23] In so ruling, the court stated:

> We fail, therefore, to understand the concern of the trial judge with the question of privity. Privity is a concept having relevance only in a contractual situation and is, of course, that concept which, as an historical matter and prior to the evolution of the doctrine of strict liability in tort, limited a consumer's warranty recourse to the party with whom he had directly dealt.
>
> ...
>
> The fact, however, remains that this action by these plaintiffs against these subcontractors was neither instituted nor prosecuted on an implied warranty theory but rather on a traditional negligence basis. Privity is hence irrelevant.[24]

The language of the *Gaston* court's holding revealed an intent to place New Jersey among those jurisdictions that hold a subcontractor directly liable in tort to an owner or developer in the absence of a direct contractual relationship, if that subcontractor's defective workmanship caused the owner to sustain property damage.

Other jurisdictions have consistently so held, recognizing a direct cause of action in negligence, irrespective of the availability of a warranty or strict liability cause of action, when the purchaser of a new house seeks to recover property damages only from a negligent subcontractor.[25]

The significance of this decision should not be overlooked. The *Gaston* decision not only creates a viable cause of action, but seems to permit a plaintiff to elude the consequences of the "economic loss doctrine," which normally prohibits tort actions when the damage is economic only (e.g., the cost to remediate mold growth). In *Gaston,* the "economic loss doctrine" was held to be inapplicable due to the fact that the action was founded on "pure negligence."[26] In so holding, the *Gaston* court stated:

> It appears that the nature of the damages here may be limited to replacement and repair of defective workmanship, a category of damages customarily referred to as "economic loss." We see, however, no impediment, conceptual or practical, to the recovery of this category of damages in a negligence action by the purchaser against the subcontractor.
>
> ...
>
> In our view, if plaintiffs sustained any economic loss by reason of the negligence of the subcontractors, they are entitled to be made whole.[27]

B. Breach of Contract

Similar to most jurisdictions, a *prima facie* breach of contract case requires the plaintiff to establish: a valid contract, defective performance by the defendant, and resulting damages.[28] Such claims can be expected in the mold context.

C. Breach of Implied Warranties

In addition to liability for breach of the express terms of a contract, contractors and subcontractors are frequently held liable for breach of the following implied warranties: (1) the implied warranty of good workmanship; (2) the implied warranty of habitability; and (3) the implied warranty of quiet enjoyment.

1. Implied warranty of good workmanship

The most common cases will involve construction defects that lead to water intrusion problems and mold growth. In conjunction with an allegation that such defects are in contravention to the express sales contract, the property owner may also allege that the faulty or substandard construction constitutes a breach of the implied warranty of good workmanship (which applies to all new homes).[29]

The implied warranty of good workmanship is not limited to the initial home purchaser. In New Jersey, subsequent buyers may also be entitled to implied warranty protections.[30]

2. Implied warranty of habitability

In certain mold cases, plaintiffs may allege that the construction defect and resulting mold growth affected the habitability of the property.[31] The implied warranty of habitability means that the property is suitable for living purposes and able to be occupied.[32] Thus, a successful breach of the implied warranty of habitability claim requires proof that some vital living element of the property was affected.[33] Such claims are likely to appear in lawsuits involving allegations of bodily injury (allergies, respiratory problems, fatigue, etc.).

3. Implied warranty of quiet enjoyment

Implied warranty of quiet enjoyment claims usually arise in the landlord-tenant context. Under the implied warranty of quiet enjoyment, any act or omission of the landlord which renders the premises substantially unsuitable for the purpose for which they were leased, or which seriously interferes with the beneficial enjoyment of the premises, is a breach of the covenant of quiet enjoyment.[34] The remedy of constructive eviction has been applied to such cases.[35]

Implied warranty of quiet enjoyment claims have often been successfully founded on circumstances regarding health and safety (e.g., claims involving noxious odors[36] or failure to heat the premises[37]). Accordingly there is no reason to believe that such claims will not be made in the mold context.

D. Fraud or Negligent Misrepresentation Claims

Fraud claims require the plaintiff to prove: (1) a material misrepresentation or omission of a presently existing or past fact; (2) knowledge of belief by the defendant of its falsity; (3) an intention that the other person rely on it; (4) reasonable reliance thereon by the other person; and (5) resulting damages.[38] Negligent misrepresentation claims require the plaintiff to prove that an "incorrect statement was negligently made and justifiably relied upon" and that the injury was sustained as a consequence of that reliance.[39] When a builder, subcontractor, landlord, property owner, or real estate professional knows of a mold problem and intentionally or negligently fails to advise the tenant or homeowner, a fraud and/or negligent misrepresentation claim is likely to be made.[40]

Beyond these common law duties, the New Jersey Consumer Fraud Act must be factored into disclosure considerations of real estate professionals.

New Jersey Courts have ruled that brokers, agents, and salespersons involved in the sale of real estate are subject to claims brought under the New Jersey Consumer Fraud Act.[41] The Act prohibits both affirmative misrepresentations and acts of omission.[42] The Act states that "the omission of any material fact with intent that others rely upon such omission, in connection with the sale...of...real estate" is an "unlawful practice."[43] Such may be the case when the nondisclosures rise to conduct equivalent to "swindling" or "shocking to the ethical sense of the community."[44] Significantly, violation of the Act permits a purchaser of real estate to recover treble damages for any ascertainable loss, plus reasonable attorney's fees.[45]

E. Workers' Compensation

Employers and their insurers are also not immune from mold litigation. Notwithstanding the fact that the link between bodily injury and mold contamination has yet to be established, claims for workers' compensation due to injuries related to mold exposure are growing. In mold-contaminated buildings, employees will often seek workers' compensation for personal injury allegedly caused by exposure to mold. When mold is identified by an employee, the employer should act accordingly to avoid allegations of "intentional harm," which permits an employee to escape the workers' compensation bar.

New Jersey is no stranger to this phenomenon. In a recent New Jersey case, a workers' compensation judge held that a teacher had suffered 10 percent permanent partial disability after working for several months in a classroom where mold and mildew were present.[46] The judge awarded the teacher $50,682 in compensation for temporary and permanent disabilities and ordered the school board to pay a penalty for denying the teacher's request for a transfer to another school following the onset of the health problems.[47]

13.3 Class Actions

Mold lawsuits will often be brought by numerous similarly situated plaintiffs who are members of a condominium association, tenants in an apartment building, homeowners in a townhouse complex, or home purchasers from a common builder. In such cases, the plaintiffs may seek class certification. To qualify as a class action, a lawsuit must satisfy the four requirements of New Jersey Court Rule 4:32-1: (1) numerosity; (2) commonality; (3) typicality; and (4) adequacy of representation.[48] Although common issues of fact and law might exist with respect to certain limited issues in a mold case, the individual issues are likely to predominate.

13.4 Potential Defenses

A. Statute of Repose

A statute of limitations sets forth the period within which an action must be commenced based on the accrual of that cause of action.[49] A statute of repose, however, operates regardless of the accrual of a cause of action.[50] New Jersey has a ten-year statute of repose which is found at N.J.S.A. 2A:14-1.1, and limits the potential liability to which architect and building contractors (among others) are subject.[51] Thus, plaintiffs instituting an action in New Jersey alleging property damage or bodily injury claims based on deficiencies in design, planning, surveying, supervision, or construction of an improvement to real property have only ten years from "substantial completion" of the improvement to real property) to file their claim.[52] Significantly, this is so even if the defect is undiscovered until some time after the improvement is made.[53]

Product design alone is not enough to trigger the applicability of N.J.S.A. 2A:14-1.1.51 The statute does not benefit manufacturers and sellers of products who were not involved in the design, planning, and/or construction of the improvement to real estate.[54] More specifically, the sale of a mass-produced item does not constitute the "design, planning supervision or construction of an improvement to real property" as envisioned by the statute.[55] However, when a manufacturer or seller of building products or components significantly participates in the installation of that product into the building, such that it constitutes an "improvement real property" within the meaning of N.J.S.A. 2A:14-1.1, that party is entitled to the protection granted by New Jersey's statute of repose.[56]

The statute of repose poses a serious risk to those representing mold plaintiffs, which is heightened by the fact that mold growth is often a slow process and not discovered until some significant time after the alleged construction defect is identified. For those representing defendants, the statute of repose offers an invaluable defense that summarily defeats a plaintiff's claim.

B. Spoliation

Fulfilling one's duty to preserve evidence is difficult in a mold case. Indeed, both the owner and the tenant will want to quickly remove and remediate any discovered mold. This is especially so in light of the propensity for mold to reoccur when improperly remediated. As part of the remediation process, owners commonly destroy and remove sheet-rock, ceiling tile, insulation, wood framing, or other affected materials. Notwithstanding the reasonableness of such conduct, the destruction of such building components may destroy valuable evidence in a subsequently brought litigation.

Depending on the specific factual circumstances involved, such spoliation of evidence could result in: (1) dismissal of the claim; (2) precluding the offending party from relying on the spoliated evidence; or (3) injecting an "adverse inference" into the jury charge.[57] Thus, owners are placed in the untenable position of having to remove mold-laden materials from the property, while at the same time having to "preserve" evidence in the event of subsequent litigation. Under the circumstances, litigators should counsel clients to notify all potentially interested parties prior to demolition.

Spoliation of evidence in a prospective civil action occurs when evidence pertinent to the action is destroyed, thereby interfering with the action's proper administration and disposition.[58] The duty to preserve evidence arises when there is: (1) pending or probable litigation involving the defendants; (2) knowledge by the plaintiff of the existence or likelihood of litigation; (3) foreseeability of harm to the defendants (or in other words, discarding the evidence would be prejudicial to defendants); and (4) evidence relevant to the litigation.[59] The duty to preserve evidence is a question of law to be determined by the court.[60] Although the scope of the duty to preserve evidence is not boundless, an opportunity for inspection should be afforded to a potentially responsible party before relevant evidence is destroyed.[61]

Significantly, the spoliator's level of intent, whether negligent or intentional, does not affect the spoliator's liability.[62] Rather, it is simply a factor to be considered when determining the appropriate sanction for the spoliation.[63] Moreover, when a party's agent (i.e., expert witness or legal counsel) engages in spoliation of evidence, there is nothing inherently unfair about imposing sanctions against a litigant for the conduct of the litigant's agents.[64]

C. Contractual Provisions

Although a party generally cannot disclaim liability for personal injury claims, defendants should be able to limit their potential liability for property damage claims.[65] As in most construction-related cases, potential defendants can limit their liability by contract.[66] This includes (1) limitation of remedy provisions, (2) limitation of damages provisions, and (3) exclusion of incidental and consequential damages provisions.[67] There is no reason to believe that such disclaimers or limitations would not be upheld by courts in the mold context.

13.5 Damages

A. Attorneys' Fees and Costs

The general rule is that litigants bear their own expenses for fees and costs, except when specifically authorized by statute, rule, or agreement.[68] Attorney fee provisions in construction contracts should be carefully considered at the time of contracting.

When the New Jersey consumer fraud statute is implicated, defendants may be held liable for attorneys' fees and costs.[69] This is so, irrespective of express contract terms.

B. Cost of Repair versus Diminution of Value

For property damage cases, the general rule is that the plaintiff is entitled to either (1) the cost to repair the damage or (2) the difference between the value of the property in its "damaged condition" versus the value of the property in its undamaged condition.[70] There is no reason to believe that the same rules will not apply in the mold context.

C. Opportunity to Repair

Although many states now have "right to cure" laws (which permit builders to make repairs prior to the filing of a lawsuit), no such legislation currently exists in New Jersey.

Although there currently is no "right to cure" law in New Jersey mold-related litigation, there may be movement toward adopting such a law in the near future. Indeed, with respect to purchaser-builder arbitrations involving new construction, New Jersey's acting governor has issued an Executive Order toward that end. On May 9, 2005, New Jersey's Acting Governor Dick Codey signed Executive Order Number 33, which provides additional protections to new home buyers. The Order also creates a single arbitration hearing that will focus on defect repair instead of monetary relief. The standard, under the Order, is that the relief should be aimed at restoring the home to "as new" condition. Thus, for new-home mold claims subject to arbitration, the builder may be provided an opportunity to repair as opposed to being subject to pure monetary damages.

D. Economic Loss Doctrine

The uncertainty created by the emerging nature of mold litigation can be partially diminished by the potential mold defendant's use of the "economic loss rule." The "economic loss rule" springs from the distinction between tort and contract.

Tort law compensates consumers for physical injury or damage to property other than the allegedly defective product itself. Contract law, on the other hand, compensates consumers for disappointed economic expectations. The economic loss rule maintains the distinction between tort and contract by requiring that claims for economic loss (e.g., disappointed economic expectations) be brought in contract. Thus, the "economic loss rule" is a judicially created doctrine that prohibits recovery in tort when a product has damaged only itself and the only losses suffered are economic in nature.[71]

Thus, building product manufacturers, or any other potential defendant in a mold case involving damage to the product itself (the structure at issue), should not be subject to the type of unlimited liability that is often associated with tort claims.

13.6 Admissibility of Scientific Evidence or Expert Testimony

The medical and scientific communities dispute over whether mold causes serious bodily injury. Accordingly, expert testimony on the relationship between mold and bodily injury is a significant element of any mold case for expert testimony to be relevant. That is, there must be a logical connection between the expert's theory and the expert's conclusion. With respect to mold litigation, this means that the expert must be able to demonstrate that exposure to mold caused the plaintiff's injury. Absent such proof, the expert's analysis is irrelevant.

To understand New Jersey's standard on the admissibility of expert testimony, one must be knowledgeable on two different standards that courts use for determining whether expert testimony is admissible—the *Frye* test and the *Daubert* test.[72] Pursuant to *Frye v. United States,* expert testimony is only admissible if it is based on scientific principles that are sufficiently established so that they have gained general acceptance in the relevant scientific community.[73] Pursuant to *Daubert v. Merrell Dow Pharmaceuticals*, expert testimony is admissible only if the judge finds the testimony or evidence to be both reliable and relevant.[74] Reliability is assessed by looking at (1) whether the theory or technique can and has been tested, (2) whether it has been subjected to peer review and publication, (3) the known or potent rate of error, and (4) whether the theory or technique has been generally accepted.[75]

New Jersey's courts utilize a *Frye/Daubert* hybrid standard. The admissibility of expert opinions is governed by New Jersey Rules of Evidence 104, 702 and 703. The New Jersey Supreme Court has charged trial courts with the responsibility in certain circumstances of conducting an evidentiary hearing pursuant to Rule 104 in cases in which "the scientific reliability of an expert's opinion is challenged."[76] The appropriate inquiry with respect to whether expert testimony is sufficiently reliable is not whether the court thinks the expert's reliance on the underlying data was reasonable, but whether comparable experts in the field would actually rely on that information.[77] The Supreme Court held in *Rubanici v. Witco Chemical Corp.* that a theory of causation that had not yet reached general acceptance in the scientific community "may be found to be sufficiently reliable if it is based on a sound, adequately founded scientific methodology involving data and information of the type reasonably relied on by experts in the scientific field."[78]

13.7 New Jersey Mold Legislation

New Jersey Senate Bill 1625, the "Toxic Mold Protection Act of 2008," introduced in the Senate, and referred to the Senate Community and Urban Affairs Committee on May 5, 2008. The same bill was introduced and referred to the Assembly Health and Senior Services Committee on October 23, 2008. New Jersey's Toxic Mold Protection Act has yet to pass; however, if this bill does pass, it would require: (1) the Department of Health and Senior Services to adopt rules and regulations establishing permissible mold exposure limits and procedures for assessment of the health risks posed by the presence of mold; (2) the Department of Community Affairs to adopt mold identification guidelines and mold remediation procedures; and (3) the establishment of "mold disclosure" rules in the context of real estate transactions.[79] Unlike mold disclosure laws of other states, New Jersey's mold disclosure statute does not provide the seller with immunity from litigation.[80]

13.8 Insurance Coverage

Mold claims and lawsuits may involve claims of negligent design and construction that are suitable for coverage under typical comprehensive general liability (CGL) policies, builders' risk policies, and errors and omissions (E&O) policies.[81] However, mold-related insurance claims are all too often met by the insurance industry's attempt to preclude coverage for these claims. With respect to policies issued prior to recent public awareness of mold-related property and bodily injury claims, insurers often based their denial of coverage on the "absolute pollution exclusion." With respect to new policies being issued, insurers are inserting mold-specific exclusionary language into their policies.

A. Absolute Pollution Exclusion

Typical policy form exclusions for pollution bar insurance coverage for bodily injury or property damage arising out of the discharge, dispersal, release or escape of smoke, vapors, soot, fumes, acids, alkalis, toxic chemicals, liquids or gases, waste materials or other irritants or contaminants or pollutants into or upon land, the atmosphere or any water course or body of water.

It is pursuant to this language that insurers argue that the "absolute pollution" exclusion bars coverage for mold claims. New Jersey courts have held that the exclusion is not applicable to certain indoor pollutants.[82]

B. Mold-Specific Exclusions

On September 11, 2003, the New Jersey Insurance Commissioner (Holly Bakke) issued a bulletin to all New Jersey P/C insurers giving specific guidelines on mold and fungus exclusions for personal and commercial lines. The bulletin, No. 03-24, replaces a previous set of guidelines contained in bulletin 02-14, issued July 8, 2002. The relevant portion of the announcement is as follows.

1. Personal lines and commercial lines property

Coverage should be offered at $10,000, on an aggregate basis, with optional increased limits of $25,000, and $50,000 made available. The $10,000 annual aggregate coverage should include loss to property caused by mold, fungi, wet or dry rot or bacteria, the cost to remove mold, fungi, wet or dry rot, or bacteria from property covered, the cost to tear out and replace any part of the building or other covered property as needed to gain access to the mold, fungi, wet or dry rot, or bacteria; and, the cost of testing of air or property to confirm the absence, presence or level of mold, fungi, wet or dry rot, or bacteria. Coverage should apply only if such mold loss results from a "peril insured against" that occurs during the policy period. The limitation does not apply to losses due to fire and lightning.

2. Personal lines liability

Liability coverage should apply, up to at least $50,000, on an aggregate basis, for the total of all damages arising directly or indirectly, in whole or in part, out of the actual, alleged or threatened inhalation of, ingestion of, contact with, exposure to, existence of, or presence of any mold, fungi, wet or dry rot, or bacteria. Increased limits up to $100,000 should be available, when requested by the insured.

New Jersey's Department of Banking and Insurance's announcement also permits companies issuing "Commercial Lines General Liability" policies to provide coverage for mold up to the policy limits, provide sublimits, or exclude the coverage completely. It also states that insurers should continue "capturing Mold Data in the statistical format currently in use for other lines," and should notify policyholders of the options "to buy up to the higher limits."

13.9 Conclusion

This text highlights the nationwide inconsistency of proposed mold legislation, the unsettled spectrum of generally accepted mold remediation standards, and the unrestrained nature of personal injury verdicts. The result is the creation of a volatile landscape for those potential mold defendants who operate in more than one state. New Jersey does not currently possess a well-established body of law on mold litigation. Nonetheless, New Jersey has developed extensive bodies of case law on legal concepts readily applicable to mold cases. An understanding of the general principles presented in this chapter should not only serve as a primer for litigators confronted with mold claims, but should also provide guidance on how to counsel clients involved in such cases.

Endnotes

1. *See Gallant v. Koskovich, et al.*, 364 N.J. Super. 418, 431, 836 A.2d 840, 847 (Law Div. 2003) (stating that "Proof of negligence requires establishment of a duty of care and a breach thereof proximately causing the harm").

2. *See* "Homeowner Says Water Problems Concealed in Disclosure Statement," *Mealey's Litig. Rep. Mold* (Vol. 3, Issue No.1, January 2003).

3. *See id.*

4. *See, e.g., Juliano v. Gaston,* 187 N.J. Super. 491 (App. Div. 1982), *cert. denied,* 93 N.J. 318 (1983) (relaxing the privity requirement in an action brought by homeowner against subcontractor).

5. *See Strawn v. Canuso,* 140 N.J. 43, 55-56, 657 A.2d 420, 426 (1995).

6. *See, e.g., Dupler v. Schwager,* No. 19625, 2003 WL 22429101 (Oh. App. 2d Dist. Oct. 24, 2003) (*caveat emptor* does not apply to latent defects); *Ray v. Clark,* No. 46277-6-I, 2000 WL 1873902 (Wash. App. Div. 2000) (finding an exception to *caveat emptor* when the landlord fails to disclose the existence of a latent defect).

7. *Id.*

8. *Id.*

9. *See* 2008 N.J. Senate Bill 1625 (213 Legislature).

10. *See* 2006 N.J. Senate Bill 1787 (212 Legislature).

11. *See* 2006 N.J. Assembly Bill 973 (212 Legislature).

12. *See Aronsohn v. Mandara,* 98 N.J. 92, 105-106, 484 A.2d 675, 682-683 (1984).

13. *See* N.J.S.A. 46:3B-2; *see also, Ingraham v. Trowbridge Builders,* 297 N.J. Super. 72 (App. Div. 1997).

14. *ld.*

15. *ld.*

16. *See* N.J.S.A. 46:3B-9.

17. *See* Melvon Aron Eisenberg, "Third-Party Beneficiaries," *Columbia L Rev.* 92:1358, 1402-1403 (1992).

18. *See* Steven B. Lesser and Amy L. Koltnow, "Liability of Construction Design Professionals and the Economic Loss Rule," *WTR Brief* 29:50 (2000).

19. *Juliano v. Gaston,* 187 N.J. Super. 491 (App. Div. 1982), *cert. denied,* 93 N.J. 318 (1983).

20. *See id.;* In *Totten v. Gruzen,* 52 N.J. 202 (1968) the New Jersey Supreme Court repudiated the "completed and accepted" rule, which was a historical bar to an action by the victim of defective workmanship after the owner's acceptance of the completed project.

21. *Id.* at 494.

22. *Id.*

23. It should be noted that the plaintiffs first instituted the same cause of action against the prime contractors and received a default judgment that was never satisfied because of the prime contractor's insolvency. Thus, while some may argue this is a case of "corrective justice," and should be limited as such, there is no such restrictive language in the opinion.

24. *Id.* at 495, 497.

25. *Id.* at 497.

26. *Id.* at 497-498.

27. *Id.*

28. *See Coyle v. Englander's,* 199 N.J. Super. 212, 488 A.2d 1083 (App. Div. 1985).

29. *See McDonald v. Mianecki,* 159 N.J. Super. 1, 386 A.2d 1325 (App. Div. 1985); *Ramapo Brae Condominium Ass'n, Inc. v. Bergen County Housing Authority,* 328 N.J. Super. 561, 746 A.2d 519 (App. Div. 2000); *Aronsohn v. Mandara,* 98 N.J. 92, 484 A.2d 675 (1984).

30. *See Aronsohn v. Mandara,* 98 N.J. 92, 99, 484 A.2d 675, 678-679 (1984).

31. *Id.*

32. *Id.*

33. *Id.*

34. *See Reste Realty Corp. v. Cooper,* 53 N.J. 444, 251 A.2d 268 (1969).

35. *Id.*

36. *See McCurdy v. Wyckoff,* 73 N.J.L. 368, 63 A. 992 (Sup. Ct. 1906).

37. *See, e.g., Higgins v. Whiting,* 102 N.J.L. 279, 131 A. 879 (Sup. Ct. 1926).

38. *See Winslow v. Corporate Express, Inc.*, 364 N.J. Super. 128, 140, 834 A.2d 1037, 1044 (App. Div. 2003); *Zorba Contractors, Inc. v. Housing Auth. of the City of Newark,* 362 N.J. Super. 124, 139, 827 A.2d 313, 322 (App. Div. 2003); *Richie and Pat Bonvie Stables, Inc. v. Irving,* 350 N.J. Super. 579, 589, 796 A.2d 899, 906 (App. Div. 2002).

39. *See Kuhnel v. CNA Insurance Companies,* 322 N.J. Super. 568, 581, 731 A.2d 564, 571 (App. Div. 1999); *Carroll v. Cellco Partnership,* 313 N.J. Super. 488, 502, 713 A.2d 509, 516 (App. Div. 1998).

40. *See, e.g., Strawn a Canuso,* 140 N.J. 43, 55-56, 657 A.2d 420, 426 (1995) (holding that under certain circumstances a professional seller of real estate's "silence may be fraudulent").

41. *See* N.J.S.A. 56:8-1 et seq.; *Strawn v. Canuso,* 140 N.J. 43, 55-56, 657 A.2d 420, 426 (1995).

42. *See Strawn v. Canuso,* 140 N.J. 43, 60-61, 657 A.2d 420, 428-429 (1995).

43. *Id.*

44. *Id.*

45. *See Strawn v. Canuso,* 140 N.J. 43, 60-61, 657 A.2d 420, 428-429 (1995).

46. Diego Graglia, "Teacher Gets $61,000 in Mold-Related Case," the *Star Ledger* (February 13, 2004).

47. *Id.*

48. *See Strawn v. Canuso,* 140 N.J. 43, 55-56, 657 A.2d 420, 426 (1995).

49. *See Greczyn v. Colgate Palmolive, et al.*, 367 N.J. Super. 385, 390-391, 842 A.2d 895, 898 (App. Div. 2004).

50. *Id.*

51. *See Cyktor v. Aspen Manor Condominium Ass'n et al.*, 359 N.J. Super. 459, 470, 820 A.2d 129, 137 (App. Div. 2003).

52. N.J.S.A. 2A:14-1.1.

53. *Id.*

54. *Wayne Township Board of Education v. Strand Century, Inc., et al.*, 172 N.J. Super. 296 (App. Div. 1980); see also, *Hall v. Luby Corp.*, 232 N.J. Super. 337 (Law Div. 1989).

55. *Rolnick v. Gilson & Sons, Inc.*, 260 N.J. Super. 564, 567-68, 617 A.2d 288 (App. Div.1992).

56. *See Wayne Township Board of Education v. Strand Century, Inc., et al.*, 172 NJ. Super. 296 (App. Div. 1980); see also, *Hall v. Luby Corp.*, 232 N.J. Super. 337 (Law Div. 1989).

57. *See, e.g., Manorcare Health Services, Inc. v. Osmose Wood Preserving, Inc.*, 336 N.J. Super. 218, 226 (App. Div. 2001).

58. *Manorcare Health Services, Inc. v. Osmose Wood Preserving, Inc.*, 336 N.J. Super. 218, 226 (App. Div. 2001).

59. *Id.*

60. *Id.* at 226; *Aetna Life and Casualty Co.*, 309 N.J. Super. 358, 365 (App. Div. 1998).

61. *Hirsch v. General Motors*, 266 N.J. Super. 222, 251, 264 (Law Div. 1995) (holding that "a report prepared at plaintiff's request with prospective litigation in mind without affording defendant's experts an opportunity to inspect the same best evidence and prepare a defense is substantially prejudicial to defendants").

62. *Manorcare*, 336 N.J. Super at 226; *see also, Aetna*, 309 N.J. Super. at 368; *Hirsch*, 266 N.J. Super. at 256.

63. *See Id.*

64. *Hewitt v. Allen Canning Company,* 321 N.J. Super. 178, 185 (App. Div. 1999) *(citing Nerney v. Garden State Hospital,* 229 N.J. Super. 37 (App. Div. 1988)).

65. *See, e.g., Alloway, III v. General Marine Indust., L.P.,* 149 N.J. 620, 630, 695 A.2d 264, 269 (1997) (stating that "the U.C.C. allows manufacturers to limit their liability through disclaimers, except for personal injuries"); *Saltiel v. GSI Consultants, Inc.*, 170 N.J. 297, 788 A.2d 268 (2002) (stating that Prosser & Keeton distinguish between tort and contract claims through the rule that "tort obligations may not be disclaimable"); *New Mea Construction Corp. v.*

Harper, 203 N.J. Super. 486, 494, 497 A.2d 534, 538 (App. Div. 1985) (also stating that Prosser & Keeton distinguish between tort and contract claims through the rule that "tort obligations may not be disclaimable").

66. *See, e.g., Marboro, Inc. v. Borough of Tinton Falls,* 297 N.J. Super. 411, 417, 688 A.2d 159, 162 ("Our courts have traditionally upheld contractual limitations of liability").

67. *See, e.g., General Motors Acceptance Corp. v. Jankowitz,* 216 N.J. Super. 313, 327, 523 A.2d 695, 702 (App. Div. 1987) (a seller may limit or exclude consequential damages); N.J.S.A. 12A:2-719 Contractual modification or limitation of remedy.

68. *Velli v. Rutgers Casualty Ins. Co.,* 257 N.J. Super. 308, 309 (App. Div.), *cert. denied,* 130 N.J. 597, 617 A.2d 1220 (1992); *Josantos Const. v. Bohrer,* 326 N.J. Super. 42 (App. Div 1999).

69. *See* N.J.S.A. 56:8-1 et seq.

70. *See Berg v. Reaction Motors Division, Thiokol Chemical Corp.,* 37 N.J. 396, 412, 181 A.2d 487, 495 (1962) ("In its treatment of the measure of damages when harm is done to personal property, the Restatement of Torts provides that the plaintiff be given an option to recover either the diminution in value or the reasonable cost of repairs.")

71. *See Goldson v. Carver Boat Corp.,* 309 N.J. Super. 384, 707 A.2d 193 (App. Div. 1998).

72. *Frye v. United States,* 293 F. 1013 (D.C. Cir. 1923); *Daubert v. Merrell Dow Pharmaceuticals,* 509 U.S. 579 (1993).

73. 293 1013 (D.C. Cir. 1923).

74. 509 U.S. 579 (1993).

75. *Daubert v. Merrell Dow Pharmaceuticals,* 509 U.S. 579 (1993).

76. *Kemp ex rel. Wright v. State,* 174 N.J. 412, 425-27, 809 A.2d 77 (2002).

77. *See* 2008 N.J. Senate Bill 1625 (213 Legislature).

78. *See Rubanici v. Witco Chemical Corp.,* 125 N.J. 421, 449, 593 A.2d 733, 74748 (1991).

79. *See* 2004 N.J. Senate Bill 1249 (211 Legislature).

80. *See, e.g.*, The "Montana Mold Disclosure Act" Montana Code. Ann., Tit. 70, Ch. 16, Pt. 7 § 701 *et seq*. (2003).

81. It should be noted that in general ten states have statutes that provide new homeowners with what is sometimes referred to as homeowner warranty insurance or guarantees which are provided through a new home builder or a state sponsored program. *See generally* Connecticut (C.G.S.A. § 47-116); Florida § 634.327); Indiana (IC 32-15-7-1); Louisiana (LSA-R.S. 9:3141); Maryland (Code, Real Property, § 10-601); Mississippi (Miss. Code Ann. § 83-58-1); New Jersey (N.J.S.A. 46:3B-1); South Carolina (Code 1976 § 40-29-190); Virginia (Code 1950, § 55-70.1). In general, homeowner warranty programs may impose certain time restrictions for claims and limit a builder's liability to the purchase price of the home should a new homeowner elect to participate in the program. *See, e.g.*, N.J.S.A. 46:3B-4, 46:3B-9.

82. *Byrd ex rel. Byrd v. Blumenreich,* 317 N.J. Super. 496, 722 A.2d 598 (App. Div. 1999) (holding that "Penn National's absolute pollution exclusion clause is uncertain or ambiguous and susceptible to differing interpretations as to whether a claim for personal injury caused by the *indoor* residential ingestion of lead paint chips, flakes, or dust is excluded from coverage. Such uncertainty or ambiguity is fatal to Penn National's position.") (emphasis added). *NAV-ITS, Inc. v. Selective Ins. Co. of America,* 183 N.J. 110, 121 (2005) (finding Pollution Exclusion to be limited to "traditional environmentally related damages," which did not include fumes from floor sealant).

Chapter 14

An Overview of Toxic Mold Litigation in New York

Richard J. Valladares, Esq. and Ryan C. Grelecki, Esq.

Synopsis

14.1 Introduction

Although certain jurisdictions may have experienced a decline in the filing of toxic mold lawsuits, the same cannot be said for the State of New York. Indeed, as late as November 28, 2008, in the case of *Ventimiglia v. Tishman Speyer Archstone-Smith*, the United States District Court for the Eastern District of New York found that defendants had properly removed their class action toxic mold case to federal court under 28 U.S.C. § 1332(d) and the Class Action Fairness Act of 2005.[1] In order to establish such jurisdiction, the court, in part, found that the putative class of tenants suing the defendant landlord of a luxury apartment complex, "easily place[d] $5 million in controversy."[2] The plaintiffs' complaint in *Ventimiglia* seeks damages for a variety of claims including property damage, personal injury, medical monitoring, economic damage, caused by defendants' alleged breach of the covenant of quiet enjoyment, breach of the warranty of habitability, and alleged deceptive acts in violation of New York law. Although *Ventimiglia* is one of many toxic mold lawsuits filed within the last three years within the State of New York, the significance of *Ventimiglia*, due to the amount in controversy and class action issues, should not be disregarded. Indeed *Ventimiglia* could be a harbinger of renewed mold litigation activity in New York. Accordingly, the following provides a summary of recent mold litigation activity and the general legal principles relevant to toxic mold cases filed in New York.

14.2 Tort Actions

A. Negligence

The most common mold claims concern a property owner or maintenance company's failure to maintain or repair a toxic mold condition in a residence. Such cases require the traditional negligence elements of proof: (1) duty; (2) breach; (3) causation; and (4) damages.[3]

That said, and as further set forth below, negligence cases concerning toxic mold often present unique issues concerning the statute of limitations, causation, notice, etc.

In *Donna Reid v. Gateway Sherman, Inc. et al.*, the defendant purchased a residential apartment building on October 7, 2005, and was sued on August 17, 2006, by tenant plaintiffs for damages for personal injury allegedly arising out of a toxic mold condition in the premises.[4] The defendant moved to dismiss the complaint asserting that it purchased the building "more than three years after the alleged toxic condition arose and that, subsequent to the purchase, it had insufficient notice of the condition to be found negligent for failing to correct it."[5]

The Court denied the defendant's motion to dismiss. In so holding, the Court held that although the mold condition may have existed prior to the sale, the complaint alleged that "the condition persisted until the date of the complaint, August 17, 2006."[6] Thus, the purchase date alone "was not sufficient to establish [defendant] did not have notice of the allegedly dangerous condition or a reasonable opportunity to repair it."[7]

B. Misrepresentation

In addition to negligent real estate maintenance claims, mold litigation also touches upon the sale and purchase of real estate. In that regard, buyers often seek to hold sellers liable for toxic mold growth experienced immediately, or shortly, after the purchase date.

In *Kagan v. Freedman*, plaintiffs, who were buyers of a single-family residence, asserted causes of action for fraud and breach of contract, against defendant sellers, alleging that the residence was contaminated with toxic mold and defendants dissuaded them from conducting a mold inspection of the basement prior to sale.[8] The court granted summary judgment to defendants holding:

> The defendants made a prima facie showing of entitlement to summary judgment by demonstrating that the real property purchase contract contained a specific disclaimer that the contract was executed in reliance upon contrary oral representations as to the condition of the property and that the property was sold "as is."[9]

Moreover, the court stressed that even if plaintiffs' allegations were true, the contract's specific disclaimer barred plaintiffs' reliance on oral representations of the seller at the time of sale.[10]

C. New York Consumer Protection Statute

In addition to common law negligence claims, toxic mold defendants may confront statutory-based fraud claims as well. General Business Law § 349 prohibits deceptive and misleading business practices, and its scope is broad.[11] The following practices are defined as deceptive practices under § 349:

> (a) Deceptive acts or practices in the conduct of any business, trade or commerce or in the furnishing of any service in this state are hereby declared unlawful.
>
> * * *
>
> (g) This section shall apply to all deceptive acts or practices declared to be unlawful, whether or not subject to any other law of this state, and shall not supersede, amend or repeal any other law of this state under which the attorney general is authorized to take any action or conduct any inquiry.

General Business Law § 349 "on [its] face appl[ies] to virtually all economic activity and [its] application has been correspondingly broad."[12] To state a cause of action under General Business Law § 349 "a plaintiff must plead: 'first that the challenged act or practice was consumer-oriented; second, that it was misleading in a material way; and third, that the plaintiff suffered injury as a result of the deceptive act.'"[13]

Thus, the sale or lease of any property in New York without disclosing that the property previously experienced, or is currently experiencing, toxic mold contamination, could expose the seller to potential consumer fraud claims.

A claim under the New York Consumer Protection statute may be brought by the Attorney General "in the name and on behalf of the people of the state of New York to enjoin such unlawful acts or practices and to obtain restitution of any moneys or property obtained directly or indirectly by any such unlawful acts or practices."[14] However, in addition to the right of action granted to the Attorney General, "any person who has been injured by reason of any violation of this section may bring a private action in his own name to enjoin such unlawful act or practice, an action to recover his actual damages or fifty dollars, whichever is greater, or both such actions."[15]

"The court may, in its discretion, increase the award of damages to an amount not to exceed three times the actual damages up to one thousand dollars, if the court finds the defendant willfully or knowingly violated this section."[16] "The court may also award reasonable attorney's fees to a prevailing plaintiff."[17]

D. Medical Monitoring Claims

The injuries or ailments resulting from exposure to toxic substances are sometimes not open and obvious upon immediate contact with that toxic substance. In fact, days, weeks, months or even years may pass the exposure date, before such injuries become evident. Accordingly, plaintiffs who are exposed to toxic substances but cannot show immediate injury or prove that they will necessarily suffer from an injury linked to the toxic exposure, seek damages nonetheless for the anticipated costs associated with future medical monitoring of their health. Such claims are known as medical monitoring claims and are often asserted in toxic mold cases.

In *Allen v. General Elec. Co.*, the Appellate Division of New York resurrected the viability of medical monitoring claims in the state when it reinstated a plaintiff's medical monitoring claims after summary dismissal.[18] Thereafter, in *Sorrentino v. ASN Roosevelt Center, LLC, et al.*, wherein former tenants of a luxury apartment complex brought a putative class action against the landlord for mold-related claims, the United States District Court for the Eastern District of New York stated:

> [T]he federal courts in this district have found that "in cases involving exposure to toxic materials, the New York Court of Appeals would recognize an independent cause of action for medical monitoring."[19]

Accordingly, medical monitoring claims persist in New York. In fact, such claims have been raised in the recent class action of *Ventimiglia v. Tishman Speyer Archstone-Smith,* as noted above.[20]

To recover "medical monitoring costs following exposure to a toxic substance..., a plaintiff must establish both that he or she was in fact exposed to the disease-causing agent and that there is a 'rational basis' for his or her fear of contracting the disease....This 'rational basis' has been construed to mean the clinically demonstrable presence of [the toxic substance] in the plaintiff's body, or some indication of [toxin]-induced disease, i.e., some physical manifestation of [toxic] contamination."[21]

To defend against such claims a defendant must present evidence "that the medical monitoring plaintiffs were not exposed to the disease-causing agent or that there is no rational basis for their fear of contracting the disease."[22]

14.3 Contract Actions

New York recognizes a warranty of habitability, pursuant to N.Y. Real Property Law § 235-b:

> In every written or oral lease or rental agreement for residential premises the landlord or lessor shall be deemed to covenant and warrant that the premises so leased or rented and all areas used in connection therewith in common with other tenants or residents are fit for human habitation and for the uses reasonably intended by the parties and that the occupants of such premises shall not be subjected to any conditions which would be dangerous, hazardous or detrimental to their life, health or safety.

Section 235-b provides tenants with a cause of action sounding in breach of contract.[23] The statute, however, does not impose strict liability upon a landlord for personal injury sustained by a tenant due the condition of or defect in the premises.[24] Accordingly, tenants must still prove fault, causation, and notice in actions based on injuries resulting from conditions of and defects in the premises.[25] It is important to note that the tenant cannot waive the statutorily-created warranty of habitability.[26]

With regard to condominiums, the warranty of habitability does not apply to an individual unit within a condominium.[27] Moreover, an individual condominium unit owner cannot withhold payment of common charges and assessments required under the condominium association bylaws due to defective conditions in the unit itself or common areas.[28] The warranty of habitability also does not extend to commercial leases.[29]

14.4 Potential Defenses to Mold Claims

A. Defenses to Personal Injury Claims

1. Statute of limitations

The applicable statute of limitations for claims of personal injuries arising from mold claims is governed by CPLR § 214-c which provides that such an action "must be commenced within three years from the date of discovery of the injury by plaintiff or from the date when through the exercise of reasonable diligence such injury should have been discovered by the plaintiff, whichever is earlier.[30] Because toxic mold injuries often involve the aggravation or exacerbation of pre-existing respiratory ailments, defendants may argue that the statute of limitations begins to run from the date of first experiencing such pre-existing ailments. However, New York courts appear to reject that argument as it relates to mold cases:

> The salient question is when did the plaintiff discover any symptoms caused by her exposure to toxic substances emanating from the subject [property]. The fact that the plaintiff may have discovered some ailments prior to moving to the subject [property] may be relevant to the issue of causation, it is irrelevant to the issue of timeliness of the claim.

In New York, under certain circumstances, CPLR § 214-c(4) may extend a statute of limitations period. In that regard, CPLR § 214-c(4):

> ...permits a plaintiff who did not discover the cause of the illness until up to five years after manifestation of the injury to bring an action within one year after discovery of its cause, *only* where the plaintiff can both plead and prove "that technical, scientific or medical knowledge and information sufficient to ascertain the cause of his injury had not been discovered, identified or determined prior to the expiration of the period within which the action or claim would have been authorized.[31]

However, in *Martin v. 159 West 80 Street Corp., et al.*, the court cast doubt on whether CPLR § 214-c(4) may be relied upon to extend the statute of limitations period in a typical toxic mold case when it stated:

> That provision cannot be relied upon here, because plaintiff has not alleged that the medical or scientific community in general lacked information that molds such as those in the apartment could be the cause of her illness.[32]

The present status of the law in New York, at least in New York's First Department, post-*Martin v. 159 West 80 Street Corp.*, appears somewhat unsettled.

2. Causation

To establish a relationship between an individual's illness and a toxin suspected of causing that illness, a plaintiff must establish (1) the level of exposure to the toxin; (2) that the toxin is capable of causing the alleged illness and the level of exposure to the toxin that will engender that illness; and (3) the probability the toxin caused the injuries.[33] New York courts have held that it is not always necessary for plaintiff to quantify exposure levels precisely or use the dose-response relationship, provided that whatever methods an expert uses to establish causation are generally accepted in the scientific community.[34] In the absence of expert testimony on the issue of causation, toxic mold plaintiffs are unable to establish a *prima facie* personal injury tort case as against a toxic mold defendant.[35] In addition, because of the common nature of many allergic symptoms of mold exposure, it is often the case that plaintiffs confront causation proof problems by their failure to exclude other possible causes of the plaintiff's ailments.[36]

In *B.T.N. v. Auburn Enlarged City School District*, students instituted an action against a school district alleging that they suffered injuries because of exposure to harmful airborne substances in a school building.[37] Defendant moved for summary judgment and to exclude plaintiff from presenting medical evidence, contending that plaintiffs could not meet the *Frye* test, on the basis that they could not establish through generally accepted scientific principles that the alleged exposure to the harmful airborne substances caused their injuries.[38] In support of its motions, defendant submitted an expert affidavit stating that there "was no scientifically-based causal relationship between plaintiff's exposure and symptoms...."[39] The trial court denied defendants' motions and defendants appealed. The appellate court upheld the trial court's holding. In so ruling, the appellate court found the following evidence submitted by plaintiff to be sufficient to meet the requirements of *Frye*: (1) epidemiological evidence to support a finding of general causation, i.e., that the atypical molds found to be present in the school building can cause plaintiff's symptoms[40]; and (2) an expert affidavit that determined specific causation by the use of scientifically-accepted methodology of differential diagnosis.[41] Significantly, the court held that, "[t]here is no requirement that an expert precisely quantify exposure levels or establish a dose-response relationship."[42]

In *Fraser v. 301-52 Townhouse Corp.*, plaintiffs were former residents of a unit in a cooperative apartment building owned by defendants, and sued defendants seeking damages for personal injuries (e.g., respiratory problems, rash and fatigue) allegedly caused by dampness and mold infestation in the subject apartment building.[43] Defendants moved for summary judgment and to preclude plaintiffs' expert evidence related to causation between the dampness and mold and plaintiffs' alleged injuries. After conducting a *Frye* hearing on the causation issues, the trial court ruled in favor of defendants, precluding the plaintiffs' expert evidence and dismissing the personal injury claims. The appellate court affirmed the lower court's ruling. In so affirming, the appellate court held that plaintiffs' expert merely established an *association* between mold and the alleged health problems, but failed to establish a causal relationship:

> While there is general agreement that indoor dampness and mold are "associated" with upper respiratory complaints, defendants' expert took the position, consistent with the literature they submitted, that the observed association between such conditions and such ailments is not strong enough to constitute evidence of a causal relationship. In other words, "'association' is not equivalent to 'causation'"[44]

In so holding, the *Fraser* court made clear that its holding did "not set forth any general rule that dampness and mold can never be considered the cause of a disease" but instead, that such causation was not demonstrated by the evidence submitted by plaintiffs in that particular case.[45] Specifically, plaintiffs' causation evidence was found to be deficient because: (1) the medical literature submitted by plaintiffs' expert did not identify any study showing that indoor dampness and mold have been shown to cause upper respiratory symptoms such as plaintiffs;[46] (2) plaintiffs' experts failed to "specify the threshold level of exposure to dampness or mold needed to produce" the plaintiffs' alleged injuries;[47] (3) plaintiffs' expert's claim to have established causation by means of "differential diagnosis" is unavailing;[48] and (4) plaintiffs "failed to offer a reliable measurement of the level of mold in the subject apartment."[49]

In *Spalma v. Lawrence Towers Apartments, LLC,* plaintiff was a tenant of defendants' residential apartment building and sued for damages for alleged injuries caused from exposure to mold and other toxic substances, including aggravation of chronic obstructive pulmonary disease, obstructive airway disease, bronchial asthma, other respiratory problems, aggravated psoriasis, anxiety and mental anguish.[50] Defendants moved for summary judgment, claiming that plaintiff's injuries were not caused by exposure to mold or any other substances at the subject property. In support of its motion for summary judgment defendants submitted evidence from an allergist that conducted plaintiff's independent medical examination and reviewed plaintiff's medical history and related records. The allergist asserted that causation could not be established by plaintiff because: (1) plaintiff was admitted to a hospital on 12 separate occasions prior to moving into the subject property for many of the injuries alleged in the complaint;[51] (2) plaintiff was tested and was found to have no allergy to mold or any other substance found in the subject property;[52] and (3) plaintiff experienced no improvement in her symptoms after leaving the subject property.[53] Plaintiff rebutted defendants' expert with a contrary opinion submitted by its own doctor. However the court found plaintiff's rebuttal expert opinion to be insufficient to defeat summary judgment because it contained only conclusory assertions that "plaintiff's deteriorated health condition [was] due to mold in [the subject property]."[54]

B. Defenses to Property Damage Claims

A landlord may only be liable for failing "to repair a dangerous condition, of which it has notice, on leased premises if the landlord assumes a duty to make repairs and reserves the right to enter in order to inspect or to make such repairs."[55] Plaintiff bears the burden of proving that the landlord had notice of the dangerous condition and a reasonable opportunity to repair it.[56] Moreover, the notice must be specific as to the alleged mold growth and notice may not be sufficient if it is merely of the condition that may lead to, or cause, mold growth (*e.g.*, notice of leaky pipe was insufficient, in and of itself, to constitute notice of subsequent mold growth;[57] notice of brown discoloration spot and surrounding wetness on a wall does not as a matter of law constitute notice of potential mold growth).[58]

Merely because a premises is exposed to toxic mold does not mean that a tenant can unilaterally terminate a lease under a constructive eviction theory. Indeed, where a landlord has timely abated a toxic mold condition and can show that the premises does not pose an environmental hazard, a landlord may recover unpaid rent if a tenant vacates a premises prior to the expiration of their lease agreement.[59]

14.5 Insurance

Property owners should look to their insurance policies for coverage in the event of a mold claim or loss. It is well established under New York law that a policyholder bears the burden of showing that the insurance contract covers the loss.[60] A viable insurance coverage claim, therefore, requires proof that the loss occurred during the coverage period. Although the policyholder must establish coverage, the insurer bears the burden of establishing any applicable policy exclusions.[61]

Even absent a specific mold exclusion, insurance policies generally only cover a "fortuitous event" and thus implicitly exclude coverage for intended or expected harms.[62] New York courts have construed the term "fortuitous event" to mean an event "happening by chance or accident."[63] With regard to mold claims made under a policy of insurance, insurers often look to deny coverage on the basis that such mold was not caused by a "fortuitous event."

In that regard, the case of *Catalano v. State Farm Ins. Cas. Co.* is instructive. In *Catalano*, plaintiff sued his insurer for denying a mold contamination claim under his homeowner's policy.[64] The insurer denied coverage for the mold contamination losses by claiming that the mold was not caused by a fortuitous loss but instead caused by long-term maintenance and ventilation problems. The federal district court granted the insurer's request for summary judgment and no coverage for the plaintiff's mold losses was found. In so holding the *Catalano* court stated:

> The evidence before the Court is uncontroverted that the mold contamination was not caused by a fortuitous event, but was the result of "long term moisture migration;" and a "long-standing ventilation problem" caused by inadequate maintenance. Accordingly, the loss does not fall within the policy's coverage "for accidental direct physical loss."[65]

14.6 Conclusion

In New York, mold litigation continues to be vigorously litigated, and rapidly developing case law is further clarifying the standards for plaintiffs and defendants in mold and related insurance litigation.

Endnotes

1. 588 F. Supp. 2d 329 (E.D.N.Y. 2008).

2. *Ventimiglia v. Tishman Speyer Archstone-Smith,* 588 F. Supp. 2d 329, 335 (E.D.N.Y. 2008).

3. *Alvino v. Lin*, 751 N.Y.S.2d 585 (N.Y. App. Div. 2002) ("To establish a *prima facie* case of negligence, a plaintiff must establish the existence of a duty owed by a defendant to the plaintiff, a breach of that duty, and that such breach was a proximate cause of injury to the plaintiff").

4. N.Y. Slip Op. 01969, 2009 WL 708907 (N.Y. App. Div. Mar. 17, 2009).

5. *Id.* at *1.

6. *Id.*

7. *Id.*

8. 866 N.Y.S.2d 216 (N.Y. App. Div. 2008).

9. *Id.* at 217.

10. *Id.*

11. *Lonner v. Simon Property Group, Inc.*, 866 N.Y.S.2d 239 (N.Y. App. Div. 2008).

12. *Id.*

13. *Id.*; *Singh v. Queens Ledger Newspaper Group*, 770 N.Y.S.2d 99, 100 (N.Y. App. Div. 2003) (quoting *Stutman v. Chemical Bank*, 709 N.Y.S.2d 892 (N.Y. App. Div. 2003)).

14. General Business Law § 349(b)

15. *Id.* at § 349(h)

16. *Id.*

17. *Id.*

18. 821 N.Y.S.2d 692 (N.Y. App. Div. 2006).

19. 579 F. Supp. 2d 387, 390 (E.D.N.Y. 2008).

20. 588 F. Supp. 2d 329, 335 (E.D.N.Y. 2008).

21. *Allen v. General Elec. Co.*, 821 N.Y.S.2d 692 (N.Y. App. Div. 2006) (citing *Abusio v. Consolidated Edison Co. of N.Y.*, 656 N.Y.S.2d 371(N.Y. App. Div. 1997).

22. *Allen v. General Elec. Co.*, 821 N.Y.S.2d 692 (N.Y. App. Div. 2006).

23. *German v. Federal Home Loan Mortg. Corp.*, 885 F. Supp. 537 (S.D.N.Y. 1995).

24. *Id.*; *Alharb v. Sayegh*, 604 N.Y.S.2d 243 (N.Y. App. Div. 1993).

25. *Curry v. New York City Housing* Authority, 430 N.Y.S.2d 305 (N.Y. App. Div. 1980)

26. *Spatz v. Axelrod Management Co., Inc.*, 630 N.Y.S.2d 461 (N.Y. Civ. Ct. 1995).

27. *Matter of Abbady (Mailman)*, 629 N.Y.S.2d 6 (N.Y. App. Div. 1995).

28. *Id.*

29. *Polak v. Bush Lumber Co.*, 566 N.Y.S.2d 757 (N.Y., App. Div. 1991).

30. *Spalma v. Lawrence Towers Apartments, LLC,* No. 11311/07, 2008 WL 5505515, at *3 (N.Y. Sup. Ct. Nov. 25, 2008); *Martin v. 159 West 80 Street Corp.*, 770 N.Y.S.2d 720 (N.Y. App. Div. 2004).

31. *Martin,* 770 N.Y.S.2d at 721.

32. *Id.* at 722.

33. *LeBoeuf v. Safeguard Ins. Co.*, No. 9202/04, 2007 WL 4151551, at *2 (N.Y. Sup. Ct. Oct. 25, 2007).

34. *See id.* at *2.

35. *Id.*

36. *Krasnow v. JRGB Mangement, Corp.,* 808 N.Y.S.2d 75 (N.Y. App. Div. 2006)

37. 845 N.Y.S.2d 614 (N.Y. App. Div. 2007).

38. *B.T.N. ex rel. Netti v. Auburn Enlarged City School District*, 845 N.Y.S.2d 614 (N.Y. App. Div. 2007).

39. *Id.* at 615.

40. *Id.*

41. *Id.*

42. *Id.*

43. 870 N.Y.S.2d 266 (N.Y. App. Div. 2008).

44. *Id.* at 268.

45. *Id.*

46. *Id.* at 268-69.

47. *Id.* at 269-70.

48. *Id.* at 268.

49. *Id.* at 270.

50. *Spalma*, 2008 WL 5505515, at *1.

51. *Id.* at *6.

52. *Id.*

53. *Id.* at *6-7.

54. *Id.* at *6.

55. *Litwack v. Plaza Realty Investors, Inc.*, 869 N.Y.S.2d 388, 389 (N.Y. 2008).

56. *Id.*

57. *See Lark v. Leon B. DeMatteis Assocs.*, 851 N.Y.S.2d 529 (N.Y. App. Div. 2008)

58. *Litwack v. Plaza Realty Investors, Inc.*, 835 N.Y.S.2d 151 (N.Y. App. Div. 1st Dep't. 2007).

59. *NPR, LLC v. K.A.B.B., Inc.*, 25 A.D.3d 674, 811 N.Y.S.2d 706 (N.Y. App. Div. 2006)

60. *Morgan Stanley Group, Inc. v. New England Ins. Co.*, 225 F.3d 270, 276 (2d Cir. 2000); *Consolidated Edison of N.Y., Inc. v. Allstate Ins. Co.*, 98 N.Y.2d 208, 218 (N.Y. 2002).

61. *See Nova Cas. Co. v. Central Mut. Ins. Co.*, 872 N.Y.S.2d 603, 604-05 (N.Y. App. Div. 2009).

62. *Catalano v. State Farm Ins. Cas. Co.,* No. 04-CV-452A, 2007 WL 295321 at *4 (W.D.N.Y. Jan. 30, 2007) (citing *Consolidated Edison of N.Y., Inc. v. Allstate Ins. Co.*, 98 N.Y.2d 208 (N.Y. 2002)).

63. *Catalnao*, 2007 WL 295321, at *4.

64. *Id.*

65. *Id.* at *5

Chapter 15

An Overview of Toxic Mold Litigation in Oregon*

Kelly Vance, Esq.

Synopsis

15.1 Introduction

Oregon mold cases are a relatively recent development, despite the long rainy winters and the construction industry's longstanding proclivity to build year-round in Oregon. There is a growing awareness in the Northwest that substandard construction practices and landlords who refuse to properly maintain their apartment buildings, can be responsible for mold problems.

With respect to mold problems arising in a landlord-tenant context, landlords often benefit from the fact that tenants do not have sufficient funds to hire experts to conduct testing, or to testify in court that an apartment or rental home actually made them ill. As to homeowners who are the victims of deficient construction,

*Reprinted with permission from the author, Kelly Vance.

they often find themselves having to move out of a house that makes them ill, conduct the appropriate testing and, if possible, repair their homes. Moreover, most Oregon homeowners insurer's policies have exclusions for faulty and defective construction or repairs. Accordingly, they must look to the construction contractor who built their homes for a remedy. Still a latent defect can go undiscovered for many years, and Oregon has a ten-year statute of repose, which bars any claims against the contractor ten years after the house was built. In addition, under a new "Right to Repair Law"[1] Oregon homeowners are required to give written notice of the defects in the house to the contractor and provide the contractor an opportunity to inspect and repair the damage or offer a settlement.

15.2 Insurance Issues Affecting Oregon Mold Claims

Oregon law has not traditionally recognized third-party bad faith claims. It has, however, recognized first-party bad faith claims against the insurer only in the narrowest of circumstance, such as the situation where an insurer has undertaken to defend its insured in a liability action and then puts its interests ahead of its insured. This most often arises where the insurer rejects an offer to settle a claim within policy limits and then a verdict exposes the policyholder to liability above her coverage limits.[2]

Oregon has adopted the "efficient proximate cause" doctrine. An "efficient proximate cause" is "an action that sets in motion a train of events and which brings about a result without the intervention of any force, starting and working actively and efficiently from a new and independent source."[3] In *Gowans v. N.W. Pac. Indem.* Co., the court stated:

> It is an established rule of insurance law that where a peril specifically insured against sets other causes in motion which, in an unbroken sequence and connection between the act and final loss, produces the result for which recovery is sought, the insured peril is regarded as the proximate cause of the entire loss.[4]

Oregon courts have also adopted the "substantial factor" causation standard in cases where there are multiple defendants.[5] In *McEwen v. Ortho Pharmaceutical*, the court held that "[t]he respective liability of multiple defendants depends on whether the negligence of each was a substantial factor in producing the complained of harm."[6] The court explained that the plaintiff need not show that each defendant's negligence was "sufficient to bring about plaintiff's harm by itself; it is enough that [each defendant] substantially contributed to the injuries eventually suffered by [the plaintiff.]"[7]

Fleming v. United Service Automobile Association, although not a mold case, strictly speaking, deserves mention here because of the way it impacted, or at least had a potential to impact on, mold coverage cases in Oregon.[8] *Fleming* involved the application of ORS 742.246(2), legislation which responded to a practice by insurers conducting business in Oregon employing misleading policy language. The statute provides, in part, that:

> Any provision restricting or abridging the rights of the insured under the policy must be preceded by a sufficiently explanatory title printed or written in type not smaller than eight-point capital letters.

The policy at issue in *Fleming* contained a section entitled "PERILS INSURED AGAINST," which consisted of two statements that the policy insures against "risk of direct loss to property described in Coverages A and B," and "direct physical loss to the property described in Coverage C." Those statements were followed by a list of losses that were *not* covered. The policy did not explain that there were provisions appearing under title "PERILS INSURED AGAINST" that actually restricted or abridged an insured's right to coverage. Accordingly, the policy violated ORS 742.246(2), which provides that:

> Any insurance policy issued and otherwise valid which contains any condition, omission or provision not in compliance with the Insurance Code, shall not be thereby rendered invalid but shall be construed and applied in accordance with such conditions and provisions as would have applied had such policy been in full compliance with the Insurance Code.

The pollution exclusion clause in *Fleming* limited the right to coverage, but appeared under that title, "PERILS INSURED AGAINST." The insurer relied on that clause in denying coverage for plaintiff's loss. In this circumstance, construing the policy as though it did not contain the pollution exclusion clause was the remedy imposed by the Oregon Supreme Court. In other words, the policy was applied as if the pollution exclusion did not exist.

Interestingly, despite the seemingly clear mandate of the statute, the plaintiff lost at every step of the case, including at the trial court level, before the Court of Appeals and even the Oregon Supreme Court. Plaintiff, after receiving an adverse decision at the Oregon Supreme Court, filed a successful motion for reconsideration. Accordingly, insurers have been forced to rewrite their policies to comply with the statute or risk having their exclusions being held unenforceable.

15.3 Standard of Proof for Experts in Oregon

Section 702 of Oregon's Evidence Code (OEC) sets the standard for admission of scientific evidence:

> If scientific, technical or other specialized knowledge will assist the trier of fact to understand the evidence or to determine a fact in issue, a witness qualified as an expert by knowledge, skill, experience, training or education may testify thereto in the form of an opinion or otherwise.

According to the court in *State v. Brown*, expert testimony is admissible if it is relevant under OEC 401, would assist the trier of fact under OEC 702 and is not subject to exclusion under OEC 403.[9] Scientific evidence "draws its convincing force from some principle of science, mathematics and the like[, and,] [t]ypically, but not necessarily, scientific evidence is presented by an expert witness who can explain data or test results and, if necessary, explain the scientific principles which are said to give the evidence its reliability or accuracy."[10] The *Brown* court utilized a number of factors in determining whether scientific evidence is probative under OEC 401 and OEC 702:

- The technique's general acceptance in the field;
- The expert's qualifications and stature;
- The use which has been made of the technique;
- The potential rate of error;
- The existence of specialized literature;
- The novelty of the invention; and
- The extent to which it relies on the subjective interpretation of the expert.[11]

These seven factors are not an exclusive checklist. Clinical diagnoses, differential diagnosis and the process of elimination also bear the marks of scientific inquiry.

> The goal of the clinician is to arrive at a diagnosis that can be used to develop a rational plan for further investigation, observation, or treatment, and ultimately to predict the course of the patient's illness. To do this, the clinician must verify or validate the diagnostic hypothesis.[12]

In *Jennings v. Baxter Healthcare Corp*, the Oregon Supreme Court noted:

> Grimm testified that he performed "a classic neurological examination" on each of the women in his study group. Grimm's hypothesis is based on his own experiences and observations, as well as on scientific methodology.... Grimm conducted his evaluations by using neurological examination techniques generally accepted by the scientific community and with an error rate of five to seven percent. In each case, Grimm made personal observa-

> tions and conducted a medical record review. He proceeded in conjunction with other specialists involved in the women's care. Grimm also studied the scientific and medical literature about silicone-related subjects.
>
> Grimm eliminated other potential causes of plaintiff's conditions through differential diagnosis, which is a generally accepted form of scientific inquiry.[13]

Grimm's study and conclusions had not been subjected to peer review and had not been published; however, the court found that neither peer review nor publication is a *sine qua non* for the admissibility of scientific evidence.[14]

In *Hawks v. Hartley*, the court considered a challenge to plaintiffs' medical expert, industrial hygienist and environmental health expert made the day before trial.[15] The court denied all three challenges, finding that not all expert testimony is "scientific" testimony. The court denied defendant's challenges to the hygienist and environmental health experts based on his review of their qualifications.[16] The court also found *Brown v. Boise-Cascade Corp.*,[17] where the trial court's exclusion of an industrial hygienist was reversed, as controlling on the admissibility of the hygienist testimony. In another toxic mold case, *O'Hara v. Cockram*, the court allowed the same medical expert to testify that toxic mold in plaintiffs' home was a cause of their medical and health problems.[18]

15.4 Negligence, Breach of Contract and the Economic Loss Rule

In *Securities-Intermountain, Inc. v. Sunset Fuel Co.*, the question of whether certain construction defect claims sounded in tort or contract was important to a statute of limitations analysis.[19] The first and third counts of the complaint in *Securities-Intermountain* alleged breaches of contract. The second count alleged breach of the common law duty of workmanship. The court noted that an allegation of breach of this common law standard could state a claim in either contract or tort. "By inclusion of the phrase 'unworkmanlike manner,' this allegation appears to invoke a negligence standard or general professional duty of due care and skill rather than a contractual standard."[20] The court then allowed the claim to be construed as a contract claim, and therefore subject to the six-year limitations period for contract rather than the shorter two-year period for tort claims.[21] Notably, the defendant argued that the allegation of breach of the duty to construct the building in a "workmanlike manner" sounded in negligence.

Since *Securities-Intermountain*, it has become almost routine for defendants in construction negligence claims to argue that plaintiffs must show a "special relationship" between themselves and a defendant in order to proceed. The special relationship doctrine is an offshoot of the economic loss doctrine.[22] In *Onita Pacific Corp. v. Trustees of Bron*son, the question was whether Oregon was going to recognize a negligent misrepresentation claim in a commercial context involving parties dealing at arms length. It was significant to both the court's approach and the result of that case that the alleged damages were *purely economic*, as distinguished from property damage or personal injury. The court noted that negligence cases between contacting parties involving purely economic losses are more limited than the latter type of cases, stating that one "ordinarily is not liable for negligently causing a stranger's purely economic loss *without injuring his person or property*...."[23]

Onita specifically cited *Securities-Intermountain* and reaffirmed that "professional or contractual relationships may also give rise to a tort duty to exercise reasonable care on behalf of another's interests"[24] In fact, the court observed that construction professionals such as architects and engineers "may be subject to liability to those who employ (or are the intended beneficiaries of) their services and who suffer losses caused by professional negligence...." [25] The court further noted that one may rely upon advice given by an agent, realtor, or an insurer engaged in protecting an insured from excess liability, because all of those actors are seeking to further the economic interests of the client.[26] The court distinguished these fiduciary-like relationships from one involving parties in an arms-length commercial dealing.[27] Cases following *Onita* have been inconsistent. Some decisions have noted the pure economic loss rule while permitting cases to proceed because the claims also involved property damage or personal injuries. Most decisions have ignored the *Onita* distinction between the types of damages suffered altogether and have focused on the fact that the claim was based on a duty outside of the contract.[28]

In *Harris v. Suniga*, the Oregon Supreme Court, made it clear that the "economic loss doctrine" did not prevent an action in negligence against a contractor:

> Here, plaintiffs seek recovery because **defendants' negligence caused dry rot in the apartment building** that plaintiffs own. The allegations in the complaint are thus quite different from the kinds of damages that this court has characterized as "economic losses" in other cases—the reduced stock price in *Oregon Steel Mills*, the monetary gift to a beneficiary in *Hale*, or the "indebtedness incurred or return of monies paid" in *Onita Pacific Corp.* **Plaintiffs here seek recovery for physical damage to their real property, and this court's cases generally permit a property owner** to recover in negligence for damages of that kind.[29]

According to *Harris*, the distinction between what is and what is not an economic loss depends upon the nature of the damage which occurred.[30]

15.5 Oregon Toxic Mold Decisions

A. *Strader v. Grange Mutual Insurance Company*[31]

Plaintiffs sued their insurer for breach of contract and for personal injury arising from their insurer's handling of a first-party insurance claim. The trial court granted defendant's motion for partial summary judgment on the personal injury claim. The breach of contract claim went to trial, where plaintiffs prevailed and were awarded damages plus prejudgment interest but not attorney fees. On appeal, the Oregon Court of Appeals decided, *inter alia*, whether plaintiffs could base a personal injury claim on conduct that was a breach of contract.

Plaintiffs bought a home in September 1995 and insured it under a homeowners' policy issued by defendant. Three months later, a windstorm caused extensive water damage to the house and its contents. The insurer arranged for temporary repairs, which did not prevent further water damage or allow existing moisture to evaporate. Permanent repairs to the roof were finished a year after the storm, in December 1996, but defendant and plaintiffs could not agree on the amount due under the policy. During the winter Kathy Strader began having health problems which her physician diagnosed as asthma aggravated by mold spores. He advised her to reduce exposure to her home. Plaintiffs informed defendant of this diagnosis and showed their insurer the areas of the house containing mold. Despite this, the insurer continued to refuse to pay the amount requested to repair the water damage and get rid of the mold. Plaintiff sued.

Plaintiffs alleged breach of contract in that the insurer had not met its obligation under the policy to pay compensation sufficient to cover repair of the roof and water damage. They also asserted a negligence claim for their insurer's unreasonable delays in repairing the roof and its failure to correct the moisture problem and remove the mold. The trial court granted summary judgment to defendant on the personal injury claim. The case went to trial on the breach of contract claim, and the jury awarded plaintiffs $195,500 in damages. Plaintiffs appealed.

On appeal, the *Strader* court began its decision by correctly stating that a party seeking to assert a tort claim based on conduct that is also breach of a contract must allege that the defendant's conduct violated some standard of care that is not part of the defendant's contractual obligations. But the court went beyond *Securities-Intermountain* which recognized tort liability based on breach of the implied covenant of workmanship and held that there could be no tort liability for breach of either an explicit or implied covenant. The *Strader* court then opined "that the independent standard of care stems from a particular special relationship between the parties." Instead of finding, as Oregon courts had for years, that a tort duty of care may be based on the existence of duties outside of the contract, such as common law duties, statutory duties or duties implied by the relationship of the parties, the *Strader* Court moved an implied covenant (such as the implied covenant of workmanship recognized in *Securities-Intermountain* as supporting tort liability) into the area of tort immunity. The result was that *Strader* departed from prior precedent and seemingly immunized contracting parties that were negligent and who for over a century would have been held accountable under the law of negligence.

The *Strader* court then focused on the relationship of the parties and found that the tort of negligence could only be asserted if there was a "special relationship" thus importing the element of a negligent misrepresentation claim (right to rely because of the relationship) that had been confused since *Conway*. The court then held that the relationship between an insurer and insured is special only in the context where an insurer defends a claim that is covered under a liability policy.[32] However, it opined that in a first-party claim setting the relationship was necessarily adversarial in nature, because the parties assumed adverse postures in court. The court wrote:

> More to the point, the relationship between an insurer and its insured is special with respect to the insurer's performance of its duty to defend, so that negligent performance of that duty gives rise to a tort claim, but the same relationship is not special with respect to the insurer's refusal to settle within policy limits, which sounds only in contract; in the former context, the insurer is in something resembling a fiduciary role, whereas in the latter it and the insured are adversaries. *Id.* at 334.

As noted above, where an insurer refuses to settle within policy limits and then exposes its insured to excess liability is one scenario in Oregon where an insurer can be sued for bad faith.[33] The court focused on the insurer's duty to defend and ability to control the defense as connoting a special relationship in a liability defense situation but then said that there was "no mandate to exercise independent judgment for the sole benefit of plaintiffs" in a situation where an insurer undertakes a duty to adjust a claim and pay for repairs.

B. *O'Hara v. David Blain Construction, Inc.*[34]

The Mark O'Hara family of Eugene, Oregon, filed a toxic mold/construction defect case against the builder who remodeled their home. They asserted that, due to a defective remodeling of their previous home, they were exposed to toxic mold and micro-toxins. The case settled confidentially during trial.[35] In 2002, they decided to build a new house, taking special care to protect against toxic mold growth. They hired a construction consultant and a builder to design and oversee the construction of the new house. Construction of the house began in late 2002. However, the house was not finished when Oregon's seasonal winter rains arrived. They began experiencing medical problems after they moved in and discovered mold in the house. They hired remediation specialists to remove the mold and remedy other defects.

Plaintiffs sued their builder and building consultants for personal injury and property damage in September 2004. They alleged defective construction that resulted in their damages and breach of the agreements for the construction and consulting services. They alleged that their consultant breached the duty to inspect and ensure that the residence was constructed as designed. The case went to trial in July and August 2005. The jury returned a verdict finding that the builder defendants were negligent, but that the consultant was not negligent. The jury also found that the builder had not breached the contract. Plaintiffs obtained judgment against the builder defendants in the amount of $31,620, and the trial court also awarded costs in the amount of $6,215. Plaintiffs appealed, arguing that the trial court erred when it denied their motion to file a second amended complaint approximately 30 days before the date of trial. The proposed amendment sought to add a claim for damages of $2.5 million for loss of income and the increased cost of obtaining similar housing. It also would have added nine new specifications of negligence against some of the defendants. The trial court denied the motion to amend, holding that the timing and scope of the amendment would "make it really impossible to try this case in the time frame that it will be tried in." On appeal, the Court of Appeals affirmed the trial court decision, stating that the trial court did not abuse its discretion in denying the late amendment.[36]

Plaintiffs also argued that the trial court erred in excluding evidence that Blain did not carry insurance providing coverage for toxic mold damage. Plaintiffs' contract with the Berry defendants included the requirement that Berry obtain a certification that Blain carried such insurance. After leave to file a second amended complaint was denied, plaintiffs tried to claim that this allegation was alleged within a previous version of their complaint. The trial court and Court of Appeals disagreed, finding that the prior version of the complaint did not include such allegation.[37]

Plaintiffs argued that the trial court erred in excluding testimony by any witness offering an opinion as to whether Katelyn O'Hara's endometriosis was a result of exposure to toxic mold. But defendants had asked plaintiffs to produce medical records in December 2004 and January 2005. Plaintiffs provided some documents but no information that indicated that endometriosis was a condition that resulted from defendants' alleged negligence.[38] Under ORCP 44 D(2), a trial court has the discretion to exclude a physician's testimony for a party's failure to comply with ORCP 44 C. The trial judge excluded evidence of whether plaintiff Katelyn O'Hara's endometriosis was a result of exposure to toxic mold and the Court of Appeals held that it was within the trial court's discretion to do so.

Plaintiffs also assigned error to the trial court's refusal to reopen evidence after both sides had rested to allow their medical expert, who had returned to Arizona, to testify by telephone. Defendants had cast doubt on the validity of the testing procedures relied on by plaintiffs' expert, Dr. Michael Gray in the defense's case-in-chief. Plaintiffs sought leave to allow Gray to testify by telephone from Arizona in rebuttal and to present a letter from him explaining why the issues raised by defendants in their case-in-chief had no bearing on the specific subject matter of his testimony. The trial court denied plaintiffs' motions and, again, the Court upheld that decision as lying within the trial court's discretion to regulate the conduct of a trial.

Plaintiffs argued on appeal that the trial court erred when it entered a verdict for a total of $31,620 instead of awarding that amount each to Mark and Mary Jane O'Hara. The Court of Appeals noted that the verdict form was patently ambiguous. It could be reasonably interpreted to inquire "what are each individual plaintiff's damages" or to inquire "what total damages should plaintiffs, as a group, receive." But the Court of Appeals found that plaintiffs' failure to object to the verdict before the jury was discharged deprived the trial court of the opportunity to address that question to the jury, so the issue was not preserved for appeal.

C. *Haynes v. Adair Homes, Inc.*[39]

Perhaps the most significant mold case in Oregon, from the standpoint of a notable jury verdict, is *Haynes v. Adair*, believed to be the first case in the Northwest that actually went through a full jury trial to a significant verdict for the plaintiffs. Most cases before and since have either resulted in a settlement, a defense verdict, or a relatively small jury verdict for property damage but not personal injury. The jury in the *Haynes* case awarded damage not only for property damage and personal injury but also neurological damage to the Haynes children. That made it one of the first verdicts in the country to recognize neurological damage from mold intoxication.[40]

Paul and Renee Haynes were the owners of five acres in Sandy, Oregon, on which they had a small older house. They contacted Adair Homes, Inc., a company that markets lower cost "starter" homes and builds hundreds of houses a year in the Northwest. The Haynes family planned to upgrade into a somewhat larger house. Adair Homes, Inc. showed them a house package that cost around $67,000 to erect on site. Adair's program usually requires the homeowner to provide the land and do certain finish work such as painting and final landscaping.

Adair commenced construction in the winter of 2001, one of the wettest winters in recent memory. The Hayneses videotaped the house and took many photos during construction, never expecting that they were documenting evidence to be used against Adair in court later. Their photos and videos showed standing water on the floor decking. At trial they were able to prove that Adair closed up and insulated the walls before the house was thoroughly dried out. As a result, mold began to grow inside the wall cavities. When the Haynes family moved into the house in March, they began to feel ill and their symptoms worsened with time. Finally, they discovered the mold in what Renee Haynes described in court as a "happy accident."

In July 2002 Mr. Haynes used a small backhoe to landscape around the house. He was momentarily distracted by his son's scream while playing with his brother and accidentally rammed the machine into the wall, knocking a stud off center and popping open a panel of drywall inside a bedroom. Upon assessing the damage, he discovered slimy mold growing inside the wall cavity. Further inspection revealed that the home was contaminated by toxigenic mold, including *Stachybotrys chartarum, Chaetomium, Curvularia, Cladosporium, Alternaria, Aspergillis niger*, various forms of *Penicilium* and other forms of toxigenic fungi. Moisture tests of the framing wood at floor level revealed a moisture content of 32 percent, in July 2002, months after the house was completed, and after several months of hot, dry weather.

The Haynes family put the contractor on notice and asked it to honor the warranty. When the builder refused, the Haynes filed suit. At that point, Adair commenced an arbitration claim against them with Construction Arbitration Services ("CAS") out of Dallas, Texas, and moved to stay the court case pending arbitration. Adair claimed that the Haynes family was contractually bound to arbitrate their dispute, but the contract had both an arbitration clause and an attorney fee provision allowing fees for any pretrial, trial or appellate work. Mr. and Mrs. Haynes submitted affidavits saying that their Adair salesman represented to them (and other Adair customers) that Adair's arbitration clause only applied to disputes that occurred in the course of construction and that any disputes that occurred after the house was completed were to be resolved in court. Adair's arbitration claim alleged that they breached their contract by not arbitrating and sought unspecified damages of $15,000. Adair had been fully paid for its contract work. In the year between when the house was completed and the dispute arose, Adair never once asserted that it was due any money from the homeowner.

The court stayed part of the case involving claims between Mr. and Mrs. Haynes and Adair, but allowed the claim by Michael Haynes to proceed in court. On August 21, 2003, Adair and the Hayneses attended an arbitration hearing, where Adair's alleged "damages" were shown to be nothing but a claim for attorney fees incurred in connection with the motion to stay. Because Adair had requested those fees at the court hearing, but had not received an award, the Haynes's counsel was able to show that the court had already rejected Adair's "damages." The arbitrator said during the hearing that he viewed Adair's dispute resolution provision as applying only to disputes which arose during construction, and not to post-construction disputes. On August 26, 2003, before the arbitrator could issue a written decision, Adair voluntarily withdrew from arbitration and CAS refused to proceed.

The trial resulted in a jury verdict for plaintiffs and a general money judgment in their favor for an aggregate $498,417.94. The Haynes family also received a supplemental judgment for their attorney fees and costs in the amount of $291,353.77. Adair's appeal on the merits was dismissed but the appeal of the fee award is pending as of this writing. The prevailing party on appeal is also entitled to attorney fees.

1. Economic loss doctrine

There were many issues raised in this case, besides the question of arbitrability. One of the issues raised by Adair before trial was whether a claim for negligent construction was barred under the economic loss doctrine. As discussed above, that doctrine had held, *inter alia*, that a party who had a contract with a defendant must seek his contract damages by way of a breach of contract claim, instead of a negligence claim. But the negligence claim in *Haynes v. Adair* did not merely include claims that Adair breached provisions of the contract or warranty. The negligence claim asserted by the Haynes family fell outside the four corners of the agreement. The allegation that Adair failed to perform to the standard of care or workmanship prevailing in the construction industry was based not on the specific terms of the contract, but upon standard imposed by the law and which is implicit in every contract. The Hayneses relied upon *Securities-Intermountain*, discussed above.

The court made an interesting decision, which predated *Harris v. Suniga* by three years. The court decided to allow any claim for property damage or cost of repair to be pursued on a breach of contract theory, and any claim for tort damages, such as personal injury, other personal property damage or consequential losses to be pursued on a negligence theory. This essentially split the Hayneses' causes of action and the various categories of damages they had suffered. The court seemed to agree that the negligence claim was not defeated by the seeming lack of any special relationship between the Haynes family and their builder. The Oregon Supreme Court has apparently ratified this approach in *Harris v. Suniga*, discussed above.

2. Challenges to plaintiff's medical expert

The defense attorney in the *Haynes* case, as most defense counsel are wont to do, tried to exclude plaintiffs' medical experts from testifying. The lead medical expert was the late Dr. Vincent Marinkovich, a renowned immunologist formerly of Stanford University Medical School. Dr. Marinkovich had treated thousands of mold victims over his career and was well qualified to render an expert opinion based on his experience and training. The defense seized upon the idea that he had invented a new kind of blood test for mold antibodies, using a thread upon which mold antigens were imbedded. Other blood tests utilized different means to introduce the blood to mold antigens, such as a porous jell or plastic plate. But the essence of all bloods tests was to see if the blood reacted with the antigens. If a reaction occurred, then the body had been exposed to the mold because it had started developing an immunological response (antibodies). Dr. Marinkovich had developed this thread test and sold it to a private entity because he did not want to be accused of having a conflict of interest when he used his own test. That company had not marketed it effectively, leading the defense to claim that the test was not genuinely accepted in the medical community.

The Haynes family introduced several different blood tests from different doctors who were mold experts and who used different labs to interpret the results. All of the plaintiffs' blood tests were high for several kinds of mold found in the house. The defense used OHSU in Portland and its blood tests came back negative. The jurors rejected the OHSU test results and one juror was physically angry when the defense expert introduced the negative result.

3. Attorney fees

The Haynes family was entitled, as prevailing parties, to an award of their reasonable attorney fees. The defense objected to the amount requested, but conceded that the plaintiffs were entitled to some fee award. After briefing and a full evidentiary hearing, the court awarded the Haynes family every penny of their documented costs and fees. [41] One of the reasons for this was that the Haynes's attorney charged a very modest rate ($170 to $190 per hour) compared with other attorneys (defense counsel billed $225) and wrote off almost 70 hours of time to try to relieve financial pressure on his clients. The plaintiffs' expert at the attorney fee hearing testified that, in his experience, a plaintiff's attorney usually has twice as much time into a case than defense counsel because plaintiffs' counsel has to do more work to sustain the burden of proof. The plaintiff's attorney billed only slightly more than the defendant's attorney in the *Haynes* case.

On appeal, Adair claims that the trial court should not have awarded the Haynes children any fees because the children were not parties to the contract. The trial court at the attorney fee hearing pointed out that Adair's attorney fee clause is extremely broad and authorizes an award of fees for claims that arise out of "the construction of the structure." Therefore, Mrs. Haynes had a right to attorney fees related to prosecuting the negligence claim and any work involving the children also arose out of construction of the project. The work performed by plaintiffs' counsel in furtherance of the negligence claim was also common to the contract claim, for which Adair admits fees are recoverable. Under Oregon law[42] the trial court need not apportion fees between claims involving common issues. Adair's second assignment of error on appeal was that mediation and filing a claim in arbitration was a condition precedent to a right to seek an attorney fee award.

D. *Murdock v. Hood Custom Homes, LLC*

On August 11, 2009 an Oregon homeowner succeeded in obtaining an arbitration award of $318,418.82 against a homebuilder in another defective construction case prosecuted by the author of this chapter. The case, entitled *Murdock v. Hood*

Custom Homes, LLC, was filed with the Arbitration Service of Portland, case no. ASP 090120-2. The three member arbitration panel consisted of retired judges, who rendered a decision less than one hour after the close of evidence at the hearing. Mr. Murdock proved that the builder constructed his house in wet winter weather and did not adequately dry the home before enclosing the walls with insulation and drywall. As a result, the exterior siding and OSB sheathing deteriorated and the interior became compromised. Mr. Murdock became ill while living in the house. Upon an investigation, he found mold inside the house's wall cavities. Plaintiffs' experts were Dr. Gordon Baker, M.D. of Burien, Washington, and Amy Siedliecki and the Mold Reporters from Portland, Oregon.

Endnotes

1. ORS 701.560 *et. seq.*

2. *Georgetown Realty v. The Home Ins. Co.*, 313 Or. 97, 106, 831 P2d 7 (1992); *Farris v. U.S. Fidelity & Guar. Co.*, 284 Or. 453, 587 P2d 1015 (1979); *Employers' Fire Ins. Co. v. Love It Ice Cream Co.*, 64 Or. App. 784, 670 P2d 160 (1983).

3. Couch on Insurance 2d, § 74:711 (Rev ed. 1983).

4. 260 Or. 618, 621, 489 P.2d 947, 491 P.2d 1178 (1971).

5. *See, e.g, Dewey v. A. F. Klaveness & Co.*, 233 Or 515, 541, 379 P2d 560 (1963) (causation standard was whether the defendant's conduct was a "substantial factor" in physically producing the injury).

6. 270 Or. 375, 418528 P.2d 522 (1974).

7. *Id.*

8. 329 Or. 449, 988 P2d 378 (2000).

9. 297 Or. 404, 409, 687 P.2d 751 (1984).

10. *Id.* at 407-08.

11. *Id.* at 417.

12. *Reference Guide on Medical Testimony* 463-64. *See also O'Key,* 321 Or. 283, 292, 899 P.2d 663 ("The scientific method is a validation technique, consisting of the formulation of hypotheses, followed by observation or experimentation to test the hypotheses.").

13. 331 Or. 285, 308, 14 P.3d 596 (2000).

14. *See id. See also O'Key,* 321 Or. at 304 ("In some cases, valid but innovative theories or propositions will not have been published, either because they are too particular, too new, or of limited interest.").

15. Lane County Circuit Court, Case No. 16-99-08461.

16. The key case relied on was *State v. Trager*, 158 Or. App. 399 (1999). That opinion lays out the differences between scientific testimony and other expert testimony, with an easier standard of admissibility for non-science evidence.

17. 150 Or. App. 391 (1997).

18. Lane County Circuit Court, Case No 16-00-12848.

19. 289 Or. 243, 611 P.2d 1158 (1980).

20. *Id* at 263.

21. *Id.*

22. *See Onita Pacific Corp. v. Trustees of Bron*son, 315 Or. 149, 159, 843 P.2d 890 (1992).

23. *Id. (citing Hale v. Groce*, 304 Or. 281,284, 744 P.2d 1289 (1987)) (emphasis added).

24. *Id.* at 160.

25. *Id.* at 161 (*citing Ashley v. Fletcher,* 275 Or. 405, 550 P.2d 1385 (1976); *Bales for Food v. Poole,* 246 Or 253, 256, 424 P2d 892 (1967)).

26. *Id.* at 161.

27. *Id.*

28. *See, e.g., Securities-Intermountain,* 289 Or. at 262; *Georgetown Realty v. The Home Ins. Co.*, 313 Or. 97, 106, 831 P.2d 7 (1992).

29. Oregon Supreme Court, Case No. S054549, March 20, 2008 (emphasis added).

30. *Id.*

31. 179 Or. App. 329, 39 P.3d 903 (2002).

32. The *Strader* court also ignored *Crosby v. SAIF Corp.*, 73 Or.App. 372, 378, 699 P.2d 198 (1985) where the Oregon Court of Appeals recognized a special relationship in a first party insurance setting.

33. Oregon bad faith law is limited to scenarios where an insurer refuses to settle within policy limits thus exposing its insured to excess liability. See e.g. *Farris v. U.S. Fid. and Guar. Co.*, 284 Or. 453, 587 P2d 1015 (1978).

34. 216 Or. App. 384, 173 P.3d 1257 (2007).

35. This is the case mentioned above in the discussion of medical evidence and expert admissibility. This discussion is about a second case that followed after the *O'Hara v. Stangeland* case.

36. Citing *Safeport, Inc. v. Equipment Roundup & Mfg*., 184 Or.App. 690, 699-701, 60 P.3d 1076 (2002), *rev. denied*, 335 Or. 255 (2003) (setting out applicable abuse of discretion standard).

37. Oregon's code pleading system embodied in ORCP 18 requires a plain and concise statement of the ultimate facts constituting a claim for relief and not simply notice pleading followed in other jurisdictions and federal courts. If you are an out-of-state attorney not familiar with code pleading, you should associate an Oregon attorney to navigate this dangerous area of the case.

38. Under ORCP 44 C, in a civil action where a claim is made for damages for injuries to a party, "upon the request of the party against whom the claim is pending, the claimant shall deliver to the requesting party a copy of all written reports and existing notations of any examinations relating to injuries for which recovery is sought."

39. Clackamas County Case No. CCV0211573.

40. Because of the author's familiarity with this case, having been the Haynes's attorney, a more thorough discussion of what transpired is possible here.

41. A cautionary tale to mold victims everywhere is when you litigate against a big defense firm, expect the fees to escalate dramatically. The fee award was in the amount of $291, 353.77.

42. *Bennett v. Baugh*, 164 Or App 243, 248, 990 P2d 917 (2000).

Chapter 16

An Overview of Toxic Mold Litigation in Pennsylvania

Douglas F. Schleicher, Esq. and Julie Beddingfield, Esq.

Synopsis

16.1 Introduction

There have been few enforcement actions or lawsuits in Pennsylvania relating to mold. Accordingly, this chapter provides a general overview of the mechanisms available to government agencies at the state and local level to regulate mold-related exposure. In addition, various legal theories of liability in private actions, based on both statutory and common law, will be discussed in order to help the reader anticipate where future private litigation may be focused.

16.2 State and Local Enforcement Authority

Pennsylvania has not enacted legislation specifically addressing mold issues. Notwithstanding the foregoing, there are several governmental bodies which may have enforcement authority relating to mold growth, exposure and remediation.

A. Pennsylvania Department of Environmental Protection

Pursuant to several sections of the Administrative Code of 1929, the Pennsylvania Department of Environmental Protection (PADEP) has broad authority to "protect the people of [Pennsylvania] from unsanitary conditions and other nuisances."[1] This includes the power to examine and survey property in the state with respect to "nuisances."[2] If such conditions are identified, PADEP may order the alleged nuisance to be abated or removed.[3] Thereafter, if the owner or occupant of the property fails to respond to the order, PADEP also has the statutory right to enter the premises, abate the nuisance itself and later seek recovery of its costs in doing so.[4] With respect to tenements, lodging or boarding houses, PADEP also has the authority to condemn the property for unsanitary conditions.[5]

B. Local Regulations

The Pennsylvania legislature has enacted several laws authorizing cities and municipalities to promulgate local regulations regarding the sanitation and inspection of all forms of improved real estate. With this grant of power most local entities have enacted housing and building regulations requiring that properties be kept in a sanitary condition. Many of these local regulations empower local sanitary officers with entry, inspection and abatement authority similar to those available to PADEP. Local regulations also generally provide that a local municipality has the right to condemn properties that constitute an ongoing public nuisance or are otherwise uninhabitable.

16.3 Potential Private Rights of Action

To date, there has been little mold litigation in Pennsylvania. However, the following summarizes some of the relevant private rights of action that may be applicable in a mold-related lawsuit in Pennsylvania.

A. Contract Claims

1. Contractual claims for economic loss

The specific terms of a contract govern any contract claim. That being said, even absent a mold-specific provision, certain types of claims can be expected. Economic loss may include: (1) failure to receive fair value (e.g., unsanitary housing or commercial space) in real property transactions; (2) lost profits from down time associated with the presence of mold; and (3) expenses related to mold enforcement actions or remediation programs.

2. Implied warranty of habitability (residential)

In the absence of express contractual provisions, residential leases are subject to an implied warranty of habitability.[6] Therefore, the landowner has an implied obligation to provide a tenant with improvements that are safe and sanitary, even if the lease language itself does not explicitly speak to such issues.

Although a local housing code violation does not, by itself, establish a breach of the warranty, such violations can generally be used as evidence to show a material breach of the obligation.[7] The materiality of a landlord's breach is a question of fact and the factors that Pennsylvania courts have traditionally established for assessment in this regard include the following: does the condition violate a housing code, law or regulation; the nature and seriousness of the condition; the effect of the defect on safety and sanitation; the length of time during which the defect has persisted; and the age of the improvement.

In addition to proving that a material breach has occurred, the plaintiff must show notice to the landlord of the defect or condition; that the landlord had a reasonable opportunity to make the necessary repairs; and that the landlord failed to do so.[8]

Assuming that a plaintiff is successful in proving breach of the implied warranty of habitability, standard contractual remedies apply. Recoverable economic damages include rent rebates and amounts spent on reasonable repairs to make the property "habitable" again. In addition, at least one federal court sitting in Pennsylvania has authorized a damage award for "deprivation and humiliation" related to a breach of warranty of habitability claim.[9]

3. Implied warranty of habitability (commercial)

As a general matter, Pennsylvania courts have been unwilling to read a warranty of habitability into commercial leases because the leases are assumed to be the result of arms length negotiations between parties with roughly equal bargaining power.[10]

Pennsylvania courts have, however, also held that general contract law no longer binds commercial lessees to the "independence of obligations" doctrine, under which a tenant had only one remedy if the landlord was in material breach of the lease: surrender the premises and be relieved of the obligation to pay rent.[11] Under more recent Pennsylvania case law, at least two other options exist, including performing remediation on behalf of the landlord and reducing rent for the costs associated with same; or deducting from the rent the difference between the rental value of the premises as leased and the value of the property if the lease had been complied with (e.g., rent abatement).[12]

In light of the foregoing, sophisticated commercial tenants should seek affirmative representations, warranties and covenants from the landlord regarding the sanitary condition of their space and other common areas of the building. In addition, they should consider identifying in the lease specific remedies that would be available in the event of a breach.

4. Implied warranty of construction in a good and workmanlike manner

Under Pennsylvania law, construction contractors are deemed to provide an implied warranty that the construction work was performed in a reasonably workmanlike manner and that the finished product is fit for the purpose intended.[13] This warranty is based in contract law and provides regular contract damages available to the plaintiffs. However, there is no contractual privity requirement in order to assert such a claim.[14] Pennsylvania courts have also held that the warranty of workmanship will be implied with respect to both residential and commercial properties.[15]

5. Breach of lease

At least one court in Pennsylvania has interpreted specific lease provisions as they pertain to the presence of mold in a building. In *Hirsh v. Carbon Lehigh Intermediate Unit #21*, a school district terminated a lease with its landlord due to a recurring mold condition.[16] In response, the landlord filed suit asserting that the school district breached its non-residential lease agreement and sought to recover unpaid rent for the remainder of the lease term. The court held that the presence of mold did not constitute a breach of the casualty provision of the lease because it did not totally destroy or extensively damage the premises, notwithstanding that the school was vacated during the school year for a short period of time to allow for remediation. The court found that the school district bore part of the responsibility for the mold's presence, since it decided not to install an HVAC system as part of the construction of the building. Further, the court noted that the school district failed to notify the landlord of the mold's recurrence, which precipitated the district's unilateral attempt to terminate the lease. Accordingly, the court held that the district breached its lease, and awarded damages to the landlord.

B. Pennsylvania Unfair Trade Practices and Consumer Protection Law

Pennsylvania courts have held that the Unfair Trade Practices and Consumer Protection Law (UTPCPL) provides a private right of action related to sales and leases of real estate.[17] The act prohibits "unfair or deceptive acts or practices," which are further defined by a specific list of activities, including actual and implied misrepresentations to the public.[18] For the claims of fraud under the UTPCPL, the elements of proof are the same as those for a common law fraudulent misrepresentation claim: there must be a material representation; made with knowledge of its falsity, or recklessness as to its truthfulness; an intent to mislead the aggrieved party; justifiable reliance on the misrepresentation; and resulting injury that was proximately caused by the justifiable reliance.[19] With respect to claims of "deception" under the UTPCPL, however, Pennsylvania courts have not settled the question of whether all of the elements of fraud must be met, or whether "deception" may be established by a less restrictive standard.[20] If a property owner is aware of mold growth on the property and fails to disclose it to the purchaser or lessee, therefore, a seller may be liable for a violation of the act.

The statute generally provides that a private plaintiff can seek redress for "any ascertainable loss of money or property" that results from a violation of the act.[21] In addition to traditional tort remedies, the UTPCPL also provides trial courts with authority to grant up to three times the actual damages sustained, along with associated costs and reasonable attorney fees.

C. Residential Real Estate Disclosure Law

The Real Estate Seller Disclosure Law (RESDL), 68 Pa.C.S.A. § 7301 *et seq.*, was enacted in December 2000. It pertains to sales of residential properties of one to four units.[22] The RESDL requires sellers of subject properties to disclose to the buyer all known material defects pursuant to a form promulgated by the State Real Estate Commission.[23] Although there is no required disclosure on the form relating to mold, there are required disclosures relating to water, roof and related building conditions and hazardous substances, many of which may give rise to a required disclosure pertaining to mold. A real estate transfer covered by RESDL may not be invalidated solely because of a failure by a party to comply, but that party is subject to liability for the actual damages suffered by the buyer as a result of any violation, and a court may impose such additional damages or remedies as may otherwise apply.[24]

D. Tort Actions

Pennsylvania courts have yet to render any significant decisions in tort cases addressing the alleged health effects related to mold exposure. However, personal injury and property damage suits against property owners or property management companies in Pennsylvania may be premised on several well-recognized tort theories. In addition to property owners, entities such as design professionals (e.g., architects and engineers) and contractors may be targeted in suits based on allegedly defective construction or design of buildings or HVAC systems.

1. Negligence (premises liability)

Mold personal injury and property damage cases can arise under many factual scenarios. One frequent context involves premises liability. Pennsylvania recognizes premises liability claims based in negligence. A defendant's standard of care usually depends on its relationship to the plaintiff. Differing standards of care by Pennsylvania courts have been applied to licensees, public invitees and business invitees of the entity who owns or controls the property.[25]

In *Reed v. Dupius*, the Pennsylvania Superior Court allowed negligence claims for a landlord's failure to repair water intrusion problems which the plaintiff alleged caused her sinus and respiratory problems, and damage to her personal property.[26] In *Reed*, the tenant had notified the landlord of water intrusion problems, offered to replace wet carpet or hire a professional cleaner, but the landlord promised, and then subsequently failed, to make the necessary repairs. Mold eventually grew in the wet basement and throughout the home, allegedly causing personal injuries and property damage to the tenant. The lower court granted a demurrer based on the "gist of the action" doctrine (that the claims were improperly based in negligence when they arose out of a failure to perform a contractual obligation). The Superior Court reversed, holding that landlord's obligation arose from her awareness of, and promise to rectify the water intrusion problem. This created a legal duty on the part of the landlord to *exercise reasonable care* in fulfilling her promise to repair that is separate and distinct from her contractual duty to repair.[27]

Other Pennsylvania cases, although not dealing specifically with mold, are instructive, because they deal with similar indoor air quality issues. For instance, in *Wright et al. v. McDonald's Corp.*, plaintiffs alleged various personal injuries as a result of the inhalation of carbon monoxide at a franchised premises leased from McDonald's.[28] The court noted that under Pennsylvania law, a landlord out of possession is generally under no duty to maintain and repair leased premises. However, the landlord has such a duty when 1) the dangerous condition existed at the time of the leasing; 2) the landlord knew or should have known of the condition; and 3) the tenant could not have discovered the condition with a reasonable examination. In *Wright,* the judge denied the defendant's motion for summary judgment. In so holding, the court found that the plaintiffs had shown sufficient evidence that McDonald's designed and constructed a hot water heater ventilation system with a latent defect, of which it should have been aware. The court further found that the plaintiffs could not have discovered the defect upon reasonable inspection.

A residential or commercial landlord may be subject to liability if it has knowledge of a mold condition in a space to which the tenants do not have access, such as the basement, utility or other areas. Depending on the design of the particular building or the equipment in it, air may also be drawn from the basement or ground floor areas and dispersed throughout the building thereby potentially providing an exposure pathway to tenants. Evidence of such circumstances could establish a duty upon a landlord or property manager to respond to mold problems that arise as a result.

In *William Penn School District v. Workers' Compensation Appeal Board,* the Commonwealth Court upheld the decision of the workers' compensation judge awarding damages to an instructional assistant who claimed disabilities resulting from exposure to bacteria and fungus in the school basement classroom in which she worked.[29] The workers' compensation judge found that the claimant had sustained work-related injuries in the nature of an aggravated and exacerbated asthmatic condition and that she was totally disabled. While the claimant's own expert testified that there were a number of contributing causes, including a history of smoking, the Commonwealth Court determined that there was "substantial evidence" in the record to support the workers' compensation judge's findings. William Penn School District was ordered to pay wage loss benefits and outstanding medical bills.

2. Professional negligence

Personal injury claims attributable to mold may arise as a result of the negligence of architects or engineers in the design, supervision or construction of a building, its HVAC systems, building envelope or other features.[30] The Superior Court of Pennsylvania has generally recognized that "an architect may be held liable for negligence in failing to exercise the ordinary skill of his profession, which results in the erection of an unsafe structure whereby anyone lawfully on the premises is injured."[31] Other Pennsylvania cases confirm that design professionals have a duty to unrelated third parties for damages arising from faulty building designs.[32]

The duty of the design professional was addressed in the context of a property damage claim in *City of Allentown v. O'Brien and Gere Engineers, Inc.*[33] In *City of Allentown*, the federal district court reviewed "the conduct expected of a reasonably competent engineering firm with respect to recommending, designing and supervising the construction of a structure appropriate for the client's needs." The court provided three qualitative measures for fact finders to use when assessing the conduct of a design professional: (1) did the professional use the reasonable care and diligence expected of a design professional in considering and evaluating all information pertinent to the project undertaken; (2) did the professional apply the knowledge reasonably expected of a design professional to make appropriate design recommendations to the client in accordance with sound design principles; and (3) did the professional apply the skill and knowledge reasonably expected of a design professional to design a structure or facility that is reasonably likely to accomplish the purpose for which it was retained.[34]

3. Intentional infliction of emotional distress

Mold exposure may give rise to intentional infliction of emotional distress (IIED) claims. In the residential housing context, Pennsylvania courts have refused to dismiss the theory that evidence of uninhabitable conditions at a leased premise can be used as the basis of a claim for IIED.[35] To prove an IIED claim, a plaintiff must show that the landlord must have acted intentionally or with reckless disregard of the consequences of its acts; the landlord's conduct must have been extreme or outrageous; the lessee must have suffered severe emotional distress; and the landlord's conduct was the cause of the emotional distress. In *Fair v. Negley*, the court found that plaintiffs had adequately pleaded a case for IIED and would have an opportunity to prove that defendant's actions in allegedly breaching the warranty of habitability was outrageous behavior sufficient to support a claim for IIED.[36] Although the *Fair* case did not involve mold, it arose from indoor air quality problems allegedly caused by an improperly ventilated gas hot water system and space heaters on the premises.

4. Strict products liability

In addition to targeting entities that own, manage, design or construct buildings, personal injury plaintiffs have also targeted manufacturers of exterior cladding systems using strict product liability theories.[37]

Pennsylvania courts have historically recognized an action of strict products liability under Section 402A of the Restatement (Second) of Torts (1965).[38] The requisite elements of a strict products liability claim are that the product was sold in a defective condition unreasonably dangerous to the public; that the defect existed when it left the hands of the defendant; and that the defect caused harm to the plaintiff.[39] As a practical matter, the "unreasonably dangerous" requirement was deemphasized by the Pennsylvania Supreme Court in *Berkebile v. Brantly Helicopter Corp.*, wherein the court noted that this qualification was only provided to prevent a manufacturer from being held liable where the product is not defective.[40] Accordingly, once a product is shown to be defective and that the defect has caused injury, the "unreasonably dangerous" requirement has been met.[41]

Pennsylvania courts have regularly followed §402A and applied the doctrine to property damages.[42] In *Cumberland Valley Joint School Authority v. Haldeman, Inc.*, a roof coating of "silicone asbestolite" was defective and caused water ingress and resultant damage to the plaintiff's roof.[43] The defendant wholesaler asserted that the claim was barred by the economic loss doctrine. The court denied the defendant's motion to dismiss, noting that the plaintiff had properly alleged resultant property damage.[44] Although it is not a mold case, *Cumberland Valley* provides guidance and support for future mold plaintiffs who can trace their damage to water ingress or mold growth directly caused by a defective building product.

5. Medical monitoring damages

In addition to personal injury damages such as medical expenses and lost earnings, Pennsylvania has recognized a separate claim for medical monitoring costs. In *Redland Soccer Club, Inc. v. Department of the Army*, the court noted that a common law claim for medical monitoring exists if a toxic tort plaintiff proves: (1) an exposure greater than normal background levels; (2) to a proven hazardous substance; (3) caused by the defendant's negligence; (4) as a proximate result of the exposure the plaintiff has a significantly increased risk of contracting a serious latent disease; (5) a monitoring procedure exists that makes the early detection of the disease possible; (6) the prescribed monitoring regime is different from that normally recommended in the absence of the exposure; and (7) the prescribed monitoring regime is reasonably necessary according to contemporary scientific principles.[45]

In *Heller v. Shaw Industries, Inc.*, plaintiffs alleged personal injury (sick building syndrome) caused by excessive levels of volatile organic compounds (VOC) that were released into the air in the plaintiffs' home from carpeting manufactured by the defendant. The plaintiffs asserted a claim for medical monitoring damages.[46] However, the trial judge made the following determination:

> ...plaintiffs have adduced no evidence that defendant's carpets emitted VOCs at concentrations harmful to health, that the levels of VOCs detected by [the consultant] are higher than the normal background presence, that plaintiffs suffer increased risk of contracting a serious latent disease as a result of their exposure to the levels of VOCs detected by [the consultant], or that the medical monitoring would be beneficial to the treatment and early detection for a serious latent disease.[47]

Although the *Heller* case does not specifically address mold, it is instructive as to the difficulty a mold plaintiff may have in trying to make out a claim for medical monitoring expenses. At this time, there is little conclusive, peer-reviewed evidence that mold is generally toxic or that it is the cause of any serious latent disease.

6. Negligent misrepresentation (professional)

Mold litigation often includes disputes between contractors and professionals with respect to responsibility for the specific conditions leading to mold growth. Contractors may allege defects in the design professional's work on the project via claims based on the Restatement (Second) of Torts §552 arguing that the design professional's plans and specifications incorporated "negligent misrepresentations." In order to state a claim for negligent misrepresentation a contractor must show a misrepresentation of a material fact; that the defendant either knows it is a misrepresentation, makes it without knowledge of its truth or falsity, or makes the representation under circumstances in which it ought to know of its falsity; that the defendant must intend the representation to induce another to act on the misrepresentation; and that the contractor suffered an injury acting in justifiable reliance on the misrepresentation.[48]

At this time, there are no reported cases in Pennsylvania involving a contractor's claims of negligent misrepresentation against a design professional related to mold. It is also unclear whether a contractor will ultimately be successful making these claims because of the economic loss doctrine, which bars tort claims seeking exclusively economic damages. For example, a property owner may choose to sue only the contractor for its mold-related property damages. The contractor may, thereafter, attempt to add the design professional as a third-party defendant, alleging negligent misrepresentation. Such a claim would likely be barred by the economic loss doctrine.

7. Implied warranty of fitness for intended purpose (professionals)

Although a contractor's action for negligent misrepresentation against an architect may be precluded by the economic loss doctrine, design professionals may find it difficult to extricate themselves from the net of liability. Typically, a design professional impliedly warrants that its plans and specifications will result in a structure reasonably fit for its intended purpose.[49] It has been determined that third parties may rely on this implied warranty.[50] Therefore, a contractor can be expected to assert a breach of implied warranty claim against a professional arguing that the mold-related damage is the result of the professional's errors or omissions.

8. Negligent construction

Contractors and construction managers are likely to be targeted directly by owners in property damage claims related to mold and moisture conditions.[51] To date, there are no reported Pennsylvania opinions discussing claims that can be brought against contractors arising from mold. However, Pennsylvania courts generally recognize several different theories of redress against contractors for construction defects, including an action for "negligent construction."[52]

9. Intentional misrepresentation/failure to disclose (sale of property)

Intentional misrepresentation is actionable if the following is shown: (1) a representation; (2) which is material to the transaction at hand; (3) made falsely, with knowledge of its falsity or recklessness as to whether it is true or false; (4) with the intent of misleading another into relying on it; (5) justifiable reliance on the misrepresentation; and (6) the resulting injury was proximately caused by the reliance.[53] The tort of intentional non-disclosure has the same elements as intentional misrepresentation, except that with non-disclosure the party intentionally conceals, rather than affirmatively misrepresents, the material fact.[54] While concealment may be fraudulent, mere silence is not sufficient in the absence of a duty to speak.[55] A real estate broker, in addition to a seller, can be liable for the torts of fraud and intentional non-disclosure.[56]

Historically, fraudulent concealment has not been actionable unless there is active concealment.[57] However, in *Roberts v. Barbagallo*, a far-reaching decision with potentially significant ramifications, the Superior Court held that liability for fraudulent concealment extends to failure to provide generally available information about an allegedly toxic substance.[58] In *Roberts*, the court held that a broker was liable for fraudulent concealment because it failed to disclose to the buyer material information concerning the possible health effects from urea formaldehyde foam insulation (UFFI) and thereby prevented the buyer from investigating the insulation in the house prior to her signing the agreement of sale.[59] The court found that the information concerning UFFI was material because: (1) there was a federal ban on UFFI; (2) there were known potential health risks from the use of UFFI; and (3) the local board of realtors had recommended that information concerning UFFI that was material to real estate transactions, should be disclosed to both buyers and sellers and that an effort should be made to try to ascertain the use of UFFI in properties being listed for sale. All of these facts were known to the broker.[60] The court did not satisfactorily explain how the failure to disclose the material information prevented the buyer from investigating UFFI in the house. The court's decision may be attributable to the court's belief that the individual realtor was on notice that insulation was in the house, and that she did not sufficiently investigate its composition. Nonetheless, the court refused to hold that the brokerage or the individual realtor had an obligation to investigate the nature of the insulation. The *Roberts* decision suggests that residential real estate brokers should at least strongly consider providing written information to prospective purchasers concerning the potential dangers arising from mold.

In addition, Pennsylvania courts have held that sellers have an affirmative duty to disclose known termite infestations, *see,* e.g., *Qhashnock v. Frost*, and other "serious and dangerous latent defects."[61] In A*nderson v. Harper,* 622 A.2d 319, 323 (Pa. Super. 1993), the Superior Court found that a seller of real property was obligated to disclose to his seller a malfunctioning sewage disposal system that caused sewage to surface to the top of the residential lot because it could pollute the environment, including water supplies, and might create potential health and safety problems.[62] The homeowner believed he had fixed the ongoing septic problem, but was deemed to know that the problem had not been fixed, and therefore had to be disclosed, because the seller did not obtain the permit required to fix the system and he did not properly fix it under existing regulations.[63] Although the subsequent passage of the RESDL in 2000 may undermine the holdings in these Pennsylvania disclosure cases related to termite damage and septic systems,[64] they are instructive as to potential mold liability, which is not directly addressed in the RESDL. Because at present there are no regulations which specify what constitutes a complete remediation of mold conditions, good practice suggests that sellers obtain an independent third-party opinion of a qualified consultant that remediation has been completed before failing to disclose a pre-existing mold or moisture condition.

10. Negligent misrepresentation (sale of property)

To state a claim for negligent misrepresentation, the plaintiff must show: (1) misrepresentation of a material fact; (2) made under circumstances in which the misrepresenter ought to have know its falsity; (3) with an intent to induce another to act on it; and (4) which results in injury to a party acting in justifiable reliance on the misrepresentation.[65] Unlike intentional misrepresentation, the speaker need not know her words are untrue, but must have failed to make a reasonable investigation of their truth. In addition, there must be a duty owed by one party to another.[66] Without ruling on the issue, the court in *Bortz v. Noon*, opined that real estate brokers might be subject to claims of liability under this theory, as well.[67] To date, no reported Pennsylvania case has found a duty to investigate conditions relating to mold.[68]

11. Innocent misrepresentation (sale of property)

An innocent misrepresentation is actionable if it is material to and the basis of a transaction, and the purchaser is justified in relying on the misrepresentation.[69] However, the remedy for an innocent misrepresentation is rescission, not monetary damages for tort recovery.[70]

16.4 Insurance Coverage

There are not many reported decisions in Pennsylvania addressing insurance coverage for mold. One notable case is *Deede Smith Kemmerer v. State Farm Insurance Co.*, in which the plaintiff sought coverage for mold-related property damages allegedly attributable to a toilet leak in her home when she was on vacation.[71] One of the covered perils was "sudden and accidental discharge or overflow," which the court stated would have justified recovery under the policy. However, the plaintiff's expert did not speak to the issue of causation. The insurance carrier submitted expert testimony that the property damage was caused by multiple uncovered causes of loss, including high humidity, stagnant air, a wet basement, dampness in the powder room from a neighboring greenhouse, and humid summer weather. The court determined that the issues of causation in the case were complex and required expert testimony. Because the plaintiff had offered no such testimony, summary judgment was awarded to the defendant.

Endnotes

1. 71 P.S. § 510-17.

2. *Id.*

3. *Id.*

4. *Id.*

5. 71 P.S. § 510-19.

6. *Pugh v. Holmes*, 405 A.2d 897 (Pa. 1979).

7. *See Pugh*, *supra* at 906.

8. *Id.*

9. *See In re Clark*, 96 B.R. 569 (Bankr. E.D. Pa. 1989).

10. *Hirsh v. Carbon Lehigh Intermediate Unit #21*, 65 Pa. D.&C. 4th 390 (Pa. Com. Pl. 2003).

11. *McDanel v. Mack Realty Co.*, 315 Pa. 174, 172 A. 97 (1934).

12. *See Pawco, Inc. v. Bergman Knitting Mills, Inc.*, 424 A.2d 891 (Pa. Super. 1980).

13. *Elderkin v. Gaster*, 288 A.2d 771, 777 (Pa. 1972).

14. *Spivak v. Berks Ridge Corporation Inc. et al.*, 586 A.2d 402, 405 (Pa.Super.1991).

15. *Pittsburgh Nat'l Bank v. Welton Becket Associate et al.*, 601 F. Supp. 887 (W. D. Pa 1985); *Sports Management Group, Inc. v. Allensville Planning Mill, Inc.*, 16 Pa. D. & C.3d 760, 765 (1980).

16. 65 Pa. D.&C. 4th (Pa. Com. Pl. 2003).

17. *See Skurnowicz et al. v. Lucci et al.*, 798 A.2d 788 (Pa. Super. 2002); *Commonwealth of Pennsylvania v. Monumental Properties, Inc., et al.*, 329 A.2d 812 (Pa. 1974).

18. 73 Pa.C.S. §201-2(4).

19. *Skurnowicz, supra* at 793.

20. *See, e.g., In re Partners Group Financial, LLC,* 394 B.R. 68 (Bankr. E.D. Pa. 2008) and *Chiles v. Ameriquest Mortgage Co.* 551 F.Supp.2d 393 (E.D. Pa. 2008)(adopting the view that in order for the addition of the terms "or deception" to be given effect, not all elements of common law fraud need to be proven for allegations of deceptive conduct); and *Skurnowicz, supra* at 793 and *Collaizzi v. Beck,* 895 A.2d 36, 39 (2006)(requiring a plaintiff to prove all elements of common law fraud).

21. 73 Pa C.S. §201-9.2(a).

22. 68 Pa.C.S.A. § 7302(a); 68 Pa.C.S.A. § 7103(a).

23. 68 Pa.C.S.A. §§ 7303-7304(a).

24. 68 Pa.C.S.A. § 7311(a).

25. *See Cresswell v. End,* 831 A.2d 673 (Pa. Super. 2003); *Gutteridge v. A.P. Green Services, Inc. et al.*, 804 A.2d 643 (Pa. Super. 2002).

26. 920 A.2d 861 (Pa. Super. 2007).

27. *Id.* at 866.

28. No. 91 Civ. 2061, 1993 WL 53582 (E.D. Pa. March 2, 1993).

29. 717 A.2d 589 (Pa. Commw. 1998).

30. *See Bonnette, et al. v. Tunica-Biloxi Indians*, No. 02-919, 2003 WL 21229282 (La. Ct. App. May, 28, 2003) (several groups of plaintiffs filed suit against construction defendants, including an architect and an engineering firm, for personal injuries from alleged mold exposure at a casino and its related child care facility).

31. *Young v. Eastern Engineering and Elevator Company, Inc.*, 554 A.2d 77, 79 (Pa. Super. 1989); 97 A.L.R.3d §2(a) (1980); 5 Am.Jur 2d, Architects §25; *see also Prost v. Caldwell Store, Inc.*, 187 A.2d 273, 276 (Pa. 1963).

32. *See, e.g., McKonley v. Franco,* 12 Pa. D. & C.3d 105 (1979) (subsequent owners of building were able to maintain suit against architect in negligence after roof collapsed without privity of contract).

33. No. CIV. A. 94-2384, 1997 WL 256050 (E.D. Pa. May 8, 1997).

34. *Id.; Bloomsburg Mills v. Sordoni Construction Co.*, 164 A.2d 201 (Pa. 1960).

35. *See Fair v. Negley*, 390 A.2d 240 (Pa. Super. 1978); *Beasley v. Freedman,* 389 A.2d 1087 (Pa. Super. 1978).

36. 390 A.2d 240 (Pa. Super. 1978).

37. *See Gropper, et al. v. STO Corporation, et al.*, 552 S.E.2d 118 (Ga. App. 2001) (homeowners filed suit against builder, stucco subcontractor and stucco manufacturer asserting claims of strict products liability for mold-related personal injuries and property damage due to use of synthetic stucco product on the exterior of their home).

38. *See Webb v. Zern*, 220 A.2d 853 (Pa. 1966).

39. *See DeSantties v. Frick Co.*, 745 A.2d 624 (Pa. Super. 2000).

40. 337 A.2d 893 (Pa. 1973)

41. *Id.*

42. *See Cumberland Valley Joint School Authority v. Haldeman, Inc.*, 23 Pa. D. & C.3d 616 (1982); *2-J Corporation v. Tice Construction Co. et al.*, 126 F.3d 539 (3rd Cir. 1997).

43. 23 Pa. D. & C.3d 616 (1982)

44. *Id.*

45. 696 A.2d 137(Pa. 1997).

46. No. Civ.A. 95-7657, 1997 WL 535163 (E.D. Pa. Aug. 18, 1997), *aff'd* at 167 F.3d 146 (3d Cir. 1999).

47. *Id.* at *21.

48. *See Borough of Landsdowne v. Sevenson Environmental Services, Inc. et al.*, 2000 WL 1886578 (E.D. Pa.) *citing Williams Controls, Inc. v. Parente, Randolph et al.*, 39 F. Supp.2d 517 (M.D. Pa. 1999).

49. *See, e.g., Bloomsburg, supra* at 203; *Metropolitan Edison Co v. United Engineers & Constructors, Inc.*, 4 Pa. D & C.3d 473 (1977).

50. *See, e.g., Spivak, supra* at 405.

51. *See Centex-Rooney Const. Co., Inc. v. Martin County*, 706 So.2d 20 (Fla. App. 4 Dist. 1997)(Florida appellate court upheld $8.8 million dollar breach of contract award against construction manager for failing to properly supervise construction).

52. *See Spivak, supra* at 405 (contractor has a common law duty to perform its work in a reasonable manner); *see also Sports Management Group, Inc. v. Allensville Planning Mill, Inc.*, 16 Pa. D. & C.3d 760 (1980).

53. *Bortz v. Noon*, 729 A.2d 555, 560 (Pa. 1999)

54. *Id.*

55. *Sevin v. Kelshaw*, 611 A.2d 1232, 1236 (Pa. Super. 1992); *Smith v. Renaut*, 564 A.2d 188, 192 (Pa. Super. 1989).

56. *Bortz v. Noon*, 729 A.2d at 560.

57. *See Anderson v. Harper*, 622 A.2d 319, 323 (Pa. Super. 1993).

58. 531 A.2d 1125 (Pa. Super. 1987).

59. *Id.* at 1131.

60. *Id.*

61. 622 A.2d 319, 323 (Pa. Super. 1993).

62. *Id.* at 324.

63. *Id.*

64. *See, e.g., Growall v. Maietta*, 931 A.2d 667, 673 n.4 (Pa. Super. 2007) (noting that viability of cases decided prior to the enactment of the RESDL "might rightly be called into question").

65. *Bortz*, 729 A.2d at 561.

66. *Id.*

67. *Id.* at 563.

68. *See generally Gibbs v. Ernst*, 647 A.2d 882, 893 (Pa. 1994)

69. *Bortz*, 729 A.2d at 564.

70. *Id.*

71. No. 01-5445 (E.D. Pa. Jan. 16, 2004).

Chapter 17

An Overview of Toxic Mold Litigation in South Carolina

Eric Fosmire, Esq.

Synopsis

17.1 Introduction

South Carolina has a temperate environment which can be conducive to fungal growth. The combination of average annual precipitation and moderate daily temperatures are factors in South Carolina's ranking for relative mold risk. South Carolina did not experience the rush of mold cases which seemed to follow *Ballard*. Nonetheless, substantial mold claims have been brought in the past and will likely continue to be brought in the future.

17.2 Right to Cure Residential Construction Defects

Mold cases in South Carolina, which arise in the residential context, must be considered in light of the South Carolina Residential Right to Cure Act ("Right to Cure Act").[1] If the mold claim arises from construction defects, the complaining party needs to comply with the act before filing suit. The notice and opportunity for the right to cure applies only to: (a) single family homes; (b) duplexes; and (c) multi-family units comprised of no more than 16 units and no more than three stories in height.

Under the Right to Cure Act, a claimant may not file suit for a construction defect or deficiency arising out of design specification, surveying, planning, supervision, or observation of construction without first giving the contractor or subcontractor notice of the claim. If the claimant files suit without providing notice and an opportunity to cure, upon motion of the affected defendant, the court shall stay the case until the claimant complies with the requirements of the Act.

Upon receiving notice, the contractor or subcontractor has 30 days to inspect the premises, to which claimant shall provide reasonable access for the purposes of inspection. After inspection, the contractor or subcontractor may serve an offer of resolution upon the claimant. The claimant must respond to the contractor's offer within ten days. The contractor's or subcontractor's failure to respond to the initial notice of claim is deemed a denial of the claim.

If the parties cannot resolve the dispute pursuant to notice and opportunity to cure, or if the contractor or subcontractor does not respond, the claimant may proceed with a civil action. Offers of settlement or concessions made pursuant to the Right to Cure Act are not admissible.

17.3 Statutes of Limitations and Repose

A party with a cause of action must bring the suit within the applicable the statute of limitations in South Carolina. There is a three-year statute of limitations for most causes of action, including: (a) wrongful death; (b) personal injuries; (c) damage to real or personal property; (d) contract actions; (e) actions on insurance policies; (f) shareholder derivative actions; and (g) fraud. There is a two-year statute of limitations for intentional torts such as: (a) libel and slander; (b) assault; (c) battery; and (d) false imprisonment.

It is important to note that South Carolina employs the discovery rule for when a cause of action accrues. Pursuant to the S.C. Code Ann. §15-3-530, the statute of limitations begins to run from the date a party either knows or should have known, by exercise of reasonable diligence, that a cause of action exists for wrongful conduct causing injury.

Anyone considering an action arising out of improvements to real property must also consider the ultimate statute of repose.[2] South Carolina legislatively modified its statute of repose in 2005. The statute of repose applies to actions for damages resulting from defective or unsafe conditions in an improvement to real property. A 13-year statute of repose applies to structures that achieve substantial completion before July 1, 2005. An eight-year statute of repose applies to structures that achieve substantial completion after July 1, 2005.

Application of the statute of repose requires evidence of substantial completion. A certificate of occupancy or certificate of completion of final inspection constitutes proof of substantial completion, unless the contractor and owner, by written agreement, establish a different date of substantial completion.

The statute of repose applies to: (a) breach of contract to construct or repair real property; (b) negligent construction of real property; (c) personal injury, death, or property damage as a result of defective or unsafe real property; (d) actions for contribution or indemnification; (e) actions against sureties or guarantors or current or prior owners; (f) actions against owners or manufacturers of components incorporated into real property or persons who perform designing or planning, surveying, supervision, or testing, or repair or improvement to real property. The major exceptions to the statute of repose include: (a) fraud; (b) gross negligence; and (c) recklessness.

17.4 Insurance Issues

A. Trigger of Coverage

South Carolina utilizes an injury-in-fact trigger of coverage. Coverage is triggered at the time of the injury-in-fact and continuously thereafter to allow coverage under all policies in effect at the time of the injury-in-fact during the progressive damage. This will allow the allocation of the risk among insurers when more than one insurance policy is in effect during the progressive damage.[3]

B. Duty to Defend

The determination of whether an insurance company is obligated to defend an action under its policy provisions is based on the allegations of the complaint.[4] "If the underlying complaint creates the possibility of coverage under an insurance policy, the insurer is obligated to defend."[5] An insurer may not defend only covered claims. Even if there is only one aspect of the claim that could possibly be covered, the insurer must defend the entire suit.[6] An insurer has no duty to defend an insured where the damage was caused for a reason unambiguously excluded under the policy.[7]

South Carolina has developing case law as to whether a commercial general liability (CGL) insurance policy provides coverage for construction defects. When considering either the prosecution or defense of a mold claim, counsel should first examine whether there is a potentially applicable policy of insurance and whether the policy of insurance contains mold or environmental hazard exclusions.

Regarding the alleged coverage for defects themselves and resulting damages, counsel must closely read *L-J, Inc. et al. v. Bituminous Fire & Marine Ins. Co.*,[8] and *Auto Owners v. Newman.*[9]

In the *L-J v. Bituminous* case, the South Carolina Supreme Court noted that it had not previously addressed whether faulty workmanship itself constitutes an occurrence under a CGL policy. The court did note that it had previously decided "that a CGL policy is not intended to cover economic loss resulting from faulty workmanship. *Century Indemnity Co. v. Golden Hills Builders, Inc.*, 348 S.C. 559, 561 S.E.2d 355 (2002)." In addition, the South Carolina Court of Appeals found that faulty workmanship is part of the insured's contractual liability, not an insurable event under a CGL policy.[10] In *L-J*, after making a factual specific analysis, the court found that the faulty workmanship by the road contractor did not constitute an occurrence.[11] After so finding, the court specifically added a footnote which stated "the CGL policy may, however, provide coverage in cases where faulty workmanship causes a third-party bodily injury or damage to other party, not in cases where faulty workmanship damages the work product alone."[12] The court then referenced that the analysis of the New Hampshire Supreme Court in *High Country Assoc. v. New Hampshire Ins. Co.*, 139 N.H. 39, 649 A.2d 474 (1994), was useful, wherein the New Hampshire court found that a CGL policy provided coverage for damage caused by continuous exposure to moisture resulting in property damage and not merely negligent construction to the work product itself.[13]

In rehearing *Auto Owners*, the South Carolina Supreme Court may further clarify whether a CGL policy of a homebuilder covers damages caused by the negligence of a subcontractor. Though the opinion is under reconsideration by the court, the analysis addresses whether the negligent construction was an occurrence under the policy and has, thus far, stated "it should be clear that this court intended the 'third-party' language to refer to subcontractors who are not a party to the CGL policy between the insurer and contractor."[14] The court found that the subcontractor's negligence led to an occurrence implicating the policy, thus finding coverage because there was resulting property damage to other property, not the work product.

17.5 Joint and Several Liability

When faced with multiple defendants whose actions joined together to injure the plaintiff, the plaintiff may sue them in one action or in separate actions; however plaintiffs are limited to only one full recovery for their injuries.[15] South Carolina follows the common law rule that joint tortfeasors are jointly and severally liable to the plaintiff.[16]

As of July 1, 2005, joint and several liability has been legislatively modified to avoid the inequitable result wherein a defendant who minimally contributes to the cause of plaintiff's injuries should not be required to pay for the entirety of plaintiff's damages.[17] Now, a defendant must be at least 50 percent at fault to be held jointly and severally liable for the whole of the damages. If a defendant is less than 50 percent at fault, then he is only liable for the percentage of his negligence. The modification to joint and several liability does not apply to a defendant whose conduct is willful, wanton, reckless, grossly negligent, or intentional, or where the conduct involves the use, sale, or possession of alcohol or drugs. The jury, or the court if it is a non-jury trial, will specify the amount of damages and determine the percentage of fault upon a special verdict on percentage of liability.

17.6 Theories of Liability in Mold Actions

Negligence claims may exist against architects, engineers, general contractors or those involved in the construction trade for faulty design and construction. The implied duty to perform a job in a workmanlike manner may cause contractors to be liable to tenants, building managers or landlords.

Breach of contract claims may arise between the building owner and architects, or engineers or general contractors or subcontractors or any combination thereof for defective construction. The usual allegation is that the defendant in question failed to perform the design or construction work in compliance with contract plans, specifications and conditions. There is often a question as to whether a defect is the result of the design or the contractor's defective workmanship.

Breach of warranty claims may also exist. South Carolina recognizes both express and implied warranties in law. In the context of construction defect claims, the implied warranty is that the work of the professional will conform to the standard of their profession. The particular facts and circumstances of each case must be examined to determine whether there was an express or implied warranty or whether the conduct is actually the equivalent of negligence.

Plaintiffs may also seek recourse under the South Carolina Unfair Trade Practices Act ("the Act"). Under the Act, if a plaintiff can demonstrate unfair methods of competition or deceptive acts or practices in the conduct of any trade or commerce and there was an ascertainable loss of money or real property as a result, an individual may bring a cause of action for violation of South Carolina Code Annotated § 39-5-10, *et seq*. Note that a violation of the Act allows the plaintiff to recover treble damages and costs and attorneys fees.

17.7 Class Actions

Class action claims may also arise from a situation where mold developed. Class actions in South Carolina are controlled by Rule 23 of the South Carolina Rules of Civil Procedure. Rule 23(a) requires the following prerequisites to a class action: (1) the class is so numerous that joinder of all members is impractical; (2) there are questions of law or fact common to the class; (3) the claims or defenses of the representative parties are typical of the claims or defenses of the class; (4)

the representative parties will fairly and adequately protect the interest of the class; (5) in cases in which the relief primarily sought is not injunctive or declaratory with respect to the class as a whole, the amount in controversy exceeds $100 for each class member.

Rule 23 is modeled on, but is different from, Rules 23 of the Federal Rules of Civil Procedure 23. Regardless, an examination of the cases discussing the application of Rule 23(a) reveals that South Carolina courts tend to adopt procedures established in the federal court system.[18] As under Fed. R. Civ. P. 23(a), certification under South Carolina law requires a showing by the Plaintiffs of numerosity, commonality, typicality and adequacy of representation. Rule 23 of the South Carolina Rules of Civil Procedure also inherently requires that the class action be manageable and superior to other forms of action, and class certification should be denied if the class action would not be manageable.[19] Otherwise, an action certified as a class is at risk of degenerating into an unmanageable quagmire of individual issues and affirmative defenses.

Certification of a class in South Carolina requires a rigorous analysis by the court to determine that the plaintiffs have met their burden of demonstrating the presence of all essential elements mandated by Rule 23. Plaintiffs bear the burden of establishing that each of the elements of Rule 23(a)(1) through (5) can be met.[20] Plaintiffs' failure to satisfy any one of the prerequisites is fatal to class certification.[21] The trial court is charged with undertaking a rigorous analysis to ensure that the certification requirements are satisfied.[22] In undertaking this analysis, the Court may not engage in speculation or conjecture, nor may it guess whether at some future date evidence may be forthcoming to support any essential element.[23]

In conducting its analysis, the court may look beyond the bald allegations in the Complaint, but does not decide the merits of the underlying claim.[24] The court conducts its analysis by taking "into account the substantive elements of plaintiff's claims and it looks to the proof necessary to those elements so as to envision the form trial on those issues would take."[25] However, the court may not look to the merits in deciding whether to certify a class.[26]

In making its analysis, if the Court foresees a trial where the basic elements of the alleged claims and corresponding defenses cannot be proven on a class-wide basis by the evidence and, instead, resolution of the class members' claims would require evidence from, or individual determinations about, each class member, then certification is inappropriate.

17.8 Experts

The following provides a comparison of South Carolina's evidentiary rules to the federal rules, as they relate to admissibility of expert testimony:

South Carolina State Court	Federal Court
Rule 702—Testimony by Experts. If scientific, technical, or other specialized knowledge will assist the trier of fact to understand the evidence or to determine a fact in issue, a witness qualified as an expert by knowledge, skill, experience, training or education may testify thereto in the form of an opinion or otherwise.	Rule 702—Testimony by Experts. If scientific, technical or other specialized knowledge will assist the trier of fact to understand the evidence or to determine a fact in issue, a witness qualified as an expert by knowledge, skill, experience, training, or education, may testify thereto in the form of an opinion or otherwise, if (1) the testimony is based upon sufficient facts or data, (2) the testimony is a product of reliable principles and methods, and (3) the witness has applied the principles and methods reliably to the facts of the case.
Rule 703—Basis of Opinion Testimony by Experts. The facts or data in the particular case upon which an expert bases an opinion or inference may be those perceived by or made known to the expert at or before the hearing. If of a type reasonably relied upon by experts in the particular field in forming opinions or inferences upon the subject, the facts or date need not be admissible in evidence.	Rule 703—Basis of Opinion Testimony by Experts. The facts or data in the particular case upon which an expert bases an opinion or inference may be those perceived by or made known to the expert at or before the hearing. If of a type reasonably relied upon by experts in the particular field in forming opinions or inferences upon the subject, the facts or data need not be admissible in evidence… Facts or data that are otherwise inadmissible shall not be disclosed to the jury by the proponent of the opinion or inference unless the court determines that their probative value in assisting the jury to evaluate the expert's opinion substantially outweighs their prejudicial effect.

South Carolina State Court	Federal Court
Rule 704—Opinion on Ultimate Issue. Testimony in the form of an opinion or inference otherwise admissible is not objectionable because it embraces an ultimate issue to be decided by the trier of fact.	Rule 704—Opinion on Ultimate Issue. (a) Except as provided in subdivision (b), testimony in the form of an opinion or inference otherwise admissible is not objectionable because it embraces an ultimate issue to be decided by the trier of fact. (b) No expert witness testifying with respect to the mental state or condition of a defendant in a criminal case may state an opinion or inference as to whether the defendant did or did not have the mental state or condition constituting an element of the crime charged or of a defense thereto. Such ultimate issues are matters for the trier of fact alone. (As amended October 12, 1984.)
Rule 705—Disclosure of Facts or Data Underlying Expert Opinion. The expert may testify in terms of opinion or inference and give reasons therefor without first testifying to the underlying facts or data, unless the court requires otherwise. The expert may in any event be required to disclose the underlying facts or data on cross-examination.	Rule 705—Disclosure of Facts or Data Underlying Expert Opinion. The expert may testify in terms of opinion or inference and give reasons therefor without first testifying to the underlying facts or data, unless the court requires otherwise. The expert may in any event be required to disclose the underlying facts or data on cross-examination.

17.9 South Carolina Toxic Mold Case Law

There is one South Carolina case that actually references "toxic mold." In *Roland v. Heritage Litchfield, Inc.*, the issue was whether there was sufficient evidence of habitability of the condominium units in question to preclude summary judgment in favor of the plaintiffs.[27] The Court found that the evidence demonstrated that, although the buildings were under construction, sheetrock in the firewall became wet from rainfall as the roof had not yet been completed. As a result of a subsequent plumbing leak, which required the opening up of the firewall, mold was discovered within the firewall. There was a dispute as to whether the mold in the firewall rendered the units uninhabitable. The court held that:

> The "habitability" of a dwelling does not turn on whether a person actually lives there; rather habitability is defined as "[t]he condition of a building in which inhabitants can live free of serious defects that might harm health and safety…"

The court further found that, despite some evidence that the units had been rented and that only if the firewalls were disturbed would the mold become problematic, it was not sufficient to preclude summary judgment.

In *Taylor, Cotton, & Ridley, Inc. v. Okatie Hotel Group, LLC*, a mechanic's lien was brought by a subcontractor against a property owner and a general contractor.[28] The owner requested that the trial court consider improper installation of insulation allegedly resulting in $651,551 in mold damages. The trial court excluded evidence of mold damage as inapplicable to the mechanic's lien at issue, and the trial court's ruling was upheld on appeal.

Endnotes

1. S.C. Code § 40-59-810, *et seq.*

2. S.C. Code § 15-3-640.

3. *Joe Harden Builders, Inc. v. Aetna Cas. and Sur. Co.*, 326 S.C. 231, 486 S.E.2d 89 (1997); *Century Indemnity Co. v. Golden Hills Builders, Inc.*, Op. No. 25426 (S.C. March 11, 2002).

4. *R.A. Earnhardt Textile Mach. Div., Inc. v. South Carolina Ins. Co.*, 277 S.C. 88, 90, 282 S.E.2d 856, 857 (1981).

5. *Isle of Palms Pest Control Co. v. Monticello Ins. Co.*, 459 S.E.2d 318 (Ct.App. 1994).

6. *Id.*

7. *Falkosky v. Allstate Ins. Co.,* 311 S.C. 369, 429 S.E.2d 194 (Ct. App.1993), aff'd as modified, 312 S.C. 210, 439 S.E.2d 836 (1993).

8. 366 S.C. 117, 621 S.E.2d 33 (2005), reh'g. den. (Nov. 10, 2005).

9. No. 26450, 2008 WL 648546 (SC Mar. 10, 2008). Note that rehearing was granted in *Auto Owners v. Newman* and arguments were held on November 6, 2008. The South Carolina Supreme Court has not issued a subsequent opinion modifying, withdrawing, or otherwise explaining the decision of March 10, 2008, as of the date of this document.

10. *Isle of Palms Pest Control v. Monticello Ins. Co.*, 319 S.C. 12, 459 S.E.2d 318 (Ct. App. 1994).

11. *L-J*, 366 S.C. at 123.

12. *Id.*

13. *Id.*

14. Auto Owners, 2008 WL 648546, at *3.

15. *Atlantic Coastline Railroad Co. v. Whetstone*, 132 S.E.2d 172 (1963).

16. *Pendleton v. Columbia Railway, Gas & Electric Co.*, 133 S.C. 326 (1926).

17. S.C. Code § 15-38-15.

18. *See Gardner v. Newsome-Buick, Co.*, 304 S.C. 328, 404 S.E.2d 200 (1991)(Where there is no South Carolina law, courts should examine federal court construction.)

19. *See McGann v. Mungo*, 287 S.C. 561, 340 S.E.2d 154, 159 (1986)(class must be cognizable and manageable). *See also* James Flanagan, South Carolina Civil Procedure 179, 183 (2d. ed. 1996).

20. *See Waller v. Seabrook Island Property Owners Ass'n*, 300 S.C. 465, 467, 388 S.E.2d 799, 801 (1990), citing *Windham v. American Brands, Inc.*, 565 F.2d 59 (4th Cir. 1977) *cert. denied*, 435 U.S. 968 (1978).

21. *Id.*

22. *Id.* (citing *General Ťelephone Co. of Southwest v. Falcon*, 457 U.S. 147 (1982)).

23. *Id.*

24. *General Ťelephone*, 457 U.S. at 160 ("[I]t may be necessary for the court to probe behind the pleadings before coming to rest on the certification question."); *Castano v. American Tobacco Co.*, 84 F.3d 734, 744 (5th Cir. 1996) ("Going beyond the pleadings is necessary, as a court must understand the claims, defenses, relevant facts, and applicable substantive law in order to make a meaningful determination of certification issues") (internal citations omitted).

25. *Elliott v. ITT Corp.*, 150 F.R.D. 569, 572 (N.D. Ill. 1992) (citation omitted).

26. *Tilley v. Pacesetter Corp.*, 333 S.C. 33, 43, 508 S.E.2d 16, 21 (1998).

27. 372 S.C. 161, 641 S.E.2d 465 (Ct. App. 2007)

28. 641 S.E.2d 459 (Ct. App. 2007).

Chapter 18

An Overview of Toxic Mold Litigation in Texas

Stephen Pate, Esq. and Rhonda M. Sigman, Esq.

Synopsis

18.1 Introduction

Any recent article regarding mold litigation in the United States will invariably raise the infamous *Ballard* case tried in Austin, Texas.[1] In that 2001 case, a Texas jury handed down a $32.2 million verdict against the insurer of a house that was worth $750,000.[2,3] Though the Austin Court of Appeals reduced the award to $4 million plus interest and attorneys' fees,[4] the verdict was the harbinger of a new era in mold litigation.

Although *Ballard* was not the first "toxic mold" case, it uniquely attracted significant media attention because of its enormous jury award. Media frenzy ensued and prompted the Commissioner of the Texas Department of Insurance to warn that fear and publicity were feeding upon each other to cause a mold dilemma.[5]

From 2000-2001, near the time *Ballard* was decided, insurance claims for mold damage in Texas increased exponentially, rising from 1,050 claims in the first quarter of 2000 to 14,706 claims in the fourth quarter of 2001.[6] The number of claims made per 1,000 policyholders in Texas rose from 1.7 in the first quarter of 2000 to 23.57 in the fourth quarter of 2001.[7] By 2002, Texas, with only 8 percent of the national population, generated 75 percent of all mold claims.[8]

Insurance companies in the Texas homeowners insurance market were caught off guard by the surge in claims and the resulting hemorrhage of payouts.[9] In 2001, many of the larger insurers, including Allstate, State Farm, and Farmers Insurance Group refused to issue new policies covering water-related claims.[10] By 2002, Farmers Insurance Group announced that it would not renew Texas homeowners' policies and several other insurers threatened to withdraw from the Texas homeowner's market. These moves were suspended only because of agreements made with the Texas Department of Insurance.[11]

At about the same time, insurance companies raised their rates. The average cost of insuring a home in Texas went from $786 a year in 2000 to $1,201 a year in 2003. In comparison, the nationwide average cost of insuring a home went from $508 a year to $569 a year during the same period of time.[12] The insurance companies attributed the higher rates in Texas to unwarranted lawsuits and higher claims for mold and storm-related losses.[13] The dramatic increase in mold claims corresponds directly with an increase in the number of mold-related lawsuits, against insurance companies in particular.

This chapter outlines the issues related to mold litigation and summarizes the current mold legislation in Texas. Particular attention is paid to issues regarding accrual of action, admission of expert testimony in physical injury claims, and, in the insurance law arena, issues regarding trigger of policy coverage and ensuing loss clauses.

18.2 Mold Litigation in Texas

In mold-related lawsuits, plaintiffs have available to them numerous causes of action against a vast group of potential litigants. For example, if a plaintiff alleges that physical injury or property damage was caused by a defect in building construction, potential defendants could include builders, contractors, subcontractors, construction managers, property managers, architects, designers, construction component suppliers, and building owners. If a plaintiff alleges that mold damage was caused by faulty repair of household appliances or plumbing, the service person could be liable for the resulting damage, including property damage or physical injury. Some causes of action available to a plaintiff include breach of contract, breach of warranty, negligence, gross negligence, negligent misrepresentation, intentional or negligent infliction of emotional distress, and violations of the Texas Deceptive Trade Practices Act (DTPA).

As described earlier, homeowner insurers are likely the most often targeted defendants. Damages that may be claimed against insurers include the cost of mold remediation, compensation for property damage, physical injury, and the insurer's misconduct, if any, in handling the insured's claim. An insurer's misconduct in claims denial cascades beyond contractual claims involving the insurance policy and includes extracontractual claims. In such cases, a plaintiff may assert against an insurance company—in addition to common law torts—actions for bad faith, unfair settlement practices, and unfair or deceptive acts under Texas Insurance Code chapters 541 and 542 (formerly article 21.21).

This subsection discusses the issues of when causes of action accrue for purposes of limitations periods, the difficulties in bringing claims for physical injury because of the difficulty in submitting expert opinions, and particular issues in claims against insurance companies, including statutory claims, coverage triggers, and ensuing loss clauses.

A. The Statute of Limitation and Accrual of Action Issues

Determining when a cause of action accrues—or for purposes of insurance coverage, determining when a policy is triggered—for mold-related damage is a challenging issue in mold litigation. Mold often grows in places where it is not easily discoverable by the building occupants. To deal with the particular challenges and circumstances related to injuries not easily discoverable, the Texas legislature has enacted statutes, and the courts have developed common law, to determine when an action should accrue.

For certain causes of action, the Texas Civil Practice and Remedies Code (CPRC) provides clear guidance regarding the period of limitations. Under the CPRC, most causes of action for personal injury and property damage have a two-year limitations period.[14] There is, however, an extended limitations period for improvement to building construction where injury or damage that may not be discoverable until many years after the improvement was completed.

Suits claiming personal injury or property damage against architects, engineers who furnish design, planning, or inspection of construction of improvements to real property, and suits against persons furnishing construction or repair of improvements may be brought within ten years after substantial completion of the improvement.[15] This ten-year limitations period applies regardless of when the defect is discovered.[16] The actions against these statutory defendants accrue when the improvements are substantially completed.[17]

Although the CPRC provides clear guidance as to accrual of action for claims against designers and builders of real property improvements, accrual of action for claims against other potential defendants are not so neatly resolved. Because mold damage may not be apparent until years after occurrence of the act or event that caused the mold to proliferate, determining when a cause of action accrues for the purpose of usual two-year limitations period is crucial.

Generally, a cause of action accrues when a wrongful act causes some legal injury, regardless of when the plaintiff learns of the injury.[18] A party needs only be aware of enough facts to make her cognizant of her right to seek judicial remedy.[19] For mold-related damage, however, some questions have arisen regarding how to determine when the legal injury occurs. This is because injury resulting from the wrongful act may not be readily apparent at time the wrongful act leading to mold damage was committed.

To combat some of the uncertainties associated with the accrual of action when the injury is not readily apparent, Texas courts have formulated what is known as the "discovery rule," which is applied when the damage or injury was "inherently undiscoverable" and when the evidence of the damage or injury is objectively verifiable.[20] The discovery rule is a judicially conceived exception to the statute of limitations and is used to determine when a cause of action accrues where a plaintiff was unable to know of his injury at the time it occurred.[21] When applicable, the discovery rule tolls the running of the limitations period and defers the accrual of a cause of action until a plaintiff discovers, or through the exercise of reasonable care and diligence should discover, the nature of his injury.[22] The discovery rule imposes upon the plaintiff a duty to exercise reasonable diligence to discover facts of negligence. The limitations period thus begins when the plaintiff knew or should have known of the facts giving rise to his cause of action.

Application of the discovery rule, however, is not always straightforward. Even when the discovery rule applies, it is still a question of fact when the plaintiff should have known the facts giving rise to his injury. The cases of *Booker v. Real Homes, Inc.* and *Palmer v. Sears, Roebuck & Co.* offer guidance on identifying the events triggering the accrual of a cause of action.

In *Booker*, the plaintiffs (the Bookers) first experienced water leakage problems due to construction defects in September 1997.[23] By November 1997, the Bookers began to notice a "musty" odor inside their home. They reported this odor to the builder of the house, but the builder did not take any remedial action until the Bookers asked the builder to remedy the problem again in June 1998. In September 1998, the builder discovered water damage, including moisture and mold, and determined that the windows were the source of the water leaks. The builder and the window installer repaired the problem in November 1998, but the odor returned. In July 1999, the Bookers discovered wet and rotten wood. The seepage from the window had apparently caused extensive water damage inside the walls of the house, and the water damage led to the eventual mold infestation. The mold, in turn, as the Bookers alleged, caused them health problems.

In October 1999, the Bookers sued the home builder and the window installer, claiming breach of contract, breach of warranty, negligence, gross negligence, negligent misrepresentation, intentional infliction of emotional distress, and violations of the Texas DTPA.[24] The trial court found, and the appellate court affirmed, however, that the Bookers' claims were barred by the two-year statute of limitations. In affirming the defendants' summary judgment, the appellate court applied the discovery rule and found that the limitations period had run. That court explained that all that was required to commence the running of the limitations period was the discovery of an injury and its general cause, not the exact cause in fact and the specific parties responsible.[25] Thus, the court found that the discovery rule applied to toll the running of the statute until September 1997, the date on which the Bookers actually knew of the leaks, not when the Bookers determined the specific cause of the leaks. Accordingly, the *Booker* court held that the period of limitations had run on the Bookers.[26]

A different situation was presented in the matter of *Palmer v. Sears, Roebuck & Co.*[27] In *Palmer*, Sears performed repairs on Palmer's air conditioner in April 1993. One month later, Palmer discovered a leak in the air conditioning unit where repairs were made that caused water to accumulate in the unit. In October 1994, Palmer became ill. A preliminary determination was made that mold and sporing from the air conditioner leak was the cause of Palmer's injuries. Palmer filed suit in September 1996.

Palmer acknowledged that he knew of his property damage, the first injury for which he could sue, in May 1993, more than two years before he filed suit. He insisted, however, that he could not have known of his physical injuries until they first manifested themselves in October 1994, within the two-year limitations period.

The court, however, found that Palmer's cause of action accrued at the time Sears negligently performed the repairs to his air conditioner and not on the date when the extent of the resulting damages were fully ascertainable.[28] Palmer's legal rights, property and physical, were invaded the moment water began leaking from the supposedly repaired air conditioner and damaged his property. In so holding, the court concluded that:

> [o]nce injury results there is but a single tort and not a series of separate torts, one for each resultant harm. The cause of action thus created is for all the damage caused by a single legal wrong, and a plaintiff may not split

> this cause of action by seeking damages for some of his injuries in one suit and for later-developing injuries in another. The cause of action 'inheres in the causative aspects of a breach of a legal duty, the wrongful act itself, and not in the various forms of harm which result therefrom...'[29]

Thus, under the discovery rule, a cause of action accrues when the plaintiff actually knows of the injury. It is not necessary for the plaintiff to determine the specific cause of the injury. Further, under the discovery rule, a cause of action accrues when the initial injury is discovered, not when subsequent injuries are later exposed.

B. Difficulties in Maintaining Personal Injury Claims

Plaintiffs in mold-related litigation often claim physical injury resulting from occupying a mold-infested building. There are, however, particular difficulties in maintaining physical injury claims when the injuries are allegedly the result of exposure to mold. These difficulties include the plaintiff's burden to prove both general and specific causation. In other words, a plaintiff must first prove that mold is capable of causing a particular injury or condition in the general public and then prove that the mold to which the plaintiff was exposed caused that plaintiff's injury.[30] Proving both types of causation has shown to be a difficult hurdle for the plaintiffs to overcome in Texas. In particular, proof of general causation has been problematic because few studies have been done on the effect of mold on physical health.

1. General requirements

The causation hurdle has proved to be difficult to overcome in Texas because Texas has adopted the *Daubert* standard for expert testimony in *E.I. Du Pont de Nemours and Co. v. Robinson*.[31] Under *Robinson*, the trial judge acts as the gate-keeper of expert testimony evidence. The expert testimony must be sufficiently relevant and reliable to be admitted.

To prove general causation, a plaintiff generally must submit scientific evidence, including epidemiological studies, to show that mold is capable of causing the particular type of injury from which plaintiff suffers. Both *Daubert* and *Robinson* provide some factors in guiding the Texas courts in evaluating whether the proposed scientific evidence is reliable.[32] The *Daubert* and *Robinson* reliability requirement for scientific evidence of physical injury from mold is difficult to overcome because there have been few scientific studies done on the subject. Further, while epidemiological studies are generally used by experts where scientific evidence showing proof of causation is lacking, the Texas Supreme Court has mandated specific requirements for admission of epidemiological studies.[33]

2. Expert testimony

In Texas, for an expert witness's testimony to be admitted under the Texas Rules of Evidence, the expert must be qualified, the proposed testimony must be scientific knowledge (i.e., reliable), and the proposed testimony must assist the trier of fact to understand the evidence or to determine a fact in issue (i.e., relevant).[34] Of these three requirements, reliability of the expert testimony is the most challenged requirement for cases relating to physical injury claims in mold-related litigation.

In Texas, reliability of an expert's testimony may be challenged on four grounds—the foundational facts of the expert's opinion, the methodology the expert employed, whether there is an "analytical gap" between the expert's conclusion and the underlying data, and whether the expert accounted for other plausible causes of the damage.[35]

Further, the Texas Supreme Court enumerated a nonexclusive list of six factors to assist the trial court in determining the reliability of expert testimony: (1) extent to which the theory has or can be tested; (2) extent to which the theory relies on expert interpretation; (3) whether the theory has been subject to peer review; (4) the technique's potential rate of error; (5) the technique's acceptance by the relevant scientific community; and (6) the technique's non-judicial uses.[36]

a. Few studies exist to show the causal link between mold toxins and physical injury

The presence of mold, by itself, is not believed to necessarily cause harmful effects to human health. It is the toxin that mold releases during sporing, or "mycotoxins," that is the suspected culprit behind human ailments some believe result from exposure to mold. Thus, the mere presence of mold in a building does not necessarily mean the occupants will ultimately be exposed to mycotoxins. For a person to be exposed to the mycotoxins, mold spores must be released into the air and inhaled, contacted, or ingested. However, virtually all information related to diseases caused by mycotoxins concern ingestion of foods contaminated with mold.[37] There has been a paucity of studies done to examine the exposure to mycotoxins through inhalation.

Although epidemiological studies have been done, and those studies have consistently detected an association between respiratory symptoms and mold growth in homes, causality in those studies has not been established.[38] In September 2002, the Texas Medical Association (TMA) adopted a report from its counsel that concluded that adverse health effects from exposure to *Stachybotrys* spores (spores from the *Stachybotrys chartarum* strain of mold) were not supported by available peer review reports in medical literature.[39] The TMA instead concluded that the "probability or possibility" of causation or exacerbation of medical conditions due to exposure to mold in an indoor environment was limited to those individuals who have respiratory allergies to *Stachybotrys* spores or those rare individuals who have rare inflammatory lung diseases.[40] The author of that report acknowledged that there was a "fundamental disconnect" between what the public was being told by the media and consensus within the scientific community.[41]

Consistent with the TMA's finding, the U.S. Environmental Protection Agency has not set standards or Threshold Limit Values (TLVs) for airborne concentrations of mold or mold spores. Currently, there are no EPA regulations or standards for airborne mold contaminants.[42] The EPA thus far only recognizes that molds can trigger asthma episodes and allergies in sensitive individuals.[43]

A recent study conducted by the Institute of Medicine, on behalf of the U.S. Centers for Disease Control and Prevention, concluded that toxins from mold and bacteria can cause coughing and wheezing but that there is no evidence linking mold to more serious ailments such as cancer, fatigue, or neurological problems.[44] Even the study's conclusion linking the association between mold and coughing and wheezing must be considered with prudence because the study did not specify which agents were present in the damp buildings occupied by the research subjects.[45] Bacterial toxins could very well have been in the buildings, and in fact were expected to be in the buildings, in addition to mycotoxins from molds. While the study found that it is *biologically plausible* that toxins from *Stachybotrys chartarum* could cause effects in humans, the study cautiously urges validation from more extensive research before conclusions are drawn.

b. Case law regarding admission of expert testimony on the effects of mycotoxins on human health

The lack of reliable scientific studies demonstrating the link between mycotoxins and human health effects makes it difficult for a plaintiff to admit expert testimony on the issue of causation. Cases in Texas generally reflect this difficulty.

In *Flores v. Allstate Texas Lloyds Co.*, the plaintiffs (the Floreses) sued their homeowner's insurance company, claiming that the mold in the home caused allergic health effects.[46] The Floreses attempted to designate their family physician as a causation expert on the health effects of the household mold. The court examined the proposed expert testimony against the four *Daubert* factors. The court first concluded that plaintiffs' theory that their allergies were caused by mold in their homes was not tested by their designated expert or any other expert. Second, the expert's proffered testimony failed the "peer review" inquiry of *Daubert* because he was not able to point to publications or studies that supported his hypothesis that household molds cause allergies. Third, the potential for error in the proposed expert's technique was "virtually limitless" because the expert did not conduct tests on the plaintiffs nor was the expert able to identify any scientific study that demonstrated that the type of mold found in plaintiffs' home more likely than not caused them any health effects. Finally, the court found that the expert failed to present evidence as to the acceptance of his theory in the scientific community. Based on this four-part *Daubert* analysis, the Texas court held that the Floreses failed to prove general causation.

Further, the court found there was no specific causation because no one in the plaintiffs' household had undergone any testing to determine allergies to household mold, and the expert failed to account for other factors that may have caused the plaintiffs' health problems, such as cigarettes, dust mites, fibers, mesquite, or other environmental allergens. Specifically, the expert never conducted allergy tests on the plaintiffs or evaluated plaintiffs' exposure to mold in their home. The court thus excluded the expert's testimony.

The *Ballard* case is perhaps the most instructive case showcasing the high hurdle that potential expert witnesses must overcome before an expert can be found sufficiently reliable to testify on a subject matter. In *Ballard*, the plaintiff's husband, Allison, was diagnosed with a type of brain damage called toxic encephalopathy.[47] Two leading experts in the study of health effects of mold and mycotoxins testified on behalf of Allison and agreed that exposure to mold caused his toxic encephalopathy. The trial court, however, found that even though the foundational data used by the experts to prove general causation met the requirements of *Daubert/Robinson*, it was unreliable according to the factors propounded by the Texas Supreme Court in *Havner v. Merrell Dow Pharmaceuticals, Inc.*[48]

In *Ballard*, Allison's causation experts had presented an epidemiological study that the court found to be a "crucial underpinning" of their opinions. The court read *Havner* to hold that for an epidemiological study to be reliable foundation, it must be (1) unbiased in its design and show that exposure to the allegedly toxic substance more than doubles the risk of injury; and (2) capable of repetition with the same results 95 percent of the time (a confidence interval of 95 percent). The *Ballard* court found both elements lacking in the epidemiological study relied upon by Allison's experts. The experts had failed to show that exposure to mold more than doubled the risk of injury and further could not show that their technique was generally accepted. Allison's experts also could not provide a confidence interval because there had not been sufficient studies done. One of Allison's experts admitted that "there are very few case reports that toxic molds inside homes can cause unique or rare health conditions....These reports are rare, and a causal link between the presence of toxic mold and these conditions has not been proven."[49]

Even though the *Ballard* court seems to suggest that the requirements for proof of a 95 percent confidence interval and proof that exposure to mold more than doubles the risk of injury are necessary only if the expert relies on epidemiological studies, it found that the study was a "crucial underpinning" of the experts' opinions. At this time, it is not yet clear whether potential experts will be able to demonstrate reliability of their testimony without presenting epidemiological studies. If so, plaintiffs may be able to bypass the stringent requirements that *Havner* appears to impose on epidemiological studies before these studies may be admitted as evidence. It remains likely, however, that epidemiological studies will continue to be crucial to mold experts' opinions due to the absence of studies showing a direct causal link between mold and physical injuries.

A possible counterexample to the stringent reliability requirements espoused in *Havner* is the more recent case of *Caldwell v. Curioni.*[50] In *Caldwell*, the plaintiffs (the Caldwells) became ill soon after they moved into a rented house. An examination of the house revealed a large amount of mold.

The Caldwells had offered as evidence a report by one of their experts that confirmed the presence of *Stachybotrys*. The report concluded that *Stachybotrys* produces a mycotoxin that has been documented as toxic to humans. Further, the Caldwells offered affidavits of doctors they had consulted who testified that they observed a multitude of physical problems in the Caldwells that were caused by mold infestation. The court appeared to have accepted the experts' opinion that the Caldwells' physical injuries were caused by mold. The court did not specifically go through the *Robinson* and *Havner* analysis, and the defendant did not appear to have challenged the reliability of the Caldwells' expert testimony. The court did appear to accept that the Caldwells provided at least some evidence of general and specific causation, and the court found that the defendant's failure to eliminate the mold before the Caldwells occupied the house was the proximate cause of their physical injuries.

The *Caldwell* case appears to demonstrate that courts are at least willing to consider expert testimony of the adverse health effects of mycotoxins without undergoing the rigorous analysis set forth in *Robinson* and *Havner*. However, the lack of scientific evidence that mold causes serious health problems probably dooms these efforts.

C. Insurance Litigation

As noted earlier, no industry is affected greater by the rise in mold litigation than insurance companies, who are the targets of most of the litigation resulting from mold damage. Not only are the insurance companies liable for first-party claims under homeowner insurance policies, they are often also liable for third-party claims under comprehensive general liability policies issued to builders and contractors.

Texas has one of the most heavily regulated insurance industries in the country. Until 2003, only two basic forms for the homeowner's insurance policy were allowed: HO-A and the more comprehensive and more popular, HO-B.[51] Thereafter, because of the insurers' threats to withdraw from the Texas homeowner's insurance market and skyrocketing insurance premium rates, the Department of Insurance now permits additional forms that provide for more explicit exclusions and inclusions of claims regarding mold, as well as specific policy endorsements for mold coverage.[52]

Although much controversy surrounds what is covered under a policy, significant mold verdicts against insurers almost always involve bad faith or poor claims-handling issues. For example, in *Ballard*, the defense attorney referred to the case as a mold case, but the jurors pointed out that it was a bad faith case.[53] It is the breach of extracontractual duties that leads to the large awards that have grabbed the headlines. In addition to common law causes of action, the Texas Insurance Code provides stiff penalties against insurers for misconduct against insureds.

This section briefly discusses some of the possible statutory claims under the Texas Insurance Code and two particular issues that have arisen in regards to litigation involving insurance companies—the trigger event of an occurrence policy and the "ensuing loss" provision common in homeowner's insurance policies. These areas represent two unsettled areas of insurance law in Texas regarding mold-related litigation.

1. Statutory claims under the Texas Insurance Code Chapters 541 and 542 (Formerly Articles 21.21 and 21.55)

Chapter 541 (formerly Article 21.21) of the Texas Insurance Code is the primary source of law for bad faith and misrepresentation claims against insurers in Texas. Under Chapter 541, insurers are prohibited from unfair or deceptive trade practices.[54] Section 541.060 of the Chapter provides a laundry list of approximately nine prohibited acts and practices that Chapter 541 defines to be unfair settlement practices.

For example, Section 541.060(a)(2) prohibits insurers from failing to attempt in good faith to effectuate a prompt, fair, and equitable settlement of a claim to which the insurer's liability has become reasonably clear. This is the standard "bad faith" claim that insureds bring against their insurers for failing to pay a claim, and the standard is identical to the common law bad faith standard.[55]

The statutory claim, however, provides for an award of up to three times actual damages if the insurer's wrongful conduct is committed "knowingly."[56] The prevailing claimant may also recover court costs and reasonable attorneys' fees.[57] Further, Chapter 541 provides that if a plaintiff can show that she relied on an insurer's misconduct to her detriment, the plaintiff can bring an action under the Texas DTPA, provided that other prerequisites for bringing an action under the DTPA are met.[58]

2. Trigger of insurance coverage

A significant point of contention in insurance coverage disputes is often with regard to determining the trigger event of an occurrence policy. Most homeowner insurance policies are occurrence policies for which coverage is triggered by the occurrence of a covered event. Similar to the problem associated with accrual of action, a difficulty exists in determining when mold damage "occurred" and when coverage is triggered.

For first-party property damage claims, some Texas courts have adopted the "relaxed" manifestation theory to designate the trigger of an occurrence policy.[59,60] Under the relaxed manifestation theory, a loss or damage occurs when it manifests or when it becomes readily apparent, not when the wrongful act was committed.[61] A loss or damage is considered apparent when it is "capable of being easily perceived, recognized and understood."[62] This theory has a striking resemblance to the discovery rule for deferral of the accrual of causes of action.

American Home Insurance Co. v. Unitramp illustrates the application of the manifestation theory in Texas.[63] In *Unitramp*, the claimed injury was the receipt of fuel diluted with water onto a ship. The issue was whether the injury to the purchaser of the fuel manifested when the watered-down fuel was received (which was prior to the relevant policy period) or when the watered-down nature of the fuel became apparent (which was during the policy period). Because no one knew the fuel was diluted when it was loaded onto the ship, the court held that the resulting damage did not manifest until tests revealed that the fuel was diluted. Prior to the testing of the fuel, the damage to the purchaser was not readily apparent or easily perceivable.

Similarly, in mold-related cases, the presence of mold would most likely be considered to trigger coverage in an occurrence policy only when it is manifested or becomes readily apparent, not when it is actually discovered or when the causal act was committed. The benefit of the relaxed manifestation theory lies in the balance of providing insureds relief from having to discover harm when it is not discoverable yet placing the insureds on notice of their duty of diligence in discovering the harm.

For a comprehensive general liability (CGL) policy, however, there is authority that the exposure theory is used to determine trigger of coverage where a triggering occurrence includes continuous or repeated exposure to conditions under the policy.[64] Under the exposure theory, coverage is triggered in any policy period in which *exposure* to the cause of the injury occurred.[65] Time of discovery or manifestation of damage is irrelevant. Further, while the manifestation theory is applied only to property damage claims under first-party policies, for a CGL policy, the exposure theory is applied to both physical injury and property damage.[66]

3. "Ensuing loss" provisions

Until three years ago, one of the most unsettled areas of Texas insurance law regarding mold damage was the "ensuing loss" provision in insurance policies. A typical policy contains a clause that expressly excludes certain perils, for example:

> Loss caused by wear and tear; deterioration; rust, rot, mold or other fungi; dampness of atmosphere, extremes of temperature; contamination; vermin, termites, moths or other insects;

This exclusionary clause is usually modified by an "ensuing loss" provision, for example:

> The foregoing Exclusions shall not apply to ensuing loss caused by collapse of building, or any part thereof, water damage or breakage of glass which constitute a part of the building, provided such losses would otherwise be covered under this policy.[67]

On its face, the ensuing loss provision does not appear to provide coverage for mold loss. As an illustration, the above sample of provisions expressly excludes loss from mold. The ensuing loss provision thus reads that mold loss would not be excluded from policy coverage if that mold loss is a loss that ensues from, for example, water damage, and only *if* the mold loss would otherwise be covered under the policy. Mold loss, however, is not otherwise covered under the policy because it is expressly excluded by the exclusionary clause. Thus, the ensuing loss provision would not provide coverage for mold loss. Under this interpretation, the ensuing loss provision does not alter the exclusion against mold damage.

This is most clearly illustrated in the case of *Fiess v. State Farm Lloyds*, a decision by the Texas Supreme Court that came to it on a certified question from the United States Court of Appeals for the Fifth Circuit.[68] In *Fiess*, Tropical Storm Allison flooded the Fiesses' house and, in turn, caused mold to proliferate in the house.[69] Although mold was expressly excluded by the Fiesses' homeowner's policy, the Fiesses argued that the mold exclusion did not apply because their mold damage falls within an exception to the exclusion as an ensuing loss caused by water damage under the policy. The Texas Supreme Court, however, held that the ensuing loss provision in the standard Texas Homeowners Form B ("HO-B") policy did not provide coverage for mold contamination caused by water damage that was otherwise covered under the policy.[70] The court reasoned that "ensuing loss" referred to the loss that was a consequence of an excluded loss, not loss that causes an excluded loss.[71] Under this reasoning, loss caused by mold would not be covered. However, if mold caused water damage (or any of the other enumerated losses in the ensuing loss provision), the loss that results from the water damage, that was itself caused by mold, would be covered. In other words, if mold causes water damage, which in turn causes loss, the loss is the "ensuing loss" that is covered by the provision. The loss, which is ultimately caused by mold, would be covered, despite the exclusion of mold damage.

The Supreme Court began its opinion by emphasizing that its decision would be based solely on the language in the insurance policy and that, perhaps more importantly, its decision would *not* be based on notions of a "mold crisis" in Texas:

> The question in this case is not whether insurers should provide mold coverage in Texas, a public policy question beyond our jurisdiction as a court. The question instead is whether the language in an insurance policy provides such coverage—no more and no less.
>
> The rules for construing insurance policies have been around for a long-time, long before this dispute arose. Those rules require us to construe a policy according to what it says, not what regulators or individual insurers thought it said. Ambiguities in the plain language must be settled in favor of consumers, but they must appear in the policy itself—we cannot create ambiguities from previous policies, an agency's interpretation, or a "mold crisis."
>
> The policy here provides that it does not cover 'loss caused by mold.' While other parts of the policy sometimes make it difficult to decipher, we cannot hold that mold damage is covered when the policy expressly says it is not.[72]

In interpreting the ensuing loss provision, the Supreme Court reiterated the well-settled rule that all parts of a policy must be read together, "giving meaning to every sentence, clause, and word to avoid rendering any portion inoperative."[73] In applying this longstanding rule to the case before it, the Supreme Court stressed that it could not disregard the fact that the policy provision begins by unambiguously stating, "We do not cover loss caused by mold," even though the policy provision ends with, "We do cover ensuing loss caused by water damage."[74]

The Supreme Court's view was grounded on a prior Texas case that dealt with the settlement of a foundation. In *Lambros v. Standard Fire Insurance Co.*, subsurface water in the plaintiff's home caused the building's foundation to settle, which in turn caused the plaintiff's loss.[75] The plaintiff's policy excluded loss caused by settling of a foundation but contained an ensuing loss clause that excepted losses caused by water damage from the exclusions. The court found no coverage because the settlement of foundation was caused by water damage and not vice versa. Giving the ensuing loss exception its "ordinary meaning," the court concluded that "an ensuing loss caused by water damage is a loss caused by water damage where the water damage itself is the result of a preceding cause."[76] Thus, the ensuing loss exception comes into effect when an excluded loss causes water damage, which in turn causes a loss. In other words, the ensuing loss exception would not cover an otherwise excluded loss unless the otherwise excluded loss caused one of the enumerated damages in the ensuing loss provision which in turn caused the claimed loss.

The Supreme Court found *Lambros* particularly instructive because the Texas Supreme Court refused writ on that case, meaning that the Supreme Court implicitly found the judgment of the court of appeals, and the legal principles announced in the opinion, to be likely correct.[77] This theoretically gives *Lambros* the same force and effect as an opinion of the Texas Supreme Court.[78] Accordingly, in order for the Supreme Court to accept the interpretations proffered by both the Fiesses and the Texas Department of Insurance, the court would have to overrule *Lambros*. The Supreme Court, however, declined the invitation to overrule *Lambros*, finding it strange that, although *Lambros* had been decided for nearly a quarter century, insurance regulators had done nothing to change the HO-B policy.

Also, in deciding how to construe the ensuing loss provision, the Texas Supreme Court examined the overall purpose of a homeowners policy. The Texas Supreme Court expressed concern that, because the excluded risks—mold, wear and tear, termites, etc.—damage a house incrementally and are extremely common, interpreting the ensuing loss provision to cover all of these risks would effectively "convert it from an insurance policy into a maintenance agreement."[79] Instead, the Texas Supreme Court found that the ensuing loss provision was intended to provide coverage only if these common risks lead to relatively uncommon and disastrous loss, such as building collapse, glass breakage, or water damage. The Texas Supreme Court found that by interpreting the ensuing loss provision in the above manner, the meaning of this provision would reflect the reason for which homeowners obtain insurance: to provide coverage for uncommon and catastrophic losses.

Finally, the Texas Supreme Court looked to decisions from other jurisdictions for guidance. The Texas Supreme Court explained that to accept the Fiesses' argument that an ensuing loss provision can cause an excluded loss to become a covered loss would be to give ensuing loss provisions in Texas "a different meaning from what they have in most other American jurisdictions."[80]

In light of the above reasons, the Texas Supreme Court held that the ensuing loss provision could not be interpreted as providing coverage for mold caused by water damage that was otherwise covered under the policy and, therefore, answered "no" to the certified question asked by the Fifth Circuit. In its concluding remarks, the Texas Supreme Court made clear that, should the political branches of the Texas government disagree with the court's decision to exclude coverage for mold in Texas homeowners' policies, they had the means to provide otherwise, but that "Texas courts must stick to what those policies say, and cannot adopt a different rule when a 'crisis' arises."

Thus, despite its previous status as one of the most unsettled areas of Texas insurance law regarding mold damage, the Texas Supreme Court's decision in *Fiess* has resolved the issues arising from several inconsistent holdings in Texas concerning the ensuing loss provision in homeowner's insurance policies.[81] Accordingly, the *Fiess* decision is required reading for any attorney confronted with mold-related litigation in Texas.

D. Texas Mold Legislation

The increase in public awareness (or, in some parties' view, unmitigated fear) of the effects of mold has caused a corresponding increase in the number of industrial hygienists and mold remediators. Industrial hygienists inspect buildings for presence of mold. Remediators remove and clean building structures, materials, and personal belongings contaminated with mold. In Houston alone, there are approximately 300 businesses that offer remediation services. This cottage industry is formed by water extractors, asbestos removal experts, contractors, and, as some have termed, the "get rich quick off of mold" group.[82] The previous lack of standards and regulations in this area caused some to worry about fraud on frightened consumers by unscrupulous remediators or inspectors.

The Texas legislature responded to these concerns by enacting Chapter 1958 of the Texas Occupations Code and Chapter 544 of the Texas Insurance Code. Chapter 1958 of the Texas Occupations Code provides for rules regulating mold assessors and remediators and clarifies liability of property owners, and Chapter 544 of the Texas Insurance Code prohibits insurer discrimination against buildings previously contaminated by mold.[83,84]

Chapter 1958 of the Texas Occupations Code prohibits individuals from inspecting or investigating buildings for the presence of mold unless the individual has a mold assessment license and prohibits individuals from remediating mold without a mold remediation license.[85] Since January 1, 2005, all remediators and inspectors must have the proper licenses to conduct mold-related activities. To obtain a license, an individual must successfully complete a training program offered by a trainer accredited by the Texas Department of Health and pass a licensure examination.[86] Pursuant to Chapter 1958, the Texas Board of Health adopted the Mold Assessment and Remediation Rules, which specifically lay out how remediators and inspectors are regulated.[87] These Mold Assessment and Remediation Rules also include a Code of Ethics.[88]

Chapter 1958 mold remediators must also prepare a "remediation work plan" to the consumer before mold remediation begins.[89] Chapter 1958 also seeks to protect consumers by requiring mold assessors to provide a certificate of mold remediation to the property owner, which must include a statement that the mold contamination identified for the project has been remediated as outlined in the mold remediation plan.[90] Importantly, Chapter 1958 exempts property owners from civil liability derived from damages related to a decision to allow someone to occupy a building after mold remediation has been performed on the property.[91]

Finally, Chapter 544 of the Texas Insurance Code prohibits insurers from making underwriting decisions regarding residential property insurance policies based on previous mold damage or claims for mold damage.[92] This chapter governs all insurers that underwrite residential property insurance in Texas. If the insurance applicant has property that is eligible for homeowners insurance but that has previously suffered from mold damage, the insurer cannot discriminate against the applicant in issuing insurance policies if the property has been remediated and current inspection reveals no evidence of mold damage.

Endnotes

1. *Ballard v. Fire Ins. Exch.*, No. 99-05252 (250th Dist. Ct., Travis County, Tex., June 1, 2001).

2. *Id.*

3. *See Allison v. Fire Ins. Exch.*, 98 S.W.3d 227 (Tex. App.—Austin 2002, pet. denied).

4. *Id.*

5. Texas Department of Insurance, Commissioner Montemayor Statement to Consumers and Consumer Groups, Sept. 18, 2001, https://wwwapps.tdi.state.tx.us/inter/asproot/commish/news/clips2001.asp?id=88.

6. Texas Department of Insurance, Mold Data-All Claims (1/1/2000 to 12/31/2001), June 14, 2002, https://wwwapps.tdi.state.tx.us/inter/asproot/commish/news/clips2002.asp?id=84.

7. *Id.*

8. Mary Sit-DuVall, *The Mold Toll: Claims Boost Insurance Rates, Fraud*, HOUSTON CHRONICLE, June 30, 2002, *available at* http://www.chron.com/CDA/archives/archive.mpl?id=2002_3560239.

9. *Id.*

10. *See, e.g.*, Terrence Stutz, *Allstate halts new policies: Insurer is latest in Texas to cite mold losses in homeowners market*, DALLAS MORNING NEWS, Sept. 29, 2001, at 1A, *available at* 2001 WLNR 11701579.

11. *See* Sandra Fleishman and Sabrina Jones, *One Claim Too Many?; Insurance's New Policy: Use It and Lose It*, THE WASHINGTON POST, NOV. 10, 2002, Sunday Correction Appended, at H01.

12. Christopher Clausen, *Texas Consumers Fight High Cost of Home Insurance*, THE BEAUMONT ENTERPRISE, Apr. 23, 2004.

13. *Id.*

14. TEX. CIV. PRAC. & REM. CODE § 16.003 (Vernon 2007).

15. TEX. CIV. PRAC. & REM. CODE §§ 16.008-16.009 (Vernon 2007).

16. *See Trinity River Auth. v. URS Consultants, Inc.*, 889 S.W.2d 259, 260 (Tex. 1994).

17. *See* TEX. CIV. PRAC. & REM. CODE §§ 16.008-16.009.

18. *See Moreno v. Sterling Drug, Inc.*, 787 S.W.2d 348, 351 (Tex. 1990).

19. *See Murray v. San Jacinto Agency, Inc.*, 800 S.W.2d 826, 828 (Tex. 1990).

20. *See Velsicol Chem. Corp. v. Winograd*, 956 S.W.2d 529, 531 (Tex. 1997).

21. *See Moreno*, 787 S.W.2d at 351.

22. *See id.; HECI Exploration Co. v. Neel*, 982 S.W.2d 881, 886 (Tex. 1998).

23. *Booker v. Real Homes, Inc.*, 103 S.W.3d 487, 490 (Tex. App.—San Antonio 2003, pet. denied).

24. *See id.*

25. *See id.* at 492.

26. The court, however, found that there was evidence of fraudulent concealment on the part of the builder and reversed the summary judgment in favor of the builders. Fraudulent concealment estops a defendant from using limitations as an affirmative defense and suspends the running of the limitations period after it has begun. *See Booker*, 103 S.W.3d at 493.

27. *Palmer v. Sears, Roebuck & Co.*, 969 S.W.2d 582 (Tex. App.—Fort Worth 1998, no pet.).

28. Though the court held that the action accrued when the repair was made, subsequent language suggests that the action accrued when Palmer detected the leakage, one month after the repair was made. Having the action accrue when Palmer detected the leakage would be in line with the court's reasoning.

29. *Palmer v. Sears, Roebuck & Co.*, 969 S.W.2d at 585 (quoting *Gideon v. Johns-Manville Sales Corp.*, 761 F.2d 1129, 1136-37 (5th Cir. 1985)).

30. *See Merrell Dow Pharm., Inc. v. Havner*, 953 S.W.2d 706, 714 (Tex. 1996).

31. *See E.I. Du Pont de Nemours & Co. v. Robinson*, 923 S.W.2d 549 (Tex. 1995).

32. *See id.* at 557-58.

33. *See Havner*, 953 S.W.2d at 717.

34. *Robinson*, 923 S.W.2d at 556.

35. *Allstate Tex. Lloyds v. Mason,* 123 S.W.3d 690, 698 (Tex. App.—Fort Worth 2003, no pet.).

36. *Robinson*, 923 S.W.2d at 557.

37. U.S. Environmental Protection Agency, Indoor Air Pollution: An Introduction for Health Professionals: Mycotoxins, 1994, http://www.epa.gov/iaq/pubs/hpguide.html.

38. James Guy, Risks and Liabilities Associated with Toxic Molds, Address at the 2001 Environmental Law Update Seminar (Oct. 2001).

39. O. Edwin McClusky, Report of Council on Scientific Affairs: Black Mold and Human Illness, http://www.nwinsurance.org/members/mold_texstudy.pdf.

40. *See id.*

41. *See id.*

42. U.S. Environmental Protection Agency, Mold Resources: Indoor Air Regulations and Mold, http://www.epa.gov/iaq/molds/moldresources.html.

43. U.S. Environmental Protection Agency, Mold Resources: Asthma and Mold, http://www.epa.gov/iaq/molds/moldresources.html.

44. INSTITUTE OF MED., COMM. ON DAMP INDOOR SPACES AND HEALTH, DAMP INDOOR SPACES AND HEALTH 9-10 (The National Academies Press 2004), *available at* http://www.nap.edu/openbook.php?isbn=0309091934.

45. *Id.* at 9.

46. *See Flores v. Allstate Tex. Lloyd's Co.*, 229 F. Supp. 2d 697, 699 (S.D. Tex. 2002).

47. *See Allison*, 98 S.W.3d at 239.

48. *See id.*; *see also Havner*, 953 S.W.2d at 714-15.

49. *Ballard v. Fire Ins. Exch.*, No. 99-05252 (250th Dist. Ct., Travis County, Tex., June 1, 2001).

50. *See Caldwell v. Curioni*, 125 S.W.3d 784 (Tex. App.—Dallas 2004, pet. denied).

51. The Texas HO-B policy was problematic for insurers because it did not require water discharge to be sudden and accidental, as is required by standard insurance policies issued in most states. Krik Hansen, *Mold: The Fungus Among Us is Difficult to Evict,* INSURANCE JOURNAL, May 5, 2003, *available at* http://www.insurancejournal.com/magazines/west/2003/05/05/partingshots/28748.htm.

52. The Texas Department of Insurance now allows more forms of homeowner's insurance policies. (The policies in Texas now specifically exclude mold, and consumers can purchase mold endorsements separately). Most policies do not cover mold remediation beyond that necessary to repair or replace property damaged by water loss otherwise covered by the policy. The HO-A policy offers no coverage for mold remediation or for damage caused by water leaks, although some companies offer coverage for sudden and accidental water leaks as an endorsement to the base HO-A policy. Insurance companies, however, are required to offer mold remediation coverage. The HO-B policy is much more expensive and covers mold damage only if the mold is on property physically damaged by sudden water and accidental water. This includes hidden and concealed damage that is reported within 30 days of detection. However, even the HO-B policy does not cover cost of testing or remediation. Additional endorsements would have to be purchased.

53. Fred Hagans and Jennifer Rustay, *Mold Bad Faith Cases: Tools and Strategies*, The Brief, Fall 2003 at 13, *available at* http://www.hbb-law.com/badfaith2.pdf.

54. *See* TEX. INS. CODE. § 541 *et seq.* (Vernon 2007).

55. *See Mid-Century Ins. Co. v. Boyte*, 80 S.W.3d 546, 549 (Tex. 2002).

56. *See* TEX. INS. CODE § 541.152(b) (Vernon 2007).

57. *Id.*

58. *Id.*

59. The Texas Supreme Court described the theory prescribed by the Dallas Court of Appeals in *Dorchester Dev. Corp. v. Safeco Ins. Co.*, 737 S.W.2d 380, 383 (Tex. App.—Dallas 1987, no writ) as a "pure" manifestation approach. *See Am. Physicians Ins. Exch. v. Garcia*, 876 S.W.2d 842, 853 n.20 (Tex. 1994). The approach taken in *Dorchester*, however, was actually the "relaxed" manifestation approach, as a later Dallas Court of Appeals case clarified. *See Cullen/Frost Bank v. Commonwealth Lloyd's Ins. Co.*, 852 S.W.2d 252, 257 (Tex. App.—Dallas 1993, writ denied).

60. The "pure" manifestation rule triggers coverage upon actual discovery of injury, whereas the "relaxed" manifestation rule triggers coverage in the first policy period during which discovery of injury is possible. *See Am. Physician Ins. Exch.*, 876 S.W.2d at 853 n.20.

61. *Am. Home Assurance Co. v. Unitramp Ltd.*, 146 F.3d 311, 313 (5th Cir. 1998); *Dorchester*, 737 S.W.2d at 383.

62. *Unitramp*, 146 F.3d at 314.

63. *Id.* at 313-14.

64. *Pilgrim Enter., Inc. v. Marland Cas. Co.*, 24 S.W.3d 488, 496-98 (Tex. App.—Houston [1st Dist.] 2000, no pet.).

65. *Am. Physician Exch.*, 876 S.W.2d at 853 n.20 (emphasis added).

66. *Pilgrim Enter., Inc.*, 24 S.W.3d at 497-98.

67. *See, e.g., Merrimack Mut. Fire Ins. Co. v. McCaffree*, 486 S.W.2d 616 (Tex. Civ. App.—Dallas 1971, writ ref'd n.r.e.).

68. *Fiess v. State Farm Lloyds*, 202 S.W.3d 744 (Tex. 2006) (hereinafter "*Fiess II*").

69. *Fiess v. State Farm Lloyds*, 392 F.3d 802, 804-05 (5th Cir. 2004).

70. *Fiess II*, 202 S.W.3d at 745.

71. *See id.* at 749 ("'Ensuing loss caused by water damage' refers to water damage which is the *result*, rather than the *cause*, of" one of the types of damage enumerated in the exclusion) (emphasis in the original); *see also Lambros v. Standard Fire Ins. Co.*, 530 S.W.2d 138 (Tex. Civ. App.—San Antonio 1975, writ denied).

72. *Fiess II*, 202 S.W.3d at 745.

73. *Id.* at 746.

74. *Id.* at 748.

75. *Lambros v. Standard Fire Ins. Co.*, 530 S.W.2d 138 (Tex. Civ. App.—San Antonio 1975, writ ref'd).

76. *Id.* at 141.

77. Texas Rules of Form, Texas Law Review, Tenth Edition, Appendix A.

78. *See id.*; *see also Fiess II*, 202 S.W.3d at 749.

79. *Fiess II*, 202 S.W.3d at 750.

80. *Id.* at 752-53. The Supreme Court emphasized that the Fiesses' argument had been rejected by courts in Alabama, Arizona, California, Florida, Illinois, Massachusetts, Minnesota, New York, North Carolina, New Hampshire, Ohio, Pennsylvania, Vermont, Washington, and Wisconsin.

81. These inconsistent holdings occurred after *Lambros* but before *Fiess II* and involved several Texas courts interpreting the ensuing loss provision to cover mold loss. *See Flores v. Allstate Texas Lloyd's Co.*, 278 F. Supp. 2d 810, 814 n.3 (S.D. Tex. 2003); *Coury v. Allstate Texas Lloyds*, Cause No. H-02-2238 (S.D. Tex. March 31, 2004); *see also Aetna Cas. & Sur. Co. v. Yates*, 344 F.2d 939, 941 (5th Cir. 1965).

82. Mary Sit-DuVall, *The Mold Toll: Claims Boost Insurance Rates, Fraud*, HOUSTON CHRONICLE, June 30, 2002, *available at* http://www.chron.com/CDA/archives/archive.mpl?id=2002_3560239.

83. TEX. OCC. CODE § 1958.001 *et seq.* (Vernon 2007).

84. TEX. INS. CODE § 544.301 *et seq.* (Vernon 2007).

85. TEX. OCC. CODE § 1958.101.

86. §§ 1958.105-1958.106.

87. §§ 1958.053-1958.054.

88. § 1958.059.

89. § 1958.152.

90. § 1958.154.

91. § 1958.303.

92. TEX. INS. CODE § 544.301 *et seq.*

Chapter 19

An Overview of Toxic Mold Litigation in Washington*

Kelly Vance, Esq.

Synopsis

19.1 Introduction

There are few reported mold litigation decisions in the State of Washington. It appears that most cases filed in court settle in advance of trial or verdict. Of the few reported "mold cases" in Washington, the large majority of them concern mold-related insurance coverage claims. The following is a general overview of Washington law with respect to mold-related litigation.

19.2 Construction Negligence Claims in Washington

In *Davis v. Baugh Industrial Contractors, Inc.*, the Washington Supreme Court abandoned the "completion and acceptance" doctrine and adopted the Restatement (Second) of Torts rule, which holds building contractors liable in negligence for defective workmanship.[1] The completion and acceptance doctrine placed the burden on the buyer to inspect the house after completion and decide whether or not to accept it. If the house was accepted, the buyer's remedies for defects was limited to whatever warranty the builder provided.

*Reprinted with permission from the author, Kelly Vance.

Prior to *Davis v. Baugh*, it was unclear whether a cause of action for construction defect existed beyond a claim for breach of contract or breach of warranty. However, in *Davis v. Baugh* the Washington Supreme Court abandoned the completion and acceptance doctrine. Instead, the court adopted the Restatement (Second) of Torts rule arguably holding Washington building contractors liable for negligent workmanship, especially if it causes personal injury.

Some defense attorneys had traditionally cited Washington's "economic loss" rule in asserting that there was no cause of action for construction negligence in Washington.

The economic loss rule was designed as a boundary between the law of contracts, which is designed to enforce expectations created by agreement, and the law of torts, which is designed to protect citizens and their property by imposing a duty of reasonable care on others.[2] An "economic loss" is described in Washington as "those damages falling on the contract side of the line between tort and contract."[3] Under Washington law, economic loss is distinguished from physical harm or property damage.[4]

This rule was developed to allow parties to allocate risk of pure economic loss by contract.[5] If, for example, a contractor walks off the job, leaving the owner to hire another to complete the project at greater expense or if she overcharges the owner, the law of contracts establishes the aggrieved party's remedy to recover the economic loss of the additional expense of completion. She can sue for breach of contract and receive the benefit of her bargain—a structure completed for the price she agreed to pay. This is often referred to as "expectation damages." She is entitled to the result which she had a right to expect when she made the contract with the breaching party.

However, it is not generally expected that a builder will perform negligently. In fact, the expectation is just the opposite. Therefore, the law needed to provide a remedy for such unexpected malfeasance. If, for example, a contractor, through his negligence, damages the building or makes the owner sick because the building gives off toxic gases or is contaminated by mold due to bad workmanship, the cost to repair and other consequential damages are not perceived as economic losses, but damages flowing from the negligent acts or omissions of the builder.

Contrary to the arguments routinely made by defense attorneys, an argument can be made that, even before *Davis v. Baugh*, Washington law has acknowledged a negligence cause of action in construction defect cases. For example, Washington's statutes, RCW 4.16.300 et seq., require that a consumer give written notice of construction defects to a builder 45 days before filing a construction defect suit. In addition, RCW 4.16.326 sets up a defense of comparative fault to a consumer claim based on construction defect. Obviously, there would be no need to have a comparative negligence statute if Washington did not at least implicitly recognize construction negligence claims. This statute, moreover, states that this comparative fault defense was not applicable in a case where a person suffered personal injury from a construction defect. The statute states in pertinent part that it:

> "[D]oes not apply to any **civil action in tort** alleging personal injury or wrongful death to a person or persons resulting from a construction defect."[6]

Plaintiffs in Washington also have the ability to rely on the Washington Consumer Protection Act if builders misrepresent the quality and nature of their services.[7]

There is no case setting forth the specific elements of a negligent construction claim in Washington. It remains for future cases to flesh out the changing law in this area.

19.3 Washington Standards for Admissibility of Expert Evidence

Mold cases are very expert intensive. Typically, a mold victim will seek medical attention, starting with their family doctor. Depending on their symptoms, they may be referred to specialists who conduct, for example, pulmonary function and blood testing. They also need to document the state of the contaminated building, requiring an expert on mold testing and possibly a construction expert as well. Often a neurological expert is required if symptoms such as depression, and extreme emotional distress result. The defense at trial will challenge these experts' ability to testify on a number of grounds.

Washington follows a standard for admissibility of scientific and medical evidence set forth in *Frye v. United States*, which held that expert testimony is only admissible if it is generally accepted in the relevant scientific community.[8] Washington's Supreme Court implicitly adopted the *Frye* standard in *State v. Woo*.[9] Although the court may not weigh evidence, it does have the discretion to determine whether a witness qualifies as an expert, and whether her testimony would be helpful to the trier of fact.[10] Additionally, new scientific evidence is subject to the *Frye* test for admissibility.[11]

Under *Frye*, a court is to determine if the evidence in question has a valid, scientific basis. Because judges do not have the expertise required to decide whether a challenged scientific theory is correct, they defer this judgment to scientists. This inquiry turns on the level of recognition accorded to the scientific principle involved, so courts look for general acceptance in the appropriate scientific community. If there is a significant dispute between qualified experts as to the validity of scientific evidence, it may not be admitted. Evidence deriving from a scientific theory or principle is admissible if that theory or principle has achieved general acceptance in the relevant scientific community. But scientific opinion need not be unanimous for scientific evidence to be admissible. The difference of opinion is why both sides hire experts and let the jury decide which side's view it believes is more valid.

Once a methodology is accepted in the scientific community, then application of the science to a particular case is a matter of weight, not admissibility. Washington's evidentiary rule, ER 702, allows qualified expert witnesses to testify if scientific, technical, or other specialized knowledge will assist the trier of fact.[12]

The question of admissibility is not based on reliability, but whether it is generally accepted in the scientific community. Blood tests have been accepted in the scientific community for many decades, yet defense attorneys will sometimes try to suppress blood tests showing the presence of mold antibodies in a mold victim's blood. For example, a defense attorney may challenge the circumstances under which the test was taken or the test mechanism itself. In Washington, whether a given scientific technique has been performed correctly in a particular instance (i.e., whether laboratory error has occurred) goes to its weight, not admissibility.[13]

Ultimately, the admission of expert testimony is within the trial court's discretion. Under ER 702, expert testimony may be admitted if the witness qualifies as an expert and the expert testimony will be helpful to the jury. On appeal, reviewing courts examine this evidentiary ruling *de novo*, and substitute their own judgment for the trial courts, if appropriate.

19.4 Reported Mold Cases

There are few reported decisions involving mold cases in Washington.

In *Kelsey Lane Homeowners Association v. Kelsey Lane Co., Inc.*, a condominium homeowners association sued Kelsey Lane Co. (KLC), after construction defects caused severe water damage to the condominium buildings.[14] The Association contended that KLC fraudulently concealed from prospective purchasers the fact that building envelope components were missing or improperly installed. The trial court dismissed the complaint, finding no genuine issue of material fact about the developer's actual knowledge of the defects without considering claims that relied on a "should have known" standard. Plaintiffs introduced no evidence suggesting that KLC had actual knowledge of the defects, or that it breached its fiduciary duty while it controlled the homeowners association. The court rejected a "should have known" standard.

In *Ramos v. Arnold*, the Ramos family purchased a home in Lynnwood in 2001.[15] Before making an offer, they noticed that a three-foot portion of the hallway ceiling was sagging. They questioned their real estate agent about this defect and the agent stated that it was likely a "PUD package," apparently referring to insulation added to conserve energy. A cousin who worked in the drywall and ceiling business looked at the hallway ceiling and told the Ramoses that the sag may have been caused by water damage. The Ramoses nevertheless made an offer on the home on September 24, 2001, conditioned on a satisfactory home inspection. Their inspector noted that the roof was in "very poor condition with decay under the trees and missing shakes on the south faces and east face." The inspector's report advised that the roof would not last much longer but did not mention the sagging ceiling in the hallway.

After the inspection, the Ramoses waived the contingencies and proceeded with the purchase. Their lender ordered an appraisal. The appraiser made a visual inspection of both the inside and exterior of the home in order to estimate the property's market value. The appraiser did not report noticing any apparent defects either inside or outside the home and did not communicate with the Ramos family or send them a copy of the appraisal.

The sale closed on October 15, 2001. Several days later, after the Ramos family moved in, the roof began leaking during a storm. Water damaged the roof and ceiling and caused mold growth. The ceiling started crumbling and material containing asbestos fell into the house, causing Ms. Ramos and her two children to experience respiratory problems.

The Ramoses filed a claim under their homeowner's insurance policy. Their claim for water damage was accepted and paid, but their claim for mold damage was rejected. They then filed suit against several defendants, including claims against the appraiser for breach of contract, negligence in conducting the appraisal, and violation of the Consumer Protection Act. The appraiser moved for summary judgment arguing that the Ramoses were actually aware of the sagging ceiling before purchasing the home and that the Ramoses could not show that they had relied on the appraisal report when they decided to purchase the house. Ms. Ramos admitted that she did review the contents of the appraisal before the purchase, which she apparently contradicted in her deposition. The Ramoses' claimed that the appraiser committed an unfair or deceptive act by failing to include major defects in the residence in the appraisal report, which kept the paperwork clean on the residence. They alleged that this prevented further investigation, and caused the Ramoses to enter into the purchase and sale agreement for the residence.

Both parties cited the same case to support their respective positions: *Schaaf v. Highfield.*[16] In *Schaaf*, the trial court found that while the appraiser owed a duty of care, the plaintiff did not demonstrate justifiable reliance on the appraisal report and already knew *before* he bought the house that it needed a new roof. He could not blame the appraiser for failing to report what he already knew to be true.[17] Lack of reliance on the appraisal report barred Schaaf's claim. In *Ramos,* their claim failed under the negligent misrepresentation analysis detailed in *Schaaf,* because without proof of reliance there is no basis upon which to find that any breach by the appraiser proximately caused their damages.[18]

The Court of Appeals held that there was no claim against the appraiser under the Washington Consumer Protection Act, stating that the purpose of the Consumer Protection Act is to "complement the body of federal law governing restraints of trade, unfair competition and unfair, deceptive, and fraudulent acts or practices in order to protect the public and foster fair and honest competition."[19] The term "trade" as used by the Act only includes the entrepreneurial or commercial aspects of professional services, not the substantive quality of services provided.[20] Entrepreneurial aspects include how the cost of services is determined, billed, and collected and the way a professional obtains, retains, and dismisses clients. Claims directed at the competence of and strategies employed by a professional amount to allegations of negligence and are exempt from the Consumer Protection Act.[21] The Ramoses' allegations concerning the inadequacy of the appraisal amounted to an allegation of negligence, not an implication of entrepreneurial or commercial aspects of professional services. The Court of Appeals upheld the trial court dismissal of the Consumer Protection Act claim on summary judgment.

The Ramoses also appealed the trial court's dismissal of their breach of contract claim contending that, even though they had no contract with the appraiser, they were third-party beneficiaries to her contract with their lending bank. Under Washington law, as in most states, a party is a third-party beneficiary only if the contracting parties intend to create such a relationship at the time the contract is formed.[22] The test of intent is an objective one, for which the key is whether performance of the contract would necessarily and directly benefit the party claiming to be a third-party beneficiary.[23] Although the appraisal report identifies the Ramoses as potential borrowers, the report was written for the benefit of the lender, which wanted to determine if the house was worth what the lender was lending for its purchase. There was no evidence the bank intended for the appraiser to assume a direct obligation to the Ramoses or that they would necessarily benefit from the terms of the contract between the bank and the appraiser. The Court upheld the trial court's dismissal of the contract claim, concluding that the Ramoses were not third-party beneficiaries to the appraisal contract between the appraiser and the lender.

In *Mercer Place Condominium Association v. State Farm*, Mercer Place discovered structural rot to its wood frame structures in late 1996.[24] A structural engineer determined that Mercer Place was in a state of progressive structural decay. After Mercer Place notified State Farm of the damage, the insurer conducted investigative tears of the structure to determine which portions were in a collapsed state. State Farm recognized that coverage could be provided for such damage under the policy's "collapse" provision. But State Farm only wanted to extend coverage for parts of the buildings facing "imminent" collapse, not deteriorating parts that may collapse in the future.

The condominium association sued State Farm contending that coverage for loss under its insurance policy was not limited to damage involving collapse that occurred during the policy period. It argued that coverage also extended to that damage not yet in a state of collapse during the policy period but that will eventually reach a point of collapse, unless repaired.

The trial court found that the language of the policy only extended coverage to those portions of the property shown to be in a state of collapse during the policy period. The court granted partial summary judgment to State Farm, and conducted a bench trial limited to the issues of the extent of "collapse damage" that occurred during the policy period and whether State Farm fulfilled its obligation to investigate the Mercer Place's claim fully and fairly. The court determined that State Farm fully and fairly conducted its investigation, that State Farm paid for all collapse loss which occurred during the policy period, and that there was no credible evidence of any collapse loss "which has not been reasonably and adequately investigated and repaired" by State Farm. The decision was appealed.

The Court of Appeals held that although the policy covers loss commencing during the policy period, the loss that is covered is "collapse" or substantial impairment of structural integrity. It further held that the trial court correctly observed "collapse cannot commence before it occurs. The structure is either in a 'collapse' condition or it is not." Looking at the policy as a whole, the court found that adopting the Mercer Place's argument would defeat the purpose of the policy's exclusionary provisions. The policy specifically excludes those losses flowing from such conditions as decay, continuous or repeated seepage or leakage of water, or faulty construction or design, except to the extent that such conditions are found to have created substantial impairment of structural integrity during the policy period. The result is that the trial court decision stood, and State Farm's responsibility was limited.

The case of *DePhelps v. Safeco Ins. Co. of America* concerned an insurance coverage case where the homeowner had converted the use of the home to a bed and breakfast.[25] The homeowner's policy insured the dwelling for use principally as a private residence, but the policy also covered various aspects of room rentals.

In March 1997, heavy accumulations of snow and ice on the roof shifted, which loosened part of the metal roof. The homeowner attempted to fix the damage himself, but realized the damage was more extensive than he had originally estimated. He reported the damage to his insurance carrier, Safeco, and submitted a claim. He also submitted a contractor's estimate of $40,000 to repair the roof. Safeco inspected the damage and approved the estimate. It paid $28,432 for the repairs in November 1998. However, additional damage appeared. Mr. DePhelps and Safeco argued over the extent of that damage. Safeco paid an additional $49,163 in August 1999. But the roof still leaked. The owner's contractor temporarily repaired it. Safeco paid for those temporary repairs. In December 1999, the home and its contents were found to be contaminated by toxic mold caused by water leaks resulting from defective repairs. In January 2000, the homeowners moved out of the house and submitted more claims for mold damage and loss of use.

Safeco estimated the repair costs at over $600,000 and paid $536,446.86. The DePhelpses submitted a repair claim for $1,724,650 and sued for breach of contract, bad faith, and Consumer Protection Act (Chapter 19.86 RCW) violations. Both sides moved for partial summary judgment on the coverage issues. The trial court held that the claim was not covered by the policy. The Court of Appeals reversed the trial court's decision. The Court of Appeals held that the policy anticipated that rooms will be rented out and defined the limits of Safeco's liability in the event they are. Nothing in the policy suggested that the presence of renters limited Safeco's liability for structural damage. The policy did not distinguish between "business pursuits" and "rental or holding for rental."

Because the homeowners lost income from renting out the premises, they claimed that lost income under the "loss of use" provisions of the policy. Safeco argued that they were only entitled to loss of their use as a residence, not lost rental income. The Court noted that, in a tort action, loss of income is recoverable "if the proof is adequate."[26] Proof of lost profits or business income may be considered as evidence of the value of the loss of use in an action for damages.[27] The DePhelps' policy provided that, in the event of a claim, the insured must provide "records supporting the fair rental value loss." But the policy contained separate loss of use provisions: one for the loss of the insureds' own housing and another for lost rental income. The court then held that the DePhelpses could recover the rental value of the home as a single-family rental, or recover the reasonable cost of equivalent housing for themselves (as reduced by the rental activity), plus an estimate of the amount they would have earned from the rented portions.

The court took an actual cash value approach to the loss of the building. The policy defined actual cash value as "the market value of property in a used condition equal to that of the destroyed property, if reasonably available on the used market." The court then held that additional costs to upgrade the house to comply with new building code provisions applicable to use of rental premises or hotels were not covered. Replacement cost considerations—such as building code upgrades—did not apply. The court stated that a determination of market value of the destroyed property will depend on whether it was saleable as a bed and breakfast when the damage occurred. This depended upon whether it was in compliance with the then existing building codes for that purpose, and whether that code compliance would pass to a buyer—or whether the county could or would require upgrades as a condition of sale (as well as for reconstruction). The key holding was that cash value applied to the property as it stood at the time of loss. Replacement costs, including code upgrades, were not included.

The matter of *Gifford v. Majteka* resulted in an unreported decision on a question of whether or not there was sufficient evidence to go to a jury.[28] The trial court had granted summary judgment to the sellers of a house, which the buyer had leased to the plaintiffs. The plaintiffs sued the seller, saying that the seller misrepresented the condition of the house to their landlord, saying that bleach stains on the walls and carpet was an effort to clean up children's markings, not mold or mildew. They later developed symptoms consistent with mold exposure and had the house tested.

Mrs. Gifford's complaint alleged that exposure to the mold in the house caused her to suffer an allergic reaction and asthma. She presented her own affidavit as well as a declaration from her physician and a toxicologist's air quality report showing elevated levels of *Penicillium* in the house, which exceeded that found in outdoor samples. Her toxicologist opined that there were likely undiscovered reservoirs of mold within the wall cavities. Her doctor said in his declaration that her symptoms were consistent with asthma attacks which could have resulted from mold exposure. The toxicologist's report noted that her symptoms improved when she moved out of the house and followed an antifungal treatment regimen. He opined that it was more probable than not that her symptoms were caused by mold.

The defendant submitted counter affidavits from an industrial hygienist saying that this type of mold was found everywhere in the world and a doctor saying this type of mold does not cause the type of symptoms that Mrs. Gifford experienced. He went so far as to say that most people do not have any symptoms with exposure to *Penicillium*.[29]

The trial court found that the plaintiffs did not present medical evidence sufficient to establish that their symptoms were caused by mold. The Court of Appeals reversed this decision, saying that the toxicologist's opinion that her symptoms were more likely than not caused by mold exposure was within his area of expertise. The court also noted that her medical doctor noted her asthma attacks. The court found that Mrs. Gifford was entitled to a trial and to let a jury decide which experts they believed. The opinion is of little use in court as Washington courts do not accept unreported decisions as legal precedent.

19.5 Insurance Issues

Although this section is not designed to be an overview of all insurance issues arising in mold litigation, a brief discussion of insurance issues is appropriate to illustrate the importance of insurance in mold cases.

Mold cases also arise in the context of first-party homeowners' insurance claims. Typically a loss occurs where a homeowner has suffered a roof leak or a burst water pipe, which may or may not be covered by their homeowner's policy. Usually a homeowner notifies his insurer of the loss and the insurer investigates the problem and determines whether or not the loss is covered. The insurer then either arranges for repair work (if coverage exists) or sends the customer a letter saying the loss is not covered. An insurance coverage dispute may ensue after a denial of coverage has been forwarded to the insured.

Under most homeowners' policies, where a loss is to the dwelling itself, the loss is usually presumed to be covered unless specifically excluded. This is an "all risk" type of policy. However, that coverage rule does not apply regarding personal property insured by the same policy. Where the loss relates to personal property in the house, the property must usually be specifically named as a covered item or category of items under the policy's personal property coverage. This is usually referred to as "named perils coverage."[30] Unless a specific item of personal property is named in the policy, it may not be covered. As with any generalization there can be exceptions, but generally the building damage is presumed to be covered unless excluded and personal property loss is presumed to be excluded unless specifically "named" in the policy.

Most homeowner's policies exclude damage caused by construction defects, unworkmanlike repairs or design defects. The general idea is to lay responsibility for such problems at the feet of the contractor who caused them, not the homeowner's insurer. Often those exclusions have an exception for ensuing losses that arise from the defect. The ensuing loss clauses in some states allow the exclusion to govern a roof leak resulting from a shoddy roofing job. Moreover, the homeowner's insurer can be called upon to repair ensuing damage to the house even in the wake of the faulty repair. Generally, these clauses result in the homeowner insurer not being required to repair the shoddy workmanship, but to repair ensuing losses resulting from it. Washington takes a narrow view of the "ensuing loss" doctrine. In Washington, ensuing losses must be more or less unrelated to the initial defect to extend coverage.[31]

Some courts have held that policies which exclude coverage for damage caused by mold nonetheless insure damage resulting from a covered peril, even if that damage was mold-related. In those cases, mold was found to be both the damage and a cause. At least some courts held that such policies covered the loss, despite the exclusion. Insurers began writing mold exclusions into their policies around 2002, after the celebrated Texas verdict in the *Ballard* case against Farmers Insurance. A policy excluding coverage for damage "caused by mold" would not seem to exclude mold damage *resulting* from a covered peril which is the efficient proximate cause of the loss. There are no cases in Washington addressing this issue.

Endnotes

1. Case No. 76696-7, decided January 18, 2007

2. *Berschauer/Phillips Constr. Co. v. Seattle Sch. Dist. No. 1*, 124 Wn.2d 816, 821, 881 P.2d 986 (1994).

3. *Id.* (quoting *Washington Water Power Co. v. Graybar Elec. Co.*, 112 Wn.2d 847, 861 n.10, 774 P.2d 1199, 779 P.2d 697 (1989)).

4. *Stuart v. Coldwell Banker Commercial Group, Inc.*, 109 Wn.2d 406, 420, 745 P.2d 1284 (1987).

5. *Id.* at 822.

6. RCW 4.16.326 (emphasis added).

7. *See* Washington's Consumer Protection Act, RCW 19.86 *et seq.*

8. 293 F. 1013 (D.C. Cir. 1923).

9. 84 Wn.2d 472, 527 P.2d 271 (1974).

10. *See In re Pers. Restraint of Young*, 122 Wn.2d 1, 57, 857 P.2d 989 (1993) ("The determination of whether expert testimony is admissible is within the discretion of the trial court.").

11. *See, e.g., State v. Gregory*, 158 Wn.2d 759, 829, 147 P.3d 1201 (2006).

12. *See also State v. Copeland,* 130 Wn.2d 244, 263, 272, 922 P.2d 1304 (1996) (citing *State v. Cauthron,* 120 Wn.2d 879, 886, 846 P.2d 502 (1993).

13. *Copeland, supra*, 130 Wn.2d at 270.

14. 125 Wn. App. 227, 103 P.3d 1256 (2005).

15. WACA 58679-3–071607 (2007).

16. In *Schaaf*, the homeowner discovered that the roof leaked and sued the appraiser. He claimed the appraiser negligently failed to note the defective roof in the appraisal report. The trial court concluded that the appraiser owed no duty to the prospective homebuyer and granted the appraiser's motion for summary judgment. On appeal, Schaaf argued that lack of contractual privity with the appraiser did not negate the fact that the appraiser owed him a duty of care. The Court concluded that under the law of negligent misrepresentation, an appraiser does owe a duty of care to third parties. *Schaaf*, 127 Wn.2d at 21.

17. *Schaaf*, 127 Wn.2d at 30.

18. The court noted that where there was a conflict between deposition testimony and a subsequent affidavit, this conflict in a witness' testimony did not create a question of fact sufficient to defeat summary judgment.

19. RCW 19.86.920.

20. Citing *Haberman v. Washington Pub. Power Supply Sys.*, 109 Wn.2d 107, 169, 744 P.2d 1032 (1987) where the court stated that to prevail in a private Consumer Protection Act action, a plaintiff must establish five distinct elements: (1) unfair or deceptive act or practice; (2) occurring in trade or commerce; (3) public interest impact; (4) injury to plaintiff in her business or property; and (5) causation.

21. Citing *Short v. Demopolis*, 103 Wn.2d 52, 61-62, 691 P.2d 163 (1984).

22. *Burke & Thomas, Inc. v. International Organization of Masters*, 92 Wn.2d 762, 767, 600 P.2d 1282 (1979).

23. *Lonsdale v. Chesterfield*, 99 Wn.2d 353, 362, 662 P.2d 385 (1983).

24. 104 Wn. App. 597, 17 P.3d 626 (2000).

25. 116 Wn. App. 441, 65 P.3d 1234 (2003).

26. *Straka Trucking, Inc. v. Estate of Peterson*, 98 Wn. App. 209, 211-12, 989 P.2d 1181 (1999) (quoting Dan B. Dobbs, Law of Remedies § 5.15(2), at 876 (2d ed. 1993)).

27. *King Logging Co. v. Scalzo*, 16 Wn. App. 918, 928, 561 P.2d 206 (1977).

28. Case No. 25886—2-II, Washington Court of Appeals, Division II, on July 20, 2001.

29. Actually *Penicillium* is one of the most dangerous molds around. Some species produce mycotoxins such as *Ochratoxin*, *Citrinin*, *Gliotoxin* and *Patulin*. Some species also produce penicillic acid, peptide nephrotoxin, viomellin and other substances that are harmful to humans.

30. In *Bowers v. Farmers Ins. Exchange*, , 991 P.2d 734 (Wash. App. Div. 2000), Farmer's Insurance Exchange denied coverage for an insured who rented a house. Tenants, without the insured's knowledge, converted the house into a marijuana growing operation. The operation caused a sauna-like atmosphere in the basement and excessive water condensation, which led to mold damage. The court held that the tenant's acts fell within the covered peril of vandalism and were, therefore, included within coverage rather than excluded by the mold exclusion.

31. *See e.g. McDonald v. State Farm Fire & Casualty Co*, 119 Wn 2d 724, 837 P2d 1000 (1992).

Chapter 20

Table of Toxic Mold Case Law in Other States

Richard J. Valladares, Esq., Ander Krupa, Esq.,
Ryan C. Grelecki, Esq., Kristy Byrd, Esq.,
and Stephanie L. Oginsky, Esq.

State	Case Name	Year	Prevailing Party	Ruling	Holding
CT	*Williams v. Abrams*, No. X04CV054005263S, 2007 WL 806084 (Conn. Super. Ct. Feb. 20, 2007)	2007	Defendants	Granted defendants' motion to strike	Plaintiff's claim for "intentional misconduct" against real estate agents who did not warn him before he inspected the premises that there was toxic mold present failed because they did not allege a purposeful intention to cause harm.
CT	*Nangle. v. National One, LLC*, No. X01CV044004344, 2005 WL 3292534 (Conn. Super. Ct. Oct. 19, 2005)	2005	Plaintiffs	Granted prejudgment remedy	Probable cause existed to sustain commercial tenant's application for prejudgment relief against landlord for negligent creation of condition that promoted growth of mold and microtoxins where it was not clear that the landlord's liability insurance included coverage for such claims.
KY	*Walker v. Cabinet for Health Services*, No. 2006-SC-0360-WC, 2007 WL 542144 (Ky. Feb. 22, 2007)	2007	Defendants - Appellees	Affirmed denial of worker's compensation benefits	Evidence did not compel a finding that plaintiff's work for defendant was a cause of her neurotoxicity when physician's report did not consider whether she was exposed to any chemicals that led to this condition at her second place of employment.
LA	*Arthole v. Trinity Universal Insurance Company of Kansas*, 3 So. 3d 611 (La. Ct. App. 2009)	2009	Defendants-Appellees	Affirmed dismissal of Plaintiffs' claims	Claims for damages from toxic mold infestation at workplace were barred by statute that required claims to be brought within one year of the end of employment, and no exception applied because plaintiffs had actual knowledge of their symptoms sufficient to invoke an inquiry into the cause.
LA	*Bayer v. Omni Hotels Management Corp.*, 995 So. 2d 639 (La. Ct. App. 2008)	2008	Defendant-Appellee	Affirmed grant of summary judgment in favor of developer	Plaintiffs presented no evidence that toxic mold conditions existed while developer owned building or that developer had knowledge of the condition when they owned the building.

State	Case Name	Year	Prevailing Party	Ruling	Holding
LA	*Barnett v. Watkins*, 970 So. 2d 1028 (La. Ct. App. 2007)	2007	Defendant-Appellee	Affirmed grant of partial summary judgment	Plaintiffs' claims against general contractor for toxic mold growth were dismissed, except those brought under the New Home Warranty Act, which provided the exclusive remedy for Plaintiffs because the builder did not agree in the building contract to increase the warranties.
LA	*Harper v. Grand Casino Coushatta*, 940 So. 2d 911 (La. Ct. App. 2006)	2006	Defendant-Appellee	Affirmed grant of summary judgment	Plaintiff's medical evidence did not support assertion that his symptoms were related to his work for defendant and the worker's compensation judge did not err in weighing the credibility of the expert witnesses.
LA	*Watters. v. Department of Social Services*, 929 So. 2d 267 (La. Ct. App. 2006)	2006	Plaintiffs-Appellees	Affirmed in part and remanded in part the grant of class certification	Trial court did not err in granting class action certification where mold exposure occurred during insurer's policy period; however the court remanded with instruction to determine whether a causal connection existed between the exposure to the toxic substance and the injury so that the class could be redefined so that it was not vague.
LA	*Gallo v. St. Tammany Parish Hospital*, 906 So. 2d 1276 (La. Ct. App. 2005)	2005	Defendant-Appellee	Affirmed judgment for defendant	Workers' compensation court did not err in finding plaintiff failed to prove causation and that they suffered from an occupational disease after their alleged exposure to toxic mold at work.
LA	*Hemstad v. Jefferson Parish School Board*, 916 So. 2d 1174 (La. Ct. App. 2005)	2005	Defendant - Appellee	Affirmed grant of summary judgment in favor of insurer	There was no insurance coverage because the insurance policy's Employers' Liability Exclusion barred claims for injuries to employees from exposure to toxic substances.

State	Case Name	Year	Prevailing Party	Ruling	Holding
LA	*Snyder v. Belmont Homes, Inc.*, 899 So. 2d 57 (La. Ct. App. 2005)	2005	Defendants-Appellants	Reversed denial of exception of prematurity for failure to arbitrate	Agreement to arbitrate "a dispute, controversy or claim of any kind or nature arising between the parties" includes toxic mold injury claim, and plaintiff was required to arbitrate claim.
LA	*Caracci v. Cobblestone Village Condominium Association*, 877 So. 2d 1000 (La. Ct. App. 2004)	2004	Defendant-Appellee	Affirmed grant of preliminary injunction to defendant	Condominium association was entitled to injunction to allow access to condo unit to perform remediation work to eliminate toxic mold.
LA	*Smith v. State Farm Insurance Cos.*, 869 So. 2d 909 (La. Ct. App. 2004)	2004	Defendants-Appellees	Affirmed dismissal of claim against inspector	Inspector hired by insurance company owed no duty to warn plaintiffs directly of mold in plaintiffs' home.
MD	*Montgomery Mutual Insurance Co. v. Chesson*, 923 A. 2d 939 (Md. 2007)	2007	Defendants-Petitioners	Vacated and remanded with instruction to hold hearing pursuant to defendants' motion in limine	Plaintiffs' expert's testimony should have been the subject of a *Frye-Reed* to determine whether the expert's theory regarding mold exposure and illness, and the techniques employed to reach medical conclusions, were generally accepted in the medical community.

State	Case Name	Year	Prevailing Party	Ruling	Holding
MD	*Davis v. State Auto Property & Casualty Insurance Co.*, No. C2003-86729, 2004 WL 3313611 (Md. Cir. Ct. Dec. 2, 2004)	2004	Plaintiffs	Declaratory judgment in favor of plaintiffs	Plaintiffs were third party beneficiaries of builder's insurance policy and thus plaintiffs were entitled to recover for toxic mold injuries sustained because of faulty work of subcontractors of builder.
MI	*Aladdin's Carpet Cleaning, Inc. v. Farm Bureau General Insurance Co.*, No. 278605, 2009 WL 499209 (Mich. Ct. App. Feb. 26, 2009)	2009	Plaintiff-Appellee	Affirmed grant of summary judgment in favor of plaintiff on issue of the duty to defend	Insurance company had a duty to defend against homeowner's toxic-mold-related negligence claim, which was an unintentional and unexpected accident and was therefore an "occurrence" within the meaning of the policy.
MI	*Conant v. State Farm & Casualty Co.*, No. 260524, 2006 WL 1411216 (Mich. Ct. App. May 23, 2006)	2006	Plaintiffs-Appellees-Cross-Appellants	Affirmed jury verdict in favor of plaintiffs	There was sufficient evidence to support the jury's verdict awarding damages for loss to personal property, lost equity in the home and additional expenses after a contractor hired by the insurer cut holes in the wall of plaintiffs' home to locate the source of water damage to determine whether it was covered by the homeowner's policy and cause caused the disruption of mold spores and the severe contamination of the home; the insurer did not meet its burden of proving plaintiffs' failed to mitigate their damages when they abandoned the home and most of their personal property.

State	Case Name	Year	Prevailing Party	Ruling	Holding
MI	*Huffman v. City of Marlette*, No. 260283, 2006 WL 2683309 (Mich. Ct. App. Sep. 19, 2006)	2006	Plaintiff-Appellee	Affirmed denial of defendant's motion for summary disposition	Plaintiff's allegation of intermittent but inevitable water run-off resulting in black mold caused by the city's improvement of the street in front of her house stated a claim for inverse condemnation, and governmental immunity did not apply.
MI	*Ortiz v. Allstate Insurance Co.*, No. 254777, 2006 WL 889378 (Mich. Ct. App. Apr. 6, 2006)	2006	Defendant-Appellant	Reversed denial of defendant's motion for summary disposition	Insurance company was entitled to summary disposition because the contract unambiguously excluded coverage for mold damage.
MI	*Williams v. V.R. Thomas Construction Co.*, No. 263309, 2006 WL 515443 (Mich. Ct. App. Mar. 2, 2006)	2006	Defendant-Appellee	Affirmed dismissal of claims for personal injury and property damage; reversed dismissal of contract claim	Statute of limitations barred plaintiffs' toxic mold-related claims for personal injury and property damage and the discovery rule did not apply because plaintiffs failed to demonstrate that their injuries were latent in nature; contract claims should not have been dismissed because plaintiffs were the intended beneficiaries of the contract.

State	Case Name	Year	Prevailing Party	Ruling	Holding
MI	*Cross v. Harbor Club North Association, LLC*, No. 261399, 2005 WL 2659528 (Mich. Ct. App. Oct. 18, 2005).	2005	Defendant-Appellee	Affirmed summary disposition in favor of defendant	Plaintiff failed to show that defendant developer had notice of a toxic mold problem in the building before plaintiff purchased her condominium when the record showed that defendant only had knowledge that wood in the crawl space showed signs of being damp for extended periods.
MI	*Nalepka v. James Hnatio*, No. 262000, 2005 WL 2249088 (Mich. Ct. App. Sept. 15, 2005)	2005	Defendants-Appellees	Affirmed summary disposition in favor of defendants	Plaintiffs, buyers of a property, did not reasonably rely on defendants' failure to inform them about the presence of toxic mold on the property since plaintiffs hired their own expert for inspection. Thus, plaintiffs did not establish a prima facie claim for fraudulent misrepresentation.
MI	*Hayley v. Allstate Insurance Co.*, 688 N.W.2d 273 (Mich. Ct. App. 2004)	2004	Defendant-Appellant	Reversed denial of defendant's motion for summary disposition	Insurance policy clearly excluded losses caused by mold and losses consisting of mold damage, thus, plaintiffs were not entitled to coverage for toxic mold discovered in home after home sustained water damage.
MO	*Haney v. Fire Insurance Exchange*, 277 S.W.3d 789 (Mo. Ct. App. 2009)	2009	Defendants-Appellees	Affirmed dismissal	Insurer and adjuster owed no duty to warn contractors repairing home damaged by tornado of toxic mold in home; environmental consultant owed no duty to disclose findings of mold in home to contractors.
NC	*Cameron v. Merisel Properties, Inc.*, 652 S.E.2d 660 (N. C. Ct. App. 2007) (*see also* previous case listed below)	2007	Plaintiffs-Appellees	Affirmed jury verdict in favor of plaintiff	Issue of whether toxic mold in workplace caused employee's bilateral vestibular dysfunction was for the jury; and the jury verdict of $1,600,00 in lost earnings was not excessive in light of expert testimony.

State	Case Name	Year	Prevailing Party	Ruling	Holding
NC	*McCoy v. Coker*, 620 S.E.2d 691 (N.C. Ct. App. 2005)	2005	Plaintiff-Appellee	Affirmed in part and reversed in part denial of defendants' motions for dismissal and summary judgment	Building inspector's allegedly negligent inspection of home resulting in toxic mold growth was an "accident" within the meaning of defendant County's general liability policy, and thus, the coverage under the policy resulted in a waiver of governmental immunity in homeowner's suit against County and inspector in his official capacity; the inspector was public official immune from liability in his individual capacity.
NC	*Cameron v. Merisel Properties, Inc.*, 593 S.E.2d 416 (N.C. Ct. App. 2004)	2004	Plaintiffs in part; Defendants in part	Affirmed in part and reversed in part defendants' motion to dismiss	Trial court erred in applying one-year statute of limitations to claims where catch-all three-year statute of limitations applied to claim against employer for intentional exposure to toxic workplace conditions and three-year statute of limitations for willful negligence applied to claim against co-employee. Exceptions to the exclusivity rule in workers' compensation cases apply when co-employee acts willfully and wantonly or employer intentionally engages in misconduct knowing it is substantially certain to cause serious injury or death. Here, plaintiffs sufficiently alleged a claim against co-employee whose actions resulted in exposing plaintiff to toxic environment; however, plaintiff failed to allege claim against employer because the allegations did not sufficiently allege that employer had knowledge of a "substantial certainty" of "serious injury." Plaintiffs sufficiently alleged a premises liability claim.

State	Case Name	Year	Prevailing Party	Ruling	Holding
NC	*Satorre v. New Hanover County Board of Commissioners*, 598 S.E.2d 142 (2004)	2004	Defendants-Appellants	Reversed denial of defendants' motion for summary judgment	County did not waive sovereign immunity from negligence claims brought by courthouse employees arising from alleged injuries obtained due to the presence of mold, carbon monoxide, and other chemicals and irritants in courthouse by purchasing insurance, where insurance policy excluded coverage for the negligent acts alleged in employees' complaint and summary judgment should have been granted.
OH	*Herzner v. Fischer Attached Homes, Ltd.*, No. CA2007-08-090, 2008 WL 2004473 (Ohio Ct. App. May 12, 2008)	2008	Defendants-Appellees	Affirmed summary judgment in favor of defendant builder	Trial court did not abuse its discretion in excluding expert testimony from family practitioner who purportedly specialized in toxic molds where data showed that mold spores existed in condominium that could produce mycotoxins, but no tests were performed to determine whether mycotoxins in fact existed; the gap in data could not support purported expert's finding that plaintiff's injuries caused by toxic mold.
OH	*Meyer v. Chieffo*, 904 N.E.2d 560 (Ohio Ct. App. 2008)	2008	Plaintiff in part; Defendant in part	Affirmed in part, reversed in part, and remanded for new trial.	Purchaser was not entitled to damages for personal injury as a result of exposure to mold on premises absent expert testimony showing that purchaser's allergy was to that particular form of mold or that such mold was the cause of purchaser's symptoms; seller breached installment contract by failing to treat mold, thus jury award of zero damages in favor of purchaser was against the weight of the evidence and a new trial was warranted.

State	Case Name	Year	Prevailing Party	Ruling	Holding
OH	*Cross v. Classic Collision Repair, Inc.*, No. CA2006-12-106, 2007 WL 4555783 (Ohio Ct. App. Dec. 28, 2007)	2007	Defendants-Appellees	Affirmed summary judgment in favor of defendants	Plaintiff failed to demonstrate issue of material fact relating to damages and proximate cause where results of mold test were excluded by trial court because the tests were not properly authenticated and could not be introduced through plaintiff's affidavit when the tests were conducted by a non-party.
OH	*Terry v. Caputo*, 875 N.E.2d 72 (Ohio 2007)	2007	Defendants-Appellants	Reinstated grant of summary judgment	Plaintiffs could not establish prima facie case of toxic mold exposure without expert testimony concluding that toxic substance in fact caused the claimant's medical condition.
OH	*Polk v. The Landings of Walden Condominium Association*, No. 2004-P-0075, 2005 WL 1862126 (Ohio Ct. App. Aug. 5, 2005)	2005	Defendants-Appellees	Affirmed grant of summary judgment in favor of defendants	Claims against insurers failed because mold exclusion provision in homeowner's insurance policy excluded losses caused by mold regardless of the initial or proximate cause of the mold; plaintiffs claims were also barred by one-year statute of limitation.
OH	*Googash v. Conrad*, No. 20184, 20191, 2004 WL 2445236 (Ohio Ct. App. Oct. 15, 2004)	2004	Plaintiff-Appellee	Affirmed jury verdict in favor of plaintiff	Plaintiff presented sufficient evidence to establish a causal connection between her diseases and her place of employment to warrant submission of her claims to the jury by offering testimony that her condition became evident while she worked for school, tests showing that toxic molds existed in the school building,.
TN	*Morrow v. Ronnie Bull*, No. E2007-00606-COA-R3-CV, 2008 WL 539017 (Tenn. Ct. App. Feb. 27, 2008)	2008	Plaintiffs-Appellants	Reversed summary judgment in favor of defendants	A material issue of fact was created regarding whether negligent construction of new house resulted in toxic mold infestation where plaintiffs presented combination of lay and expert testimony.

State	Case Name	Year	Prevailing Party	Ruling	Holding
TN	*Wagner v. Washington County Department of Education*, No. E2007-00868, 2008 WL 880287 (Tenn. Apr. 3, 2008)	2008	Defendants-Appellants	Reversed and adopted opinion of special workers' compensation appeals panel dismissing plaintiff's claim	Plaintiff failed to establish that her exposure to toxic mold occurred in her workplace where the only actual data supplied indicated the presence of mold was significantly lower at the workplace than in plaintiff's home.
VA	*Kayes v. Keyser*, No. CL06-313, 2007 WL 6007198 (Va. Cir. Ct. Mar. 8, 2007)	2007	Plaintiffs in part; Defendants in part	Demurer overruled in part and sustained in part	Plaintiffs' allegations of excessive levels of moisture resulting in toxic mold infestation were sufficient to establish cause of action for breach of warranty; plaintiffs did not state a cause of action for conspiracy.
WI	*3305-05 Marina Road, LLC v. Zennet Properties, LLC*, 724 N.W.2d 273 (Wis. Ct. App. 2006)	2006	Defendants-Appellees	Affirmed grant of summary judgment in favor of insurers	There was no insurance coverage for damages related to real estate agent's failure to disclose toxic mold infestation.
WI	*Eddy v. B.S.T.V., Inc.*, 696 N.W.2d 265 (Wis. Ct. App. 2005)	2005	Intervenors-Respondents (Insurers)	Affirmed grant of summary judgment in favor of insurers	Coverage for real estate brokers' failure to disclose mold contamination in house was barred by the professional services exclusion of the brokers' insurance policies.

Internet Resources

www.aaaai.org—American Academy of Allergy, Asthma and Immunology. News and information resource for the Academy of Allergy, Asthma and Immunology.

www.abms.org—American Board of Medical Specialties. Identifies the 24 approved medical specialty boards. Provides good reference information regarding certification within the specialties which may allow you to check an "expert's" licensing and qualifications.

www.acaai.org—American College of Allergy, Asthma and Immunology. Reference material and news relating to the full range of topics which would come within the American College of Allergy, Asthma and Immunology.

www.cdc.gov/mold—National Center for Environmental Health. Website includes introductory scientific information for a variety of molds. Provides links to government and private websites relating to mold.

www.eima.com—EIFS Manufacturer's Association. Industry website for manufacturers, distributors and contractors, architects and associate members. Also has good information about EIFS facts.

www.epa.gov/iaq/molds/moldresources.html—Environmental Protection Agency. Federal Government website providing access to mold-related government publications. Topics include clean-up, health, floods, indoor air regulations, schools, homes and commercial buildings.

www.helpstopfraud.org/—Pennsylvania Insurance Fraud Prevention Authority. Helpful statistical information with tabs and reference material.

www.iii.org—Insurance Information Institute. Website covers the entire range of the insurance industry but within the site has mold-related information.

www.namic.org—National Association of Mutual Insurance Companies. Wide range of information available, both in the public area and member center relating to the insurance industry including recent mold developments. www.namic.org/archives/default.asp

www.nicb.org—National Insurance Crime Bureau. Provides helpful information related to fraud. Reference section with the newsroom and materials and publication links.

www.mold-help.org—Scientific information and mold-related news, appears Plaintiff-oriented.

www.moldnews.net—Wide range of mold-related news stories. Claims to be the "ultimate toxic mold news story provider."

http://palimpsest.stanford.edu/bytopic/mold—Stanford University Library Preservation Department. Website provides conservation information and leads to a wide variety of academic and scientific sources relating to mold geared toward document preservation but has very good health-related information.

www.themoldsource.com—Wide range of mold-related topics. Legal, scientific and health-related coverage.

About the Editors

Joel L. Herz of the Law Offices of Joel L. Herz in Tucson, Arizona, concentrates in complex environmental and related litigation matters. He graduated from the University of Michigan with honors in 1985, and the University of Michigan Law School in 1987. From 1987 to 1994, Mr. Herz practiced in the environmental and litigation practice groups with the New York office of Fried, Frank, Harris, Shriver and Jacobsen. Over the past 22 years, he has handled more than 100 mold and other environmental proceedings or litigations for clients, including NL Industries, 3M, and Fruit of the Loom. His litigation practice includes cases under Superfund, environmental insurance, and various state environmental laws, as well as toxic tort and mold actions. He has achieved substantial victories for private clients in environmental cases, such as *In re FV Steel and Wire Co.*, 372 B.R. 446 (Bankr. E.D. Wis. 2007) and *Halliburton v. NL Industries, Inc.*, 553 F. Supp 2d (S.D. Texas 2008) affirmed per curium. He also counsels and assists clients concerning environmental compliance and how to limit environmental risks in transactions.

Mr. Herz is admitted to practice in Arizona, New York and New Jersey, as well as the United States District Courts for the District of Arizona, Southern District of New York, Eastern District of New York, District of New Jersey, Northern District of Texas, Southern District of California, Eastern District of Wisconsin, the Second, Fifth and Ninth Circuit Courts of Appeal, and the United States Supreme Court. Mr. Herz has made several seminar presentations on environmental and real estate topics. He is a contributing author of *Brownfields: A Comprehensive Guide To Redeveloping Contaminated Property* published by the American Bar Association Section of Natural Resources, Energy and Environmental Law (First Edition, 1997, Second Edition, 2002, and Third Edition, 2009). He was also the original co-editor of *Toxic Mold Litigation* (Lawyers & Judges Publishing, 2005). Joel L. Herz is AV rated by Martindale-Hubbell.

Ernest L. Greer is Managing Shareholder of Greenberg Traurig, LLP's Atlanta office and Chair of the Atlanta Litigation Practice Group. His practice consists of the representation of clients in various complex litigation matters, including class action, construction, commercial, products liability, and employment litigation.

He serves as construction counsel for numerous corporations and government entities and has wide-ranging trial experience representing construction industry clients in multi-million dollar actions.

Mr. Greer graduated from Harvard University with a Bachelor of Arts degree. He graduated with a law degree in 1991 from Northwestern University School of Law, where he was appointed as a Patricia Roberts Harris Fellow and Northwestern University Fellow. Following graduation, he served as a judicial clerk to the Honorable Damon J. Keith, United States Court of Appeals for the Sixth Circuit. He is admitted to practice in Georgia. Mr. Greer was listed by *Chambers & Partners USA Guide* in 2009. He has been selected as one of "Georgia's Legal Elite" by *Georgia Trend* magazine in 2008, as a "Georgia Super Lawyer" in 2007, 2008 and 2009, and as one of "Georgia's Super Lawyers Rising Star" in 2005 and 2006.

Richard J. Valladares is a Shareholder in the Litigation Practice Group of Greenberg Traurig, LLP's Atlanta office. He has experience in numerous areas of litigation, including construction, products liability, insurance coverage, complex commercial, class action, and personal injury defense. Mr. Valladares' litigation and trial experience extends throughout all phases of a dispute, including pre-litigation negotiations, administrative investigations, trial, and appeal. In addition, he advises a wide array of clients, from Fortune 500 companies to the smallest entrepreneur, on dispute resolution and litigation avoidance techniques.

Mr. Valladares co-authored "An Overview of Mold Litigation in New Jersey," *Molds: A Comprehensive Guide to Litigating Mold Damage and Injury Cases* (Lawyers & Judges, 2005.) He was a contributing editor, William S. Greenberg, *Trial Handbook for New Jersey Lawyer*s, West New Jersey Practice Library Series, 3rd and 4th Eds. (West Publishing Co., 2001-2004). Mr. Valladares received his J.D. from Seton Hall University in 2001 and his undergraduate degree from Rutgers University in 1995. He is admitted to practice in Georgia and New Jersey.

Ryan C. Grelecki is an associate in the Commercial Litigation group of Greenberg Traurig, LLP's Atlanta office. His practice focuses on a variety of complex commercial and business-related litigation, including construction litigation. Ryan has had a variety of experiences in all aspects of the litigation and dispute resolution processes, including the taking of fact and expert witness depositions, drafting and arguing various substantive motions and hands-on experience in trial, mediation and arbitration. Ryan received his J.D. from the Florida State University College of Law, where he served as Notes & Comments Editor and Writing & Research Editor for the *Florida State University Law Review*. He also served as a judicial extern to the Honorable Robert L. Hinkle, Chief Judge of the United States District Court for the Northern District of Florida. Ryan received undergraduate degrees in Marketing and Religion from The College of William & Mary.

About the Contributors

Sean P. Abbott, Ph.D. is a mycologist specializing in indoor microbial contamination issues and is President of Natural Link Mold Lab, Inc. in Reno, Nevada. He received his Ph.D. from the University of Alberta, and with over 20 years experience in the field of Indoor Air Quality and mycology, has published on fungal biology and systematics, airborne biological hazards, microbial contamination of the indoor environment, and opportunistic human pathogenic fungi. Dr. Abbott has had extensive involvement with industry organizations, providing expertise to assist in the development of acceptable standards of care in the industry, including serving as a committee chair and contributing author of the IICRC S520 Standard and Reference Guide for Professional Mold Remediation (Second Edition, 2008). Over the last six years, he has provided expert witness consultation and testimony for plaintiffs and defendants in state and federal cases involving growth of mold and bacteria in buildings, residual microbial contamination, sampling methodology, laboratory analysis, aerobiology, and medical mycology.

Julie Beddingfield is an associate and member of the Environmental Group of the Philadelphia law firm of Klehr, Harrison, Harvey, Branzburg & Ellers. Her practice covers a broad range of environmental matters including Brownfields redevelopment, contaminated site assessment and remediation, environmental issues in real estate transactions, solid and hazardous wastes, underground storage tanks, and water and wetlands regulation. Julie is also one of the few attorneys in Pennsylvania to qualify as a LEED AP (Leadership in Energy and Environmental Design Accredited Professional), and spearhead's the firm's green building and energy group, including the legal and environmental implications in upgrading existing buildings to new energy efficient standards.

Barry L. Bellovin, Esq., Attorney and Counselor at Law, has been a shareholder in Bellovin & Karnas, P.C. since 1985 (formerly Siegel, Bellovin & Karnas P.C.) in Tucson, Arizona. His practice focuses extensively on plaintiff personal injury, medical malpractice, class action, product liability and toxic tort litigation. Since 1995, Mr. Bellovin has served as Judge for the Juvenile Court Commissioner,

Pima County Juvenile Court in Tucson. Mr. Bellovin has also served as Judge to the Special Pima County Superior Court Commissions and Special Magistrate in Tucson, and has taught law, business law and social science at the Pima Community College and University of Phoenix in Tucson.

Mr. Bellovin is a member of the State Bar of Arizona, California State Bar, New York State Bar, U.S. Supreme Court Bar, U.S. Court of Appeals (9th Circuit), U.S. District Court of Arizona, U.S. District Court of California (Northern, Eastern, Central and Southern Districts), U.S. District Court of New York (Southern and Eastern Districts), American Bar Association, Association of Trial Lawyers of America, Arizona Trial Lawyers, Pima County Bar Association, and the Hastings College of Law Alumni Association. He is also active in community service serving as president or board member for numerous organizations. In 1996, Mr. Bellovin received the Pima County Bar Association's Pro Bono Attorney Award.

Marianne E. Brown has over 16 years of experience in a broad range of complex litigation, including first chair jury trial experience in real estate, construction, and engineering matters, toxic tort, title insurance, and environmental litigation. Ms. Brown is a graduate of the University of Pennsylvania Law School and Haverford College. Ms. Brown is rated AV® by Martindale-Hubbell.

Ms. Brown's experience includes the case preparation and final negotiation of a $38 million settlement of the Paoli Railyard Superfund dispute on behalf of the Southeastern Pennsylvania Transportation Authority and Conrail. This settlement was the second largest verdict or settlement in the State of Pennsylvania in 2005.

Mark P. Buttner, Ph.D., is an Associate Research Professor at the University of Nevada, Las Vegas. He is the Director of the Microbiology Division. He earned a Ph.D. in Environmental Science and Health from the University of Nevada, Reno, in 2000.

Kristy M. Byrd, Esq. is an associate in the Litigation Department in Greenberg Traurig's Atlanta office. Ms. Byrd's practice includes a variety of litigation matters including class actions, complex contractual disputes, insurance coverage and technology.

Abigail A. Clapp, Esq. is a senior litigation associate in the Chicago office of the international law firm of Greenberg Traurig, LLP. Ms. Clapp's practice consists primarily of commercial litigation and white collar criminal defense.

Edward Eshoo, Jr., Esq. is a founding partner of Childress Duffy Goldblatt, Ltd. in Chicago, where his areas of practice include insurance coverage, insurance producer malpractice, mold litigation, commercial litigation and construction defects. Mr. Eshoo has lectured extensively on a variety of topics related to mold litigation, including seminars on "Mold Litigation from the Policyholder's Perspective," "Making Your Insurance Company Pay for Toxic Mold," "Anatomy of a Mold Case," and "Challenging Mold-Related Exclusions and Limitations in Homeowners Insurance Policies." He is a member of the American, Illinois State, and Chicago Bar Associations, the National Association of Public Insurance Adjusters, the National Fire Protection Association, the Illinois Trial Lawyers Association, and the Association of Trial Lawyers of America, for whom he has co-chaired the Toxic Mold Litigation Group. Over the past 19 years, he has lectured on insurance-related topics and has authored articles and publications on first-party property insurance issues, including chapters four and ten of the *Illinois Institute of Continuing Legal Education Property Insurance Practice Handbook.*

Eric S. Fisher practices in the Litigation Department of Greenberg Traurig's Atlanta office. Mr. Fisher's practice includes a variety of litigation matters including real estate, entertainment, complex contractual disputes, product defect, intellectual property, bad faith, and labor and employment issues. He is licensed to practice in both Georgia and California.

Eric G. Fosmire is a shareholder of Collins and Lacy in Columbia, South Carolina. He is a trial lawyer who practices in the area of construction defects, premises and alcohol liability. His practice also includes insurance coverage and catastrophic personal injury litigation. He has tried numerous condominium construction defect cases. Eric has been a speaker at numerous construction defect and mold seminars and claims handling training sessions. He received his Bachelor of Arts degree from Wofford College in 1986 and his Juris Doctor from the University of South Carolina in 1989. He is a former law clerk for The Honorable Don S. Rushing of South Carolina's Sixth Judicial Circuit. He served as an assistant solicitor in the Fifth Judicial Circuit, prosecuting a range of major violent crimes and drug offenses. He is a member of the South Carolina Bar, South Carolina Defense Trial Attorneys Association, and the Defense Research Institute.

David M. Governo has a national reputation as a leader in the fields of indoor air quality and complex civil litigation. Mr. Governo represents clients throughout the United States in cases involving mold, lead, asbestos and chemical exposure claims.

With respect to indoor air quality and mold, Mr. Governo advises business owners, including remediators, and represents both plaintiffs and defendants in mold-related litigation. In 2001, he developed and chaired Mealey's National Mold Litigation Conferences in California and Florida and over the past eight years, he has been invited to present papers on mold at legal and trade conferences throughout the country.

In 2004, Mr. Governo participated in the *National Institute for Environmental Health Sciences* project for the development of *Guidelines for the Protection and Training of Workers Engaged in Maintenance and Remediation Work Associated with Mold* (published May 2005). In 2004, Mr. Governo presented a paper on "Mold, Liability and HVAC Engineering" at ASHRAE's Annual Meeting, served on the faculty of the Massachusetts Continuing Legal Education (MCLE) seminar on Mold, and served on the faculty of the Harvard School of Public Health's Mold Conference.

In 2005, Mr. Governo taught several national courses for the water loss and disaster recovery industry, authored a chapter in the first edition of the textbook *Toxic Mold Litigation* published by Lawyers & Judges Publishing Co., and authored the article "Tips to Reduce Builder Liability Claims" published in *Indoor Environment Connections.* In 2006, Mr. Governo obtained a defense verdict as co-counsel for a property owner in the first "toxic mold" case tried in Rhode Island. He also chaired a seminar on mold litigation in Boston sponsored by MCLE. In 2008, Mr. Governo presented a seminar on mold at the Crawford Contractor Connection conference.

Mr. Governo has published articles on many aspects of mold including remediation, liability, insurance coverage and claims handling. He is a member of numerous bar and technical associations, including the American Society of Heating, Refrigerating and Air Conditioning Engineers (ASHRAE), the Indoor Air Quality Association, ACGIH, ASTM and the Editorial Board of *Indoor Environmental Connections.* He holds Martindale-Hubbell's highest rating (AV) and has been voted a New England Super Lawyer for 2008 and prior years.

Ander Krupa is an associate in the Atlanta office of Greenberg Traurig, LLP. His practice focuses on a variety of corporate and transactional law matters with a particular concentration on mergers and acquisitions. Ander earned his law degree, *cum laude*, from Georgia State University College of Law and holds a bachelor's degree in Business Administration from the University of Georgia.

Dr. Ryan Kuhn, Ph.D. is the Director of Industrial Hygiene Services for Dominion Environmental Consultants, Inc in Phoenix, Arizona. Dr. Kuhn received his doctorate degree from New Mexico State University in Biology (environmental microbiology emphasis) in 2001. Since graduating from New Mexico State, he has worked as an environmental consultant specializing in environmental microbial contamination. Dr. Kuhn has published research articles and given numerous presentations on issues related to mold in indoor environments. Dr. Kuhn has performed mold investigations and designed remediation plans for numerous residential and commercial properties across the country. Dr. Kuhn has extensive litigation support experience and has been retained as an expert witness on over 250 mold cases nationwide and provided expert testimony in a number of states.

Matthew J. Levinstein, who expects to graduate with High Honors from Chicago-Kent College of Law in 2009, has accepted a position as an associate at the law firm Greenberg Traurig, LLP. During his time at Chicago-Kent, Mr. Levinstein was the Managing Editor of The Chicago-Kent Law Review. Mr. Levinstein received a BS with Honors in Mechanical Engineering from the University of Illinois at Urbana-Champaign.

Kimberly A. Mello is a Shareholder in the Tampa office of Greenberg Traurig LLP and a member of the firm's Appellate Practice Group. She devotes her practice to appeals and other complex litigation in both state and federal courts involving a variety of substantive areas, including environmental, mass tort, class action, products liability, and business litigation. She is a member of the Board of Trustees of the Florida Supreme Court Historical Society and the Appellate Practice Section of The Florida Bar, where she has held leadership positions, including Editor of The Record, the Section's quarterly publication, and serving on the Executive Council. Ms. Mello has also served as Chair of the Appellate Practice Section of the Hillsborough County Bar Association. She has authored numerous articles on appellate practice and other topics. Ms. Mello received her J.D., *cum laude*, from Stetson University, where she was a Member of the *Stetson Law Review*.

Stephanie L. Oginsky, Esq. is an associate in the Litigation group in Greenberg Traurig's Atlanta office. Stephanie has experience in numerous areas of litigation including complex commercial litigation, class action, construction litigation, securities litigation, products liability and international arbitration.

Sarah E. O'Leary is an experienced trial attorney who has successfully represented clients in both state and federal courts, as well as before administrative agencies. She graduated from Northeastern University School of Law in 1996. Ms. O'Leary concentrates on defending product liability and toxic tort cases.

Stephen Pate, Esq. has been a partner since 1994 in the Houston office of Fulbright & Jaworski LLP. He focuses his litigation practice on construction litigation, first-party insurance litigation, commercial coverage litigation, fraud, extracontractual and insurance litigation. Before joining the firm, Mr. Pate served as law clerk to Judge Joe J. Fisher, U.S. District Court. Mr. Pate is a past chair of the Property Insurance Committee of the Tort and Insurance Practice Section of the American Bar Association. He is a member of the Federation of Defense and Corporate Counsel and is chair of that body's Property Insurance Section. Pate was the Mid-Year Program Coordinator for the Tort and Insurance Section of the American Bar Association. He has served as a panelist at the Property Loss Research Bureau for the past several years. Pate has spoken on property insurance and bad faith issues at seminars presented by American Bar Association National Institutes, Loss Executives Association, the Defense Research Institute, the Federation of Insurance and Corporate Counsel, and the Mealy's Company. Pate serves on the Editorial Board of the *Bad Faith Law Reporter* and *The Insurance Coverage Litigation Reporter*. Pate authored the Chapter on "Inland Marine Insurance" for West's Insurance Coverage Litigation Series, and has authored the Property Insurance Survey for the *Tort and Insurance Practice Journal.* Mr. Pate is Co-editor of *Property Insurance Annotations: Fire and Extended Coverages* (Third Edition) (ABA 1998). Mr. Pate is a fellow of the Houston and the Texas Bar Foundations and has served as Director of both the Texas and Houston Young Lawyers Associations. He is listed in Who's Who in America, Who's Who in America Law, Who's Who in the South and Southwest, and Who's Who in the World. While in law school, he was research editor for the Vanderbilt Journal. Mr. Pate received a B.A., *magna cum laude*, in 1980 and a J.D. in 1983 from Vanderbilt University. He is a member of Phi Beta Kappa. He has tried over 40 cases in 12 different Texas counties.

Patrick J. Perrone, Esq. is a partner at K&L Gates LLP in Newark, New Jersey. His practice is concentrated in civil litigation, with particular emphasis on the defense of mold claims involving builders, property owners, and building product manufacturers. Mr. Perrone is currently defending a number of mold claims and has written and spoken extensively about mold litigation. Mr. Perrone has appeared in numerous courts throughout the country and has handled hundreds of building product cases. In addition to his trial experience, Mr. Perrone has performed extensive appellate work, including appeals in the New York Court of Appeals and numerous Federal Courts of Appeal. Mr. Perrone is a member of the American Bar Association, the New Jersey State Bar Association, the New Jersey Builders Association, and the National Association of Homebuilders.

Douglas F. Schleicher, Esq. is a partner at the Philadelphia law firm of Klehr, Harrison, Harvey, Branzburg & Ellers and chairs the firm's Environmental Group. He is a leading practitioner in the areas of mold remediation and indoor air quality, as well as in Brownfields redevelopment, transactional environmental issues and environmental litigation. Recently, Mr. Schleicher has represented the owner of an apartment complex in both emergent and class action litigation arising from the condemnation of buildings due to the presence of mold, as well as in the remediation, sale and insurance coverage negotiations for the facility. In addition, he has worked with numerous building and apartment owners and managers on numerous matters arising from the actual or suspected presence of mold, including investigation and remediation, tenant interaction, and development of pro-active contract, due diligence and insurance strategies. He has written articles and participated as a faculty member at a number of seminars addressing mold. Mr. Schleicher is a member of the American Bar Association's Section of Environment, Energy and Resources; the Pennsylvania Bar Association's Section on Environmental, Mineral & Natural Resources; the Philadelphia Bar Association's Environmental Law Section; the Building Industry Association; and the Apartment Association of Philadelphia. He received his J.D. from the University of Michigan Law School and his A.B. from Princeton University.

Rhonda M. Sigman is an associate at the law firm of Fulbright & Jaworski, LLP in Houston, Texas.

Ms. Sigman's practice consists primarily of complex commercial litigation, including insurance coverage, construction litigation, commercial contracts, and personal injury. She received her J.D. from the University of Texas School of Law, where she was a member of the Order of the Coif and the Chancellors' Honor Society, and a BA *cum laude* in Economics, Art History, and Managerial Studies from Rice University. She is licensed to practice law in Texas.

Linda D. Stetzenbach is a professor in the University of Nevada, Las Vegas, School of Public Health.

Ashley Turner is a law clerk at K&L Gates LLP in Newark, New Jersey. She is currently a third-year student at Seton Hall University School of Law. Ms. Turner is an Associate Editor of the Seton Hall Circuit Review. She is a Seton

Hall Chancellor Scholar as well as a Distinguished Scholar Full Merit Scholarship recipient. Ms. Turner graduated with a B.A., magna cum laude in Political Science, minor in Writing, from Loyola College in Maryland in May 2007.

Kelly Vance has, since 1984, been admitted to practice in six states, but limits his active practice to the Northwest United States. A former U.S. Marine, Kelly's mission statement is straightforward. He began his law career in Alaska, but later joined a Seattle-based firm, which opened the door to a more regional presence and a more varied practice. Although he was known as a friend of the construction industry, Kelly's heart was burdened by damage suffered by families that became exposed to toxic mold as a result of shoddy construction practices. He began to accept cases that held builders accountable for their bad workmanship. In March, 2005, Kelly secured a far-reaching toxic mold verdict in the case known as *Haynes v. Adair Homes, Inc.* That case became a rallying point for victims of shoddy construction, and was one of the main reasons that Oregon's governor appointed a task force to study construction issues and consumer complaints.

David B. Weinstein is the Managing Shareholder of Greenberg Traurig LLP's Tampa office and chairs the firm's Environmental & Toxic Tort Practice Group.

Mr. Weinstein has an active civil and criminal litigation and trial practice. In the criminal area, he represents business organizations and individuals in federal, state, and local investigations. He also has significant experience with representing clients in internal investigations involving alleged fraud, regulatory violations, and other misconduct. In the civil context, he represents clients in class action, mass tort, multidistrict, and other complex litigation. In both the civil and criminal areas, Mr. Weinstein has substantial experience in helping clients develop and implement crisis management and public relations strategies.

Mr. Weinstein lectures and publishes regularly on environmental, business, and other issues. This has included presentations to the United States Sentencing Commission, the American Bar Association, the Federal Bar Association, the Florida Chamber of Commerce, and The Florida Bar as well as articles in the *Federal Bar News & Journal, The Florida Bar Journal,* and other publications.

Mr. Weinstein is a Co-chair of the Criminal Litigation and Enforcement Subcommittee of the ABA Environmental Litigation Committee and a Vice-Chair of the Environmental Enforcement and Crimes Committee of the ABA Section of Environment, Energy, and Resources. He is listed in *The Best Lawyers in America* in both Commercial Litigation and Environmental Law as well as in *Chambers USA, Who's Who Legal: USA, Florida Trend Magazine's* "Florida's Legal Elite," and *Florida Super Lawyers.* Mr. Weinstein received his undergraduate and law degrees from the University of Florida where he was a member of Florida Blue Key and the Trial Competition Team.

Dennis I. Wilenchik, Esq. is the founding shareholder of the Phoenix, Arizona, law firm of Wilenchik & Bartness, PC. He has practiced extensively for over 30 years, principally in the areas of real estate, construction, and general commercial litigation. He is a nationally certified Civil Trial Advocate with the National Board of Trial Advocacy and a former chairman of the Trial Practice Section of the State Bar, President of the Maricopa County Bar Association Young Lawyers Division, Secretary of the State Bar of Arizona Civil Practice and Procedure Committee, and member of the Superior Court's Civil Study committee, and editorial board member of the *Arizona Bar Journal*. He is a former partner in the international law firm of Squire, Sanders & Dempsey, and a deputy County Attorney and Judge Pro Tem of the Superior Court of Maricopa County, and is a frequent lecturer on trial tactics, evidence, mold and construction defect issues.

Dennis would like to thank Jamie L. Mayrose and Adam S. Polson for their valuable assistance in preparing these materials.

Index

www.ingramcontent.com/pod-product-compliance
Lightning Source LLC
LaVergne TN
LVHW090308180526
839095LV00001B/20
* 9 7 8 1 9 3 3 2 6 4 3 7 0 *